M000195095

Healthcare Information Security and Privacy

Healthcare Information Security and Privacy

Sean P. Murphy

New York   Chicago   San Francisco
Athens   London   Madrid   Mexico City
Milan   New Delhi   Singapore   Sydney   Toronto

Cataloging-in-Publication Data is on file with the Library of Congress

McGraw-Hill Education books are available at special quantity discounts to use as premiums and sales promotions, or for use in corporate training programs. To contact a representative, please visit the Contact Us pages at www.mhprofessional.com.

Healthcare Information Security and Privacy

Copyright © 2015 by McGraw-Hill Education. All rights reserved. Printed in the United States of America. Except as permitted under the Copyright Act of 1976, no part of this publication may be reproduced or distributed in any form or by any means, or stored in a database or retrieval system, without the prior written permission of publisher, with the exception that the program listings may be entered, stored, and executed in a computer system, but they may not be reproduced for publication.

All trademarks or copyrights mentioned herein are the possession of their respective owners and McGraw-Hill Education makes no claim of ownership by the mention of products that contain these marks.

1234567890   DOC DOC   10987654

ISBN   978-0-07-183179-6
MHID   0-07-183179-7

Sponsoring Editor
Meghan Manfre

Editorial Supervisor
Patty Mon

Project Editor
LeeAnn Pickrell

Acquisitions Coordinator
Mary Demery

Technical Editors
Lori Reed-Fourquet,
Bobby E. Rogers

Copy Editors
Emily Radar, Kim Wimpsett

Proofreader
Susie Elkind

Indexer
Karin Arrigoni

Production Supervisor
James Kussow

Composition
Cenveo Publisher Services®

Illustration
Cenveo Publisher Services

Art Director, Cover
Jeff Weeks

Information has been obtained by McGraw-Hill Education from sources believed to be reliable. However, because of the possibility of human or mechanical error by our sources, McGraw-Hill Education, or others, McGraw-Hill Education does not guarantee the accuracy, adequacy, or completeness of any information and is not responsible for any errors or omissions or the results obtained from the use of such information.

ABOUT THE AUTHOR

Sean P. Murphy, FACHE, CPHIMS, CISSP-ISSMP, CIPP/IT, is currently a vice president at Leidos in the Health Solutions Group and serves as the organization's health information privacy and security officer. He is a healthcare information security expert, with nearly 20 years of experience in the field, serving at all levels of healthcare from the hospital to an international integrated delivery system. Before joining Leidos, he was a lieutenant colonel in the U.S. Air Force Medical Service Corps. He has served as CIO and CISO, but his proudest professional accomplishment was his service as a senior mentor to the Afghan National Police Surgeon General's Office in 2008–2009 in support of Operation Enduring Freedom. He has a master's degree in business administration (advanced IT concentration) from the University of South Florida, a master's degree in health services administration from Central Michigan University, and a bachelor's degree in human resource management from the University of Maryland. He's also an adjunct professor at Saint Leo University and a fellow at the American College of Healthcare Executives. He is a past chairman of the HIMSS Privacy and Security Committee and is a Fellow and contributing author for the National Cybersecurity Institute, Excelsior College.

About the Technical Editors

Lori Reed-Fourquet, MCS, is a principal at e-HealthSign, LLC, consulting in health informatics. She is the convener for ISO TC215 WG 4 on health informatics security, privacy, and patient safety. She is also a member of the IT Infrastructure Planning and Technical committees; IHE Quality, Research, and Public Health Planning and Technical committees; and HL7 Security and HL7 Public Health and Emergency Response committees. Lori has been working in medical and health informatics for more than 20 years, serving in numerous leadership capacities, creating successful collaborations involving diverse healthcare communities in competing markets. She was part of the contracting teams to the Office of the National Coordinator for Health Information Technology and the Security and Privacy and the Standards Harmonization initiatives as part of the U.S. efforts to advance nationwide interoperable health information technology. She serves as a technical assessor for the American National Standards Institute (ANSI), the U.S. Office of the National Coordinator (ONC) Approved Accreditor for the Permanent Certification Program for Health

Information Technology (HIT). She holds a master's of computer science degree from Rensselaer Polytechnic Institute.

Bobby E. Rogers is an information security engineer working for a major hospital in the southeastern United States. His previous experience includes working as a contractor for Department of Defense agencies, helping to secure, certify, and accredit their information systems. His duties include information systems security engineering, risk management, and certification and accreditation efforts. He retired after 21 years in the United States Air Force, serving as a network security engineer and instructor, and has secured networks all over the world. Bobby has a master's degree in information assurance (IA) and is pursuing a doctoral degree in IA from Capitol College in Maryland. His many certifications include the CISSP-ISSEP, CEH, and MCSE: Security.

As a veteran and Air Force retiree, I dedicate this book to those who have served this great nation and those who provide healthcare benefits to our service members, all veterans, retired patriots, and their family members.

Most importantly, I dedicate this book to my wife, Melissa. Thank you for your patience and persistence through this process. Without you, each time Murphy's Law proved true during this project I would have surrendered. You motivated and inspired me to see the future and try one more time.

CONTENTS AT A GLANCE

CONTENTS

ACKNOWLEDGMENTS

My first thanks has to go out to Lisa A. Gallagher, BSEE, CISM, CPHIMS, the vice president of Technology Solutions at HIMSS, for her friendship and support in my involvement with the HIMSS Privacy & Security Committee, its workgroups, and its task forces. For the past five years, I have had the pleasure of being involved with the Privacy & Security Committee, including serving as the chairperson in 2011–1012. Lisa is a guiding force in security and privacy in healthcare and has been a mentor to many.

Next, I would like to acknowledge Kathleen McCormick, my associate, fellow author, and friend, who connected me to McGraw-Hill Professional when she invited me to be part of a large body of subject-matter experts developing a guide for HIT certification. Kathleen's drive as it applies to providing useful education on topics relative to healthcare and workforce improvement was a large reason why I wanted to write this book.

Speaking of McGraw-Hill Professional, I can't continue without mentioning my utmost appreciation for, and undying gratitude to, Meghan Manfre—my editing consultant, acquisition editor, and taskmaster throughout the entire process. Meghan kept me on target throughout the entire process and was one of the reasons I made it through this process. There were many times during the past year or so when it seemed this book would never see the light of day. However, Meghan believed in the project, maybe even more than I did at times. These may be my words in the book, but it is her muscle that got it done. Additionally, a very sincere, special, and related debt of gratitude to the team that edited (and re-edited) this book. Thank you LeeAnn Pickrell and Emily Rader for all of your hard work and for sharing your gift of writing with me.

And although posthumously, I must acknowledge the vision and support of Mr. Lynn McNulty. I will always remember meeting Lynn in a pub and mapping out the need for healthcare-specific information protection measures of workforce competency. Yes, this was on the back of a napkin, not figuratively, literally. He believed in the concept and is the genesis of the healthcare information protection credentialing process at $(ISC)^2$ along with Hord Tipton. From their leadership, this book emerges. Lynn believed in the ramblings and passion of this healthcare information security professional when no one else did. He built the bridge between $(ISC)^2$ and the concept of credentialing healthcare information security practitioners outside of the normal information security credentialing process, with the goal of beginning to measure workforce competency in healthcare information security and privacy. Without Lynn, this day would never have come. Without him, however, I will continue on in his spirit for building relationships, growing professionalism, and securing sensitive information in healthcare. We all miss you, Lynn.

INTRODUCTION

If you are reading this introduction, you are probably one of two types of people. The first type is someone who has worked in healthcare for a few years and whose responsibilities are becoming more dependent on information technology—and therefore information security. Perhaps you work in healthcare records management, and your organization recently implemented an electronic healthcare record. You have been chosen to provide your records management expertise to the new digital system. Congratulations! You are clearly valued in your organization. And this book will serve you because it will address, in a practical manner, your concerns about moving from paper-based records to digital, networked systems.

The second type of person is someone who has worked in information technology in healthcare or an industry other than healthcare. Perhaps you are a network operator who previously worked for the local bank or supermarket. Now you have the opportunity to be the firewall administrator for the community hospital. Congratulations to you as well! You are now an important person in the delivery of healthcare. You may not consider yourself a healthcare provider, but you are, and you most certainly support directly those personnel who provide patient care. Within this book, you will learn the implications on patient care and healthcare business of providing information security and privacy in a healthcare organization. When it comes to healthcare provision, the actions or inactions of information technology practitioners can impact patient safety or clinical quality.

For those of you who do not fit into the two categories I mentioned, do not worry. This material is very much applicable to your pursuit to elevate your competency and your dedication to the profession. Having performed healthcare information security and privacy work for a decade or two, I offer this book as a collection of lessons learned as much as anything else. Here, you will find real scenarios, actual issues, and practical solutions. I name no names to protect the innocent. In sum, I grew up in healthcare information security and still maintain a "healthcare first" attitude. When perfectly acceptable information security practices are applied to healthcare without considering the impact on patient care or provider practices, healthcare often suffers. My goal is to be part of mitigating the risk that information protection can actually introduce when trying to do the right thing. Competent healthcare information security and privacy professionals can, in fact, enable better healthcare, improve outcomes, and advance organizational initiatives.

I hope you will enjoy reading this material as much as I have enjoyed constructing it. I welcome your feedback on any and all of the material. In many ways, what you will read is the result of many discussions and commiseration sessions I have had over the years with like-minded colleagues and friends. Actually, the need for this book can be described by that same feedback loop. Let me know what you think.

How to Use This Book

There are just a handful of books about healthcare information security and privacy from which to choose today. That may change over time. The title may indicate a specific focus and target audience, but this book is not limited in purpose:

- This book will help those of you who are experiencing first-hand the integration of healthcare, biomedical engineering, information security, information technology, and privacy.

- It is a terrific desk reference for those of you who already have a few years in a healthcare information security and privacy position.

- The material is valuable as part of a curriculum in healthcare information security and privacy in universities, colleges, and technical education workshops and seminars.

I would like to share some of the intentions behind how the content was assembled and delivered.

All Healthcare Is Local (Like Politics)

For the most part, we are guided more by our organizational policies and experiences than theoretical practices and higher-level regulatory pressures. That said, organizational policies and procedures should be based on those laws and directives from regulators. To be effective as a healthcare information security and privacy professional, however, you will be guided more by organizational policies and procedures. This is also why experience in the healthcare field is so important toward measuring competency. With that in mind, one of the underlying themes of this book is the role you will play in developing and implementing organizational policies. As you read this book, take the opportunity to think about your own organizational policies and procedures around information protection:

- What policies and procedures are in place?

- What are their stated purposes?

- What regulations do they comply with?

- What are the roles and responsibilities presented?

The following are some of the types of policies you should look for:

- Information security program

- Information risk management

- Incident reporting process

- Information governance (Information Management Council, Configuration Control Board, and so on)

- Notice of privacy practices

In this way, the book has a practical application. As you read and study, you may find areas that do not reflect how your organization does things. There is always room and need for some variation. By comparing and gathering internal sources, you will gain a better appreciation of the general organization and structure of information protection, which should be evident in all healthcare organizations. (If nothing else, you might identify opportunities for improvement!) Again, internal policies and procedures are typically linked to a requirement that is external to the organization, such as HIPAA or PHIPA. Therefore, this book recognizes how important internal guidance is in understanding the application of overarching national or international regulatory frameworks and directives.

Publically Available Sources Are Prioritized

The majority of the references provided in the book are publically available. In most cases, they are offered with the intent of suggesting further reading. Not only are they listed to cite a particular point made, but also to point you to a wealth of additional material you might want to also access. In this way, the book expands your knowledge base. No single book can cover every topic in sufficient detail, but narrowing the universe of information down to a manageable list of sources is possible. At the same time, obscure, hard-to-find, and proprietary sources of information are likely not available to any of us on a day-to-day basis, so these do not make up this book's source material. The sources listed are intended to augment the material and be applicable to healthcare. Some of the references include

- National Institute of Standards and Technology 800 series, with special emphasis on
  - SP 800-122, Guide to Protecting the Confidentiality of Personally Identifiable Information (PII)
  - SP 800-66, Rev 1, An Introductory Resource Guide for Implementing the Health Insurance Portability and Accountability Act (HIPAA) Security Rule
  - SP 800-61, Rev. 2, Computer Security Incident Handling Guide
  - SP 800-53, Rev. 4, Security and Privacy Controls for Federal Information Systems and Organizations
  - SP 800-39, Managing Information Security Risk: Organization, Mission, and Information System View
  - SP 800-37, Rev. 1, Guide for Applying the Risk Management Framework to Federal Information Systems: A Security Life Cycle Approach
- International Association of Privacy Professionals (IAPP) Privacy Advisor accessed at https://www.privacyassociation.org/publications/privacy_advisor

International Coverage

If you work in the United States, you undoubtedly are concerned with HIPAA and its amendments. In this book, you will find ample material to guide you in the relevant areas of HIPAA compliance. However, as the provision of healthcare becomes global and many U.S. healthcare providers expand their markets overseas, international healthcare laws and procedures become relevant to U.S.-based healthcare workers. Add to that the growing market for electronic health records and cloud-based services, to name a few, that are outside the United States and you can see that, although healthcare is still local in nature, it requires an international perspective as well.

At the same time, the target audience of this book includes all of our international colleagues in healthcare. The fact is we all share the same convergence of

- Paper-based records to digital
- Regulatory pressures to protect sensitive information
- Workforce professions with new information protection responsibilities
- Increased networking and interoperability

Because we share these common concerns, this book is inclusive of an international healthcare information security and privacy professional audience. Some may think there is too much of an international focus. Others will think it is not enough. In the end, the intent is to at least acknowledge the common concerns we all have and the similar framework and approaches we take.

Emphasis on Risk Management

One of the central responsibilities in the practice of healthcare information security and privacy is managing information risk:

- Knowing the standards-based assessment tools
- Understanding the importance of assessing the organization and third-parties
- Comprehending the process of mitigating vulnerabilities
- Communicating findings throughout the organization
- Continually assessing the organization and the risk management program for improvement

These basic concepts are foundational and a large portion of this text is dedicated to them. This is on purpose as risk management proficiency is a practical skill that you must have. I am not the first author to point out that no silver bullet exists—that there is no perfect process or technology—that will prevent all data incidents and breaches. Perfection is not the goal. It is not possible. What is key is your proficient application of risk management to your organization to protect, detect, correct, and recover as quickly as possible, with minimal impact, and at the least cost to the organization.

If you do these things, which are hard, your role as a healthcare information security and privacy professional can be rewarding and vital to improved patient care, enhanced organization-wide quality, and reduced costs over the long run. Not to mention...the work can be a lot fun!

PART I

A Healthcare Organization and Information Risk Overview

Healthcare: Organization, Technology, and Data

In this chapter, you will learn to

- Identify the organization of healthcare in the United States and select international systems
- Comprehend common elements of the healthcare relationships
- Understand the financial components of healthcare
- Recognize specific technology as it relates to healthcare
- Be aware of healthcare terminology and data standards
- Categorize foundational health data management principles

To begin the discussion of protecting information in the healthcare industry, it is necessary to introduce you to the healthcare organization and some of the information management considerations. Appreciation for the impact of applying general information protection practices without regard to the requirements of providing patient care is the foundation of this book. It is what separates healthcare information protection from any other information protection practice.

This chapter presents a general overview of the major components of typical healthcare organizations. After reading it, you will understand the concepts of patient, payer, provider, and stakeholder. Our focus includes international frameworks for healthcare delivery, which you will be able to identify and compare with the U.S. model. We introduce the basic financial operation within healthcare because payment and billing are imperatives regardless of what nation the system serves. From there, we move into a discussion of the typical technologies of healthcare. Finally, we explore ways data flows within a healthcare organization and externally between multiple providers. Throughout the chapter, we emphasize the standards and characteristics unique to healthcare. By no means is the intention of this chapter to be comprehensive; there are numerous sources of more detailed information, which we recommend at the appropriate places in the text.

The Organization and Financing of Healthcare Delivery

To be successful in protecting information in the healthcare industry, you must understand what healthcare is and is not. Words such as *unique, specialized, sensitive,* and *autonomous,* among others, are used to imply healthcare is different from other industries. These words are used appropriately because healthcare *is* a unique industry. Still, it is imperative to not accept that claim without examining the facts. How healthcare tends to be organized and financed is a good starting point.

The organization of any healthcare system originates from the interactions of several distinct groups. Generally speaking, a healthcare system consists of patients, providers, payers, and other stakeholders (such as vendors). These groups (see Figure 1-1) play certain roles that generally follow the supply-and-demand process. For instance, patients and providers exchange information in the attempt to keep, restore, or maintain health for the patient.

Patients

At the core of any healthcare scenario, the *patient* is a person who seeks assistance with matters of health (physical and mental), improvement of health status, or treatment of illness. The care they seek can be preventive in nature, interventional, rehabilitative, or in recovery from a previous incident.

Patients can be considered inpatient or outpatient. When a patient is formally admitted to a healthcare facility and they remain there for more than 24 hours, usually they are considered an *inpatient*. After these inpatients receive care, they are discharged from the healthcare facility.

The other patient status category is called *outpatient*. Outpatient status is also called *ambulatory care*. These patients receive care in numerous types of healthcare settings, including hospitals, medical clinics, associated facilities, and even their own home environment. The key is that the patient does not get formally admitted to a healthcare facility and does not stay in the facility for more than a certain number of hours to receive diagnosis and treatment. In most circumstances, 24 hours is the standard. But, a patient can be placed in an observation status for up to 48 hours without being formally admitted as an inpatient. Even some surgeries are able to be conducted in this outpatient status as regulatory guidance, reimbursement, and medical technology changes.

Figure 1-1
Healthcare
relationships

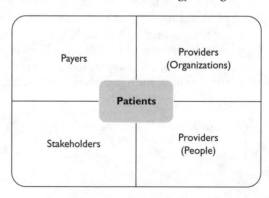

Payers

Whether healthcare is funded by a public source, such as the government, or reimbursed by private entities, such as health insurers, someone has to pay the bill for services rendered. Both in the United States and internationally, it is uncommon for an individual to "self-pay," so most payers are commonly described as *third-party payers*. In sum, a payer is almost always someone other than the patient who finances or reimburses the cost of healthcare.

NOTE In the United States, as many as 48 million individuals are uninsured.[1] By definition, these individuals would fall into the self-pay category. In some cases, the uninsured are able to fund their own care. When that is not possible, a healthcare organization may have to categorize the debt as indigent care or charity care. However, for purposes of the definition of payers, self-pay more appropriately refers to those who choose to forgo third-party payment and fund their healthcare out of their personal funds. This does not always mean the patient is wealthy. Some patients pay out of their personal funds because of a concern for their privacy.

Providers

A *provider* is a healthcare institution that exists to provide a service to patients. These can be organized as hospitals, specialized clinics, and even home healthcare. When multiple types of provider organizations, both inpatient and outpatient services, are organized into a coordinated system of clinics and hospitals, they are called *integrated delivery systems*. These systems are becoming more prevalent in healthcare to increase efficiency and reduce redundancy in providing quality healthcare. The term *provider* also is used to describe the actual people who provide healthcare. In this case, *practitioner* is an interchangeable term.

TIP In most countries, the terms *doctor* and *physician* are synonymous. In the context of daily conversation, both describe credentialed healthcare providers. In some countries such as England, there is a distinction, whereas a person is either a doctor or a physician based on level of education, specialty focus, or otherwise advanced through academic examination. Because the distinction is country-centric, you should consider the terms *provider*, *physician*, and *doctor* to be synonymous.

Stakeholders

In many areas, the local healthcare organization is probably one of the main employers of the community. It is also likely one of the most prevalent buyers and users of services, supplies, and products either directly related to patient care or indirectly related to supporting patient care operations. In addition, local government both has a direct impact on operations in the healthcare organization and is also responsive to things that happen with the hospital. In other words, a hospital that shuts down a service such as the emergency room and institutes an alternative strategy may impact the political constituency. The list of *stakeholders,* or those with an interest or impact on the healthcare organization, in such scenarios is long and diverse. A key takeaway point is that to the extent that a healthcare organization is an integral part of the community as an employer, supplier, and provider of healthcare, it is unlike most other organizations.

Healthcare Across the Globe

Even though the same elements of patient, provider, and payer must be evident in any instance of healthcare, healthcare is organized and financed differently across the globe. To highlight this, we present several major healthcare systems. Keep in mind that what follows is a high-level view and is the subject of much more in-depth discussion elsewhere. Also, within these descriptions, there is intentionally no evaluative opinion of comparable data to lead us to any conclusion. Each system has its own measure of merit and areas of improvement opportunities. The proper application of information privacy and security practices does not rely on such evaluations.

United States

The U.S. healthcare system consists of both private payers and public insurers. What sets the United States apart from the rest of the world is the extent to which healthcare costs are met by the private payers. Under the heading of private payer, there are the following considerations.

Indemnity Insurance   Basically, the model for insurance payment is based on fee-for-service. A patient receives healthcare services, pays for it at the point of care, and then submits a claim to the insurance company for reimbursement. In this scenario, the patient has the maximum freedom of choice in physicians or other restrictions to services. Of course, this scenario also results in the highest cost.

Employer-Based Insurance   The reliance on health insurance in the United States is a relatively recent development. The growth can be directly traced to employers offering coverage as an employment benefit, in addition to salary and other enticements. Employer-based coverage comes in two types: fully insured plans and self-funded plans. These two plan types were introduced after World War II with the advent of legal and tax incentives for both employers and employees. The U.S. Census recently reported that as many as 55 percent of individuals get their insurance through employer-based health insurance.[2]

- **Fully insured health plans (still, fee-for-service)**   The employer purchases government-licensed insurance that is regulated by the respective U.S. state in which it is operating and, to some extent, the U.S. federal government. The insurance company collects premiums and bears the financial risk if what the company has to pay out goes beyond the collected premiums.

  There are three primary types of government-licensed health insurance organizations.

  - Commercial health insurers
  - Blue Cross and Blue Shield plans
  - Health maintenance organizations (HMOs)
- **Self-funded employee health benefit plans**   The employer has the responsibility of paying directly for healthcare services.

Managed Care As a mechanism to control cost, improve quality, and increase access, managed care has evolved over the past 30 years. The key feature of managed care is in the integration of healthcare provision and payment within one organization. Virtually all private health coverage now involves some aspect of managed care. The organization develops financial incentives to drive patient behavior and provider treatment decisions. At the same time, the organizations rely on reliable data to develop treatment protocols that are shared to improve provider practices. Finally, one of the more contentious features of managed care is the requirement for patients and referring providers to obtain prior authorization for certain services.

The following are the four main types of managed-care options:

- **Health maintenance organization** Patients are enrolled by paying the HMO a fixed amount. They are then eligible to receive care from providers that have aligned with the HMO. Services are delivered at no additional cost to the patient. The patient typically has a small copayment for prescriptions only.

- **Preferred provider organization (PPO)** This is a fee-for-service health plan with a number of providers that have aligned with the PPO. If the patient chooses a participating provider, the cost of medical care is discounted to the enrollee. If not, the service is covered at a lesser rate. Also, the patient may incur higher deductibles and coinsurance payments. The result is more choice for the patient yet at a higher cost.

- **Point-of-service (POS)** This type of plan combines the most attractive elements of both HMOs and PPOs. In exchange for a deductible and higher coinsurance payment on a one-time basis, an HMO enrollee can choose to use a service that is outside the HMO plan. This is in contrast to a strict HMO policy of not reimbursing care received out of network (under the HMO-only model).

- **High-deductible health plan with savings option (HDHP/SO)** This type of plan usually takes the form of a health savings account (HSA). For a relatively low premium, an enrollee gets catastrophic insurance coverage. For all healthcare received up to catastrophic care, the enrollee must pay a high deductible. To offset this, enrollees are able to save wages before tax in a special type of account to be used to pay any deductibles.

The government is the primary payer in most developed countries and is integral to the overall provision of healthcare. In contrast to other countries, government spending for healthcare in the United States serves the purpose of filling in the gaps resulting from private insurance. These government-sponsored plans are also typically structured in a managed-care design:

- **Medicaid** Each U.S. state allocates the money it receives from the federal government to provide medical assistance to primarily the nonelderly, poor, and disabled. For the most part, recipients are pregnant women, children and babies, people with disabilities, and, in some cases, the elderly poor.

- **Medicare**   Medicare provides insurance coverage for individuals age 65 and older or those who are younger than 65 but have long-term disabilities. It is funded and administered by the federal government. There is no qualification related to income level, only age and disability status.

- **Department of Defense Military Health System (MHS)**   The federal government also provides funding for health benefits for active-duty service members and retired service members, as well as their dependents, through the MHS. This network has aspects of direct care (military hospitals) but also purchases healthcare from the commercial sector through a managed-care network called TRICARE. The veterans of U.S. military service also may be eligible for care through the federal Veterans Health Administration, which has a network of hospitals and treatment centers that provide care specifically to this population.

- **Indian Health Service (IHS)**   Eligible Native American Indians may receive care through the IHS within IHS facilities. They may also receive care at non-IHS facilities with payment provided by the federal government.

Depending on what services are covered and the level of reimbursement, many Americans pay premiums for more than one health insurance plan. Often plans overlap. For this reason, healthcare financing in the United States is a complex assortment of programs that can be integrated. At best, it can cover most, but not all, Americans.

Internationally, a single-payer system financed by (government) public funds is most common. A select few of those systems are presented in the following sections. Common among these, the government (with few exceptions) collects all healthcare fees and pays all healthcare costs. In short, providers in these countries bill one entity (and not the patient) for their services.

Canada

Canada is an example of a single-payer system in which the government funds universal coverage. The system is funded through taxes collected. The physicians delivering the care, however, are privately run. For example, the physicians are not government employees and provide services under a fee-for-service model. Canada has a publicly funded Medicare system, with most services provided by the private sector. Each province may opt out, though none currently does. Canada's system is known as a single-payer system, where basic services are provided by private doctors (since 2002 private doctors have been allowed to incorporate), with the entire fee paid for by the government at the same rate. The doctors submit a claim to the government (payer).

To be compliant with government mandates, all health plans in Canada must be

- Available to all residents of Canada
- Comprehensive in coverage
- Accessible without financial and other barriers
- Portable within the country and while traveling
- Publically administered

Great Britain

The government agency National Health Service (NHS) is organized and resourced to provide universal health coverage. NHS is publically funded via tax collection and is founded on the belief that all citizens have an entitlement to healthcare. The healthcare services that are included include basic services, primary care, specialty care, and inpatient care, along with radiology and laboratory services. That said, private insurance exists because there are some types of services that are not covered. These are usually elective conditions, and approximately 7 million people, or 12 percent of the population, are covered by these plans.

In terms of out-of-pocket costs, there are only a few cost-sharing arrangements for publicly covered services. Patients may pay a prescription drug copayment per prescription, while all drugs prescribed for inpatient care in NHS hospitals are free to the patient. NHS dentistry services are also subject to copayments.

European Union

The European Union does not have any administrative or authoritative role in healthcare. However, it is helpful to note that although each health system is run at an individual member-nation level, the systems are primarily publicly funded through taxation. For the most part, healthcare in the European Union is considered universal healthcare. This includes larger systems in Germany, France, Italy, and Spain. There is private funding for healthcare, which is a personal contribution toward meeting anything not funded by taxpayer contribution. This can be totally private funds paid either out-of-pocket or by personal or employer-funded insurance. That said, membership in the European Union allows citizens to carry a European health insurance card and provides reciprocal emergency healthcare funding for citizens who are visiting other member nations. In fact, this benefit extends to several other European nations that are not currently in the union.

Japan

There is measurably more government control of healthcare in Japan, which also has a universal health coverage model. At a national level, in this model, the pricing of services is set by the government. It also subsidizes local governments, third-party payers, and providers for the cost of providing healthcare (which does not actually equal what the government sets as a fee). The government does this to help these entities implement national-level policies. Japan has 47 prefectures (regions) and 1,742 municipalities that operate the nation's health system. However, all of these local healthcare entities adhere to detailed regulations set and enforced at a national level. Although funding is provided by the government, there are gaps in coverage; for instance, some hospitalization costs are not fully covered. Therefore, supplementary private health insurance is held by the majority of the adult population.

The Financial Components of Healthcare

It is a not-so-subtle point to mention that without payment, reimbursement, or fair compensation for healthcare services, the services would not happen. At least, they would not happen to the extent that the healthcare system of today uses state-of-the-art technology, highly trained professionals, and well-apportioned facilities. For these reasons, you must explore the components of how healthcare provision is financed.

Claims Processing

In the event a third party is the payer for healthcare services, claims processing comes into play. As an example, in a simplified patient-provider transaction, the provider may charge $100 for a service. The patient may pay a $25 copay as described previously. The remainder of the bill, $75, is sent to the third-party payer as a claim against the insurance or government reimbursement.

The process for claims actually begins prior to the appointment. Pre-approval is often a requirement in which the third-party payer must authorize the doctor visit, all or a portion of the services, and any of the recommended follow-on care. Without pre-approval, third-party payers can reduce the amount of reimbursement they are responsible for, or they may even deny the claim. The patient would then become fully responsible for paying the bill in its entirety.

With pre-approval, the normal process for claims would include the physician sending the bill (after copay) to the third-party claims-processing center. While providers can still submit claims manually, on paper forms, it is increasingly more common to file the claims electronically. Estimates show electronic claims are three times less expensive than submitting via paper. However, securing the electronic transaction is a concern for healthcare information privacy and security. The claims-processing center takes the patient information and any relevant documentation of the services provided and compares this to the explanation of benefits. The explanation of benefits is the policy terms and conditions. Once the third party determines all pre-approved services were delivered and covered in the policy, it will submit payment for the remaining balance to the physician.

Payment Models

In the healthcare revenue cycle, claims processing leads to payment or reimbursement for services. The models for these payments have distinct features. Discussed previously, fee-for-service where providers are paid for each service rendered to a patient is the dominant model, and it can be evident even in managed-care plans or when a government payer is involved. Without reiterating how those models work, variations of the fee-for-service model exist and should be understood by healthcare employees.

Bundled Payment

Bundled payment is a more predetermined payment model than fee-for-service. It is when a healthcare provider is compensated based on *expected* costs for each acute-care episode, not necessarily the *actual* costs. However, the parameters of the event are determined by clinical judgment. The episode must have a clear beginning and end, require defined services, and have established clinical guidelines that allow for best practices. Conditions such as cataract surgery, services for end-stage renal disease, and coronary artery bypass graphing (CABG) to improve blood flow to the heart have all proven viable bundle payment candidates. Bundled payments are central to any healthcare reform debate (in the United States) because of their ability to help reduce healthcare costs, championed by physicians and administrators alike.

Capitation

An even more predetermined compensation model, *capitation* is a payment arrangement of a set amount for each person covered by the third-party payer. Providers agree in advance to accept a capitated amount, which is a fixed amount for each person and which is called a *covered life*, based on a specified time period whether or not that person seeks care. A common way to describe this is "per member per month" for the provisions of capitation and scope of coverage to which a healthcare provider agrees. To be clear, capitation does not relate to a specific episode of care or event, like fee-for-service and bundled payments. The average, expected amount of care for each member that the payer disburses is calculated, and the payer enlists providers that agree to accept this payment. Providers accept a level of risk that they will be able to provide adequate care at some funding amount less than the capitated amount and therefore make a profit. If the amount of care exceeds the capitated amount, the provider takes the loss for excess spending—even if the care was clinically necessary.

The Evolving Payment Model (U.S.)

Even with alternatives to fee-for-service, additional models of payment (sometimes discussed as part of healthcare reform in the United States) are worth mentioning. The patient-centered medical home (PCMH) and the accountable-care organization (ACO) are presented here.

In the PCMH model, patient treatment is coordinated by a primary-care manager who makes sure the patient receives appropriate levels of care. This can mean clinically necessary referrals to specialists or diagnostic tests are vetted by the primary-care manager. As they are approved, these treatments, tests, and referrals are explained to the patient to reduce confusion and help increase the likelihood of patient compliance. Confusion and lack of patient compliance are issues that increase waste and redundancy.

PCMH has a goal of cultivating partnerships between individual patients, their personal physicians, and, when appropriate, the patient's family. There is a high degree of integration of information technology and health information exchange (requiring privacy and security considerations). All of these attempt to provide the right care at the right time at the best value to both the patient and the provider (healthcare organization).

Physicians, hospitals, and other relevant health service professionals are testing a model that joins them together contractually to provide a broad set of healthcare services. This is an ACO, which is formally organized, and is applicable currently to Medicare patients only.

Even though the ACO does not have to consist of organizations within the same corporate structure, the intent is to deliver seamless, coordinated care. In fact, as the name states, within the framework of the ACO contract, this organization is accountable to providing such care.

The payment model in healthcare must change from fee-for-service to something more efficient and effective. Churning out services for chronic diseases without regard to improving outcomes can no longer be reimbursed. An ACO (and the PCMH) model strives to improve quality and reduce hospital admissions (and re-admissions) and emergency-room visits. In return, costs are contained, and the participating providers can share in the savings.

Medical Billing

Medical billing is the process of submitting and following up on claims with health insurance companies in order to receive payment for services rendered by a healthcare provider. Providers may employ a couple different strategies in submitting their bills (or claims for payment). Depending on the size of the provider organization, larger practices tend to submit bills electronically to the payer. In smaller practices, it is more common for the forms to be completed on paper. Because the analog data must be converted to digital before submission, an entity called a *clearinghouse* receives these paper forms from multiple small practices, converts them to digital files, and submits them to the various payers.

A clearinghouse is not a healthcare provider; it is an intermediary between the provider and payer. The clearinghouse function is not limited to simply changing paper-based information to digital. Clearinghouses also serve to streamline the claims processing and revenue collection of the provider. One way by which they do this is by "scrubbing" each bill to make sure it adheres to each health plan's unique or proprietary data requirements. For a small practice, having most, if not all, bills rejected because the data fields do not conform to the payers' proprietary format can cause significant financial distress, maybe even bankruptcy.

Assuming the data elements are all present and in the correct format, another hurdle that providers must overcome in the billing process is medical necessity. Payers review bills to make sure the patient was covered and the services were a medical necessity. The guidelines for medical necessity are established by different U.S. state agencies and even by each payer, but all should find origin in the federal Medicare statute, which outlines what is reasonable and necessary. In the event a service is deemed not a medical necessity, the claim is denied or rejected, and the provider is notified, usually in the form of explanation of benefits (EOB) or electronic remittance advice.

Without going into much more detail of the billing system, it becomes clear that in the United States, medical billing is a complex process with almost countless payers and oft-changing regulations. This results in measurable additional administrative waste generated in the healthcare system.

Reimbursement

Reimbursement is the final step of the revenue cycle. As claims are processed, bills are submitted (and resubmitted), and the desired outcome from the provider perspective is to receive reimbursement for the cost of the healthcare. In a word, *reimbursement* is repayment for expense incurred. However, it is uncommon for reimbursement to equal expenses. Healthcare providers and payers continually work together to set rates of reimbursement and adjust them against a standard loosely defined as charges that are "usual, customary, and reasonable." That standard is increasingly squeezed to lower reimbursement rates that constrain providers that might have capital investments that rely on the margin between cost and repayment. But the counterargument (from payers) is that consistently squeezing reimbursement rates encourages providers to be more efficient and productive.

Technology Specific to Healthcare

Every industry employs some type of technology to make it more efficient and effective. Healthcare is no different. The fact that providers rely on medical and information technology for diagnosis and treatment of patients may be one point of difference because this goes beyond mere efficiency and effectiveness. Additionally, the impact to patient care that these technologies have is a unique concern to healthcare, especially when managed incorrectly. We cover a few of these types of technologies so you can begin to understand how important they are to healthcare.

Medical Devices

A *medical device* or technology is any item that a provider uses to diagnose, prevent, monitor, or treat a disease, injury, or physiological process. It can be hardware, software, or applications, networked or stand-alone. This includes devices such as complex capital equipment, an X-ray machine, linear accelerator, or magnetic resonance imaging (MRI), for example. Medical devices can be high-tech or low-tech. Examples range from artificial hearts to blood pressure monitors. However, what was once an easy, physical distinction between regular office automation (the personal computer) and a medical device has become almost imperceptible. Medical devices have become increasingly networked and interconnected. They operate using the same operating systems and database software that are already connected to the network infrastructure. The impact of having these devices on that same infrastructure as all other information technology assets is huge. They are sophisticated computers, yet they *are* computers, with many similar requirements and vulnerabilities from an information security perspective that must be managed. Unlike their office automation counterparts in the finance department or information technology services, these sophisticated computers are regulated by external, government agencies (in the United States, the Food and Drug Administration [FDA]),[3] and as such, the original equipment manufacturer remains obligated to maintain the device even after the sale. A partial explanation of this reality is because of the "intended purpose" in medical device management. By U.S. law, the use for which the device is intended according to the data supplied by the manufacturer on the labeling, in the instructions, or in promotional materials must remain constant. Changes to the medical device, such as updating antivirus software, may be required. Without manufacturer testing of the proposed software for any unforeseen consequences, there can be significant patient safety issues if a device malfunctions.

TIP The emergence (and convergence) of medical devices into the realm of information technology networking, both wired and wireless, has introduced a new category of employee into the field of healthcare information privacy and security. Clinical engineers, biomedical technicians, and medical technicians have all had to develop the skills and aptitude to connect their medical device systems to the healthcare network. This has integrated new terminology and concerns into traditional information technology operations.

Information Technology Networks

An *information technology network* consists of various types of computing equipment, including the medical devices mentioned previously, office automation computers, the cabling, the machines used to route and monitor traffic, and software (operating systems and so on). These myriad information technologies are connected to each other to share data. Typically based on geographical distinctions, information technology networks are classified into several categories. The most common categories found in healthcare are covered in the following sections.

Local Area Network (LAN)

The LAN is the backbone of any information technology architecture. In fact, the LAN is commonly referred to as the "backbone" when the cabling and interconnections are described. Data is transferred across the LAN operating at rates measured in hundreds of megabits per second or more, routed correctly across almost limitless numbers of devices transferring images, text, audio, and video. The distinctive features of a LAN are high speed, low error rate, private ownership, and small geographic area. Usually, those features happen all within the same physical organization and its network boundary. When LANs first were implemented, there were several configurations, called *topologies*. The first three were the star, the ring, and the bus configurations. As LANs were able to operate at higher speeds with low-cost switching technology, the point-to-point topology became more common and is the relative standard today.

 NOTE Metropolitan area network (MAN) and wide area network (WAN) are also categories of networks. The key difference between a LAN and a MAN or WAN is the connection of networks (multiple LANs) across a metropolitan area (a city) or a long geographical distance using public telecommunications lines (usually leased by organizations owning the LANs).

Body Area Network (BAN)

A BAN is a sensor (or multiple sensors) located on an individual that acts as an endpoint computing device on a network. These sensors send and receive signals wirelessly to other medical devices and LANs. BAN is a promising technology for real-time monitoring of physiological signals to support medical applications. See Figure 1-2 for an illustration of a BAN to LAN in use.

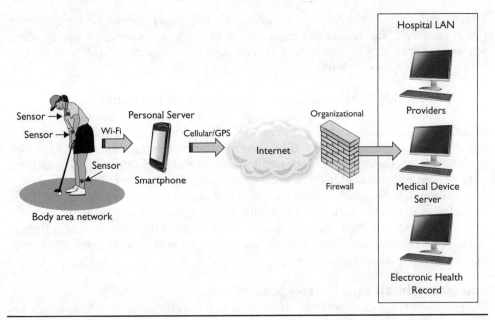

Figure 1-2 The body area network

Personal Area Network (PAN)

A PAN is a small network consisting of a communications area near an individual and may include a BAN. There are numerous devices attached to each other, primarily over wireless channels. A PAN is self-administered within a segment provided to it on the LAN of an organization or within an individual's home. Within each device is a network interface card (NIC) that makes transferring data possible, regardless of whether the senders or receivers are laptops, printers, medical devices, or network gateways.

Health Information Exchanges

The term *health information exchange (HIE)* is commonly used as both a verb and a noun. When used as a verb, HIE describes the electronic sharing of healthcare information between providers and payers. However, for purposes of this text, HIE is used to describe an object, a noun. An HIE is an organization that exists to facilitate the electronic sharing of healthcare information across multiple healthcare organizations. Typically, the organizations are not affiliated or under the same corporate structure, but they may be. In any case, the HIE supports information transfer between organization partners and within a region or community.

Disparate healthcare information systems exchanging data electronically need the HIE to move the information while ensuring the reliability of content. In this way, healthcare providers can readily access and use clinical data to improve quality, increase access, and enhance clinical practices. Public health agencies also benefit from HIEs in the analysis and surveillance of community health. Of course, because manual processes for data transfer are reduced, costs are decreased. Less paper transfer via fax machines, postal mail, and automating administrative tasks equates to savings of already scarce resources. A couple of examples of HIEs with significant impact on healthcare are covered in the following sections.

The Nationwide Health Information Network Exchange

In the United States, federal agencies; state, regional, and local health information organizations; integrated delivery networks; and private organizations are coming together to establish an HIE of HIEs, called the Nationwide Health Information Network Exchange. These stakeholders are formulating and implementing the standards, services, and policies of this framework. In this way, the electronic transfer of health information is available and reliable across more organizations equally. All the while, emphasis is placed on securing this health information exchange as it traverses the Internet. Patients will have their information follow them throughout the continuum of care, making the healthcare delivery system more patient-centered than the traditional manual, paper-based system.

European Union and United States

The European Commission's Directorate General for Communications Networks, Content, and Technology (DG CONNECT) and the U.S. Department of Health and Human Services (DHHS) have begun collaborating on a multinational, transatlantic communications framework that will strengthen transatlantic cooperation in e-health and health information technology (IT). With a kick-off meeting in June 2013,[4] the partnership established two initial areas of importance.

- Development of internationally recognized and utilized interoperability standards by identifying common vocabularies, message structures, and tools for ease of electronic health information and communication technology exchange

- Strategies for the development of a joint education and training curriculum relevant to both the European Union and the United States to increase the number of skilled health IT workforce

   Clinical experts and key stakeholders from both the European Union and the United States are joining forces to develop and implement the required action plans. The solutions will need to be innovative and involve input from government and private-sector organizations. The stated outcome (at least near-term) is to fully exploit the benefits of electronic health data transfer to

- Empower individuals
- Support patient care
- Improve clinical outcomes
- Enhance patient safety
- Improve the health of populations

Electronic Health Record

An *electronic health record* (EHR) is, in simple terms, an individual patient's medical record in digital format. It is replacing the traditional paper-based process and increasing record-keeping and analysis capabilities because of the constraints of a records system based entirely on paper charts and forms. As reliance on digital information grows and as diagnostic tools become more capable of capturing new and complex data sets, the EHR is a repository for various types of clinical information.

- Patient demographics
- Medical history such as medicine and allergy lists
- Progress reports and provider note
- Laboratory test results
- Procedure and test appointments
- Radiology images (X-ray, MRIs, and so on) and clinical photographs (endoscopy, laparoscopy, and so on)
- Prescribed and administered medications

Expanding the description, the EHR is the centerpiece of the health information system. It integrates with almost every clinical information system (for example, a radiology picture archiving and communications system [PACS]), patient registration systems, and in some cases other providers' EHRs to establish a longitudinal (over a period of time) collection of healthcare information related to an individual patient. The information must be readily available to multiple providers when they need the information no matter where they are physically located.

The EHR provides the ability to collect, store, and transfer meaningful data. It also presents the data in a way paper-based records could never do. The provider has the data in a graphical user interface (GUI) that could include everything from spreadsheets to images to simple numeric results. With any of these presentation formats, the key is that providers are able to customize the EHR within the workflow of their practice. Even more importantly, the results and displays are analyzed by the EHR to enable alerts or warnings to the provider. If a certain result signifies a drastic change in the health status of the patient, the provider's attention can be quickly drawn to that without having to review numerous, previous test results. When a prescription or treatment plan conflicts with a possible or known allergy, the provider is alerted. In emergent or urgent-care situations where the patient is not conscious or fully responsive, this can avoid a patient safety issue, possibly death.

One additional note about EHRs is that they have a profound effect on reducing medical errors. The Institute of Medicine (IOM) published an eye-opening report, "To Err is Human," in 1999 claiming that at least 44,000 patients die each year because of medical errors, and it could be twice as many due to reporting process discrepancies.[5] More recent studies and observations claim the industry has not improved by much. Central to these mistakes is the paper-based process of order entry. *Order entry* is a collective term for any type of direction a physician gives for dispensing medication and conducting tests. When these actions are done via paper, realities such as illegible handwriting can create an error. If the order is given to a nurse over the phone (a process called *verbal ordering*), data can be transcribed incorrectly. Rarely intentional, these errors introduce significant patient risk in an already risky environment. Computerized provider order entry (CPOE), found in EHRs, makes the use of paper and verbal orders obsolete. Many drug orders are conducted using drop-down lists rather than free text, for instance. In fact, with the additional control of an order "alert," the physician can be prompted to double-check an order that may be entered incorrectly in the event the physician must type the order into the system.

Personal Health Record

A *personal health record* (PHR) is sometimes confused with an EHR or is misidentified as part of the longitudinal EHR. It is not. The PHR is maintained by the patient as opposed to the provider organization. But that does not necessarily detract from a PHR's usefulness. Because the PHR is available to the patient, he or she can have timely and accurate information related to a summary of care with test results and outcomes that develop over time into a comprehensive medical history. Additionally, the PHR can be integrated with at-home patient-monitoring devices, such as wireless weight scales or blood pressure monitors that transmit via smartphone applications to augment the patient care plan. In its entirety, a PHR assists a patient to remember their own medical history and recount it correctly (for example, know exact medications or dosage currently taking). With a simple click of a button, all of that relevant data can be transmitted or saved to portable electronic media for the use of any provider.

Although PHRs may be software applications loaded on a PC or laptop, more often they are web-based solutions. These are flexible and provide better ability to integrate data from other sources (home health devices, EHRs, and smartphones, to name a few). In sum, PHRs provide a way for patients to participate in tracking and maintaining their health. They also facilitate a more efficient interaction between patient and provider. No matter how connected the health systems report are, there is still a great deal of transience and disjointed care systems that force patients to see multiple providers, which may or may not be able to share information. PHRs enable the patient to fill in any gaps that may occur.

Terminology and Data Standards

Healthcare has a distinctive language that is spoken in the healthcare environment. It is exclusive in its combination of Latin terms, jargon, and terms with organizationally specific codes. We are not going to try to identify and define all of these terms. But, at an aggregate level, several concepts relating to how healthcare professionals communicate and the information systems interact are essential for you to appreciate.

Clinical Workflow

Clinical workflow describes the various processes and patterns of actions clinicians use to deliver healthcare. In reference to electronic information and EHRs, clinical workflow describes how the data moves through the information system and by whom, to whom, when, and how often. Understanding this workflow and properly managing it leads to greater efficiency, better access to quality healthcare, and improved patient safety across care settings. Further, clinical workflow through health information systems improves health outcomes, reduces medication errors, and (in the long run) offers substantial cost savings over the manual processing of information.

Examples of clinical workflow components can include actions taken to register a patient, document patient information gathered during an appointment, develop a treatment plan, prescribe any follow-up tests and medications, provide patient education material, schedule future visits, and process bills or claims. These are not all of the processes and subprocesses involved, but they provide a general outline of how a patient moves through the physical organization. The need for electronic data related to these actions must also move in a synchronized, parallel fashion through the information systems. Figure 1-3 depicts the general idea of clinical workflow. Please note that the figure is intended to illustrate the integrated process involving clinicians, administrative personnel, and technicians. The example is not comprehensive. There are more interactions and participants in the typical clinical workflow, but one diagram probably could not depict all of it.

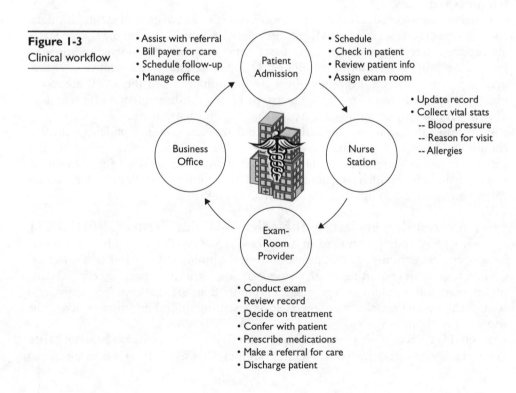

Figure 1-3
Clinical workflow

• Assist with referral
• Bill payer for care
• Schedule follow-up
• Manage office

Patient Admission

• Schedule
• Check in patient
• Review patient info
• Assign exam room

• Update record
• Collect vital stats
-- Blood pressure
-- Reason for visit
-- Allergies

Business Office

Nurse Station

Exam-Room Provider

• Conduct exam
• Review record
• Decide on treatment
• Confer with patient
• Prescribe medications
• Make a referral for care
• Discharge patient

Coding

Coding is the transformation of clinical workflow from any type of description in narrative or words into numerical data sets, or codes that are used for documenting disease description, injuries, symptoms, and conditions.

International Classification of Diseases (ICD)

For example, an International Classification of Diseases (ICD) code 382.9 stands for "Unspecified otitis media," which is a disorder characterized by inflammation (physiologic response to irritation), swelling, and redness to the middle ear.[6] Instead of having to provide all of that verbiage, medical billers can communicate that level of detail for the purposes of payment to the payers with a simple number up to six digits long that is internationally understood. Beyond facilitating the reimbursement of healthcare services, standardized codes make data analysis possible by providers and payers alike. In this way, unnecessary tests and services can be reduced, and outcome statistics are more obtainable.

In the United States, healthcare is still using the ICD-9 versions of these codes. However, the next generation of the codes, ICD-10, is already in use internationally. ICD-10 provides a more robust description of patients' medical conditions and hospital inpatient procedures than the 30-year-old ICD-9 code set does. Because ICD-10 uses up to seven digits, it will accommodate more specificity and exactness in coding. As clinical workflow and medical practices change, ICD-10 provides enough room to add new categories and codes.

Based on the ICD codes from the patient record and the patient's demographic data, another type of code set emerges. Diagnostic-related groups (DRGs) in the United States are designed to replace reimbursement based on fee-for-service billing with more of a prospective process. Basically, a group of ICD codes are established relative to "products" a provider delivers. Currently, there are more than 500 of them that are recognized. Hernia procedures for a patient age 0 to 17 and fracture of femurs are examples of DRG groups. The prevailing concept is that within each established DRG, services and processes should be similar and standard across any group of patients with that condition. Therefore, costs can be predicted. Provider organizations can adjust practice patterns to reduce variations that have minimal, if any, demonstrated clinical value. A preset payment is provided depending on what DRG applies, and the provider assumes risk for any additional costs that are more than the DRG rate.

Systematized Nomenclature of Medicine–Clinical Terms (SNOMED CT)

Another type of coding prevalent in healthcare is SNOMED CT, which is a comprehensive clinical terminology that provides clinical content and expressivity for clinical documentation and reporting. It can be used to code, retrieve, and analyze clinical data. An international standard, it is granular with more than 311,000 concepts, terms, and relationships with the objective of precisely representing clinical information across the scope of healthcare.

SNOMED CT is designed for electronic health information exchange between EHRs. This is the key difference between SNOMED CT and ICDs. SNOMED CT is so specific so as to be able to describe extensive clinical terminology that is meant more as machine language to construct the EHR. ICDs classify diagnoses and procedures suited for output to billing and data analysis functions. However, efforts are underway to integrate SNOMED CT and ICD, possibly when the ICD-11 standard is published.

Logical Observation Identifiers Names and Codes (LOINC)

To close out this introductory view of coding in a healthcare organization, LOINC is a widely accepted code system specially formulated for identifying laboratory and clinical observations. To be able to exchange observations and measurements electronically across multiple independent lab systems, LOINC uses a universal code system with a maximum field size of seven. This results in more than 71,000 LOINC values, which allows data transfer between providers, clinical laboratories, and public health authorities. How LOINC differs from ICD is in that ICD primarily exists to record diagnoses. LOINC, to reiterate, is specific to identifying test observations.

Data Interoperability and Exchange

Data sharing in healthcare is an essential component of patient care, research, and quality initiatives. Within the organization, providers consider it an imperative to be able to easily access things such as medication lists and laboratory results precisely when they need it. Even after care is provided, sharing information is important in settings such as peer record review, where procedures are reviewed and measured against organizational and clinical standards. The intent there is to discuss best practices, share common experiences, and, in the end, maximize scarce resources by reducing duplication and ineffective processes.

Many healthcare organizations conduct a tremendous amount of research and academic training as part of the healthcare they provide. Commonly, these are either purely research providers or teaching hospitals. Enabling these organizations to exchange their findings or even collaborate on research in real time advances medical care. Results become more useful with combining larger data sets on drug responses. Adding genomic data on patients to the clinical trials could really begin to predict exactly what therapies are helpful at an individual level. In sum, data sharing in research and academia reduces the traditional trial-and-error medicine that is too costly and may even be the source of patient safety risk.

One study has shown that sharing data between provider organizations has saved 92,000 lives and $9.1 billion over four-and-a-half years. Much more impressive numbers result from extrapolating data-sharing benefits across an entire nationwide healthcare system. Improving patient outcomes, streamlining processes, and reducing patient safety risks are all benefits of this data sharing.

Given the imperative for data sharing, enabling one healthcare organization to communicate with another is a challenge. There are impediments even though the language of healthcare is based on recognized clinical terminology, many standardized code sets, and a mission of diagnosis and treatment. Further, the ability to interconnect with suppliers, payers, and other stakeholders (including government agencies) can create administrative and management problems. Most often, the communication breakdowns are not technology impasses. Usually, overcoming political and personal hurdles resolves disconnects.

For instance, each healthcare organization that uses an information system to automate workflow, an EHR, or a patient administration system probably purchases that system from a commercial manufacturer. In the case of some government healthcare organizations (the military or Veterans Administration), the information systems may be government-developed. In any case, based on the agency that develops the system, interoperability is typically limited. The outcome is valuable data locked in seemingly impenetrable silos, unless the systems are all made by the same manufacturer. However, as patients typically move from one healthcare organization to another based on referrals for advanced care, for example, or healthcare organizations desire to submit bills to payers, healthcare organizations must have an ability to send and receive data independent of what proprietary system they (or their counterpart) use.

Health Level 7 (HL7)

One of the leading interconnection standards is HL7, which is a protocol developed to enable different information systems to exchange data using a standard. The organization that builds this standard is also called Health Level 7 (HL7). This international organization consists of healthcare information technology professionals, many who are subject-matter experts. It is a nonprofit, nongovernmental membership group. By developing the interconnections standard that they do, different healthcare organizations can better deliver patient care and transfer clinically significant information that typically would be unavailable because of the incompatibility of systems.

To help EHRs interconnect, a product that HL7 has published for all EHR manufacturers is the HL7 EHR System Functional Model and Standard. This defines EHRs in terms of important functionality. Using the clinical workflow expected of various patient care settings such as intensive care, emergency care, a doctor's office, or any other clinical setting, the group defined functional profiles with standard descriptions, which are applicable globally. To achieve interoperability, it is important that HL7 leads this type of effort so that providers and manufacturers develop standardized EHRs functionality with a desire for interoperability instead of trying to cobble them together after-market.

Integrating the Healthcare Enterprise (IHE)

Related to HL7, IHE is an international organization that is providing a standards framework. Its work is concentrated between the actual creation of standards, such as the EHR function standards, and how organizations implement them. IHE publishes standard implementation specifications, called *profiles*. One such collection of profiles, the Laboratory Technical Framework (LAB TF), defines specific implementations of established standards to achieve integration goals of clinical laboratories with other components of a healthcare enterprise or with a broader community of healthcare. Note that IHE does not claim to develop new or additional standards but to support the use of existing standards. The LAB TF involves standards not only from HL7 but also the College of American Pathologists (CAP) and several other standard setting organizations. Another benefit of this work is that personnel purchasing any EHR or clinical information system can refer to applicable IHE profiles, require compliance from vendors, and streamline system implementation and interoperability.

Digital Imaging and Communications in Medicine (DICOM)

When it comes to the uniqueness of healthcare with respect to interoperability of information systems, the reliance on various images captured from numerous peripheral devices in addition to numerical results and words adds extraordinary complexity to the digital medical record. Digital diagnostic imaging devices, called *modalities* (X-ray, ultrasound, computed tomography [CT], and so on), have made it necessary for a standard method for transferring images and associated information between medical devices and for use in EHRs manufactured by various vendors. Each of the imaging devices initially create the image in a proprietary format. The American College of Radiology (ACR) and the National Electrical Manufacturers Association (NEMA) formed a joint committee in 1983 to develop a standard known today as DICOM.

DICOM promotes interoperability of medical imaging equipment by specifying the protocols required for transferring digital images across the network. The device used to capture the image can be manufactured by any vendor that complies with the DICOM standard. Images are able to be stored in databases that can be interrogated using data analysis tools. Probably the most impressive accomplishment of DICOM is the advent of PACS,[7] which constitutes some of the most complex, networked medical devices in a healthcare organization. These can consist of dozens of modalities, set up in a LAN configuration connected to several different types of servers for image processing, demographic patient data integration with the images, and file transfer to end-user viewing stations. PACS is also accessible via the Web when a dedicated web server is added to the architecture. This is mainly due to providing access to providers that do not need a diagnostic quality image, unlike a radiologist. Web-viewed images have less fidelity, or image quality. In all, many healthcare organizations must accommodate a PACS as a LAN within their LAN because its footprint is large. DICOM is an evolving standard that allows the PACS both to communicate within its own component and to interface with other systems in the same organization and those distributed geographically and likely not affiliated organizationally.

The Foundation of Health Data Management

Like any industry that relies on information, healthcare organizations must adhere to proper data management principles. To do this, they should organize their information management around concepts that are considered best practices. Information in many different forms is found in every part of the healthcare organization, including written instructions, treatment plans, images, audio files, video clips, paper documents, and digital files. Successful healthcare organizations work to transform the information into a strategic asset, organizing and leveraging it into a resource as valuable as any clinical technology or financial asset it has. To have a chance at organizing and leveraging the data, healthcare data management programs will have the following components:

- **Governance**   Leadership must be applied to strategically align processes and technology. A uniform view across the organization is needed. Because data governance is not just an IT issue, a data governance committee must include senior-level executives and specialists from other business and clinical areas (along with IT representatives) who provide vision and authority to the data governance function.

- **Stewardship**   Ownership and accountability are important in managing data. Data is a valuable asset, and all personnel who have and use data must understand their individual roles in ensuring prioritization of data, maintain trust in data, and report and track data issues to resolution.

- **Quality**   Adequate checks and oversight must be in place to achieve data that is relevant, accurate, timely, and accessible, to name a few characteristics of data quality. Without these characteristics, healthcare organizations cannot begin to provide patient care without introducing significant risk of harm. They also cannot be certain their billing practices will accurately reflect work performed. Both scenarios predict critical conditions for healthcare providers.

- **Architecture**   Related to the location of data and how it flows through the organization, inventory and documentation make up the first step. Then the organization must identify the stakeholders and the relevant information life cycle. Additionally, data architecture involves defining the organization's metadata, or its data about data. An element of metadata might be "patient record" and include multiple elements such as date of birth, appointment date, prescriptions, and so on. Because this information may be used by multiple departments or even across different organizations, having metadata called *patient record number* that is uniformly defined can streamline the myriad processes that rely on these associated data elements.

- **Standards**   With all the business processes and clinical workflows that operate with healthcare, the effort to establish and maintain data with common understanding and meaning is important (and one of the reasons the coding of medical practices with ICD-9, for example, is so essential). Data standards are founded using a combination of regulations, customs, and user acceptance.

- **Security**   Assuring confidentiality, integrity, and availability of data, both in paper form or digital, is a central concern of any data management program. Within healthcare, the protection of data from unauthorized (accidental or intentional) modification, destruction, or disclosure can be a violation of law, a matter of risk to patient safety, or both.

Information Flow and Life Cycle in the Healthcare Environments

What should be clear at this point is that information is required to move along the clinical workflow of patient care. If the information is not available or reliable, patient care suffers. When critical information is not in the hands of the provider when it is needed, patient safety may be at risk. Additionally, information has a life cycle that must be managed to ensure confidentiality and integrity are maintained, as well as availability. This does not mean that confidentiality, integrity, and availability are the goals at any cost. Properly understanding information flow and information life-cycle management (ILM) is essential to reduce costs.

The ILM cycle involves the following steps:[8]

- **Creation** The information must be available, trusted, reliable, and concise from whatever source the information originates. The sources could be the patient, a provider, or any number of different medical devices and diagnostic tools.

- **Retention** The value of the information (classification) will determine how long an organization will keep the information. Policies are required to establish the length of time the records are useful and after which outdated records are discarded.

- **Maintenance** Records must be stored and protected while in the possession of the provider. A key aspect of storage is to maintain the record with the same level of availability to providers and data integrity as long as the information is useful.

- **Use** Information has to be used in a manner consistent with the reasons it was collected and never for a provider's personal gain. For example, data used for treatment typically cannot be used for published research if the patient did not consent to such use. Probably the most important feature of use within the information life cycle is protecting the information during transfer. Healthcare organizations use data. That is a given. As the data moves throughout the organization, between organizations, and between providers and payers, safeguards are needed to assure confidentiality, integrity, and availability.

- **Disposal** This is the final step in the process and the most vulnerable. Too many times data is lost or disclosed in an unauthorized manner when the organization no longer deems the information useful. During the transfer of the information to the disposal process, a data leak or breach occurs because safeguards are relaxed. Until data is destroyed, it is still necessary to protect it. There are three common disposal options whether it is paper or digital information.

  - **Overwriting** (covering up old data with new data, typically 1s and 0s)

  - **Degaussing** (erasing the magnetic field of the storage media)

  - **Physical destruction** (paper or digital shredding or incineration are choices)

 NOTE It is common to use several of these methods depending on the value of the data and the media. In some cases, such as degaussing, the process involves performing the action a number of times to completely ensure the data cannot be recovered.

A key part of any information security strategy is disposing of data once it's no longer needed. Failure to do so can lead to serious breaches of data protection and privacy policies, compliance problems, and added costs. A Tulsa, Oklahoma, hospital[9] had a 3-inch stack of medical records, consisting of patient demographics, electrocardiogram printouts, and provider notes disclosed publically. During the transfer of the paper records from the hospital to a recycler and record destruction company, proper procedures were not followed. Taking shortcuts, in this case not locking the transport box, created a data breach. This does not happen just to paper records, though. Digital information can be lost easily prior to destruction. For example, as many as 400,000 patients were put at risk when a healthcare provider failed to properly sanitize a copier/printer/fax/scanner prior to returning it after the end of its lease.[10] The names of the innocent are public knowledge but not important here. A complete list of all the examples that illustrate this topic is too long to provide here. However, the essential message to healthcare information security and privacy professionals is *this can happen to your organization*. If it does, it is most likely to happen when you let your guard down at the disposal step in the ILM.

 TIP Publically available guidance, namely, U.S. Department of Defense (DoD) 5220.22-M, is the source for one of the most used software-based data sanitization methods. The usual implementation of the hard drive overwriting is as follows:

- **Pass 1** Writes a 0 and verifies the write
- **Pass 2** Writes a 1 and verifies the write
- **Pass 3** Writes a random character and verifies the write

Health Data Characterization

Data sharing and interchange typically must be intentional. Based on law, contractual agreements, and technical compatibility, interoperability has to be a premeditated and determined effort. Beyond the concepts of data standards and the languages of healthcare, a couple other topics are important to consider, namely, data classification and data taxonomy. Even if data is technically compatible to exchange between organizations, not all data is equal. Individual organizational policies and procedures must be taken into account. Attending to health data characterization through proper data classification and data taxonomy makes information exchange feasible. To that end, another aspect to health data characterization to be mentioned is data analytics, which is an emerging trend made possible by data classification and data taxonomy done correctly.

Data Classification

As mentioned earlier, the ILM requires a healthcare organization to have a classification system, based on the value of the information. It is important to note that this type of *data classification* differs from that of computer programming, which is also called classification, but relates more to labeling the data to differentiate it into classes and sets. In the ILM context, data classification is required to apply a value relative to how sensitive and critical the information is as defined by the organization. This value will determine what level of information protection controls will be applied to information collected, maintained, retained, used, and disposed of when no longer needed.

Data Taxonomy

Data taxonomy relates to categorizing data into a standardized format with common meaning so it can be standardized. When *psychologist* means *psychologist* independent of organization and distinct from other provider professions, such as *social worker* or *counselor*, then data sharing and reuse are possible. Having a data taxonomy introduces convenience and reduces wasted efforts in trying to establish common definitions and context. Another benefit of data taxonomy is that it has proven effective in streamlining payment and reimbursement activities.

Data Analytics

Possibly the most compelling argument for proper data characterization is *data analytics*. With standard classification and taxonomy, comparative analysis on larger and larger volumes of data becomes a reality at a reasonable cost. Previously, data analytics would be constrained to individual organizations because of incompatibility of policies, procedures, and information systems. At best, data analytics were applicable only to that organization. Any comparisons most likely suffered from data latency because results could not be shared in real time. Today, alliances and data analytic firms are able to aggregate and process terabytes and petabytes of data from dozens of healthcare organizations almost instantly and simultaneously to provide outcome measures and lower costs over time.

The evolution of data analytics has information systems able to process more data faster and more economically. As organizational data becomes more compatible and standardized, a movement nicknamed Big Data has exploded in many industries. Healthcare is no exception. An example of the desire to exploit the possibilities of comparing huge volumes of health data from many different sources comes from the U.S. government, in the Big Data Research and Development Initiative.[11] The results are measurable and happening now. For instance, the State University of New York (SUNY) at Buffalo is home to one of the leading multiple sclerosis (MS) research centers. The tools and techniques available to them through Big Data analytics have enabled them to take hundreds of thousands of genetic variations, combine them with other gene products and environmental factors, and analyze the data quickly. They have successfully been able to use complex algorithms and reduce the time required to conduct analysis from 27.2 hours to 11.7 minutes.[12]

Legal Medical Record

When a medical record was completely made up of paper charts, documents, film images, and files, a *legal health record* was the entire contents related to an individual patient. That began to change with the introduction of paper to digital records conversion. Patients also have become more involved with the contents of the records related to regulatory changes, legal issues in healthcare, and patient education on the Internet.

The impact of the definition is in what is disclosed to law enforcement and for legal proceedings. Only that which constitutes a legal medical record is to be disclosed. The contents of a legal medical record should (at least) do the following:

- Support patient care decisions
- Document the care provided for the purposes of reimbursement
- Serve as evidence in legal proceedings about such care

The first challenge in defining a legal medical record is that no such standard exists.[13] Each organization is required to define the contents for itself. Some components are more obvious and universal than others. For instance, information related to medication orders, pathology reports, and emergency department records would certainly be part of any legal medical record. Administrative data and documents, however, are usually excluded. These might be items such as authorization forms for the release of information, incident or patient safety reports, and psychotherapy notes. To identify which documents can be excluded, healthcare organizations typically term these items *working documents*.

As noted, not all health information is digital. Much remains in paper format. Some of the paper records, images, and files constitute valid elements of a legal medical record. When a healthcare organization defines its legal medical record as having both paper and digital information, that record is called a *hybrid* legal medical record. Along with the location of the various databases where the electronic information resides, the medical record must have references to the sources of the paper-based information it includes.

Chapter Review

We have begun our journey. At this point, the groundwork is in place to build upon the elements that impact healthcare information privacy and security. In this chapter, we identified the organization of healthcare around patients, providers, payers, and key stakeholders. These entities make up any healthcare system, but how these systems are financed can differ. While government (single-payer) is the predominant model worldwide, the employer-based and private insurance models are present enough to be a factor.

Subsequent chapters will go into great detail about the technology and data standards specific to healthcare, but in this chapter we introduced the existence of things such as medical devices and health information networks that have particular purposes and present distinctive challenges. Medical devices especially are of concern. These special-purpose computing systems operate much like any other type of office automation. But in the end, they are regulated by external government agencies, and manufacturers maintain a level of responsibility over the life of the devices. We will revisit and expand upon these distinctions in future chapters. Finally, this chapter skimmed the surface of established categories of foundational health data management principles. Understanding these topics help shape your knowledge and use of information through its life cycle and help you properly manage products central to healthcare, for example, data analytics and the legal medical record.

Review Questions

1. If a payer is a public source, which of these would be the source of funds?

    A. Employer group

    B. Health maintenance organization

    C. Public health agency

    D. Government entity

2. (TRUE or FALSE) An inpatient is defined as an individual who checks into the emergency room and is admitted overnight for less than 24 hours.

3. Who is the primary payer in most developed countries for healthcare?

    A. Self-pay

    B. Employers

    C. Government

    D. Military

4. "Per member per month" is a common way to describe a payment model called

    A. Capitation

    B. Bundled payment

    C. Accountable care

    D. Managed care

5. Reimbursement for healthcare services must be _____, _____, and _____.

6. Of the following, which health information exchange is an example of one that is having a significant impact on healthcare?

    A. Nationwide Health Information Network Exchange

    B. Blue Cross Blue Shield

    C. Managed Care Network

    D. Electronic Health Record

7. The centerpiece of the health information system is the

    A. Medical device

    B. Provider note

    C. Electronic health record

    D. Firewall

8. (TRUE or FALSE) DICOM is the standard established to help electronic health records to interconnect.

9. (TRUE or FALSE) Assuring confidentiality, integrity, and availability of data, both in paper form or digital, is a central concern of security in the data management program.

   A. Security

   B. Governance

   C. Stewardship

   D. Standards

10. At what stage of information life-cycle management are you most likely to have a data breach?

   A. Creation

   B. Retention

   C. Use

   D. Disposal

Answers

1. **D.** An employer group or employer-based healthcare insurance would be considered a private payer. A health maintenance organization can be a method of organizing delivery of care under a government payer plan, like Medicare, but it is not a public source of funds. A public health agency is unlikely to reimburse providers for care as part of their surveillance responsibilities. Therefore, the best answer is D, a government entity that uses public tax dollars or other publically acquired funds to fund or reimburse providers for healthcare.

2. **TRUE.** A recurring appointment each day from 5 p.m. to 6 p.m. is an outpatient visit, as are appointments that do not require admissions officially into the hospital. The knee surgery with transportation to an assisted-living residence implies discharging the patient to his or her home. A sleep study, although overnight, is not an admission to a hospital. The emergency room that results in a formal admission into the hospital fits the definition of inpatient.

3. **C.** The government is the primary payer in most developed countries of the world. Only a small percentage of individuals pay out-of-pocket for their healthcare. While employers are a sizable percentage of health insurance financers in the United States, it far less common internationally. The military, as a portion of government-provided health insurance, is partially correct; it is not the primary payer.

4. **A.** "Per member per month" is a common measurement of what funds are provided to a healthcare organization for the delivery of care. The amount is preset and made available prior to the covered period of time. It has to relate

to each individual over that measured period of time. Bundled payment, accountable care, and managed care are all somewhat related to financing healthcare, but none is specifically defined or measured in terms of each covered life over a period of time.

5. **usual, customary, and reasonable.** The only correct combination of adjectives is "usual, customary, and reasonable." All of the others are not found within any typical definition of what charges are reimbursable.

6. **A.** Nationwide Health Information Network Exchange is the only answer in this category that is accurate. Blue Cross Blue Shield is a commercial health insurer, and the Managed Care Network is a generic description of connected managed-care plans (which may describe contractual arrangements as well as information technology networking). The electronic health record is an application that may be networked in an exchange but is not by definition.

7. **C.** Although the medical device category of systems is extremely important in collecting health information, it rarely does more than collect and transmit it to the electronic health record. A provider note is found within the electronic health record and is a key component. A firewall, on the other hand, should be part of any healthcare system architecture, but it should not be considered the centerpiece. The electronic health record is the repository of all the important inputs in the system to include medical devices and provider notes. Because of its value, devices such as a firewall are in place to protect it.

8. **FALSE.** DICOM is Digital Imaging and Communications in Medicine and is used to facilitate the transmission of digital images from radiology exams, for example. The only standard that fits the definition of electronic health record interconnectivity is Health Level 7 (HL7).

9. **TRUE.** By definition, security applies to the efforts to assure confidentiality, integrity, and availability of data. While the governance, stewardship, and standards are all valid health data management principles, only security exactly meets this definition.

10. Even though any stage of the information life cycle can have risk of data breach, the creation, retention, and use stages are not the most likely for data loss. When data is marked for disposal or destruction, either in paper or digital format, it is imperative to continue to apply safeguards against loss. Too many examples exist where data is no longer needed and it is no longer protected. At which point, it is stolen or lost.

References

1. Todd, Susan R., and Benjamin D. Sommers. "Overview of the Uninsured in the United States: A Summary of the 2012 Current Population Survey Report." ASPE Issue Brief. September 12, 2012. Accessed November 3, 2013, at http://aspe.hhs. gov/health/reports/2012/uninsuredintheus/ib.shtml#howmany

2. U.S. Census Bureau. "Income, Poverty, and Health Insurance Coverage in the United States: 2010." September 2011. Accessed November 2, 2013, at www .census.gov/prod/2011pubs/p60-239.pdf

3. Food and Drug Administration. "Medical Devices." Accessed October 25, 2013, at www.fda.gov/MedicalDevices/DeviceRegulationandGuidance/overview

4. European Commission. "EU and US Step up Cooperation in eHealth IT." March 22, 2013. Accessed October 22, 2013, at http://ec.europa.eu/digital-agenda/en/ news/eu-and-us-step-cooperation-ehealth-it

5. Richardson, William C. (et al.). "To Err is Human: Building a Safer Health System." Institute of Medicine. November 1999. Accessed October 14, 2013, at www.iom.edu/~/media/Files/Report%20Files/1999/To-Err-is-Human/To%20 Err%20is%20Human%201999%20%20report%20brief.pdf

6. Medishare Tools. ICD-9 Lookup. Accessed October 21, 2013, at http:// medishare.com/tools/codes/icd9/382.9#382.9?&_suid=1384529584713039419 76392909484

7. Huang, H. K. *PACS and Imaging Informatics: Basic Principles and Applications.* John Wiley and Sons. 2010. pps. 219–229.

8. National Health Service (UK). "Information Lifecycle and Records Management Policy." The Queen Elizabeth Hospital King's Lynn. March 5, 2013. Page 8. Accessed October 20, 2013, at www.qehkl.nhs.uk/IG-Documents/information-lifecycle-records-management-policy.pdf

9. Emory, Bryan. "Tulsa Medical Records Turn up on Ponca Newspaper Loading Dock." *Oklahoma's Own.* March 4, 2013. Accessed on November 13, 2013, at www.newson6.com/story/21476118/tulsa-medical-records-turn-up-on-ponca-city-newspaper-loading-dock

10. Keteyain, Arman. "Digital Photocopiers Loaded with Secrets." *CBS Evening News.* April 20, 2010. Accessed on October 30, 2013, at www.id-theft-security .com/lifelock-blog/2010/05/data-breach-4

11. Official Memo. Office of Science and Technology Policy, Executive Office of the President. "Obama Administration Unveils 'Big Data Initiative': Announces $200 Million in New R&D Investments." March 29, 2012. Accessed on October 27, 2013, at www.whitehouse.gov/sites/default/files/microsites/ostp/big_data_ press_release.pdf

12. Large Gene Interaction Analytics at University at Buffalo, SUNY. May 2013. Accessed on November 18, 2013, at www-01.ibm.com/common/ssi/cgi-bin/ssia lias?subtype=AB&infotype=PM&appname=SWGE_IM_ZN_USEN&htmlfid=IMC 14675USEN&attachment=IMC14675USEN.PDF

13. AHIMA e-HIM Work Group on the Legal Health Record. "Update: Guidelines for Defining the Legal Health Record for Disclosure Purposes." *Journal of AHIMA* 76, no.8, September 2005. pp. 64A–G. Accessed on November 12, 2013, at http://library.ahima.org/xpedio/groups/public/documents/ahima/ bok1_048604.hcsp?dDocName=bok1_048604

Healthcare: People, Roles, and Third-Party Partners

In this chapter, you will learn to

- Identify the variety of occupations and roles in a healthcare organization
- Distinguish between measures of qualifications and competency for each healthcare role
- Recognize the impact of healthcare organizational behavior on health information protection
- Comprehend the nature and importance of third-party relationships in healthcare
- Differentiate the categories of significant third parties to the healthcare organization
- Anticipate security and privacy issues related to third-party relationships

There are few organizations with more diverse workforces than healthcare organizations. To begin with, healthcare organizations employ or contract for services that result in a self-contained ecosystem. From the construction of facilities to housekeeping to dining services, healthcare organizations have staffing for power generation and full support services. This is all to enable patient care in emergency or disastrous conditions. If that is not enough diversity of workforce composition, an extremely rich mixture of highly educated and talented physicians, nurses, administrators, and medical technicians provide the direct and indirect patient care. Added to that, the numerous environments in which healthcare is delivered brings even more variety to the categories of caregivers and support personnel that are necessary. Healthcare is delivered in hospitals, clinical offices, specialty diagnostic centers, and even the home. In regard to information privacy and security, most of these categories of caregivers in all of these environments will use (and must protect) individually identifiable health information. This chapter introduces these categories of healthcare organization staff members and their various qualifications.

You will also examine the role and impact that third-party organizations play in healthcare. As mentioned, healthcare organizations require many different types of workers to accomplish their mission, and the organizations cannot have a payroll that includes all of them. That would be too expensive. A third party must provide some products and services on a contractual basis. Some of these third parties, such as medical-supply companies, serve only healthcare organizations. Others, such as data centers, serve all types of organizations with similar requirements. In either case, if the third party handles patient information for the healthcare organization, additional contractual agreements will be in place.

Identifying Workforce Dynamics: Personnel, Professions, and Proficiency

If you walk into any healthcare organization, you will find a wide variety of occupations. There are people performing roles ranging from janitorial services to open-heart surgery. There are teams cleaning rooms and others delivering babies. People perform clinical, administrative, and support services to care for patients. The variety of occupations and different levels of education and competency that exist in healthcare is unique compared to any other industry. The U.S. government identifies almost 50 categories of healthcare professionals, not including the profession of healthcare administration (finance, facility management, senior executives, and so on).[1] What is incredible is the interdependencies of these occupations. From the lowest skilled, entry-level employee to the most senior executive or seasoned physician, the entire organization works in an interconnected way to provide patient care. Technicians, professionals, and executives must work together collaboratively. One thing is certain: Information privacy and security personnel must be aware of the roles of the healthcare workforce in order to implement and maintain adequate information privacy and security.

Nurses

Because nurses can (and do) perform many tasks with a wide variety of responsibilities in any healthcare organization, they are the largest category of the healthcare workforce. In the United States alone, there are more than 2.6 million registered nurses, with 60 percent working in hospitals.[2] Internationally, many countries also have licensure for nursing. For instance, the Nursing and Midwifery Council oversee this process in the United Kingdom. Besides registered nurses, there are many other types of nurses also providing patient care in the hospital and in other care settings. Within the nursing category are numerous types of roles. Still, maybe because the need is so great, there is a bona fide shortage of skilled nurses in the United States today. Depending on the role, a nurse will receive different training and hold varying levels of competency. General categories of nursing are nurses' aides, licensed practical nurses, and registered nurses (to include nurse practitioners and certified registered nurses).

Nurses' Aides

Nurses' aides provide a great deal of patient care in a variety of healthcare settings from the physician office to the hospital to long-term care environments. A related occupation to hospital orderlies and attendants, nurses' aides perform services that include moving, repositioning, and lifting patients. You might also find them providing numerous services related to comforting patients and keeping them at ease. The education level of most nurses' aides is post–high school (a diploma or certificate). It is not uncommon for healthcare organizations to require at least a competency exam that the nurses' aide needs to pass.

Licensed Practical Nurses

The next level of nursing based on education and required training is the licensed practical nurse (LPN). These nurses must complete a yearlong (typically) certified educational program. Often these programs are affiliated with a teaching hospital that provides some hands-on experience for the students. After the students complete the program, there is an additional licensing exam. You will find LPNs in every area of healthcare provision. They work in hospitals, of course, but also may provide care in a patient's home. Through home healthcare, the continuum of care extends from the hospital into the patient's normal living environment, which has a demonstrated positive impact on outcomes.

Registered Nurses

LPNs work under the supervision of registered nurses (RNs). With more education and training requirements, RNs are at the next level of nurses providing patient care. The care they provide is more directly involved in coordinating with physicians and other healthcare providers. Whether it is in the emergency room or intensive care unit, you will see RNs at the front line of the patient care. RNs also have a large role in educating patients and the public about health status, postdischarge instructions, and a variety of other concerns related to healthcare. Of course, RNs work in the same environments as all other nurses, but because of their additional education, training, and credentialing, RNs can work independently in some nontraditional healthcare environments such as correctional facilities, schools, and summer camps. Most commonly, RNs receive a bachelor's degree in nursing. It is possible, however, to obtain RN licensure with an associate's degree in nursing or a diploma from select nursing programs. All RNs must obtain their license by passing a national RN licensing exam.

Nurse Practitioners and Certified Registered Nurses

For many reasons, healthcare professions have evolved from established roles and practices over the years. Whether the reason is new technology, staffing shortages, advances in medicine, or a combination of all these, many categories of healthcare providers have developed advanced skill sets that have blurred the lines between traditional responsibilities. Within the nursing profession, two such examples are the nurse practitioner (NP) and the certified registered nurse anesthetist (CRNA). To become an NP, one must first be an RN. Then, after additional, advanced classroom and clinical education, the RN is credentialed as an NP. NPs care for patients with acute and chronic medical conditions, and they go beyond traditional nursing care. A visit or encounter would include taking a complete history of the patient, performing a physical exam, and then ordering diagnostic tests and treatments. Depending on what their practice is, NPs can even prescribe medications and make referrals. The types of practices where you will find NPs are almost limitless. They serve in more general practices such as pediatrics, family practice, and geriatrics and in specialty care areas such as OB/GYN, oncology, dermatology, and pain management. After nurses are granted RN licensing, they must then graduate from an additional program accredited for conferring the master's of science in nursing (MSN) or the doctorate of nursing practice (DNP) degree. It does not end there. The next step is to pass a national board-certifying exam. The NP will take the exam based on what specific clinical area their educational program focused on. In other words, if the program was concentrated on geriatrics, the certification exam would also. After clearing these hurdles, the board-certified NP can apply for additional credentials, such as being able to prescribe medications and obtaining a Drug Enforcement Agency (DEA) registration number.

The second advanced nursing career track is the certified registered nurse anesthetist (CRNA). These nurses provide anesthesia to patients and can do so for any surgery or procedure that requires anesthesia. Where this responsibility was previously reserved for physicians, having CRNAs allows small-market and rural hospitals to control costs by reducing staffing expense while maintaining the standard of care. To become a CRNA, the process is similar to NP—a CRNA needs a bachelor's degree in nursing or equivalent and needs to be a licensed registered nurse. Additionally, a CRNA must have clinical experience in an acute-care setting. They need to demonstrate one year of experience in an area such as the intensive care unit as opposed to long-term care or rehabilitation units. Above all this, they also must complete an accredited nurse anesthesia educational program. Finally, to be a CRNA, the nurse has to pass a national certification examination.

In summary, nurses have long been the backbone of healthcare provision. They have impressive levels of education, training, and certification and are indispensable in every aspect of clinical workflow. They are also invaluable when serving in the administrative and executive functions of the business. They are represented in pediatrics to geriatrics, primary care to intensive care, and the exam room to the board room. Nursing professionals are highly sought after even outside the healthcare organization for their specialized understanding of healthcare and their flexibility in training. Nurses are typically the educators of patients (and other healthcare professionals), so you will find many nurses who serve outside of patient care and in health education roles.

 TIP   In the United States, one of the major impacts to labor relations in healthcare is the nursing unions. Approximately 21 percent of nurses are members of unions. In fact, nursing unionization outpaces the general unionization of other U.S. occupations, which are in decline. Some of the stated benefits to unionization are increased wages relative to peer group nurses, better patient outcomes and satisfaction because of better patient-to-nurse ratios, and an increased sense of engagement and fairness within an organization.

Physicians

The role of physician has been practiced as far back as time has been recorded, but Hippocrates around 350 BC is considered the "father of modern medicine."[3] In contrast, modern nursing began in the 19th century (although the services of nursing in patient care certainly took place as far back as there were sick and injured people). The point is that from the beginning to today, the central relationship in healthcare is between the doctor and the patient. Physicians' main role is to diagnose and treat injuries and illnesses for their patients. Surgeons, who are a specialized type of physician, treat patients by operating to treat injuries, diseases, and deformities. Almost all physicians obtain a bachelor's degree and then complete four more years in an accredited medical school. There has always been a measure of importance placed on actually performing under the guidance of a current physician. So, after medical school, on-the-job training continues via an internship for a year. Then the student must complete a residency, usually focusing on a specialty or area of increased proficiency, such as cardiology or internal medicine.

 NOTE Residency is a key difference between the requirements of nurses, including NPs and CRNAs, and physicians. This distinction is changing as more NP residencies are becoming available and recommended even if they are not required.

Like nurses, doctors must also obtain a license to practice and hold the credential of medical doctor (MD) or doctorate of osteopathic medicine (DO). It is also common for MDs and DOs to take additional exams for board certification. There are board certifications (sometimes more than one) for all the various specialties. After completing the training and licensing, they are permitted to independently prescribe medications and order, perform, and interpret diagnostic tests. In addition, each physician is also required to be credentialed specifically to practice in a particular hospital or healthcare organization. This is an internal function of the healthcare organization. Personnel verify the background and qualifications of the physician and grant the physician privileges to practice medicine within the organization.

As mentioned, a physician can be a general practitioner with responsibilities in family medicine, internal medicine, or other primary-care types of areas. Otherwise, based on additional, focused training and experience, physicians and surgeons can concentrate on a particular disease or condition or in a specific physiologic system. To help illustrate the number and variety of these specialties (the physicians are called *specialists*), Table 2-1 describes some of the most common ones.

Physician Assistants

We have already discussed healthcare providers such as the NP and CRNA and how they evolved. Another similar profession that does not originate from nursing is the physician assistant (PA). Collectively, the NP, CRNA, and PA are often called *physician extenders* because they have absorbed traditional roles and responsibilities reserved for physicians to help increase the availability of advanced care. Physician extenders have also proven invaluable by often improving quality (certainly not lessening it), reducing costs, and increasing access. The PA is recognized as another general category of healthcare professional on staff who has a license to practice medicine under the guidance of a physician. This recognition is not universal across international health systems. Primarily a U.S. healthcare physician extender, the PA may not be recognized in other countries.

Specialist	Description
Anesthesiologist	This is a doctor present during surgery. Anesthesiologists put patients to sleep safely and monitors them through the procedure.
Cardiologist	This is a doctor focused on diseases and conditions of the heart and cardiovascular systems.
Dermatologist	This is a specialist for conditions of the skin; dermatologists are important in the early detection of skin cancers.
Emergency/trauma	This is a doctor trained and ready for any variety of acute injury, trauma, emergency, and so on, 24 hours a day, every day of the year.
Endocrinologist	This is a doctor who specializes in issues with glands such as the thyroid or other hormone problems that impact growth, mood, and metabolism.
Epidemiologist	This is a doctor who identifies the spread of new diseases, determines how a virus mutates, and develops prevention and cures with immunizations and vaccinations.
Neurologist	This is a doctor who treats disorders of the brain such as Parkinson's disease and Alzheimer's disease.
Neurosurgeon	This is a related specialty to neurologist; a neurosurgeon performs surgery on central and peripheral nervous system diseases and the brain.
Obstetrician/gynecologist	This is a doctor who handles conditions related to the female reproductive system, including childbirth.
Oncologist	This is a doctor who diagnoses and treats cancer patients; an oncologist can be further specialized into one or more specific cancer types or patient categories.
Ophthalmologist	This is a doctor who treats eyes and various eye defects and blindness; an ophthalmologist also can perform eye surgeries.
Orthopedic surgeon	This is a doctor who performs examinations and surgery on bone, joint, and other related conditions, such as arthritis and osteoporosis.
Pathologist	This is a doctor who studies samples of cells for abnormalities using DNA, tissue, blood, and so on. Pathologists also perform autopsies to determine cause of death.
Pediatrician	This is a general practitioner who concentrates on the patient category of children (birth to adolescent).
Psychiatrist	This is a doctor who treats mental illnesses and behavioral health issues.
Radiologist	This is a doctor who specializes in reading and interpreting X-rays or other imaging technologies to provide diagnoses.
Plastic surgeon	This is a doctor who treats more than just cosmetic physical appearances. Plastic surgeons are consulted on a number of reconstructive physical procedures and corrective surgeries.

Table 2-1 Selected Specialist Physicians

Specialist	Description
Podiatrist	This is a doctor who concentrates on issues with gait, foot, and ankle, as well as their impact on overall physical health. Podiatrists are important in the care of diabetics with wound issues of the feet and toes.
Pulmonologist	This is a doctor who focuses on lung conditions and ventilator support for ICU patients.
Surgeon	All of the specialists may at one time or another perform surgery. However, some surgeons practice general surgery of trauma, transplant, or any number of other surgeries. Of course, they may choose to concentrate in one or two areas as well.
Urologist	This is a doctor who primarily treats urinary problems such as urinary tract infections. The male reproductive system is typically a focus.

Table 2-1   Selected Specialist Physicians

Most often, a candidate for PA already has a bachelor's degree, but some programs confer one as part of completing the PA curriculum. In any case, PA programs are approximately two to three years of schoolwork with clinical rotations in all of the areas of PA practice, such as internal medicine, family practice, ER, and so on. In some cases, a graduating PA decides to specialize in one of these clinical areas and obtains additional training and experience. The process is similar to physicians gaining specialty rotations but much shorter in length of time. PAs provide all of the same patient-care functions as a physician. But, they must work under the direction and oversight of a physician. One difference is in performing surgery, where a PA can provide assistance to a physician surgeon but not conduct the surgery independently. Identically to all nurses and physicians, there is a licensing requirement for PAs.

Medical Technicians

When you hear someone referred to as a *medical technician*, it is similarly overarching like *doctor or nurse*. There are numerous subcategories of medical technicians that fully describe the expertise and technical aptitude of any particular medical technician. For starters, the general category of medical technician describes the kind of work done in clinical laboratories performing tests and exams. A medical technician has practical knowledge and ability in a clinical area. They also must be able to understand medical data that comes from their specific equipment and how it relates to the patient. They are the first line of interpreters of results. While they do not make a diagnosis, they can certainly reduce error and rework when they recognize inaccuracies in data. You may see this in a blood bank or microbiology laboratory. Another type of medical technician operates medical devices in support of performing procedures in the specific clinical practice. This would include diagnostic imaging, cardiac catheterizations, and hemodialysis. For all of these different types of medical technicians, their reports and findings of tests and examinations are what the physicians will use to diagnose and treat the patients.

Biomedical Technicians and Clinical Engineers

Another type of medical technician is the personnel who maintain (as opposed to operate) the medical devices. These are biomedical technicians and clinical engineers. One of the key differences between these types of medical technicians and the one mentioned earlier is that biomedical technicians and clinical engineers typically do not require extensive training on human anatomy, physiology, and clinical technique. With respect to education, clinical engineers have an educational requirement that exceeds that for a biomedical technician, namely, a four-year degree at least. Biomedical technicians, much like all other medical technicians, may have a two-year degree or a certificate of training from a healthcare vocational training program. In any case, both clinical engineers and biomedical technicians work in conjunction with other medical technicians to safely operate and maintain all of the various medical devices and technologies in the healthcare organization.

Other Providers with Specific Access

Based on how they provide clinical services to the patient, several other healthcare providers and support personnel handle protected health information. All of the following are found internationally and have varying levels of licensure and certification requirements:

- **Emergency medical technicians**   These technicians have special training to provide first response to emergency situations and to handle traumatic injuries and medical care at the accident scenes.
- **Social workers**   This profession concentrates on patients' quality of life and subjective well-being. They administer to individuals, groups, and communities. Areas of practice include research, counseling, crisis intervention, and teaching.
- **Psychologists**   As MDs, psychologists provide patient care with respect to behavior and mental processes. They provide counseling services and conduct research within academic settings.
- **Pharmacists**   These people have responsibility in the proper and safe use of medications. They are an integral part of the healthcare team in that they often provide meaningful education and counseling for patients who are receiving medication.

Administration

No healthcare organization could succeed without another significant member of the healthcare workforce, the administration. Another encompassing term, *administration* describes all the various people who administratively support the provision of healthcare. At every level of the healthcare organization, from the chief executive officer to the ward clerk, these individuals provide their appropriate level of management and leadership. At the most senior level, *administration* refers to managing internal and external forces to achieve specific goals. One of the key responsibilities for senior administrators is to recruit and retain quality physicians, ensure appropriate staffing levels, and manage performance. Below this level, administration strives to achieve their objectives and allocate resources appropriately. Much like all of the other healthcare professions, administration can have general focus across many areas, like a chief operating officer or a physician officer manager. On the other hand, many administrators specialize in a given area, such as information technology or finance.

In terms of education and training, the path to an administrative position mirrors its counterparts in the other professions and categories. For more senior-level positions, at least a bachelor's degree is usually needed. In many cases, especially when in a specialty area such as information technology or finance, a graduate degree is commonly preferred. For other administrative positions, a combination of a high-school diploma and on-the-job training is required. Board certification is available to administrators of all types, from general administrators to information technology to finance. The certification of administration personnel provides a common framework for peer-to-peer relationships with healthcare provider colleagues. Sometimes, administrative personnel include professionals from other healthcare categories. For instance, many physicians move into administrative positions because of the leadership and operational issues. Most healthcare organizations will employ a chief medical officer and chief nursing officer in the administration group.

Environmental Services

Without janitorial or housekeeping services, a healthcare organization could not open its doors. The regulatory and patient safety issues that healthcare organizations face make environmental concerns important. In addition, these types of services, such as maintenance, alterations, and construction, happen in areas where patients are or will be. Environmental service personnel also provide laundry operations and linen distribution. Coupled with housekeeping services, these integrate into the overall management of beds within the organization. How quickly a room or a bed can be made ready after a patient is discharged can mean significant added revenue. Done incorrectly, the patient safety, satisfaction, and outcomes can suffer because rooms are transitioned quickly but they lack cleanliness. Infection control plays a large role, too; a huge revenue drain on healthcare organizations is the number of hospital-acquired infections and readmissions.

 NOTE With respect to credentialing and certifying cybersecurity professionals in the United States, the National Initiative for Cybersecurity Education (NICE) has been established to, among other things, set up a framework for educating the future cybersecurity workforce. This framework will draw from the credentialing and certification processes already established and recognized in healthcare and other industries, albeit not just in information technology. Expect this framework to incorporate healthcare information privacy and security professionals by calling for workers to obtain recognized certifications as the healthcare industry seeks competent and qualified information protectors. See http://niccs.us-cert.gov/footer/about-nice for more information.

Healthcare Organizational Behavior

Now that we have discussed the players and their roles, we briefly cover how they interact (and why that matters to you). In short, you will want to acknowledge the power and politics in healthcare organizations. As noted in the discussions of specific professions, these roles have long histories. The relationships and interactions have been influenced by political factors as well as clinical practice. Before the mid-20th century, the predominant healthcare roles were doctors and nurses. The relationship between the two professions is so famously intense there is a famous "game" that helps professionals explain and understand the relationship. It is called the Doctor-Nurse game, published by *JAMA Psychiatry* in 1967. The major point (not a complementary one) is to demonstrate the underlying communication issues between doctors, nurses, and, by extension, all allied health professions.[4]

In addition to the evolution of the workforce and the associated dynamics, the care setting has changed. Hospitals were not as plentiful as they are today, and patients tended to receive their care at home. The need for all of the allied healthcare professions, such as medical technicians and the variety of administrative personnel, came from the advent of clinical and information technology that required new categories of healthcare workforce. It also made patient care more complex and the need for healthcare in a hospital essential. Of course, this also created new dynamics in the interaction of all the players in healthcare provision.

As organizational behavior relates to understanding information protection in healthcare, the challenge is inevitable. The healthcare organization as an end user or customer is unlike any other. The interaction of nurses, physicians, administration, and medical technicians consists of multiple perspectives and priorities. All must be taken into account with respect to protecting information. You cannot apply information privacy and security in healthcare exactly as it is applied in the telecommunications or retail industries. To understand why is to understand the power and politics at play.

Healthcare starts with the patient. The central relationship in healthcare is the doctor-patient relationship (mentioned already). Anything that interferes with that relationship must be clinically reasonable (and legally defensible). A successful healthcare information security and privacy practitioner must account for this. For instance, installing the latest vulnerability update for an operating system considered a critical fix is a top priority in most organizations with information systems. The edict to stop work and push out the patch remotely from information technology servers may well be the industry best practice. In healthcare, that edict may interfere with patient care and can cause patient safety issues. Remember, medical devices are increasingly networked and will require that same vulnerability update. Imagine if an automatic push across the organization caused a cardiac catheterization lab system to reboot. If this is in the middle of a patient procedure, patient safety could be at risk. That is one over-simplified example; safely implementing health information technology and security has already been identified as a potential issue in healthcare adverse events (those related to patient safety).[5] The key concept is that a healthcare organization chart, a seniority list, or a corner office will not always illustrate the power within the healthcare organization. You must consider the physician (who may or may not be an employee of the organization), the nurses, and anyone else who is providing direct patient care when developing and implementing information protection strategy.

Third-Party Relationships

If you go into any city or town in the world, the odds are that the healthcare organization in that community is the largest employer, the largest customer for local businesses, and maybe even the largest property owner in terms of real estate and facilities. In some communities with multiple healthcare organizations, the economy may hinge on the business of healthcare. But even if the healthcare organization is not these things in a community, it is still the central point for the health and wellness of the population. The employees of the healthcare organization are, in fact, the community—or at least a sizable portion of it. Many of the employees, including doctors, nurses, executives, and clinicians, are highly respected people who serve in their community in a variety of ways.

While it may seem that a healthcare organization is a small, self-contained community with a large variety of personnel in its workforce, it also relies on a large number of external partners to provide supplies, services, and products. These relationships introduce information protection risk to the healthcare organization. Since we are concerned with these types of issues, it makes sense to realize that third parties that handle healthcare information for the healthcare organizations introduce risk. Note that they caused more than 33 percent of all data breaches in 2010 and 46 percent in 2011, in the United States.[6] Later, you will learn how to manage that risk, but you first must understand who the third parties are and how they interact with the healthcare organization.

Vendors

A *vendor* is someone or some entity that sells, supplies, or provides a service or product. In healthcare, vendors do business with a provider organization. They may have many different customers who are not healthcare organizations. Their service or product may or may not be healthcare related. For instance, a vendor can be an office furniture company selling all of the interior design and furnishings for a hospital waiting room, administrative offices, and conference rooms. At the same time, a medical-supply company that provides durable medical equipment, surgical supplies, or even hospital quality beds is also a vendor. The difference is the medical-supply company probably does not have any customers outside of the healthcare organization and any individual physician practice or group practices. For either of these types of vendors, the healthcare organization because of its size and purchasing power will be a significant customer. The vendor will employ members of the community based on how successful their relationship with the hospital is. For example, Henry Ford Health System in Detroit, Michigan, specifically emphasizes diversity and minority-owned business in its supply chain, which consists of more than 300 active vendors in this category.[7] Its large purchasing power works to support not only the employment rate in the community but also the minority-owned business goals. You can see how the vendor (and the community) depends on the business of healthcare.

Increased emphasis on information protection has moved healthcare organizations and industry oversight authority (including government) to establish cohesive vendor management or credentialing solutions. For instance, in Canada and relative to the Personal Health Information Protection Act (PHIPA), there are privacy and confidentiality concerns with sharing information between healthcare providers and third-party vendors. They are in the process of establishing a nationwide vendor credentialing system that will allow healthcare providers a level of assurance that third-party vendors understand PHIPA and will comply.

 NOTE While many healthcare organizations make an attempt to purchase locally or work with vendors in the community, it is not always possible. National and international companies often provide better pricing and support. In the final analysis, vendors are selected based on economic considerations as much as trying to "buy local."

Because the relationship between vendors and the healthcare organization is so important and probably a competitive one, healthcare organizations establish written policies to govern these relationships. Some of the major components of these policies include the following:

- Definition of the relationship
- Limits to gifts or gratuities
- Establishment and authority for oversight
- On-premises access rules
- Fund-raising guidelines

There are some other special considerations depending on the vendor. For instance, vendors that work with academic medical centers have provisions for publishing by employees, seminar attendance and funding, and honorariums for speaking engagements. All of these provisions are meant to establish and maintain the integrity of the relationships. Unfair advantage of one vendor over another in many communities can mean the difference between business success and failure for the vendor.

Business Partners

A *business partner* is a particular subcategory of vendor for healthcare organizations. While business partners provide a product or service for the healthcare organization, it is not a transactional type of relationship. Business partners are characterized as having longer or recurring relationships with the healthcare organization, commonly described in a contract or formal, written obligation. These relationships are particularly of interest when the business partner handles protected health information (PHI) for the healthcare organization. In the United States, a business partner is also called a *business associate*. These vendors are subject to, like the healthcare organization, industry-specific privacy laws, such as the Health Insurance Portability and Accountability

Act (HIPAA).[8] Therefore, it is crucial for the healthcare organization, as well as any business associates, to understand how to comply with the relevant regulations even if the business partner serves other industries besides healthcare. Take a data center provider as an example; the data center may serve the healthcare organization by maintaining all of the data storage, providing applications, and performing backup procedures off-site. The data center may also do this for the local public school system, the retail department store, and other nonhealthcare clients. In any case, they have to maintain their data center under the appropriate healthcare regulations, like HIPAA. This would include signing a special contract such as a business associate agreement that specifically outlines the data center's responsibilities and any provisions for noncompliance. You can imagine how complex this could be for a business partner.

The following list provides some examples of business partners, or business associates. Whether they are business associates depends, again, on whether the contract involves the use, disclosure, transmission, or maintenance of PHI.

- Electronic health records and clinical software application vendors who plan, install, and support their products.

- Any information technology vendor that provides "cloud" services to include data storage, application services, security, and hardware management.

- Utilization review and management companies that analyze referral patterns and outcomes data to help shape best and most efficient treatment options.

- Physician office answering services that interact with patients and providers on behalf of the healthcare organization.

- Data conversion, de-identification, and data analysis service providers.

- Medical billing and coding specialists who are not part of the healthcare organization as employees. In some cases, this is a work-from-home, decentralized business.

- Under some circumstances where HIPAA applies, academic healthcare researchers.

- Third-party medical transcription companies that take the provider's dictation and put it into a written or digital format.

- Health information exchanges (HIEs), e-prescribing gateways, and other health information organizations that standardize transactions and make interchange of information easier.

- Companies that destroy documents and computer drives, delete electronic equipment memory, and shred paper records as needed.

- Patient safety or accreditation organizations that require access to records for investigations.

- Third-party administrators and pharmacy benefit managers who are similar to utilization review firms.

Without question, healthcare organizations that are not subject to HIPAA (in other words, international organizations) have third parties that are business partners. The objectives of the relationships are similar to the business associate relationships in the United States. Again, these relationships tend to be a little more strategic in nature. As opposed to a vendor relationship that may supply goods and products to the healthcare organization, international business partners extend or supplement healthcare services. This integrated nature of the partnership is evident in organizations that support both U.S. and Canadian (for example) firms. They will attest to complying with HIPAA (as a business associate) as well as complying with requirements under the Personal Information Protection and Electronic Documents Act (PIPEDA).

 TIP   Under the HIPAA Omnibus Rule, as of September 23, 2013, business associates and their subcontractors (also considered business associates) are directly liable under the law, just like U.S. healthcare organizations (*covered entities*). This "downstream" relationship of business associates extends as far as there is PHI being handled. It is in effect regardless of whether the covered entity has a compliant business associate agreement in place. Absence of a signed business associate agreement does not excuse any of the downstream business associates if there is a data breach.

Government as Third Party

The role of local and national governments is a prime example of a third party with a tremendous impact on healthcare organizations. This is not reserved for U.S. health-care. While in the United States, the government, principally through Medicare and Medicaid, is the primary payer, it also regulates the industry heavily. Because the governments of most other developed nations fund healthcare completely, the oversight of government there is even more pervasive. In England, for instance, the National Health Service oversees healthcare through the Department of Health, the General Medical Council, and the Nursing and Midwifery Council. To show how pervasive governments are in overseeing healthcare, Figure 2-1 provides an overview of some leading agencies.

State and Local Government

Most likely, your interaction with the government as a third party will be at the local level. As the saying goes, politics and healthcare are local. This means that many of the decisions and events that happen at a national level really do not have as much direct impact on how you do your job as the local government decisions do. For instance, many local governments must approve the building of new facilities or the offering of new services under a provision called *certificate of need*. In the United States, as of 2011, 36 states still require the measure to control capital expenditures and, theoretically, control healthcare costs.[9] The success is arguable. However, for a healthcare organization interested in opening a cardiothoracic surgery ward to increase revenue, not obtaining a certificate of need can be a huge setback. Building the facilities or delivering the service without this local government approval can result in fines and penalties or at least render the services unreimburseable.

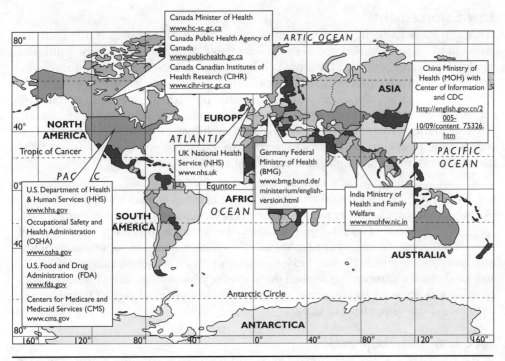

Figure 2-1   Selected government oversight agencies relative to healthcare

The local government also influences the healthcare organization positively. One way is by partnering on things such as a community health needs assessment. This helps both the local government health agencies and the healthcare organization determine a strategic plan for delivering healthcare to the various populations in the community. Local government can allocate where public resources should be expended. The healthcare organization can plan for prevention, intervention, and rehabilitation services targeted to what the community needs. The possible categories are almost infinite, but most commonly include the following:

- At-risk teens initiative
- Community asthma prevention program
- Homeless health initiative
- Injury prevention program
- Poison control center
- Wellness fairs

Law Enforcement

Since you are working in information protection, another direct impact that local government will have is in the area of law enforcement. Although every privacy and security law has a provision for law enforcement access to patient information, it is not unfettered access. Your role may be to provide the law enforcement personnel with the information they require based on organizational policies, the law itself, and need to know. For instance, disclosure under these circumstances usually must be in response to written requests from law enforcement officials. It may be difficult to refuse a police officer standing at your desk asking for access to a record of a patient who came through the emergency room last night. You may have to do just that.

 TIP Healthcare information protection depends as much on knowing the incident reporting process of your organization as it does on knowing the universe of laws that govern patient information disclosure. The most important thing you can do as a healthcare information privacy and security professional is to know your organization's data incident reporting policy. If a law enforcement official asks for disclosure of patient information that is outside of your organization's policy (as it complies with governing law), you must also know who to elevate this request to and what documented actions you need to take.

Tort Law and Malpractice

In the United States, the government as a third party, by way of the judiciary process, also plays a direct role in healthcare through tort law and malpractice. These are complex concepts and deserve much more attention than there is space in this chapter. However, an introduction to the terms and how they add to the highly regulated healthcare industry will help you understand more about how third parties impact how healthcare is provided. To start, *tort law* is comprised of civil (versus criminal) acts that provide patients with a remedy against wrongful acts committed against them. You find tort actions in the healthcare industry because of the following:

- Negligence
- Intentional torts
- Infliction of mental distress

For the information privacy and security professional, intentional tort is something to note. It is within this parameter that invasion of privacy is covered. Although a data breach may be caused by negligence and certainly may cause infliction of mental distress, tort law related to failure to assure confidentiality of patient information is related to the component of intentional acts.

This leads us to malpractice. *Malpractice* is a special kind of tort law familiar to healthcare professionals. A malpractice lawsuit is based upon negligence or carelessness by a healthcare provider. The charges can be civil or criminal based on the nature of the offense. Typically, the issue is not information security and would not involve a healthcare information privacy and security professional. However, under the law, malpractice is actually defined as a professional's improper or immoral conduct in the performance of duties, done either intentionally or through carelessness or ignorance.[10] In the near future, individuals who are in charge of protecting patient information may need to be more aware of malpractice concepts.

Nongovernment Regulators

When it is said that healthcare is one of the most highly regulated industries, this means more than just official government oversight. There are several significant examples of nongovernment regulatory third parties that shape healthcare organizations around the world. The focus on improving the safety and efficacy of patient care is one of the primary components that all accreditation organizations have in common. Through peer review and education, accreditation has proven effective in shaping healthcare organizations through this type of third-party relationship.

NOTE   In this context, accreditation is used to describe a voluntary process with findings that are not legally binding for the healthcare organization. This would be in contrast to what a government agency or regulator would conduct, such as an audit or formal inspection with findings that must be mitigated or remedied. To not comply would result in fines and penalties.

Joint Commission

Starting with arguably the most notable one, the Joint Commission (formerly the Joint Commission on Accreditation of Healthcare Organizations and previous to that the Joint Commission on Accreditation of Hospitals) is an independent, not-for-profit organization located in the United States. For about 100 years, it has accredited and certified healthcare organizations against standards of practice, and in the previous 25 years, the Joint Commission has been developing an international presence as well. It currently provides this service for more than 20,000 healthcare organizations and programs in the United States. The Joint Commission accreditation is considered mandatory to demonstrate a healthcare organization's commitment to quality and compliance with performance standards. In fact, in the United States, some reimbursement conditions are tied to having a current Joint Commission certification.

Accreditation Association for Ambulatory Health Care

Recognizing the shift from inpatient services to outpatient or ambulatory-care settings, another nongovernment third party in the United States began looking at quality and safety issues in physician groups, outpatient clinics, and any other ambulatory patient care centers. The Accreditation Association for Ambulatory Health Care (AAAHC) develops standards with regard to patient safety, quality, value, and measurement of performance. Because its focus is in ambulatory healthcare, the surveys can be more efficient and meaningful with better-equipped peer-based accreditation processes.

Accreditation Canada

In Canada, a similar organization called Accreditation Canada, formerly known as Canadian Council on Health Services Accreditation (CCHSA), accredits more than 1,000 client organizations including regional health authorities, hospitals, and community-based programs and services. Like the Joint Commission and the AAAHC in the United States, the surveyors and auditors are not government employees, nor do they take direction from the government. Both the Joint Commission and Accreditation Canada use experienced professionals, including physicians, nurses, health executives and administrators, and medical technicians from the allied health professions.

European Union

The value of accreditation of healthcare organizations is debated in the European Union. Because healthcare is fully funded by the government, outside third-party accreditation of peers is not uniformly valued or respected. Many believe the efforts should be in mandatory compliance verified through government inspection and auditing. Nonetheless, third-party organizations performing accreditation have grown rapidly in the last 30 years in Europe. To begin to objectively look at the issues, the World Health Organization (WHO) conducted one of the first international studies in 2000. This and subsequent studies have focused more on evidence of the accreditation's impact on a healthcare organization's patient care, safety, and quality improvement efforts. Currently, there are 18 national organizations active in Europe. The trend is in more programs, more participating healthcare organizations, and more surveys of healthcare organizations. Table 2-2 lists the active accreditation bodies and the member states they represent. You may note that the Joint Commission International operates in Spain particularly and across Europe. It is, in fact, part of the U.S. Joint Commission.

Public Health Reporting

Sometimes healthcare organizations collect information from patients that is legitimately needed by public health officials. These are third parties that are not vendors but are most likely government agencies. In the United States, the HIPAA Privacy Rule makes provisions for healthcare organizations to legally disclose protected health information to public health and safety agencies for the benefit of public health.[11] Provisions regarding public health reporting in the United States can be complex and vary among jurisdictions. Generally, public health requires disclosure to identify threats to the health and safety of the total community and individuals. Along with reporting of births or deaths, public health reporting may consist of the following:

- Child abuse or neglect
- Quality, safety, or effectiveness of a product or activity regulated by the FDA
- People at risk of contracting or spreading a disease
- Workplace medical surveillance when healthcare is provided at the request of the employer or as a member of the employer's workforce

Similar provisions for public health reporting are in the European Union (EU) as well, according to EU Directive 95/46/EC, which allows for data controllers to "derogate from the prohibition on processing sensitive categories of data where important reasons of public interest so justify in areas such as public health and social protection."[12]

Country (Year Established)	Organization Name
Albania (2006)	Albanian Accreditation Programme
Bosnia (2004)	Accreditation programme for health institutions and family medicine teams (AKAZ)
Bosnia (2002)	Agency for Accreditation and Health Care Quality Improvement of Republika Srpska (AAQI)
Bulgaria (2000)	Accreditation of Healthcare Establishments
Czech Republic (1998)	Spojená akreditační komise (SAK)
Denmark (2002)	The Danish Healthcare Quality Programme (DDKM)
Europe (2000)	Joint Commission International, Europe (JCI)
Finland (1993)	Social and Health Quality Service (SHQS)
France (1997)	Accreditation Program for HCOs Haute Autorité de Santé (HAS)
Germany (2001)	Kooperation für Transparenz und Qualität im Gesundheitswesen (KTQ)
Hungary (2006)	Institute for Healthcare Quality Improvement and Hospital Engineering
Lithuania (2009)	Accreditation programme for healthcare institutions
The Netherlands (1998)	Netherlands Institute for Accreditation in Healthcare (NIAZ)
Poland (1998)	Program Akredytacji (NCQA)
Serbia (2005)	Agency for Accreditation of Health Care Institutions
Spain (1996)	La Fundación para la Acreditación y el Desarrollo Asistencial - Joint Commission Internacional (FADA-JCI)
Switzerland (2001)	SanaCERT Suisse
United Kingdom (1989)	Caspe Research Knowledge Systems (CHKS) Accreditation

Table 2-2 Accreditation Organizations Active in Europe, April 2009

We find allowances for public health reporting an almost universal exception to the information protection guidelines.

Even though healthcare organizations are generally permitted (or required) to disclose patient information for public health reporting purposes, the information should be limited to only what is required. In the United States, HIPAA defines this as minimum necessary use. That is, healthcare organizations must take reasonable precautions to disclose the minimum amount of protected health information necessary to accomplish the public health purpose.

 NOTE Under HIPAA, public health agencies are not an organization directly subject to HIPAA. However, some activities are subject to the same privacy and security rules. In fact, healthcare organizations are cautious to disclose patient information under the exceptions allowed for in HIPAA. In many cases, they apply equal safeguards with an abundance of caution.[13]

Clinical Research

It is often beneficial to use patient information in clinical research. Unlike in public health reporting, researchers try to conduct clinical research after obtaining patient consent for the use of the information for that specific purpose. This is not always possible. In those cases where obtaining consent is impractical or impossible, researchers in the United States can use an internal institutional review board (IRB) or a privacy board to obtain a waiver to any required patient consent. The IRB or privacy board will have documented protocols and controls to safeguard the protected health information. This incorporates assurances that the use or disclosure of the patient information adds only a minimum of risk to privacy for the individual. The boards would require researchers to demonstrate the following:

- A plan that includes alternate measures to safeguard protected health information
- A plan to destroy patient information when no longer needed (to include any bona fide need to keep the information for research or legal reasons)
- Written statements to prohibit reuse or disclosure of patient information unless permitted by law or the IRB or privacy board
- No research without a waiver
- No research without access to and use of the patient information

For clinical research, several of the alternative steps that are taken to remove patient information from the data or at least limit it to the least amount required are important to know. You may even use these concepts outside of a formal clinical research setting in terms of simply storing and transferring data without unauthorized disclosure.

- **De-identification of patient information**   This consists of removing any individually identifying information from the data set so that you can be reasonably certain no one can identify someone based on the remaining information. There are two ways to do this. The first way is to use a person trained in rendering the information anonymous through algorithms and changes to the standard categories of identifiable data. The second way is to simply remove completely these same categories of identifiable data. The following are sources of data that may be individually identifiable information (from the National Institute of Standards and Technology [NIST] Special Publication 800-122[14]):
    - Name, such as full name, maiden name, mother's maiden name, or alias
    - Personal identification number, such as Social Security number (SSN), passport number, driver's license number, taxpayer identification number, patient identification number, and financial account or credit card number
    - Address information, such as street address or e-mail address
    - Asset information, such as Internet Protocol (IP) or Media Access Control (MAC) address or other host-specific persistent static identifier that consistently links to a particular person or small, well-defined group of people

- Telephone numbers, including mobile, business, and personal numbers

- Personal characteristics, including photographic image (especially of face or other distinguishing characteristic), X-rays, fingerprints, or other biometric image or template data (for example, retina scan, voice signature, and facial geometry)

- Information identifying personally owned property, such as vehicle registration number or title number and related information

- Information about an individual that is linked or linkable to one of the previous (for example, date of birth, place of birth, race, religion, weight, activities, geographical indicators, employment information, medical information, education information, and financial information)

NOTE When anonymizing data, a situation can occur where results that are considered outliers are so unique that they actually can be used to identify an individual. An example, take a sample size of a small 12th-grade class at the local high school (150 students). Anonymize any of the 18 individual identifiers as found in NIST 800-122, Sec 2.2, that are present in the data set. Then you may be left with data elements such as height, weight, eye color, hair color, and immunizations received. Most likely, those individuals with red hair and blue eyes would be unique enough to be identifiable with just those aggregate (albeit anonymized) data elements. These elements would still require confidentiality protection.

- **Limited data sets** This establishes that some of the patient information can be excluded and what remains is the minimum number and types of identifiers needed, if any. You would usually have a data use agreement in place for using a limited data set that would also determine who has a need to know the information and for what purposes.

- **Accounting for disclosures** Researchers must keep and be able to provide a record of all information disclosed, by whom, and to whom outside of the research organization (for example, another research organization doing similar trials) during the life of the research.

TIP Increased disclosure of patient information is authorized for the purposes of clinical research under HIPAA. When the information is used for clinical research, controls that would be required under HIPAA may be absent. Be aware of the impact of clinical research on any data use scenario.

NOTE In countries outside of the United States, other types of data may be considered uniquely identifying or protected, such as trade union membership.

Noteworthy clinical research done by a third party is through a contract research organization (CRO). This organization provides support to healthcare organizations conducting specialized types of biopharmaceutical development, preclinical research, clinical trials management, and drug safety. For the most part, these advanced research types are done by leading pharmaceutical, biotechnology, and medical device industries. CROs also support academic medical centers, the government, and international organizations. The ability to partner with CROs allows the development and evaluation of all the various trials of safety and efficacy, but they do not need to have internal staff from the healthcare organization dedicated to the research. For medical devices, the CRO gathers clinical data to support a regulatory before-market submission, drive product adoption, support product reimbursement, or monitor after-market product use. They bring expertise and streamlined processes at a much more cost-effective level than what the healthcare organization could if the healthcare organization had to do the same processes itself.

Health Records Management

Finally, you will encounter health records management organizations that are business partners to physician offices, smaller health clinics, and some other healthcare providers. Because they store and manage patient information as well as valuable business-related data, they introduce information risk that the healthcare provider must still mitigate. You will hear this many times: You cannot outsource responsibility for protecting information.

The health records management organization will typically handle the designated record set for the healthcare provider. This might be because the provider does not have adequate space or expertise. In the case of electronic information, the provider may not be able to invest in the hardware or software (such as a data center) to manage the information. Also, the healthcare organization may not be able to employ adequate privacy and security methods to maintain compliance or properly manage the information from collection to disposition. For any or all of these reasons, it is more cost-effective to outsource to a third party.

The designated records set is more than the legal medical record (discussed previously). It is defined as all the various types of patient medical and billing records used in whole or in part to make decisions on treatment, payment, and operations. The record consists of paper records, film images, electronic data, and any other medium used to store healthcare data. You might think of the difference between a legal health record and the designated record set like this: Direct patient care is recorded in the legal medical record. The designated record set has that information plus all the business information unrelated (but important) to patient care.

In the final analysis, if a healthcare organization is going to partner with a health records management third party, it will at least put a data use agreement in place to outline the use and disclosure rules. In the United States, a business associate agreement would also be required.

Administering Third Parties

So, with all of these external forces and third-party relationships that shape the healthcare organization, administering them is a fundamental element in reducing information risk (of unauthorized disclosure). We have discussed the business associate agreement, which is unique to the United States. That is one formal (written) tool to help reduce information risk. There are other agreements and documents used in the United States and internationally that you should understand. All are prenegotiated and define common understandings necessary to protect the confidentiality, integrity, or availability of patient information. A few of note are the service level agreement, the data sharing agreement, and the legal contract.

 NOTE Formal agreements between healthcare providers and third parties can cover many types of products and services other than protecting information. For instance, a healthcare organization can have agreements with transportation companies to provide support for moving furniture, equipment, and even patients. There are agreements in place to cover temporary staffing levels from employment agencies. For purposes of this book, we are limiting the content of these types of written agreements to information protection.

Service Level Agreements

The service level agreement is almost self-explanatory. It is an obligating document that outlines the support or products the third party promises to provide and relevant measures against which the healthcare organization can measure fulfillment. One such support item and its measurement would be network uptime. If the third party agrees to keep the network "up" or connected and operating for a mutually agreeable frequency, then that becomes the expectation of the healthcare organization. The measurement can be the frequency, hypothetically 99.999 percent of a full 24-hour day, 7 days a week. Not performing to that standard might cause problems for the healthcare organization. Because of this reality, service level agreements also contain remediation steps when things go wrong—escalation of complaints, financial penalties, severance of the agreement, and so on.

Data Sharing Agreements

A data sharing agreement (or data use agreement) is a similarly obligating document used to describe the access to and expectations for a third party's use of a healthcare organization's patient information. It will clearly indicate and limit the period of time the data sharing will occur, the systems the third party will access, and how the data will be used (and disposed of). Data sharing agreements can cover additional parameters. In any case, the main element of the agreement is to protect the healthcare organization by spelling out exactly how the information will or will not be disclosed. It is important to do this because, ultimately, the healthcare organization remains responsible for safeguarding the information. In a data sharing agreement, it is imperative to make sure there is a bona fide and legal need to know for the third party.

Legal Contracts

Finally, the most official and binding of the three administrative tools you will use is the legal contract. In many ways, the service level agreement and the data sharing agreement can evolve into a formal contract. Generally speaking, there are four main elements of a contract, as follows:

- The agreement must be between two or more parties.
- All parties must be competent to consent.
- The agreement must be something of value.
- The agreement must be lawful.

Where service level agreements and data sharing agreements differ from legal contracts is in the complexity and content. Both service level agreements and data sharing agreements tend to be more specifically focused on a service or product. The terms and conditions are related to measurements and quality or specific acts and tasks. However, all of the documents are used to set clear expectations, avoid costly legal actions, and provide safe handling of patient information. A formal contract would include more detail about responsibilities, resources, assumptions, and limits of liabilities over the life of the contract. In sum, often service level agreements and data sharing agreements serve as attachments to a formal, long-term contract with a third party (which may provide multiple services).

Chapter Review

Whether you work in healthcare already or are just now entering the healthcare workforce to provide information protection services, you will make your work easier if you understand the important points of this chapter. The healthcare workforce is diverse and ranges from manual labor trades to highly educated professions. All these people must work together to shape the success of the delivery of patient care. In fact, the organization may depend on these connections more than the lines of authority drawn on the organizational chart. Another major point of emphasis you must understand is that outside business partners or third parties have impactful relationships with the healthcare organization. Because of the healthcare organization's importance to most communities, the third party may be highly reliant on the business of the healthcare organization. Jobs and the local economy may depend on the partnership. In cases where the healthcare organization is reliant on the third party, especially to handle patient information correctly, the relationship may introduce risk to each of the organizations that must be addressed.

Review Questions

1. (TRUE or FALSE) Because she or he is required to practice autonomously, an independent duty nurse requires the highest level of formal education.

2. For which patients does an orthopedic specialist care?

   A. Oral conditions

   B. Foot and mouth disease

   C. Child development

   D. Joint problems

3. The most likely person to operate a magnetic resonance imaging (MRI) device is a:

   A. Nurse anesthetist

   B. Physician specialist

   C. Medical technician

   D. Nursing aide

4. To increase revenue through efficient bed management, which of the following occupational categories plays the largest role?

   A. C-suite executive

   B. Medical technicians

   C. Nursing staff

   D. Environmental services

5. Which of these words best describes a vendor to a healthcare organization?

   A. Third-party

   B. Healthcare-specific

   C. Supply company

   D. Accredited service

6. The _____ is a third-party vendor to healthcare organizations that provides accreditation for quality and patient safety standards.

7. A formal, written agreement that describes the access to and expectations for a third party's use of patient information is a _____ agreement.

8. (TRUE or FALSE) Under certain conditions, workplace medical surveillance containing patient information can be disclosed without prior individual consent because of clinical research provisions.

9. When conducting clinical research, which of the following would ensure that the research presents a plan that includes alternate measures to safeguard protected health information?

   A. Board of governors

   B. Institutional review board

   C. Medical board certification

   D. Community advocacy board

10. If you were asked to de-identify yesterday's patient appointment list containing the medical record number (MRN), patient name, and time of appointment, what action would be most appropriate?

   A. Delete all MRNs and change patient name to "PATIENT."

   B. Change the names to historical figures and delete the time of appointment.

   C. Increase each MRN by 15 and use only the last names of patient.

   D. Use only the patient name and time of appointment.

Answers

1. **FALSE.** Of these different types of nurses, a registered nurse requires as many as four years of training and education before licensure. In most cases, an RN earns a bachelor's degree as part of their academic training. The only other type of nurse offered as a possible answer that would require a specific level of formal education is the licensed practical nurse who either earns an associate degree for their two years of coursework or graduates from an equivalent hospital-based LPN program. The nurses' aides or independent duty nurses may or may not have a high-school diploma or higher. Further, an independent duty nurse can be an LPN or RN performing nursing service for a home health patient outside of the hospital.

2. **D.** An orthopedist is a specialist who is concerned with patient care of the joint, bones, muscles, and cartilage, primary for knees, ankles, and hips. Orthodontists would be more appropriate for oral conditions, while foot-in-mouth disease probably would bring in an epidemiologist or even a veterinarian. The type of specialist primarily focused on child development is the pediatrician.

3. **C.** Although it is possible that a physician specialist, such as a radiologist, may operate the MRI, a more likely scenario would involve a qualified MRI medical technician who would conduct the procedure, interpret the results for any obvious errors, and process them for use of a physician, nurse practitioner, or physician. Likewise, a nurse anesthetist would not be at the MRI controls (unless sedation of the patient was necessary). A nursing aide may be in the exam room to assist maneuvering the patient or at least calming them before the procedure but would not be responsible for operating the medical device.

4. **D.** Environmental services include housekeeping and maintenance departments. To ensure that rooms and beds are clean, ready for new occupancy, and all that is communicated as quickly as possible, environmental services are the key group of staff members. The time elapsed between patient discharge to patient admission is a terrific measurement of increased revenue if the time can be compressed. C-suite executives will play a role in overseeing the revenue measures, creating policy, and making resourcing decisions around them. Nursing staff will certainly be crucial in managing patients, and their responsibilities extend beyond admission and discharge, but the actual turnover of the room really depends on how fast the environmental services personnel do their job. Medical technicians may have a small role in some bed management processes, especially where the organization uses beds that have information technology and networking capabilities.

5. **A.** A vendor to a healthcare organization is someone or some entity that sells, supplies, or provides a service or product. Vendor will have to be a third party because they are external to the healthcare organization. However, they do not have to be healthcare specific. They may do business with healthcare organizations only. They are not required to be exclusively healthcare vendors. Some vendors are supply companies and therefore supply products, but they can also be service providers or staff augmentation. Finally, while accreditation is a service some vendors provide, it is only a description of a subset of all vendors. The best answer that covers all vendors is that they are third parties.

6. **Joint Commission.** Because a healthcare organization voluntarily undergoes Joint Commission review and the Joint Commission is not an agent of the U.S. government or any other government, their review is an accreditation. An inspection would be something formal and government directed, like an OSHA inspection. Credentialing is done for healthcare workforce personnel, such as physicians and specialists. Nurses and several other allied health professionals would test to receive licensing from educational organizations certified to confer licensing.

7. **Data sharing.** A data sharing agreement is by definition a formal, written agreement that describes the access to and expectations for a third party's use of patient information.

8. **FALSE.** Clinical research would be concerned with some types of surveillance, but by definition public health reporting is permissible under this scenario because the healthcare is provided at the request of the employer or as a member of the employer's workforce.

9. **B.** An institutional review board exists to provide this level of oversight because it may be necessary to conduct research for the benefit of the community containing patient information. In these cases, patient consent may be impossible to obtain. Rather than prohibit the research, an IRB provides oversight. A board of governors is not likely to be involved at the clinical research level of the healthcare organization. Medical board certification is not related to this scenario but is

relevant to workforce competency. A community advocacy board may get involved in research activities, especially if patient privacy is violated, but in this scenario, such an entity would not oversee the clinical research.

10. **A.** There are only two acceptable ways of de-identifying patient information. One is to create a statistically effective method so that an expert would determine no one could identify the patients. Option C is close to that type of method, but simply increasing the number by 15 would easily be deciphered. The MRN and the last name would be easy to use for re-identification. Options B and D would leave the MRN intact, which would clearly provide identification for a singular individual. Only option A would de-identify the patient information by rendering the information useless for identifying the individuals—yet would still allow for useful analysis of the data.

References

1. Bureau of Labor Statistics, U.S. Department of Labor. Accessed on December 2, 2013, at www.bls.gov/ooh/healthcare/

2. Bureau of Labor Statistics, U.S. Department of Labor, Occupational Outlook Handbook, 2012–13 Edition, Registered Nurses. Accessed on December 13, 2013, at www.bls.gov/ooh/healthcare/registered-nurses.htm

3. Lilienfeld, David E., and Dona Schneider. Public health: the development of a discipline. Volume 1, From the age of Hippocrates to the progressive era. Rutgers University Press, 2008. p. 5.

4. Stein, L. I. The Doctor-Nurse Game. *Arch Gen Psychiatry.* 1967;16(6):699–703. p. 1.

5. The Joint Commission. Sentinel Event Alert. Safely implementing health information and converging technologies. Issue 42. December 11, 2008. Accessed on December 2, 2013, at www.jointcommission.org/assets/1/18/SEA_42.pdf

6. "Managing data security and privacy risk of third-party vendors," Grant Thornton Corporate Governor, Volume 2, Fall 2011. Accessed on November 30, 2013, at www.grantthornton.com/issues/library/articles/technology/2012/TIP-2012-managing-data-security-and-privacy-of-third-party-vendors.aspx

7. Henry Ford Health System. "About Henry Ford Health System." Accessed on December 3, 2013, at www.henryford.com/body.cfm?id=48187

8. Department of Health and Human Services, Health Insurance Reform: Security Standards; Final Rule (HIPAA Security Rule), 45 C.F.R. Parts 160, 162, and 164 (2003).

9. National Conference of State Legislatures. "Certificate of Need: State Health Laws and Programs." March 2012. Accessed on November 29, 2013, at www.ncsl.org/research/health/con-certificate-of-need-state-laws.aspx

10. Bell Buchbinder, Sharon, and Nancy H. Shanks. *Introduction to healthcare management.* 2nd ed. Jones & Bartlett Learning, 2012. p. 212.

11. Department of Health and Human Services, HIPAA (Privacy Rule) 45 C.F.R. 164.512(b). (2003).

12. Directive 95/46/EC of the European Parliament and of the Council. Data Protection Directive. (34). October 1995. Accessed on November 20, 2013, at http://eur-lex.europa.eu/LexUriServ/LexUriServ.do?uri=CELEX:31995L0046: en:HTML

13. Overhage, J. Marc, Kathleen McCormick (editor), and Brian Gugerty (editor). "The Role of Healthcare IT in Improving Population Health." *Healthcare Information Technology Exam Guide for CompTIA Healthcare IT Technicians and HIT Pro Certifications*. McGraw-Hill, 2013. pp. 158–159.

14. National Institute of Standards and Technology (NIST) Special Publication 800-122. Guide to Protecting the Confidentiality of Personally Identifiable Information (PII). April 2010. p. 2–2.

Healthcare Information Regulation

In this chapter, you will learn to
- Recognize unique legal issues in healthcare information protection
- Identify applicable regulations that govern healthcare information privacy and security
- Comprehend the relationship between regulations and internal organizational guidance
- Appreciate governance frameworks to manage internal organizational policies
- Be introduced to international regulatory controls for privacy and security
- Review transnational and cross-jurisdictional issues related to information sharing

The importance of applying the proper privacy and security controls on healthcare information is probably exemplified best by the level and gravity of the regulatory environment that shapes all we do. Our efforts are deliberate and directly linked to numerous standards. From the most local policies and procedures to global practices, our work is not left to chance. Our starting point in understanding this regulatory environment is to introduce the governing process from a practical perspective. This chapter focuses on how standards apply to your organization and how they coincide with national and international standards.

Applicable Regulations

It's important to understand a few of the applicable regulations that govern healthcare. From a practical standpoint, you are most likely to need to know the local policies and procedures that govern your organization. However, you are well served to be aware of the national and international laws that shape those policies and procedures at the local level. Within the United States, state and local regulations may be even more important than the national regulations. For instance, Massachusetts has privacy laws that apply to healthcare delivered to Massachusetts residents. What follows is an overview of the pertinent higher-level regulations you need to know.

Legal Issues

The healthcare industry is highly regulated. In the United States, it is regulated at the local, state, and federal levels by rules that are often specific to healthcare. For instance, you are familiar with the Health Insurance Portability and Accountability Act (HIPAA) and its amendments—the Privacy Rule, the Security Rule, the Health Information Technology for Economic and Clinical Health (HITECH) Act, and the recent Omnibus HIPAA Final Rule. There are also numerous individual state medical privacy laws. However, healthcare also must comply with regulations that apply across other industries such as the Gramm-Leach-Bliley Act (GLBA) and the Red Flags Rule governed by the Federal Trade Commission (FTC) standards.

Internationally, much of the regulation of healthcare is found in privacy and security directives that extend across all industries. Some have specific mentions and guidance for healthcare. In general, the international view of safeguarding an individual's identifying information is a human right. So, every industry is held to a high but universal standard. Examples of these are the European Union's Data Protection Directive (DPD) Canada's Personal Information Protection and Electronic Documents Act (PIPEDA), and Australia's Privacy Amendment (Private Sector) Act of 2000. In the following sections, we discuss some of the most important areas where legal issues pertain to the work of healthcare organizations.

Medical Devices and Critical Infrastructure Issues

In addition to the normal office automation computers and local area networking equipment, healthcare organizations commonly operate special-purpose computing equipment and medical devices. These computers and devices often have operating systems and software applications identical to their office automation counterparts, but their special purpose is different. According to the U.S. Food and Drug Administration (FDA), a medical device is "an instrument, apparatus, implement, machine, contrivance, implant, in vitro reagent, or other similar or related article, including a component part, or accessory which is (in part) intended for use in the diagnosis of disease or other conditions, or in the cure, mitigation, treatment, or prevention of disease, in man or other animals."[1] In short, medical devices are an extension of the clinical care provider and integral to patient care. There are legal implications in managing them from an information privacy and security standpoint.

On one hand, actions such as updating vulnerability patches and applying any kind of additional software that is not part of the manufacturer's configuration can invalidate warranties or cause the device to malfunction. Most importantly, these updates may be the direct cause of patient harm even if the updates are considered best-practice security measures. On the other hand, both manufacturers and healthcare providers have been warned by the U.S. FDA that they have responsibilities to keep medical devices safe (to include privacy and security considerations). This creates an uneasy balance with significant government oversight.

With respect to the international concerns of medical device security, while the FDA does not have jurisdiction, it does have impact. The same concern for patient safety is a regulatory concern internationally. Medical device manufacturers that do business internationally base their requirements on the International Organization for Standardization (ISO) frameworks for securing systems. They also provide the same medical devices cleared for use in the United States through the FDA to their international customers. In this way, the FDA has an indirect reach across the globe.

Medical device manufacturers also self-regulate. An example of this is in the growing use of a form called the Medical Device Security Manufacturers' Disclosure Statement (MDS).[2] The manufacturers complete this form and provide it to customers to document the significant security features the device has. Because the form was developed in partnership with the Healthcare Information and Management Systems Society (HIMSS) and leading clinical engineering associations, the content is reflective of concerns the FDA has with medical device security. The effect is to assure a baseline security measure so that medical devices can be networked safely. Of course, vulnerabilities that may be introduced by networking the medical devices must be addressed and mitigated; this just happens differently (sometimes) than regular office automation.

When it comes to critical infrastructure, healthcare organizations certainly have a responsibility to manage the network according to standards such as NIST SP 800-34, Rev 1, "Contingency Planning Guide for Federal Information Systems," which contains standards for disaster recovery, backup operations, and continuity of operations. Healthcare organizations also have much in common with other industries that have networks that are considered critical infrastructure (as noted in Executive Order "Improving Critical Infrastructure Cybersecurity," by U.S. President Obama, February 12, 2013). There is a distinction in healthcare-critical infrastructure and the other examples with respect to the impact of network disruption. In addition to the potential loss of revenue and cost of recovery, direct patient care may be at risk during unplanned network outages. First, this has the potential to open the healthcare organization to malpractice claims if there is patient harm. Information technology outages due to cybersecurity causes in healthcare are making headlines. What is viewed as a "bug" in other information security circles is a "a disruptive, potentially dangerous major malfunction of a life-critical enterprise medical device," in a healthcare context.[2] As we become more digital and less able to revert to manual processes, the chances of patient harm increase. Second, if an unplanned outage causes an adverse event as defined by relevant healthcare accrediting agencies, in the United States and internationally (the Joint Commission, for example), it is reportable to them.

Information Accountability

Information privacy and security laws are concerned with the roles and responsibilities of those who create, use, and dispose of healthcare information. HIPAA in the United States, while enacted in 1996 *not* solely to cover privacy and security issues, began to solidify accountability for the use of medical information. HITECH concentrated even more on such concerns. To be clear, there really is no "ownership" of health information. However, patients do have legal, individual rights to access their health information and learn about disclosures of their health information. Patients are entitled to full disclosure on how their protected health information is used and disclosed. If they desire to restrict sharing of information, they can make that request. The healthcare provider does not have to honor every request, but the provider must evaluate and respond to each request. Patients also have the right to inspect and review the information, amend incorrect information, and receive a copy of health information about themselves held by the healthcare provider. The healthcare provider, in turn, has the right to use the patient information for defined reasons of treatment, payment, and operations without additional patient consent required.

TIP   Although there have been several amendments to HIPAA over the years, the term "HIPAA" commonly refers to them all. In other words, it is acceptable to reference HIPAA requirements for patient notification of a data breach even though the requirement was implemented with the HITECH rule amendment in 2009. Before that, HIPAA required the covered entity to notify the patient only if it mitigated the data loss.[3]

In the United Kingdom and the European Union, information accountability has similar parameters as in the United States. In the EU DPD, accountability stems from the roles and responsibilities of those people, or *actors*, in the information chain of custody. No one owns the information, but the EU DPD assigns roles to the actors in the information process that are similar to those in HIPAA. Table 3-1 defines these actors.

Cloud Computing

Across multiple industries, the concept of cloud computing is gaining acceptance and momentum. Cloud computing is a collection of software, platforms, and infrastructure provided as a service to consumers via the Internet from remote locations (outside of the consumer's organization). The cloud service provider hosts all the equipment on their premises and is responsible for power and availability. The consumer just logs on and uses the resources. Cloud services are offered by a variety of vendors, but some that may be the most familiar to you are Google, Amazon, and Microsoft Azure. Cloud computing presents unique risks to healthcare. These risks are magnified in that many cloud computing vendors are unfamiliar with the special requirements of healthcare. One such unique requirement is the need for all healthcare organizations to conduct a third-party risk assessment of vendors that handle protected health information (PHI) on their behalf. Because other industries may not have these assessments, or a legal

Term	Definition
Data subject	The person to whom the data pertains. Who does it identify?
Data controller	An entity (or entities) that determines the purposes for why and how any personal data is, or will be, processed. This entity can be a person, an organization, or a group of people who are not collectively an organization. The data controllers must ensure information use complies with the EU DPD.
Data processor	The person who processes the data on behalf of the data controller but is *not* an employee of the controller (such as a third-party business partner). In the European Union, these entities are not directly subject to the DPD in their role as data processor.

Table 3-1   Definitions for Information Accountability from EU DPD

requirement for assessments, vendors can be reluctant to comply with these requirements or reluctant to comply with mitigating any findings.

Another concern with cloud computing is the location of the PHI. For example, PHI
that is hosted outside the United States is a potential issue where cloud providers are
not subject to HIPAA or training of workforce members is insufficient for protection of
PHI. For this reason, many healthcare organizations require that servers hosting PHI
be located within the United States. For Canada, the transfer of data across borders
is not prohibited by PIPEDA, but more and more government agencies are requiring
that restriction in their business contracts. The location of data (even if not crossing
borders) raises concerns about requirements for audits and e-discovery. In many cloud
computing environments, resources are so co-mingled that the level of auditing and
e-discovery that supports forensics and accounting for disclosures is nearly impossible.
Cloud computing vendors may be able to accommodate these privacy and security
provisions. But when they exceed their other nonhealthcare customers' needs, costs
increase, and value to the healthcare customer may decrease.

 NOTE With the September 23, 2013, effective date of the HIPAA Omnibus
Final Rule, cloud vendors that support healthcare are mandated to sign business
associate agreements (BAAs). The larger vendors with multiple clients (many
not in healthcare) were not willing to sign these agreements. In fairness, many
saw it as an added, redundant requirement to their already rigid compliance processes
such as FISMA, SASE 16, and so on. However, according to David Holtzman from the U.S.
Department of HHS, Information Privacy Division, Office for Civil Rights, "If you use a cloud
service, it should be your business associate. If they refuse to sign a business associate
agreement, don't use the cloud service." With HIPAA updated to include strong clarification
language and statements like Holtzman's, requirements for signing a BAA for cloud
computing vendors with U.S. healthcare customers is in reality non-negotiable.

Data Breach Regulations

Many nations, including the European Union, have been considering formal government mandates for data breach notification for individuals, the data subjects. Those
efforts continue, and in reality, specific organizations already do some notification to
data subjects and data controllers. These, of course, span all industries that handle personal information.

In the United States, HIPAA mandates that the healthcare industry investigate potential and actual data breaches that may exceed other industries' standards for sensitive
personal information. For instance, to determine whether there is a data breach of
PHI, the U.S. government has determined a measurement threshold. The standard is
whether there was a risk of disclosure of the information. Previous to the HIPAA Omnibus Rule in 2013, the risk threshold was risk of harm to the individual. There is clearly a
shift in emphasis. Now a risk assessment must be done to address the following:[4]

- The nature and extent of the protected health information involved, including
  the types of identifiers and the likelihood of re-identification

- The unauthorized person who used the protected health information or to
  whom the disclosure was made

- Whether the protected health information was actually acquired or viewed
- The extent to which the risk to the protected health information has been mitigated

After these conditions have been evaluated, the healthcare organization has to report the breach unless there is a low probability that the protected health information was compromised. If the breach involves more than 500 individual records and there is not a low probability of compromise, the organization must notify the U.S. Department of Health and Human Services (HHS) of the loss, theft, or certain other impermissible uses or disclosures of unsecured PHI. Additionally, in this scenario, the organization must alert the media if the breach affects more than 500 residents of a single state. Of course, in this scenario the organization must notify the affected individuals, but in most other data breaches the healthcare organization will notify their patients as well. This risk assessment and formal process for notification differs from privacy laws governing data breach of things such as credit card information or Social Security numbers. The differences are applicable to U.S. healthcare organizations that respond to data breaches of both PHI and financial information.

Defining Protected Health Information

PHI is a separate classification of sensitive information that has several legal implications specific to healthcare organizations. PHI is built upon the existing definition of personally identifiable information (PII). This is used in international guidance, U.S. privacy law, and information security. Basically, *personally identifiable information* is information that can be used on its own or with other information to identify, contact, or locate a single person, or to identify an individual in context. In other countries with privacy protection laws, PII is typically called *personal information*. Why that matters is because the United States uses *PII* and roots the definition in the 18 identifying elements, listed next, that are defined in NIST Special Publication 800-122.

- Name, such as full name, maiden name, mother's maiden name, or alias
- Personal identification number, such as Social Security number (SSN), passport number, driver's license number, taxpayer identification number, patient identification number, and financial account or credit card number
- Address information, such as street address or e-mail address
- Asset information, such as Internet Protocol (IP) or Media Access Control (MAC) address or other host-specific persistent static identifier that consistently links to a particular person or small, well-defined group of people
- Telephone numbers, including mobile, business, and personal numbers
- Personal characteristics, including photographic image (especially of face or other distinguishing characteristic), X-rays, fingerprints, or other biometric image or template data (for example, retina scan, voice signature, facial geometry)

- Information identifying personally owned property, such as vehicle registration number or title number and related information

- Information about an individual that is linked or linkable to one of the previous items (for example, date of birth, place of birth, race, religion, weight, activities, geographical indicators, employment information, medical information, education information, or financial information)

According to the OECD and Australia's 1988 Privacy Act, for example, personal information also includes information from which the person's identity is reasonably ascertainable, potentially covering some information not covered by PII. In some cases, this can be a person's religion, union membership, or political party.

It is important to note that not all examples of PII data are automatically PII. Some, such as a Social Security number, are automatically PII because this number corresponds to one and only one person without any need of additional PII data. A piece of data such as a home address by itself may not identify one person, especially if the street address of a high-rise building does not include an apartment number. In any case, the intention of knowing these typical PII data elements helps you be aware of your information protection requirements.

To define PHI, we must begin with this definition of PII. The second component of PHI is the existence of some type of health information related to the PII. The healthcare information can relate to the following:

- The past, present, or future physical or mental health or condition

- The provision of healthcare to the individual

- The past, present, or future payment for the provision of healthcare to the individual

The third and final component of PHI is whether the PII that relates to health information of that individual is being collected, used, transferred, stored, or disposed of by an organization subject to HIPAA law. As you know, HIPAA defines two types of organizations: the covered entity and the business associate. Figure 3-1 shows an easy-to-understand illustration of different types of covered entities and business associates.

When PII is combined with health information and the organization using the information is subject to HIPAA, it becomes specially, legally protected information. Dealing with PHI requires information privacy and security policies and procedures you will not find in other industries.

Cross-Jurisdictional Impact

Those who work in healthcare organizations that have third-party business partners in other countries or care for patients around the globe may need to consider cross-border jurisdictional issues. We mentioned one earlier: You must consider jurisdictional issues when transferring or storing data using a cloud provider that has physical servers outside

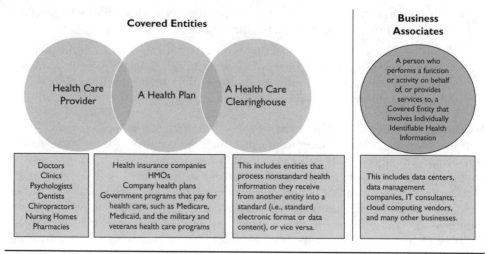

Figure 3-1 Covered entities and business associates

the United States. Of course, this can also be an issue for Canadian and EU providers. In these cases, you certainly want to ensure your local policies and procedures outline how to gain the necessary consent and approvals. Where one jurisdiction has stricter controls required than your organization's country of origin, your organization will need to assess how to comply. An example of how this process has already been addressed between the EU and foreign organizations wanting to share information is the Safe Harbor Agreement, discussed in more detail later in this chapter.

Agreements and treaties such as Safe Harbor can help bridge the jurisdictional issues. As U.S. cloud providers take on EU business partners, the U.S. companies may not fully understand the reach of the EU laws, like the DPD. From a U.S. privacy law view, the EU places additional limitations on the use of an individual's consent to permit data processing, for example, internationally. In 2013, efforts were made to strengthen the international applicability of the EU DPD in business relationships outside of the European Union. U.S. cloud providers need to adjust their standards in some cases to satisfy EU organizations. Of course, this is not specific to healthcare, but it does include EU healthcare organizations. The European Union is the most important bilateral trade area for the United States. Having a way to permit these business arrangements and adequately protect information is profoundly significant.

Another jurisdictional implication would be within various breach notification rules. Imagine an international organization getting a contract to help develop a healthcare web site in the United States. In the event the web site collected healthcare information and was hacked because of a failure to maintain proper OS vulnerability patch management, the liability may be shifted to the third-party business partner. While the actual notification of individuals may not be the responsibility of the international firm, the costs and fines certainly would be. These same liabilities and costs may not be levied in their home countries.

Conforming Policies and Procedures with Regulatory Guidance

Throughout this chapter, we briefly describe various governing regulations that apply to healthcare organizations. This chapter will complement other chapters that list applicable regulations by discussing how you may use these regulations to develop and improve your organizational policies based on relevant laws and regulation. Frankly, most of us do not refer to HIPAA or the EU DPD on a daily basis. It is far more likely that you take actions related to information sharing and protection as a result of what your internal guidance tells you to do. You must be able to determine what internal policies and procedures your organization needs. These policies must be consistent with the laws that govern your industry. Lastly, you must be able to apply the internal guidance documents to your daily work while being able to clearly articulate why the proper actions are being conducted.

An overarching control found in almost every regulation is a legal obligation for each healthcare organization to have its own internal guidelines to prevent, detect, contain, and correct information protection violations. Data protection laws mandate healthcare organizations ensure the confidentiality of patients is protected. It is not enough to have the national (or international) law or governing directive as your internal guidance. The regulations must be customized to show what your organization does and how to do it. You must apply the law to the operations of your organization and assign responsibilities according to various positions in the organization.[5] For instance, the owner of a policy must be identified. That office will have the responsibility to monitor the effectiveness of the guidance and make periodic updates as needed. The senior-level officials such as the chief information officer or chief privacy officer may have assigned responsibilities as well. Maybe these individuals enact procedures to commit resources or administer corrective actions when things do not go according to plan.

Policies

Policies are clear, simple statements of how your organization conducts business and healthcare operations. Policies are at a high level, with guiding principles to help decision making. A policy can be a few paragraphs that cover the various expectations for certain actions. For the most part, organizations use the terms *directives*, *regulations*, and *plans* interchangeably with *policies*. No matter the name, a policy in any form should have the following identifiable elements:

- **Supplemented** Policies tend to be broad statements. Proper implementation usually requires clarification procedures, forms, and other types of direction that can be used by staff. Also, rather than re-issuing policies, it is often more feasible to supplement a policy with recent improvements or additional parameters using a process of versioning. For instance, the first policy is issued as version 1. After reviewing the policy according to how often policies are reviewed for currency (such as every two years), management decides to add responsibilities for a chief information security officer (CISO). Rather than completely republish the policy, the relevant information concerning the CISO position can be added as a supplement, or version 2. This also introduces a related element common to all policies—they must be dated.

- **Visible** All policies must be available to the organization. In many cases, this happens via a web portal or intranet. But, in any case, those members of the organization who are responsible in any way for complying with the policies will certainly need to be able to access them. Training related to the policy is also important in making it visible and communicated.

- **Supported by management** This almost goes without saying, but a policy must be supported by management or it will not be followed. More to the point, management must also support the policy by overt action. They cannot circumvent the policy or ignore it and expect hospital staff to comply.

- **Consistent** Unless there is some unique aspect to the healthcare organization, such as its geographic location or community, the likelihood is that any policy will have an origin in a public law or government directive. A policy should not conflict or guide employees to violate these laws. That said, when developing a policy, you should consider fewer legal references such as organizational culture and organizational mission when writing the expectations.

Your concern is primarily information protection policies. These types of policies will have varying levels of focus within the organization. At one level, a policy is what management uses to create privacy and security programs, establish goals, and assign responsibilities. Policies can also be system-specific rules of operation, or they can simply guide managerial decisions concerning one particular issue such as e-mail privacy policy or release of information policy. Therefore, you can expect to encounter policies at different levels. According to NIST 800-15, "Generally Accepted Principles and Practices for Securing Information Technology Systems," which draws upon the OECD's guidelines for the security of information systems, your organization should have examples of policies at all levels—some governing programs, some system-specific, and some issue-specific.

Procedures

Sometimes called *standard operating procedures* (SOPs), *procedures* describe how each policy will be put into action. They are written instructions, illustrated flowcharts, or checklists covering a routine or repetitive activity. Figure 3-2 illustrates an example of a procedure flowchart for actions that should happen once a data incident or potential data breach is reported. SOPs should not replace policies but should supplement them, or at least the SOP steps should reference the governing policies. You may find terms such as *protocols*, *algorithms*, *instructions*, and *tasks* used in place of *SOP*. As long as the content is routine and repetitive and covers how the activity is carried out, these terms are synonymous.

The benefit of having SOPs to clarify policies at the varying levels is to reduce uncertainty and variation in performance. To be most effective, the SOPs must adhere to the

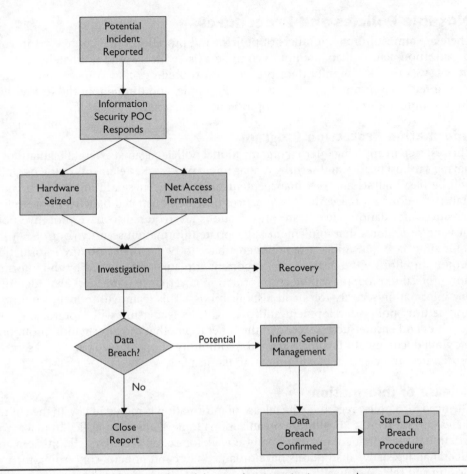

Figure 3-2 Example of flowchart of initial data incident investigation procedure

same principles mentioned earlier. Like policies, SOPs must be visible (maybe even more so), supported by management, and consistent. If they are not or if they seem to contradict the policies, caregivers and business staff will likely create alternative work-flow that may or may not be effective and efficient.

 TIP If referring to HIPAA in the United States, a special consideration is made about all internal guidance and documentation resulting from it (such as a notice of privacy practices form). All internal documentation must be implemented with the following:

Time limit You must keep the documents for at least six years (or longer if another requirement exists, such as accreditation).

Availability The organization must make internal guidance available (usually through intranet or printed pamphlets for staff).

Updates The organization must review and update the guidance periodically.

Notable Policies and Procedures

There are almost infinite numbers of policies and procedures that could exist in your organization. Rather than attempt to compile a list, which would ultimately be insufficient, we cover a few important policies and procedures that you will most likely encounter. Keep in mind that this is a small sample, and throughout the text we will address numerous other policies and procedures that are indispensable.

Information Protection Program

The first step in applying internal organizational policies against external regulations is having a robust privacy and security management process. Key elements of the program will be risk analysis and risk management procedures. These are important because standard information security best practices have demonstrated benefits in protecting sensitive information. Healthcare organizations are required to have proactive policies and procedures that implement appropriate information security controls. At the same time, cost and mission requirements have to be factored into any information protection efforts. One of the most important structures established by the information protection program will be an information governance framework that identifies key information security roles and responsibilities. This team will influence information security policy development and oversight. Its leadership will monitor ongoing activities and ensure success. Some of the other topics that the information protection program documentation will cover are the continuity of operations, personnel security procedures, and disposal of equipment, to name a few.

Release of Information

The need for a policy regarding the release of information is rooted in law. In the United States, HIPAA requires healthcare organizations to have a written policy in place. You will find the requirement internationally as well; for example, the United Kingdom and Australian legislative institutions have ordained laws and policies concerning the disclosure and release of health information.[6] Hospitals in these countries must develop policies and procedures based on relevant laws. The policies need to be consistent with applicable privacy rights for patients. Of course, since the release of information is a common, recurring task that is done every day, a written policy also controls the process so information is not handled incorrectly.

Although each organization's release of information policy will differ because local workflow is unique to each, every release of information policy should follow these basic principles:

- **Use and disclosure** This includes how the information is normally shared, with whom, and when specific patient consent would be needed. Otherwise, the information will be released without requiring a patient signature or additional authorization. You also need to include any situations where information cannot be shared.

- **Minimum necessary rules** Healthcare organizations must make efforts to disclose only what is needed. In a scenario where one specific encounter is under review, the entire legal medical record probably is not needed for disclosure.

- **Patient rights**   The healthcare organization has to inform patients about what rights they have concerning their information and how it is released to other entities.

- **Organizational controls and safeguards**   The release of information policy will include contingency and risk management information concerning how protected health information will be secured during business and clinical workflow interruptions.

- **Right to revoke or opt out**   In many countries, your release of information policy must allow the patient to change their mind and provide information as to how to indicate their changing preference.

The challenge for you may be in helping your organization keep their release of information policy current against the ever-changing standards and regulatory guidance. This can be mitigated by ensuring this specific policy is created and reviewed by several people in the organization that have privacy and security responsibilities and backgrounds. This is not a policy to be created by one person.

Notice of Privacy Practices

Several laws and regulatory recommendations internationally, including HIPAA in the United States, the Personal Health Information Protection Act (PHIPA) in Canada, and the Organization for Economic Cooperation and Development (OECD) in Europe, have provisions for notifying individuals of the organization's privacy practices. The notifications should clearly identify collection and use practices. It will also cover the privacy rights individuals have with respect to their personal health information.

The notice of privacy practices is similar to the release of information policy because many of the same components are found in each. Where they differ is in how they are implemented. To start, there is typically a requirement for the notice of privacy practices to specifically mention that the healthcare organization is obligated by law (if applicable) to protect the information. Under HIPAA and PHIPA, this is the case. Other differences are in the dissemination. Most often, a new patient receives a copy of the notice at the first service encounter or appointment. If the treatment is under emergency conditions, the notice is given to the individual as soon as possible after the emergency is over. The organization must have a notice of privacy practices identified and displayed in their organization for patients to view.

Beyond that, the healthcare organization provides this notice at several times. For instance, in the United States, it is provided at the time of enrollment in a health plan. Every three years or sooner, the notice is sent as a reminder or upon request. Finally, the notice is to be prominently displayed on a web site for their patients to access. As you can see, the notice of privacy practices is not as incident-specific as the release of information policy.

User Agreements

This is a general term that may be considered synonymous with confidentiality agreements, end user agreements (EULAs), or personal accountability documents. Typically, to instill a level of semiformal accountability in policies and procedures, staff members (users) are required to acknowledge understanding and willingness to comply with training, policy, or other regulatory requirements.

One of the best uses of a user agreement is to authorize a specific user to access an application or clinical system, like the EHR. In such an agreement, you will find the following general terms and conditions:

- Access to protected health information is intended only for authorized users and for legitimate purposes. All other access is prohibited.
- Users consent to monitoring and auditing of their use of the application or the system.
- Users will protect and not share their access credentials (user ID and password, for example), which would allow someone else to access the system under their login or authentication.
  - Some user agreements specifically mention that users maintain responsibility for any actions taken under their access credentials.
- If there are specific actions that are worth mentioning concerning user behavior, they can be outlined in the user agreement. Here are examples:
  - Downloading protected health information to external devices may be prohibited.
  - Transporting external media from the healthcare organization may not be allowed.
  - Computer systems must be fully powered off when not in use to ensure full disk encryption is enabled.
  - Data incident reporting procedures must be followed according to relative policy.
- Any training that is required prior to accessing the system must be completed, and proof of completion (certificate) must be provided to appropriate personnel.

User agreements can certainly have more elements than these. They should be customized based on local requirements, and they can be updated. For instance, technology exists to encrypt external USB drives (thumb drives). Leadership may want to allow protected health information to be downloaded by some users. The user agreement can be revised to make this allowance (yet, still prohibit it for some users).

Incident Reporting Policy

Despite robust prevention and monitoring procedures, data loss may happen. As a point of reference, there have been almost 800 data breaches involving 500 individual records since 2009. This results in a total of almost 30 million records, according to just the reports the U.S. HHS receives.[7] It is estimated that all other types of breaches of 1 record up to 499 equal about 80,000 events in the same period of time.

NOTE According to HIPAA, U.S. healthcare organizations are required to promptly report data breaches involving more than 500 individual medical records to the Department of HHS.

An organization that is prepared for potential and actual data loss incidents improves their overall privacy and security program, even if they cannot eliminate the risk. Knowing how to handle escalation of events and coordination among the right people is the framework of an incident reporting policy. Incidents are managed according to identified roles and responsibilities. The reason to have an incident reporting process is to minimally disrupt patient care or business processes. At the same time, every effort must be made to preserve the evidence to allow for proper forensics and analysis. The positive outcome of the policy would be to allow healthcare organizations to improve their information protection based on lessons learned from these events.

The incident reporting policy guides the organization through some general phases. First, the incident is suspected or detected. Maybe an intensive-care nurse notices that his computer has been accessed because he left it accessible. When he returned, the screen was on a web site he never visited before. Unfortunately, he was also logged into and using the EHR before he stepped away. Now there is a chance someone else viewed the record and possibly accessed any number of other records in the database. Following the detection phase, the individual must escalate the event via the alert phase. This is where the right people are identified for internal notification. This will include the identified privacy officer and probably the senior information security official. After they are alerted, others who have responsibilities in the policy may be included. This action will move the process into triage and response phases. In leading healthcare organizations, the incident reporting policy enacts a committee responsible for conducting actions including triage and response. The committee will include the privacy officer and the senior information security official as well as senior members of the information technology department. Other good additions to the team would be the physical security officer, empowered business area leaders, and maybe someone to represent clinical interests. During the triage and response phase, the committee should have interested individuals on it that have the sufficient organization authority to facilitate an investigation to completion. Keep in mind that as the investigation proceeds, it gets costly, resources may be needed, and senior leadership including the governing board may have to be notified.

Once the committee can determine an event actually happened and it takes actions to respond, the goal is to contain the spill and eradicate the cause. From there, the team begins the recovery process and schedules the follow-up tasks. These tasks would lead to external notification actions taken by third-party partners that specialize in data loss or breach notification. It might also include making a claim against any existing cybersecurity indemnity insurance the organization has. In any case, the follow-up actions integrate into additional policies the organization has that are likely outside of the incident reporting policy.

Sanction Policy

We are covering a *sanction policy* because, in the United States, HIPAA specifically requires healthcare organizations to have and demonstrate how to follow a policy to discipline employees who violate procedures for handling protected health information and because a sanction policy can be an extension of an organization's incident reporting policy. Once an incident is reported and investigated, data loss is resolved, and any external notification is done, the organization must take the next step and apply the appropriate and consistent discipline.

A good sanction policy will contain two basic components: the type of offense and the type of sanction or punishment. Management would have the flexibility to examine the nature of the offense, any previous offense, or the intent behind the offense. Then management could look at a variety of predetermined punishments that fall within a minimum and maximum depending on the offense. The punishment could range from a verbal reprimand to a written admonishment to suspension and ultimately termination.

In the end, the key points are that this type of policy provides management with a tool to make objective decisions absent of the appearance of impropriety or favoritism. The sanctions provided are not arrived at on a whim or based on emotion. Without a written policy, the organization weakens its position in any dispute from an employee who is disciplined. Most importantly, the organization can demonstrate that for given offenses equivalent sanctions are applied to all. Of course, organizations do not want to have a lot of sanctions to demonstrate compliance. It's better to have few incidents. Any sanction policy should be communicated to employees during the new-hire orientation process and then annually during retraining. An added measure to gain acknowledgment is to have employees sign to indicate their understanding of the policy and their obligations to comply.

Configuration Management Plan

In a complex healthcare information technology environment, there must be an organized, coordinated policy and a process to plan, implement, maintain, and decommission information technology assets. These assets include hardware and software. You will find a complex information technology environment in healthcare where the state-of-the-art medical devices interface with homegrown systems and applications. Often, because of the proprietary manufacturing of certain medical systems, the platforms may lag behind the latest supported platform that is preferred. When there is a patient safety risk of replacing the outdated platforms or updating them or when it costs too much to do so, healthcare information technology leaders may be forced to maintain and interconnect them with mitigating controls for privacy and security.

Configuration management is important for information assurance to provide confidentiality, integrity, and availability of data used in healthcare. You do this to manage the security features of hardware and software by controlling changes through the life cycle of the assets. Not only do the changes need to be managed, but it is important to update your documentation accordingly. The plan must include provisions for testing proposed changes to the baseline configuration prior to implementation. In fact, many plans include scenarios or regression test cases. These cases will help ensure proposed changes, even vulnerability patching, is done safely and efficiently.

You will encounter several common activities in the configuration management process.

- **Planning**   The organization will require the objectives and strategies to be documented and available for personnel to use.

- **Classifying and recording**   A good configuration management plan (and a good information security program) always starts with a proper inventory to determine the baseline configuration. As the baseline changes, the inventory process continues to document the new normal configuration.

- **Monitoring and control**   The change request process must mandate that changes are controlled by a disciplined process of request, testing, approval, and then implementation. Further, those responsible for maintaining the baseline must monitor the process to ensure unauthorized changes are not made.

    - Within the control function is release management. This is the orderly process by which new or modified changes that have been fully tested and approved are installed into the business or clinical system. Releases are classified and recorded based on whether they are major, minor, or emergency releases.

- **Performing audits**   To verify the configuration remains at the state that matches the current documentation, you will want to perform random and routine audits.

- **Preparing reports**   Probably the most important function of the healthcare information privacy and security professional is to communicate results, issues, and recommendations to senior organizational leadership. The configuration management plan must include an expectation for this important function to receive organizational attention.

In healthcare, like most industries, changes to the information systems should never be made haphazardly or absent of the administrative documentation. Changes must be tested before implemented. Otherwise, the change can be dangerous and can impact patient safety—even if the change improves the overall security posture of the information system.

 NOTE   The Department of Defense (DoD) has many important regulations that apply to protecting information. Two help to illustrate the connection of internal policies and procedures to national law, international regulations, and industry standards. DoD directive 5410.11, "DoD Privacy Program," and DoD directive 8500.01, "Information Assurance (IA)," shape the military's handling of sensitive personal information. To those who work in the defense environment, these directives are the singular, satisfactory source for protecting information. However, they are really just examples of internal policies and procedures. They are based on U.S. national law, international regulations, and best-practice industry standards. They are tailored to the mission of the DoD and outline the numerous roles and responsibilities of assigned personnel.

Governance Frameworks to Manage Policies

To develop feasible policies and procedures and expect them to succeed in protecting information in an organization, you need to understand some active governance frameworks in leading healthcare organizations. The intent of covering these in this chapter is to coordinate all the legal rules, guidance, and best practices that apply to the handling of information to facilitate compliance and continuous improvement. For the most part, common among the frameworks is a diversity of business and clinical disciplines. Really, none of the most effective information governance structures consists of information technology personnel or privacy experts only. Bringing in perspectives from all aspect of hospital operations and management helps generate agreement and better adherence to the standards. Inclusion fosters stakeholders. Not every information governance structure focuses solely on privacy and security, but they all should integrate these concerns into the entirety of technology and process management of information assets. Keep in mind that some of these boards and teams are mandated based on the regulatory guidance the healthcare organization must follow (for example, HIPAA in the United States).

Configuration Control Board

The *configuration control board* (CCB) can also be called a *configuration management board*. As such, it should play an essential role in how an organization implements and manages its information technology asset. This board is listed as a security control in prevailing standards and policies, such as NIST, HIPAA, FISMA, ISO, and so on. The asset can include the local area network, any end-point devices (including medical devices), and the various applications that are in operation. The chief information officer or another senior information technology official is usually the chair of the group because the CCB focuses on technology. However, having voting members from just about every department in the healthcare organization is crucial.

Where the CCB is most effective is in establishing the baseline configuration of the information asset. This does not mean the organization must have a standard configuration. Most healthcare organizations have legacy systems (especially medical devices) that cannot meet current standards. Often, the budget does not allow rapid upgrades or modernization to the extent you might desire. Either way, the CCB strives to know exactly what is residing on the network. From there, controlling changes through a systematic process will avoid exploiting vulnerabilities. Whether it is a patch of vulnerability or an addition of an entire new system, the CCB is integral in making proper maintenance happen. To that end, the CCB has an eye on security, and members should take every opportunity to address security concerns during every phase of configuration management.

Information Management Council

Information governance is usually managed by an information management council (IMC) that considers management and organizational issues as well as technical concerns. The IMC is a terrific source for developing information policy and procedures. You will find a requirement for an information management structure in guidance from the Joint Commission (TJC) in the United States. The IMC differs from the CCB, which is most concerned with technology at a specific system level even though it looks to standardize configuration across the entire organization. The IMC governs information management by addressing appropriate access to information, along with measuring risk of data loss and strategic alignment of information assets with healthcare operations. We cannot understate the continuous strategic alignment and improvement potential of the IMC. For instance, an initiative such as implementing an EHR would certainly be under the purview of the IMC to ensure the significant investment is done appropriately and in line with higher-level organizational initiatives. Even more so, the IMC gives senior leadership a central view of how resources are used to provide and protect information. Key to this budget oversight is a concept called *portfolio management*.

Portfolio management is sometimes also called *project management* in the sense that all current and planned initiatives, projects, and information capabilities are systematically addressed. This means the organization gathers and organizes all the various projects that were previously developed and delivered in no organized manner. Some were conducted within the structure of information technology leadership, and some were not. Think of a commercially available application that a physician in the emergency room purchases and wants implemented in her department. Imagine, as it turns out, the application is not capable of interfacing with any legacy systems in the hospital. This may be an issue the CCB would address; or, depending on the cost, impact, and perceived value of the application working properly, the IMC could have prevented this scenario by managing it as part of the entire portfolio or list of approved projects.

This scenario hints at the real promise of portfolio management. The ability to quantify previously informal efforts based on having the IMC prioritize and value each initiative gives senior leadership an idea of investment and return on investment.

Data Incident Response Team

Also a security control required by various standards and policies such as HIPAA, NIST, ISO, and FISMA, the *incident response team* is something that should be chartered prior to any data loss or breach occurring. Unfortunately, too many organizations fail to have an active or tested team before they need one. According to the American National Standards Institute, 44 percent of organizations do not even have a plan.[8] The point is that once there is a potential for a breach or an actual breach has happened, there is little time to pull together the right team members and conduct an investigation. Having a team ready to go when needed and knowing their roles allows an organization to have an accelerated, effective, and organized response. Not all reports of data loss are matters that require reporting outside of the organization, such as to government regulators or to the patients themselves, but all suspected data losses must be investigated and the outcomes documented. Done correctly, the data incident team can prevent a serious loss of profits, public confidence, or information assets.

The chief information security officer or senior physical security official likely heads the team. Other members of the team will come from information technology, legal, finance, senior medical representatives, risk management, internal auditing, human resources, and public relations. Of course, based on your organization, it may be important to augment this core group with subject-matter experts in data forensics, health information management, patient admissions, and so on. Ultimately, those who are selected as members of the team must have written roles and responsibilities that are understood and tested via periodic mock data loss exercises. Prior to actual events, team members must be given the necessary authority to control resources that help them carry out their duties.

Institutional Review Board

If you work in a dedicated healthcare research organization or in an organization that conducts research as part of its academic mission, you will interact with an *institutional review board* (IRB), also called *independent ethics committees* or *ethical review boards*. They are formal, chartered committees that approve, monitor, and review biomedical and behavioral research involving humans. The primary purpose of the IRB is to protect human subjects from physical or psychological harm. Much like the first rule of privacy is to determine not to collect information unless you need it, the first rule of the research is to determine whether the research should be done. The IRB determines this for the organization through a risk-benefit analysis.

 TIP In the United States, IRBs are accountable for important observation and control functions for research conducted on human subjects that are "scientific," "ethical," and "regulatory." They are empowered by the Department of Health and Human Services (specifically the Office for Human Research Protections) to conduct research and approve waivers to certain HIPAA provisions such as prior patient authorization to use PHI.

The following are the guiding principles of any IRB:[9]

- **Respect for people** People should be treated as autonomous agents (individuals), and those with diminished autonomy must be protected.

- **Beneficence** The well-being of study participants should be protected by adhering to "do no harm" and maximizing benefits while minimizing potential damages.

- **Justice** Participants should have equal opportunity to be selected because even if there is a benefit, there is probably a burden some people will have to bear.

 NOTE In the United States, the IRB is governed by 45 Code of Federal Regulations (CFR) part 46 (Department of HHS regulations for the protection of human subjects) and 21 CFR parts 50 and 56 (FDA regulations on the protection of human subjects). Closely related to IRBs is the provision under HIPAA, specifically the Privacy Rule, which has a provision for a privacy board. Both the IRB and the privacy board are permitted to allow PHI disclosure without additional patient consent for research. You can find this provision at 45 CFR parts 160 and 164, specifically, section 164.508. Privacy boards differ from IRBs, though. Privacy boards have no other authority within human subject research or FDA-sponsored research like the IRB does.

International Regulations and Controls

Protecting healthcare information is a global concern. In the United States, specific laws are in place to govern the handling of healthcare information. Internationally, laws address healthcare information specifically, though typically within the context of protecting all personal information. Privacy regulations and controls cover individually identifying information and health information is included in this. A comparison of some select international frameworks with prevailing U.S. standards is useful.

Organization for Economic Cooperation and Development Privacy Principles

The Organization for Economic Cooperation and Development (OECD), headquartered in France, has developed policy around the general principles all 29 member countries should follow with the aim of fostering international trade. The United States is a member of the OECD and is one of the largest funders of its $200 million annual budget.

The OECD framework categorizes fair information practices for collecting, storing, and using individually identifiable information. It aims to help individuals participate in the use of their own information. The principles assign responsibility for protecting information to the entities that collect and maintain it. As you familiarize yourself with U.S. and international data protection law, you will find the following principles well-integrated:[10]

- **Collection Limitation Principle**   There should be limits to the collection of personal data, and any such data should be obtained by lawful and fair means and, where appropriate, with the knowledge or consent of the data subject.

- **Data Quality Principle**   Personal data should be relevant to the purposes for which it is to be used and, to the extent necessary for those purposes, should be accurate, complete, and kept up to date.

- **Purpose Specification Principle**   The purposes for which personal data is collected should be specified no later than at the time of data collection, and the subsequent use should be limited to the fulfilment of those purposes or any occasions that are not incompatible with those purposes and as specified on each occasion of change of purpose.

- **Use Limitation Principle**   Personal data should not be disclosed, made available, or otherwise used for purposes other than those specified except in the following cases:

  - With the consent of the data subject

  - By the authority of law

- **Security Safeguards Principle**   Personal data should be protected by reasonable security safeguards against such risks as loss or unauthorized access, destruction, use, modification, or disclosure of data.

- **Openness Principle**   There should be a general policy of openness about developments, practices, and policies with respect to personal data. Means should be readily available for establishing the existence and nature of personal data and the main purposes of its use, as well as the identity and jurisdiction of the data controller.

- **Individual Participation Principle**   An individual should have the right to do the following:

  - Obtain from, or otherwise, obtain confirmation of whether the data controller has data relating to him

  - Have communicated to him data relating to him, within the following parameters:

    - Within a reasonable time

    - At a charge, if any, that is not excessive

    - In a reasonable manner

    - In a form that is readily intelligible to him

  - Be given reasons if a request made by an individual to access their information is denied and be able to challenge such denial

  - Challenge data relating to him and, if the challenge is successful, have the data erased, rectified, completely amended, or annotated in the case where the patient and provider are not in agreement

- **Accountability Principle**   A data controller should be accountable for complying with measures that give effect to the principles stated earlier.

Safe Harbor Agreement

Related to the OECD principles and their impact on international trade is the regulatory framework of a Safe Harbor Agreement. From the EU perspective, data transfer can happen only if there is a determination of "adequacy," or, in other words, the entity that is collecting the data has adequate privacy processes and safeguards in place. The European Union does not automatically grant that assurance of adequacy for non-EU member nations, like the United States or Canada does. To facilitate data transfer, to enable international trade, and to bridge any privacy differences, the European Union and United States, through the Department of Commerce, has developed a Safe Harbor framework that satisfies the adequacy requirement.[11] See Figure 3-3 for an overview of the Safe Harbor gap assessment process.

To be certain, there are different approaches to privacy and security between the United States and the European Union. However, both have a commitment to protecting the information. This Safe Harbor process does not mean the United States lacks privacy and security controls. The United States uses an industry perspective. There are specific laws governing each industry (HIPAA for healthcare, for example). The governing approach is a combination of these laws and a measure of voluntary self-regulation.

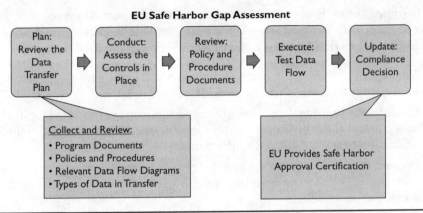

Figure 3-3 Process to address the privacy gap between U.S. and EU data transfer

The European Union, however, considers privacy a human right, and protections are directed and monitored by the national governments (across health and all industries). Therefore, there is significant control over data collection with comprehensive legislation in the European Union. Independent government data protection agencies are prevalent, and data controllers must register their databases with those agencies. In some cases, the government must provide prior approval before personal data processing may begin.

Keep in mind, the Safe Harbor framework applies to more industries than healthcare. But for healthcare organizations that need to transfer data between the United States and the member nations of the European Union, Safe Harbor is something to appreciate. It can help avoid experiencing disruption to patient care or prosecution under European law. U.S. healthcare organizations can be certified to the Safe Harbor requirements.

 TIP Safe Harbor can be easily confused by those who work in the U.S. healthcare industry because specific actions that are taken "in good faith" are usually exempted in most U.S. laws, called *Safe Harbor provisions*. HIPAA, governing healthcare, provides several Safe Harbor provisions such as using full-disk encryption to render protected health data unreadable. In the event a laptop is lost or stolen with PHI but is full-disk encrypted, the data loss is generally not reportable. The use of Safe Harbor in terms of internal policies likely applies to Safe Harbor as it is governed by the EU.

Many healthcare organizations have integrated EU-U.S. Safe Harbor policies into their existing policies. Additionally, healthcare vendors that conduct business internationally have signed up for EU Safe Harbor provisions. Annually, organizations conduct a self-certification and submit a letter to the EU to appear in the list of Safe Harbor participants.

To become EU Safe Harbor certified, a U.S. organization must comply with the following seven principles, which should look familiar with respect to the privacy principles found in the OECD guidance, although they are not identical:[12]

- **Notice**   The organization must let the individual know why it is collecting the information and how it will be used.

- **Choice**   The individual must have the opportunity to opt out of the information collection, and the organization must inform the individual of the resulting alternatives to not providing the information.

- **Onward transfer**   Safe Harbor–certified organizations can transfer information to third parties only if those organizations also agree to follow adequate information protection principles.

- **Access**   Individuals must be able to access their information. When it is inaccurate, they must have remedies available to them to correct or delete it.

- **Security**   There must be reasonable controls in place to protect personal information from loss and unauthorized disclosure.

- **Data integrity**   Organizations must limit information collection to only that which is relevant to its use. The information must be protected so that it remains reliable for that use.

- **Enforcement**   Organizations must have procedures to enforce these principles. For instance, sanctions must be convincing enough to encourage compliance.

EU Data Protection Directive

The EU DPD (officially Act 95/46/EC) regulates the processing of personal data within the European Union. EU member states are subject to the act and do not need national-level law. The EU DPD is an important component of EU privacy and human rights law. The prevailing principle of the DPD is that the first consideration is to not collect personal data at all. But when that is not possible, certain conditions must be met. This is consistent with the idea of limiting collection of personal data found in other frameworks, like the OECD. The conditions that must be met for necessary collection fall into three categories: transparency, legitimate purpose, and proportionality.[13]

- **Transparency**   The data subject has the right to be informed when his personal data is being processed. The controller must provide his name and address, the purpose of processing, the recipients of the data, and all other information required to ensure the processing is fair.

- **Legitimate purpose**   Personal data can be processed only for specified explicit and legitimate purposes and may not be processed further in a way incompatible with those purposes.

- **Proportionality**   Personal data may be processed only insofar as it is accurate, relevant, and not excessive in relation to the purposes for which they are collected and/or further processed.

  - **Accurate**   The data must be up to date, and every reasonable step must be taken to ensure that data that is inaccurate or incomplete is erased or rectified.

  - **Relevant**   The data shouldn't be kept in a form that permits identification of data subjects for longer than is necessary for the purposes for which the data was collected or for which it is further processed. Member states shall lay down appropriate safeguards for personal data stored for longer periods for historical, statistical, or scientific use.

  - **Excessive**   Only the minimum amount of identifying data that is needed should be collected.

 NOTE   When it comes to healthcare, there are some considerations. EU member states should adhere to the principle of limiting collection *except* where the data is needed for preventive medicine, medical diagnosis, or the provision of care or treatment. Additionally, the data must be handled by a healthcare entity that is subject to national laws, rules, or obligations for professional confidentiality (privacy) or the equivalent level of obligation of confidentiality.

This provision impacts data transmitted to the United States. As mentioned, this transfer is initially prohibited. The European Union considers the United States lacking in the national or equivalent level of obligation to ensure individually identifying information is kept confidential. This is why the Safe Harbor provisions are so important. Between adhering to HIPAA and certifying through the Department of Commerce, the U.S. healthcare entities can also satisfy the EU DPD requirement to demonstrate adequacy of safeguarding personal information. If you work for a U.S. healthcare business and your work includes data transfer between the United States and European Union, you will want to make sure your compliance with the HIPAA final privacy and security rules is complemented by certification under Safe Harbor.

International Organization for Standardization

The International Organization for Standardization (ISO) is an international standard-setting body that consists of qualified subject-matter experts from more than 150 countries that attempt to integrate national standards like those from the American National Standards Institute, ISO Technical Committee (TC) 215 Health Informatics, the BSI Group from the United Kingdom, and the Standards Council of Canada, to name a select few. We are mentioning ISO standards here because you should familiarize yourself with their existence and their relationship to other regulations. These standards are copyrighted and not distributed for free. However, draft ISO standards are available during review periods, and some versions of standards can be found online through various sharing agreements.[14] As a tool for daily use, the concepts and principles found in the ISO guidance are sufficiently available in other sources as well. However, they are important to acknowledge and, when available, reinforce the processes and procedures required for safeguarding individually identifiable information. For our purposes, we will talk about a few relevant standards related to managing risk, provide a brief description, and summarize their relevance. Here we will look at governance standards for information privacy and security:

- **ISO 27001: Information Security Management System**   This standard helps organizations implement security as a system versus numerous controls put in place to solve seemingly isolated issues. The standard includes handling of electronic information as well as paper-based information. From the management perspective, this standard, main contribution is to formalize the concept of risk assessments and organize information security as a quality improvement activity. The standard includes the plan-do-check-act (PDCA) concept as well as the principle of continually assessing the organization, not just episodically.

- **ISO 27799: Health Informatics**   This defines information security management in health, which uses ISO/IEC 27002 and augments the requirements of 27002 with healthcare-specific considerations for information security management.

- **ISO 29100: Privacy Framework**   This defines requirements for properly safeguarding personally identifiable information used by a data collector. The standard introduces terminology, outlines roles and responsibilities, and describes the following 11 privacy principles:

  - Consent and choice
  - Purpose legitimacy and specification
  - Collection limitation
  - Data minimization
  - Use, retention, and disclosure limitation
  - Accuracy and quality
  - Openness, transparency, and notice
  - Individual participation and access
  - Accountability
  - Information security
  - Privacy compliance

  One of the other salient points about this standard is it defines identifiability and related terms. The extent to which information serves to identify an individual is identifiability. Of course, there are varying degrees of identifiability. There is full anonymity (not identifiable) to full verinymity (positively identified). This is related to the concept of linkability, which is the extent to which you can link various data elements together to positively identify someone. Unlinkability means that, even after complex combinations and attempts, you cannot determine identity by linking the information. The other concept the standard introduces is observability. This is the extent to which you can identify or link an identity to a system by virtue of an individual's use of the system. It includes a consideration of factors such as time, location, or data contents.

- **ISO 29101: Privacy Reference Architecture** A tactical guide, this standard contains best practices collected from the industry for processing personally identifiable information. The guidance delivers consistent, technical implementation of privacy requirements. By using the guide, you can build a privacy reference architecture with the necessary privacy safeguarding measures built into the system functionally and systematically across the entire enterprise. The goal is to include all relevant systems and integrate with already existing safeguarding controls.

- **ISO 29190: Privacy Capability Assessment Model** This standard gives an organization the tools to determine their level of maturity in their processes for collecting, using, disclosing, retaining, and disposing of personal information. The level of maturity is assessed based on whether the organization has evidence of processes related to information governance, risk assessments, third-party management, and relevant policy among other areas of concern.

Generally Accepted Privacy Principles

The generally accepted privacy principles (GAPP) are rooted in the principles found in the OECD and ISO guidance. They also attempt to regulate the collection and use of PII in adherence with fair information practices and prevailing law. One of the biggest proponents of GAPP is Canadian privacy practitioners. That is likely related to the fact that the principles were developed by the American Institute of Certified Public Accountants (AICPA) and the Canadian Institute of Chartered Accountants (CICA).

Generally accepted privacy principles are founded on the following privacy objective:

> "Personal information is collected, used, retained, and disclosed, and disposed of in conformity with the commitments in the entity's privacy notice and with criteria set forth in Generally Accepted Privacy Principles issued by the AICPA/CICA."[15]

The following are the ten generally accepted privacy principles:

- **Management** The entity defines, documents, communicates, and assigns accountability for its privacy policies and procedures.

- **Notice** The entity provides notice about its privacy policies and procedures and identifies the purposes for which personal information is collected, used, retained, and disclosed.

- **Choice and consent** The entity describes the choices available to the individual and obtains implicit or explicit consent with respect to the collection, use, and disclosure of personal information.

- **Collection**   The entity collects personal information only for the purposes identified in the notice.

- **Use, retention, and disposal**   The entity limits the use of personal information to the purposes identified in the notice and for which the individual has provided implicit or explicit consent. The entity retains personal information for only as long as necessary to fulfill the stated purposes, or as required by law or regulations, and thereafter appropriately disposes of such information.

- **Access**   The entity provides individuals with access to their personal information for review and update.

- **Disclosure to third parties**   The entity discloses personal information to third parties only for the purposes identified in the notice and with the implicit or explicit consent of the individual.

- **Security for privacy**   The entity protects personal information against unauthorized access (both physical and logical).

- **Quality**   The entity maintains accurate, complete, and relevant personal information for the purposes identified in the notice.

- **Monitoring and enforcement**   The entity monitors compliance with its privacy policies and procedures and has procedures to address privacy-related complaints and disputes.

Chapter Review

The dynamic regulatory environment in healthcare can be overwhelming. The protection of information is rooted in national privacy and security laws. Those laws typically match international governing directives, although most countries do not have healthcare-specific laws like the United States. Where U.S. law and international laws differ and healthcare information must be shared, agreements such as Safe Harbor have been enacted to help bridge the differences. However, on a day-to-day basis, most of us rely on local, internal policies and procedures to govern our use of protected health information. In that sense, your focus is on your organization, but you must be familiar with prevailing national and international guidance.

Review Questions

1. The potential for a malpractice lawsuit because of a network outage most likely results from:

   A. Providers using manual processes that are not peer reviewed

   B. Hospitals diverting patients to other hospitals with fewer capabilities

   C. Out-of-date disaster recovery plans with invalid backup data

   D. Medical device patient monitoring functions impeded

2. (TRUE or FALSE) Federal law is the best source for day-to-day reference of healthcare information privacy and security practices.

3. _____ is required to be provided to inform individuals of their privacy rights with respect to their personal health information?

4. A data incident reporting policy would identify that breaches of at least what number of individual records must be promptly reported to the U.S. Department of Health and Human Services?

   A. All breaches

   B. More than 500

   C. More than 5000

   D. A number based on hospital average daily census

5. What is the governance board that oversees information protection of research called?

   A. Information management council

   B. Configuration control board

   C. Incident response team

   D. Institutional review board

6. Of the following, which would be found within the Organization for Economic Cooperation and Development (OECD) privacy principles?

   A. Collection limitation

   B. De-identification

   C. Onward transfer

   D. Choice and consent

7. (TRUE or FALSE) A data controller that should comply with measures found in the Organization for Economic Cooperation and Development (OECD) principles fits the definition of accountability.

8. To bridge any privacy differences between the European Union and United States, the _____ was developed.

   A. Fair information principles

   B. Privacy Rule

   C. Generally acceptable privacy principles

   D. Safe Harbor

9. The international standard that requires that data collection meet the conditions of transparency, legitimate purpose, and proportionality is the _____.

   A. EU Data Protection Act

   B. ISO 29100: Privacy Framework

    C. Health Insurance Portability and Accountability Act

    D. Generally acceptable privacy principles

10. ISO 27001: Information Security Management System outlines the concept and implementation of risk _____.

    A. assessment

    B. tolerance

    C. measurement

    D. perspective

11. Which of the following is based on the privacy objective of using personal information in conformity with an organization's privacy notice?

    A. Fair information principles

    B. Generally acceptable privacy principles

    C. Purpose Specification Principle

    D. Internal governance directives

Answers

1. **D.** Because medical devices are regulated by the FDA, healthcare organizations have additional responsibilities to ensure their special-purpose computing platforms have either high availability or adequate continuity procedures. Otherwise, it may be considered negligence, and therefore malpractice, if a network outage impedes the monitoring of a patient. The other responses are incorrect because these actions probably would happen but would not necessarily put patients at additional direct risk.

2. **FALSE.** While all of the answers are valid sources for how you conduct an information protection program, a recurring theme of this chapter is for day-to-day information protection practices, so the best source should be internal policies and procedures. Of course, these policies and procedures should be built upon the principles and standards found in local, national, and, in some cases, international law. Industry standards are based upon law, but in some cases, these standards reflect best practices or controls with voluntary compliance. In any case, they are valid sources for internal policies and procedures.

3. **Notice of Privacy Practices.** The correct answer is a notice of privacy practices, which is the policy (and form) healthcare organizations must comply with to notify patients of their privacy rights.

4. **B.** This is a straightforward question that is fundamental to understanding and reporting healthcare data breaches. HHS has determined that 500 is the number that delineates prompt notification. After 500 records, various additional actions must happen, including notifying patients and the local media in some cases. Of course, more than 5,000 records would also meet

this requirement, but the phrase "at least" makes option B the correct answer and matches the HIPAA law. All breaches are eventually reported in aggregate. Because this data incident reporting procedure is not established by any internal considerations, a measure such as average daily census is not applicable. But, knowing this fundamental number (500) helps you take the proper internal steps to respond to data breaches and mitigate any data loss.

5. **D.** The institutional review board (IRB) is the only choice that is relevant to research. When information protection in healthcare research with human subjects is referenced, there must be a governing IRB in place. The other choices are legitimate groups of internal staff members and leadership in a healthcare organization with information protection responsibilities, but none is specifically required for the research of human subjects.

6. **A.** Knowing and differentiating between the frameworks and international principles is difficult; they are similar. However, in some organizations and countries, it is required to be able to distinguish the principle and the source. That said, de-identification is a process of taking PHI and either removing all the identifiers or creating an algorithm to change the identifiers to make them unconnected to a person. Onward transfer is a concept covered under Safe Harbor, and choice and consent is a principle under GAPP. If your responsibilities do not include memorizing the principles and their sources, concentrate on knowing the definitions of the principles themselves.

7. **TRUE.** This is a better example of knowing the definition of the principles versus memorizing which set of standards they came from. Accountability is the OECD principle that says data controllers should be accountable for compliance with OECD and laws that follow those principles.

8. **D.** The fair information principles, in this context, are related to the OECD framework that represent widely accepted concepts concerning protecting privacy. The Privacy Rule is an amendment to U.S. HIPAA law and is not applicable to the European Union. While generally acceptable privacy principles are internationally recognized, they are more prevalent in U.S. and Canadian data exchange. The correct answer is Safe Harbor, which is the method to address any perceived gap in the privacy practices of the United States from the EU perspective.

9. **A.** As we introduce the EU DPD in this chapter, the guiding conditions of transparency, legitimate purpose, and proportionality foreshadow the finer details covered later in the book. Of course, the DPD starts with a caution to collect personal information only if you must, and otherwise do not. The ISO Privacy Framework does not include these components, and the Health Insurance Portability and Accountability Act is not international. Finally, the generally acceptable privacy principles have similar concepts, but because the EU DPD specifically frames itself around these conditions, the EU DPD is the right answer.

10. **A.** ISO 27001 is the central source from the ISO family of standards that introduces and formalizes the process of risk assessment in organizations. Because tolerance is a way to mitigate or deal with risk, it is a response to issues found in the risk assessment. Measurement and perspective are at best synonymous terms for assessment or mitigation (of risk) but are not used by ISO 27001.

11. **B.** Internal governance directives can (or should) conform with an organization's privacy notice, and vice versa, but the question defines the foundation of the generally acceptable privacy principles. The Purpose Specification Principle is one of the principles in the OECD framework, while the fair information principles are the basis of the OECD framework.

References

1. U.S. Food and Drug Administration. "Is The Product A Medical Device?" Accessed on January 12, 2014, at www.fda.gov/MedicalDevices/DeviceRegulationand Guidance/Overview/ClassifyYourDevice/ucm051512.htm

2. Silver, Jonathan D., "Computer outage at UPMC called 'rare': Systemwide disruption potentially dangerous, expert warns." *Pittsburgh Post-Gazette.* December 24, 2011. Accessed on January 23, 2014, at http://old.post-gazette. com/pg/11358/1199140-53-0.stm?cmpid=news.xml#ixzz2sNyCu9SQ

3. U.S. Department of Health and Human Services. "HIPAA Breach Notification Rule," 45 CFR Section 164.400-414. 2009. Accessed on January 20, 2014, at www.gpo.gov/fdsys/pkg/FR-2009-08-24/pdf/E9-20169.pdf

4. U.S. Department of Health and Human Services. "Modifications to the HIPAA Privacy, Security, Enforcement, and Breach Notification Rules Under the Health Information Technology for Economic and Clinical Health Act and the Genetic Information Nondiscrimination Act; Other Modifications to the HIPAA Rules; Final Rule," 45 CFR Parts 160 and 164. p. 78. 2013. Accessed on January 5, 2014, at www.gpo.gov/fdsys/pkg/FR-2013-01-25/pdf/2013-01073.pdf

5. Adapted from "Security and Privacy Controls for Federal Information Systems and Organizations." NIST Special Publication 800-53, Revision 4. pps. X, XI. Accessed on February 1, 2014, at http://nvlpubs.nist.gov/nistpubs/SpecialPublications/ NIST.SP.800-53r4.pdf

6. Yarmohammadian, Mohammad. "Medical record information disclosure laws and policies among selected countries; a comparative study." J Res Med Sci. 2010 May-Jun. 15(3). pps 140-149. Accessed on January 3, 2014, at www.ncbi. nlm.nih.gov/pmc/articles/PMC3082803

7. U.S. Department of Health and Human Services. "Breaches Affecting 500 or More Individuals." Accessed on January 20, 2014, at www.hhs.gov/ocr/privacy/ hipaa/administrative/breachnotificationrule/breachtool.html

8. American National Standards Institute (ANSI). "The Financial Impact of Breached Protected Health Information: A Business Case for Enhanced PHI Security." 2012. Accessed on January 3, 2014, at http://webstore.ansi.org/phi

9. U.S. Department of Health and Human Services. The Belmont Report. "Ethical Principles and Guidelines for the Protection of Human Subjects of Research." Part B. April 18, 1979. Accessed on February 1, 2014, at www.hhs.gov/ohrp/humansubjects/guidance/belmont.html#xbasic

10. Organisation for Economic Co-operation and Development (OECD). "Guidelines on the Protection of Privacy and Transborder Flows of Personal Data (2013)." Part 2. pps. 4–6. Accessed on January 27, 2014, at www.oecd.org/sti/ieconomy/2013-oecd-privacy-guidelines.pdf

11. Swire, P. P., S. Bermann, & International Association of Privacy Professionals (2007). Data Sharing and Transfer. In Information privacy: Official reference for the Certified Information Privacy Professional (CIPP). p. 250. International Association of Privacy Professionals.

12. U.S. Department of Commerce. "Safe Harbor Privacy Principles." 2000. Accessed on January 15, 2014, at http://export.gov/safeharbor/eu/eg_main_018475.asp

13. Official Journal of the European Communities. Directive 95/46/EC of the European Parliament and of the Council. 1995. Accessed on January 20, 2014, at http://eur-lex.europa.eu/LexUriServ/LexUriServ.do?uri=CELEX:31995L0046:en:HTML

14. An example of relevant ISO standards that are made publically available found at http://standards.iso.org/ittf/PubliclyAvailableStandards/index.html. Accessed on January 18, 2014.

15. Generally Accepted Privacy Principles. American Institute of Certified Public Accountants, Inc. and Canadian Institute of Chartered Accountants. 2009. Accessed on January 19, 2014, at www.aicpa.org/InterestAreas/InformationTechnology/Resources/Privacy/GenerallyAcceptedPrivacyPrinciples/DownloadableDocuments/GAPP_PRAC_%200909.pdf

PART I

Information Risk Decision Making

In this chapter, you will learn to

- Understand the basics of risk-based decision making
- Look at leading information risk management frameworks for their use in healthcare
- Comprehend the concept of risk tolerance and methods of handling residual risk
- Address categories of information asset controls
- Know the importance of communicating risk management activities and findings
- Learn how to support third-party relationships and minimize their risk to the healthcare organization

The concept of risk in healthcare organizations has several definitions depending on where you work. From a clinical perspective, risk is the measurement of the quality and safety of healthcare provided. Risks that put patients at harm are identified, and actions are taken to prevent or control the risks. Because here we are concerned with information protection, *risk* is defined as the potential harm caused by a purposeful or accidental event that negatively impacts the confidentiality, integrity, or availability of the information. Information risk can also result in patient harm. As you read this chapter, note that the use of the term *risk* will apply to information risk unless otherwise specifically mentioned. We cover the organized, systematic approach to managing risk and decision making in information protection. There are several frameworks for doing this important work. Once you understand what your risks are, you can begin to decide what you want to do about it. We cover several approaches to managing risk. For example, organizations must decide whether to mitigate, accept, or transfer risk. There are a few other approaches to managing risk that we will introduce. In the end, your role is to measure the risk and communicate the alternatives to leadership with regard to how information protection integrates with business strategy, clinical practices, and third-party relationships.

Using Risk Management to Make Decisions

Making decisions about managing information requires a systematic and organized approach. Otherwise, emotions or personal preferences can influence actions and actually increase the chances of an event happening or increase the extent of the impact. No matter what format you ultimately choose to make decisions about risk, you must use some methodology. Before we introduce some of the leading risk frameworks, we need to define the following terms:

- **Threat**   A specific source of information loss or damage relevant to your organization
- **Vulnerability**   A weakness that may expose the organization unnecessarily to the threat
- **Probability**   The likelihood that a threat can happen (increased based on vulnerability)
- **Impact**   The extent of damages expected by a threat event happening
- **Mitigation and controls**   Actions or processes put in place to either prevent (control) or lessen (mitigate) the impact of exploited threats

When structuring a decision that measures risk around these variables, you can use a risk management framework, discussed next, to weight cost against benefit or risk versus reward. In all cases, you can ensure that you are implementing controls that are relevant and cost-effective to the assets you are trying to protect. Figure 4-1 introduces

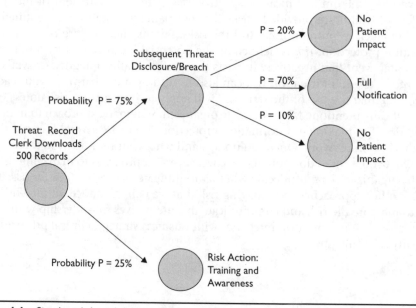

Figure 4-1   Simple risk-based decision tree

the overall concepts underlying decision making using risk measurement to choose between alternatives, which is a foundational concept behind any information risk management framework.

Information Risk Compliance Frameworks

In several chapters to follow, we explore the more technical aspects of information risk compliance frameworks. Rather than duplicate the information, this section introduces you to some leading examples and discusses their intended use for making decisions about information risk. For now, you need to recognize how each framework approaches one of the most foundational concepts of healthcare information privacy and security: information risk. You will see that no matter what tool you desire to use, the objective is to measure risk by identifying vulnerabilities, assigning a likelihood of occurrence, and assigning a value of the impact to your organization. From there, you can begin to design and implement controls to mitigate the likelihood of risk, minimize the impacts, and thereby manage risk.

Measuring and Expressing Information Risk

Here are some risk equations you may be familiar with:

Risk = Likelihood × Impact

Risk = Threat × Vulnerability × Expected Loss

Risk = Probability × Consequence

The previous "risk equations" do not mean risk is always measured in objective terms (numbers, percentages, data results, and so on). It can certainly be expressed in subjective terms such as a management value or priority measurement (low, medium, high, and so on). In healthcare, the impact of risk may be measured in monetary cost, reputation loss, and (most importantly) adverse patient events. As an illustration, an organization called Open Web Application Security Project (OWASP) is an emerging body of standards-setting organizations and experts from around the world. The organization uses a combination of simple measures to calculate risk. Based on subjective values (0–9, with 9 being the highest), assessments are made against threats and vulnerabilities to achieve an estimation of impact.[1] These notional values are plotted on a chart to quickly identify the level of overall risk severity of the issue (Figure 4-2).

Generally speaking, the common points made by almost all credible information risk management frameworks highlight these important steps:

1. Identify a person or people who are responsible for privacy and security issues.

2. Perform an information risk assessment (using a standards-based framework).

3. Have up-to-date policies that cover the proper use of sensitive information assets.

4. Charter a formal board or committee that oversees information risk management.

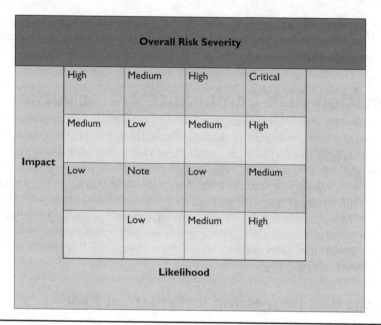

Figure 4-2 OWASP methodology for making risk-based decisions

5. Communicate findings and remediation progress through that group to senior leadership (and the entire organization, as needed).

6. Manage third-party risk by assessing their proper use of sensitive information.

7. Maintain an active privacy and security awareness training program for employees.

8. Have an obvious incident reporting process for employees to follow.

National Institute of Standards and Technology

One of the most commonly cited risk management sources is the risk management process defined in the National Institute of Standards and Technology (NIST) Special Publication 800-39, "Security Risk: Organization, Mission, and Information System View." However, that does not preclude the use of other, credible sources. The choices depend on your organization's mission, scope, and tolerance for information risk. NIST approaches risk management as a holistic process that must take the entire organization into account.

At a high level, NIST builds a risk management framework around the activities of a risk management program.[2]

- **Framing risk** What is the organization's risk tolerance, and how does it make decisions about risk?

- **Assessing risk** What are the values for the risk equation, and what are the results?

- **Responding to risk**   Based on the organization's risk tolerance, what alternatives will be chosen to address risk?

- **Monitoring risk**   This is a continuous process. How will the organization oversee changes and respond to any impacts of risk mitigation activities?

Again, these steps are at a high level. Keep in mind that the four steps NIST identifies are interconnected by as much information and communication flow as possible. The process is continuous, so the information and communication flow must contain feedback and improvement concerns.

A second source you should be familiar with is the NIST Special Publication 800-37, Revision 1, "Guide for Applying the Risk Management Framework to Federal Information Systems: A Security Life Cycle Approach." While it is intended for U.S. federal agencies, the concept of a risk management framework (RMF) is important to commercial businesses, including healthcare organizations. The NIST RMF is a disciplined, organized, and repeatable process for achieving information protection of information systems. When comparing NIST 800-37 with the RMF in NIST 800-39, you can see overlap. Both are life-cycle concepts with continuous monitoring and improvement as a central concept. NIST 800-37 has as one of its stated purposes to "...provide senior leaders the necessary information to make cost-effective, risk-based decisions with regard to the organizational information systems supporting their core missions and business functions."[3]

The two models are not redundant, though. The more detailed nature of the RMF allows flexibility to adapt the framework to industry-specific standards and guidelines. In sum, the RMF provides organizations with the flexibility needed to apply the right security controls to the right information systems at the right time to adequately manage risk. In the United States, many of the HIPAA Security Rule standards and implementation specifications correspond to the steps of the NIST RMF.[4] Approaching risk management using these NIST frameworks will help any healthcare organization comply with its risk management strategy. For a pictorial view of the NIST RMF with the relevant HIPAA standards integrated into each of its six RMF steps, see Figure 4-3.

 NOTE   As a result of U.S. Executive Order 13636, NIST published a National Cybersecurity Framework. Adoption and compliance are voluntary today. It was released in February 2014 and focuses cybersecurity efforts in five areas (identify, protect, detect, respond, and recover), with 20 subcategories of controls. Those control areas include activities such as asset management, security continuous monitoring, and improvements.

HITRUST

Developed in collaboration with healthcare and information security professionals, the Health Information Trust Alliance (HITRUST) Common Security Framework (CSF) is a security framework for protecting health information tailored for the U.S. healthcare industry. The CSF includes and integrates federal and state regulations, standards, and

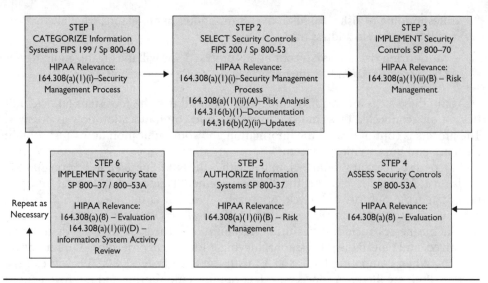

Figure 4-3　NIST RMF steps with relevant HIPAA standards

frameworks such as HIPAA, NIST, ISO, and COBIT to provide a healthcare organization with a broad and adaptable tool for assessing risk.

Because, to date, no specific risk management framework or tool has been prescribed for healthcare organizations, there is a tremendous amount of variation in risk management compliance. That means some organizations do not have a formal process, some do but it is inadequate, and some do too much just to be safe. There are few that reportedly do it correctly. The results of studies like the HIMSS annual privacy and security surveys and the judgments after data breaches reveal this. It is not the healthcare organizations' fault entirely. In an effort to allow for flexibility in the guidance to accommodate organization size, mission, complexity, and capabilities, the guidance ends up being too open to interpretation. For instance, HIPAA calls for controls for protecting information that is "reasonable and appropriate." Depending on the healthcare organization, the decision makers involved, and the level of information risk tolerance, these are terms with overly broad definitions, resulting in vulnerabilities that are not addressed, wasted resources, and ineffectiveness.

This is where a framework like HITRUST CSF has proven beneficial. The CSF is a product of collaboration among healthcare and IT professionals. The approach is to be more prescriptive because the diverse set of existing requirements from NIST, HIPAA, and so on, are integrated into an efficient set of standards that make sense to healthcare. By prescriptive, this does not mean inflexible. The CSF accommodates the diversity of information systems found in healthcare organizations. Built into the CSF is a concept of approved alternate controls to meet risk mitigation or compensation strategy against an identified vulnerability when the prescribed control is infeasible. As the CSF grows in use and popularity, it will be more of a trusted benchmark for compliance, rather than the current state of healthcare testing itself to be "reasonable and appropriate," with each organization for itself.

International Organization for Standardization

The International Organization for Standardization (ISO) is an international standards-setting board with prominence and one we discuss for its role as a governance board later in this chapter. At this point, it is introduced in the context of how it approaches information risk management. For those who work outside of the United States or in U.S. healthcare organizations that do business internationally, having an awareness of ISO standards is important. Since 1947, when it started, it has published 19,500 standards for business and technology industries. From an information risk management perspective, two leading standards apply. The first, ISO 27001: Information Security Management Risk Management Systems (ISMS), presents best-practice information security management principles, a framework, and a process for managing risk. The guidelines are applicable to any sized organization or mission and can be used by any organization regardless of its size, activity, or sector. This standard approaches risk by focusing improvement of objectives by identifying opportunities and threats. From there, the organization can allocate resources to deal with the risk effectively. If you use ISO 27001 or any of the ISO 27000 family of standards, you will learn to define risk not as a chance or probability of loss but via the effect uncertainty has on your objectives.

 NOTE   In the previous chapter, we mentioned ISO 27799: Health Informatics – Information Security Management in Health. It is relevant to include it in this discussion as well because ISO 277799 uses ISO 27002 and augments the requirements of 27002 with healthcare-specific considerations for information security management.

The ISO 27000 family of standards also introduces the final step in the risk management process, risk treatment. Under this guidance, an organization can address risk in the following ways:[5]

- **Avoid**   Do not do the action causing the risk.
- **Accept**   The probable cost of the occurrence is less than the value of the objective.
- **Retain**   Provided informed consent and potential loss are minimal, you can budget for risk.
- **Remove**   Remove the vulnerability or source of risk.
- **Change**   Change the likelihood of occurrence or the consequences (mitigation).
- **Share**   Share the cost through insurance, contracting, or other third-party agreement (outsource).

The second primary ISO source for information risk management is ISO 27005: Risk Assessment. Every source of risk management guidance should have risk assessment at the core of the processes. However, keep in mind that risk assessment is a piece of the entire risk management process. ISO 27005 focuses on information systems' risk and expands on effectively and efficiently conducting just the risk assessment. Starting with selecting the proper risk assessment techniques, this standard guides the assessor through the proper steps. Going back to the risk management process focusing on objectives, risk assessment helps risk managers recognize the risks that could affect the achievement of objectives as well as the adequacy of the controls already in place. Keep in mind that like all good processes, the system needs constant communication to and from stakeholders, and it is cyclical. Once the last step of the risk management process, risk treatment, is completed, it is time to begin again with establishing the context. In all of the better risk management processes, always start with a baseline assessment or an inventory. The ISO 27001 and 27005 standards are no different.

Common Criteria

The applicability of the Common Criteria within this topic area of risk management frameworks is because it has standards and controls built in. These controls are used by independently licensed testing and evaluation laboratories to assess the effectiveness of various hardware and software tools. The output or list of evaluated products can be used by healthcare information privacy and security personnel to select, purchase, and implement "approved" products. The approval that the Common Criteria list offers allows users to be more confident in what they use. They can be assured testing was conducted in a rigorous, standard, and repeatable manner. The products will provide adequate security so long as users choose and implement products rated for a level of protection ability sufficient for the organizational threat environment. That said, authorities behind the Common Criteria make it clear that their approval is not a guarantee.

The Common Criteria is international standard ISO/IEC 15408. It is honored by many countries, including the United States, United Kingdom, Canada, Australia, Japan, Germany, France, Spain, and Italy, to name a few. Product evaluations through the Common Criteria program are recognized by all the countries who have signed up to this agreement, called the Common Criteria Recognition Arrangement (CCRA). Most often, Common Criteria considerations are part of government system implementations and critical infrastructure.[6]

The output of the Common Criteria traditionally has been the evaluation assurance level (EAL). This is a numerical value (EAL 1–7) that corresponds to the level of security requirements a product has been tested against. In recent years, the group has begun to move away from having EALs in favor of a more flexible assurance criteria based on the product profile. For day-to-day purposes, this philosophy is of little impact. What remains important is the idea of applying a risk management framework around products and applications. From there, an evaluation or accreditation is provided.

Factor Analysis of Information Risk

One of the drawbacks of using risk management frameworks is they are not typically good at giving the results much context. Of course, subjective input based on organizational mission, culture, risk tolerance, and cost are identified as variables to prioritize the categories of vulnerabilities. Also, most every risk management framework calls for the use of alternative controls or compensating controls when a prescribed control just is not feasible because of the variables just mentioned. Another way to integrate this tailored approach into a risk management program is to understand the *factor analysis of information risk* (FAIR), which is a categorization of the factors that contribute to risk and how they affect each other. In short, FAIR concentrates the risk manager on what is more probable versus all that is possible.

Putting FAIR into practice, imagine the information assets in an organization. In the United States, a mobile device with protected health information stored on it is a vulnerability. If it is lost or stolen, it can be a data breach. Loss or theft of a mobile device is highly probable. Without protected health information (PHI) stored on it, the value might be thousands of dollars. Controls to prevent loss or damage to it should not equal more than a fraction of that value. However, with PHI stored on it, its value after loss or theft will total in the millions of dollars. This would increase the feasibility of investing more heavily in securing the devices from their vulnerabilities. In fact, the cost of providing full-disk encryption of the device probably amounts to negligible costs compared to the likely scenario of fines and penalties after the breach. According to some accounts, the cost of encrypting an end-point device is about $400, while a breach of that device can cost the organization an average of $2.4 million per incident.[7] Of course, in addition to monetary fines and penalties, device loss or theft would place the healthcare organization in the position of loss of reputation, patients delaying care or seeking it elsewhere, and costs relating to patient notification and credit monitoring. Adding full-disk encryption to the scenario, that same mobile device, if lost, is almost assuredly not considered a data breach. In this scenario, a risk management decision around whether to implement a Bring Your Own Device (BYOD) program to the healthcare organization in the United States is supported by integrating the FAIR probability thought process.

Responses for Risk-Based Decision Making

A risk management framework is effective only if it drives organizational decisions and behavior. Running decisions through the framework to categorize information assets and identifying levels of risk are the first couple steps. This data must progress to the next steps. The organization needs to identify and prioritize the actions it will take to address the risk it has identified. An organization that stops at this point of identifying risk is probably going to be considered negligent by regulators. In the event there is data loss and one or more of the identified risks were exploited when the organization failed to implement a response to the risk, the organization can expect increased fines and penalties.

Residual Risk Tolerance

To understand the response to risk an organization will take, a key factor is the residual risk tolerance. In short, this is the level of comfort an organization has for the likelihood and potential impact of a threat that exploits a vulnerability. Among the considerations are how the response to the risk fits with the organizational mission and objectives. A point we make often in this book is that the healthcare industry is different from other industries with information privacy and security concerns. Residual risk tolerance is a prime example of where this is true. For instance, in managing networked computing equipment, a proper risk management approach is to load software, particularly antivirus management, on the devices as part of a standard configuration. With this software, vulnerability patches can be pushed out remotely and automatically by system administrators. Computing devices stay at protected levels, keeping risk of virus infiltration low at a reasonable cost to the organization. However, with medical devices such as digital X-ray and smart infusion pumps also connected to the network, special care must be taken to *not* load any additional software on the machines. Each device manufacturer must test and approve software additions, updates, and deletions to these special computing devices, which typically cannot be included in the automated patch management process. This does not mean they cannot be secured. There must be an alternate process that reflects the concept of residual risk tolerance because the organization accepts that one size does not fit all. Maybe the medical devices must be segmented into a private networking scheme or enclave. Maybe software patches can be loaded manually only. This might inflate cost and level of effort, but it is an effort required within a healthcare-savvy information protection program.

Risk Treatment Identification

Based on the residual risk tolerance, you can take several approaches to address the risks found in the risk assessment.[8]

- **Avoid**   The least tolerance for these categories of risk causes the organization to try to sidestep the risk completely. Alternatives to the original process or technology must be found and implemented. A simple example might be prohibiting group accounts for authentication. Group accounts have long been prohibited in most information security standards, but healthcare providers still have them, especially in small medical practices where "appointments" may allow access for two or three personnel. In risk avoidance, an alternative to these group accounts that satisfies individual identity to an account must be implemented.

- **Transfer**   Two approaches to this category are prevalent. First, the organization shifts the risk to a third party. This is usually as a function of a contractual document or language in an agreement that holds harmless the healthcare organization from any exploitation of a risk. This risk transfer process is termed *indemnification*. The second risk transfer approach is to buy an insurance policy to cover the financial costs relative to the impact of the breach. In healthcare, cybersecurity insurance is growing in popularity to help defray the financial burden of conducting investigations, notifying patients, and doing things such as providing credit monitoring patient credit histories. In fact, depending on the type of cybersecurity insurance, the coverage can include paying for fines and penalties. Of course, cybersecurity insurance cannot reimburse an organization for costs related to lost business, damaged reputation, and time wasted on breach remediation. All of this must factor into the approach to addressing risk.

PART I

 TIP A business associate agreement in the United States is an example of an administrative control that transfers some risk to the third party that handles the protected health information on behalf of the healthcare organization.

- **Mitigate** If you cannot avoid the action that increases risk, you may choose to mitigate the chances of negative impact. Implementing administrative, physical, and technical controls such as found in NIST Special Publication 800-53 are an example of how information privacy/security mitigates risk.

- **Accept** In some rare cases, even if vulnerability is exploited, the impact to the organization is so minimal that taking any action is either too costly or too complicated, or both. When an organization chooses to simply accept risk, it still must document this measured decision and continue to monitor the actions to ensure the risk impact, if exploited, does not increase.

Information Asset Protection Controls

Some of the frameworks introduced also include various information asset controls recommended for implementation. These controls are generally safeguards or countermeasures used to avoid, transfer, mitigate, or accept risk. In the case of accepting the risk, the information asset protection controls are better described as safeguards or countermeasures that are layered around the asset. For instance, it may not be feasible to invest in an encryption solution for backup media that never leaves the data center. However, this condition supposes controls are in place that prevent the media from leaving the data center. A locked safe inside the data center might be in place. A video surveillance system could be used to discourage theft and provide forensic evidence in case of missing backup media. When properly implemented, a combination of information asset controls will come from the following categories:

- **Preventive** These controls are used with the intent of precluding an incident from occurring. Preventive controls include perimeter security such as physical fences and door locks. They can be policies that prohibit behavior and training that teaches employees proper behavior.

- **Detective** If preventive controls do not suffice, some controls are meant to identify and characterize an incident as it happens. These are alerts and alarms that signal the organization an exploit is in progress. Alerts and alarms can be traditional fire alarms but also software-based in the form of intrusion detection systems for the local area network or end-user device.

- **Corrective** Despite best efforts, an incident may not be prevented or detected. Controls exist to limit the extent of any damage caused by the incident. Disaster recovery procedures are great examples of corrective controls.

Preventive, detective, and corrective information asset controls are categorized chronologically along the activity phases or timeline of a potential incident happening (that is, before, during, and after).

Another way to categorize information asset controls is by their functionality.

- **Physical** These are security measures of a structural or visible nature. These controls deter or prevent data loss or unauthorized access to an object (file cabinet) or geographic area (data center). Examples include fences, cipher locks, security guards, and fire extinguishers. When camera or surveillance systems are in place, physical controls can even support detective and corrective controls.

- **Administrative** These are the human factors. These are the policies and procedures that guide personnel and their actions in handling sensitive information and establish levels of access and responsibilities relative to information resources. Incident response processes, security awareness and training, employee recruitment and termination procedures, and legal and regulatory compliance policies exemplify administrative controls.

- **Technical** These are the hardware and software solutions that provide safeguards across the entire activity and phases of information protection. Implementing these standards require network authentication, encryption, antivirus software, and firewalls, to name a few tools.

Figure 4-4 illustrates the overlap and integrated nature of these controls. The figure borrows from NIST Special Publication 800-53, "Recommended Security Controls for Federal Information Systems," and the 17 families of controls it presents; the overlap of these controls is demonstrated with respect to administrative, physical, and technical measures.[9]

 TIP The terms (or *taxonomy*) for these types of controls are found in various resources (for example, NIST Special Publication 800-53, Statements on Standards for Attestation Engagements [SSAE] 16, "Reporting on Controls at a Service Organization," ISO 27002, and so on). Sometimes other words are used, such as *deterrent controls* and *operational safeguards*; these other terms are useful to know but are more of a semantic preference than a real differentiation.

- **Common controls** Rather than duplicate efforts, some security controls apply across multiple systems and can be inherited by each system. This is true in cases where each system is protected by the control sufficiently. A great example of a common control is the physical security plan for a facility that houses an EHR, a laboratory information system, and the human resources information system. All the controls (doors, alarms, fire suppression, and so on) would equally protect each of these systems (and all would require such controls).

- **System-specific controls** Where common controls end, system-specific controls begin. These are unique for each information system and are the responsibility of the system owner to implement. They can be physical controls (for instance, a locked computer cabinet or a "rack" in the data center). They also can be administrative (information security plan) and technical (authentication).

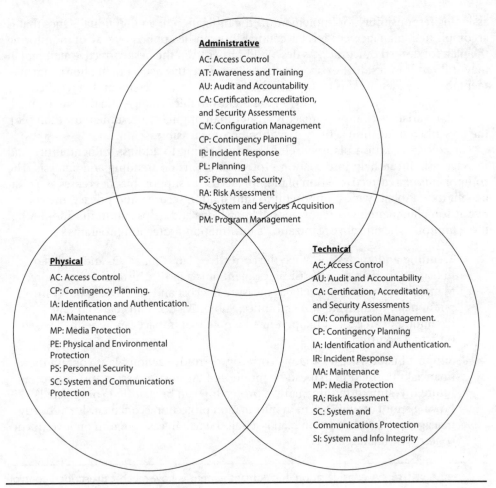

Administrative

AC: Access Control
AT: Awareness and Training
AU: Audit and Accountability
CA: Certification, Accreditation,
and Security Assessments
CM: Configuration Management
CP: Contingency Planning
IR: Incident Response
PL: Planning
PS: Personnel Security
RA: Risk Assessment
SA: System and Services Acquisition
PM: Program Management

Physical

AC: Access Control
CP: Contingency Planning.
IA: Identification and Authentication.
MA: Maintenance
MP: Media Protection
PE: Physical and Environmental
Protection
PS: Personnel Security
SC: System and Communications
Protection

Technical

AC: Access Control
AU: Audit and Accountability
CA: Certification, Accreditation,
and Security Assessments
CM: Configuration Management.
CP: Contingency Planning
IA: Identification and Authentication.
IR: Incident Response
MA: Maintenance
MP: Media Protection
RA: Risk Assessment
SC: System and
Communications Protection
SI: System and Info Integrity

Figure 4-4   Overlap of security controls

- **Hybrid controls**   Sometimes a security control can feature both common
  controls and system-specific portions. An incident response plan has elements
  of both. Some procedures are common across the entire organization while
  each system has specific steps to take if data loss is suspected.

Corrective Action Plans

A central process in risk management is to correct weaknesses or close any vulnerability gaps once they are identified. The corrective action plan is a formal, organized
management tool that identifies these discrepancies. Importantly, the plan describes
the actions needed to mitigate the risks. These actions will relate to prescribed actions
from sources such as NIST and ISO. Another key aspect of a corrective action plan is

assigning responsibility for implementing the mitigation to an individual. Once that is accomplished, management-level accountability can be applied by way of monitoring the plan for desired outcomes. As described earlier, even the best corrective action plan may still result in residual or accepted risk. The corrective action plan allows management to clearly identify this reality and document the risk assessment that resulted in a decision to accept the risk and why; in the event variables change, the risk can be readdressed. If variables change (impact is greater than originally presumed, for example), the prescribed mitigation activity may then become feasible.

The corrective action plan is useful beyond helping to address vulnerabilities and manage risk. It can help information protection efforts do trending and analysis. The components of a corrective action plan imply its use to support business cases as a cost-benefit tool. Probably most important to information security and privacy, the corrective action plan maintains organizational knowledge and helps communication. All of these improve a healthcare organization's information protection program.[10]

- **Trending and analysis**   When the corrective plan is managed and updated in concert with an annual risk assessment, it is a terrific historical data source. Management can use the data to measure the cost and effectiveness of controls put in place to mitigate vulnerabilities. Subjective decisions based on the likelihood of an exploit happening or a potential impact can be refined based on actual occurrences.

- **Support business cases**   Done correctly, corrective action plans contain the financial information that can be monitored. Against successes and failures, future investment in information protection can be justified (or rejected). Proving return on investment in information protection is often elusive. Properly managing a corrective action plan is a huge benefit in easing return on investment concerns by management.

 NOTE   A consideration in risk management is how much a prescribed control may cost to implement and maintain against the value of the asset. In addition to supporting return on investment, a corrective action plan can support decisions to not implement a control if the cost-benefit analysis of forgoing the control demonstrates the asset or the impact is not worth the investment at the time of assessment. If that analysis changes, the corrective action plan can be adjusted.

- **Maintaining institutional knowledge**   In an organization with a mature information protection program, institutional knowledge is a valued element. Otherwise, the program must rely on an individual or the competency of current workforce. A change in workforce results in a change in institutional knowledge. Having a library of corrective action plans and the analysis that goes with it ensures the organization can maintain the information protection program even if there is turnover in the workforce.

- **Facilitating effective communication**   The importance of communicating the corrective action plan to senior leadership cannot be understated. Using the tool and its related information capabilities satisfies the responsibility that information protection personnel have in creating information protection awareness, communicating to senior leadership, and documenting outcomes for compliance efforts.

Compensating Controls

In healthcare, it is often the case that prescribed controls and even alternative controls are not feasible to implement. One of the most prevalent examples of this scenario is within medical device management. There are medical devices that are imperative for diagnosing and treating patients, yet these devices cannot adhere to some of the information security requirements. In some cases, the device manufacturer has evaluated and approved only a version of operating system that is considered obsolete for regular office automation. Additionally, maybe the same medical device cannot load several software vulnerability patches because they negatively impact the device. In this case, the healthcare organization cannot knowingly allow the medical device to operate on the local area network. Disconnecting the device or upgrading it without manufacturer approval is also not an option for the healthcare organization. This is when compensating controls are implemented.

A *compensating control* is a safeguard (or several) that is a legitimate deviation from a prescribed security control. It is not a shortcut to compliance nor is it a way to get around implementing a control just because it is politically opposed or considered difficult. Before implementing a compensating control, conduct a risk analysis to document the legitimate need for a deviation (legitimate technological or documented business constraint). In the medical device scenario, the alternative controls of private network segmentation and manual patch management have already been mentioned. In addition to these for medical devices, the entire information asset in the organization can be protected via other examples of compensating controls such as backup generators, hot sites for continuing operations, and sensitive information server isolation. The intent of the original, prescribed control is met, but the bona fide considerations are addressed to balance both information protection and patient care.

In sum, a valid compensating control contains several distinct elements.[11]

- It meets the intent and rigor of the original control.
- It provides a similar level of defense as the original requirement.
- It is acceptable if the compensating control is actually more stringent than the prescribed control.
- If any additional risk is added because of the compensating control, the compensating control must meet cost-benefit or risk-reward criteria.

It may be relatively obvious, but after compensating controls are evaluated and implemented, they are usually harder or more costly than the prescribed control.

Therefore, no one should view compensating controls as a shortcut to compliance. In healthcare, it is common to meet resistance to implementing controls. Some clinicians and healthcare providers will argue a prescribed information asset control "negatively impacts patient care." Therefore, it should not be implemented. While that is always a primary concern in the cost-benefit analysis of any information protection decision, that caveat does not excuse overly relaxed controls or standards. The goal of having a healthcare-specific information privacy and security curriculum is to learn to integrate the valid concerns of caregivers with the imperatives of providing healthcare information privacy and security. This balancing act makes understanding the proper use of compensating controls a key skill to master.

Control Variance Documentation

Implementing an information asset control within any risk framework sometimes provides a range of acceptable values. After implementing a control, the outcome may not always be binary; always permit versus deny by default, for instance. Documenting and monitoring the levels of acceptable behavior or outcomes is required to measure performance against benchmarks. This way, there can be alarms or early warning notices that come from audit and logging functions.

Communication of Findings

Once the risk assessment is completed, the corrective action plan is developed, and the cost-benefit analysis is done that documents the various approaches to risk that are going to be recommended, the next order of business is to communicate the findings. This implies that communication is episodic and in a sequence of steps. It is not. Effectively, various types and levels of communication must occur in a risk management program. Certainly, once there are findings, they must be communicated.

There are no right answers on how and when the results of risk assessments are provided. In some ways, the role of information security and privacy is in marketing and sales, at least internally. To be effective or to have any chance of compliance, the information risk management program has to be understood by employees, championed by senior management, and funded adequately. The last of those three things is probably the most difficult and lacking in the healthcare industry.

Some of the more established ways risk management plans are communicated throughout the organization are through established committees. In Chapter 3, we discussed some of these. The information management council, the configuration control board, and any other cross-functional group meeting are great places to have an agenda item highlighting key findings or to provide ad hoc training on topics. In some of these groups, it is necessary (and advantageous) to introduce upcoming hardware and software initiatives. Once these are in place, providing the group updates on the return on investment is important. Take, for instance, installing a new intrusion detection system. Once it is in place, the end-user community as well as senior leadership would be interested in seeing some data on how many threats have been averted over time. Knowing that these threats probably were happening prior to the new intrusion detection system and any one of them could result in a data breach with all of that impact can be helpful in future risk management decisions. If done right, this type of marketing and sales internally can help gain organizational trust and support for adequately funding future information protection initiatives.

Provisioning Third-Party Connectivity

The operations of healthcare organizations extend well beyond the clinical care settings. In the healthcare electronic information age, there is a new type of supply chain between the healthcare organization and the vendor supplier. This new type of supply chain must be managed as a valuable asset to be protected and shared securely according to organizational, regulatory, and legal requirements. In international terms, the data controllers rely on partners who are data processors and in many cases have other data processors that must be approved to handle the sensitive information. In the United States, this relationship is the business associate and all of the downstream business associates (that is, the business associates of the business associates). As introduced earlier, the traditional vendor relationship has moved from contractual relationships to now include various, complicated interconnection agreements.

Imagine the complex relationship between the third-party organizations that manage a health information exchange (HIE) process for exchanging relevant healthcare information between (often competing) healthcare organizations that have patients in common. There might be a data center or cloud provider contracted as a third-party vendor to host the data from the healthcare organizations. The third party has access to the healthcare information and statutory and contractual responsibilities to protect the information. To develop this thought experiment, the scenario describes a chain of trust between the healthcare organization and its third-party vendors.

One reality is constant across the globe. No matter who is the third party for the healthcare organization, data controller, or covered entity (synonymous depending on country of origin), accountability for the loss of sensitive data is always the healthcare organization's responsibility.[12] The healthcare organization is the one that collected the information and made promises to the patient to protect their information (and use only as much of it as needed for intended purposes). Contractual agreements and business relationships do not change this. However, it is important that the healthcare organization put controls in place to outline expectations, define procedures, and identify matters of redress relevant to the third party's use of the information. Failing to take these interconnection actions consists of a lack of accountability to regulators. The absence of such may result in the healthcare organization facing additional civil and even criminal penalties. Keep in mind that even if an organization is found to have done everything reasonable and appropriate to prevent data loss (due diligence), civil and criminal penalties are possible. What is at issue here are increased fines and penalties by not attending to third-party relationships.

TIP The relationship with third-party entities is complex. No matter how comprehensive the risk assessment and oversight actions are that the healthcare organization may take, the ultimate responsibility for properly handling sensitive healthcare data remains the legal and ethical responsibility of the healthcare organization. That cannot be outsourced or fully transferred away based on sufficient contracting or insurance.

After considering the complexity, magnitude, and nature of the arrangement and associated risks with the third-party connection, the healthcare organization should decide how to manage the risk. There are several basic elements, listed here:

- Inventory which third-party vendors are handling PHI
- Perform a risk assessment using one of the risk management frameworks or a combination of them
- Perform due diligence in selecting a third party, considering industry ratings and past performance
- Select connection controls or a trust model for the interconnection
- Contract structuring and review appropriate to the nature of the work performed
- Conduct oversight by the healthcare organization information protection program

In building the trust with a third party, we have already discussed the risk assessment and the importance of due diligence. Additionally, this and earlier chapters have introduced senior-level involvement in third-party relationships through formal committees and boards. In the next two chapters, we will explore contractual terms and conditions structuring these relationships. What remains is a quick look at some technical controls of the third-party trust model. These models and tools are important to help formalize a level of trust with organizations that provide a valuable information service.

To formalize the chain of trust and to gain the satisfactory assurances required, you can expect to see these technical trust models in practice. By no means comprehensive, these are some leading examples:

- **PKI certificates**   For this trust model, public-key infrastructure (PKI) certificates are used to support the encrypted transfer of healthcare information. PKI is a collection of hardware, software, organizations, policies, and procedures that work together to facilitate the appropriate use of digital certificates, which make encrypting information possible. Within PKI, each user has a unique identity validated by a trusted authority. The transfer of information between two individuals with an established trust relationship under PKI is secure, and the sender and recipient have assurance that each is who they say they are (nonrepudiation).

- **Transport Layer Security (TLS) and Secure Sockets Layer (SSL)** TLS and its predecessor, SSL, are security protocols that enable the secure transport of information across protected network tunnels on the Internet. The class of certificates used are X.509 (PKI, for example). And like PKI, they allow nonrepudiation. The data is encrypted. Several versions of the protocols make possible secure applications in web browsing, electronic mail, Internet faxing, instant messaging, and Voice over IP (VoIP).

- **Virtual private networking** Through a user-created connection, remote access is made possible by a combination of passwords, biometrics, two-factor authentication, or other cryptographic methods. The remote user establishes a secure connection that extends a private network across the Internet. Data is shared just like it is all within the same organizational domain or private intranet. Logically, the connection is a virtual point-to-point connection using dedicated connections, encryption, or a combination.

Documenting Compliance

A common refrain heard in information protection and healthcare is "not documented equals not done." The impact of the statement varies across the two functions. But it is equally true that auditors and regulators across the globe will require proof of compliance for information protection activities. Admittedly, the existence of a reasonably simple set of file folders with up-to-date risk assessments, policies, and corrective actions plans would probably suffice. There are, however, several tools available that can assist. Based on complex regulatory requirements, these tools also serve to guide completeness in terms of what auditors and regulators might inspect.

NIST HIPAA Security Toolkit Application

The first tool is the NIST HIPAA Security Rule (HSR) Toolkit Application.[13] It was designed by a committee of industry volunteers and experts to help organizations assess themselves against the HIPAA Security Rule. There are hundreds of questions the survey asks. But each question provides the types of documents or actions that would count as evidence of compliance. An organization can choose to upload the documents into the tool for archiving and quick future retrieval. They can also simply provide a link or note about the file location. The tool is extensive, and healthcare organizations of significant size and mission might utilize the entire database. Other, smaller organizations can tailor the survey according to their environment. The HSR Toolkit resides on a computer desktop as an application. It is not web-based or networked to a central NIST database. The tool can be used and reused. It is not dependent on a specific hardware or software platform. Windows, Red Hat Linux, and Apple OS X are all supported.

HIMSS Risk Assessment Toolkit

Primarily for HIPAA compliance in the United States, the Health Information Management Systems Society (HIMSS) has published a risk assessment (RA) toolkit to help providers conduct a full risk assessment. It incorporates many of the popular risk management frameworks and is intentioned for smaller-sized healthcare provider organizations with limited resources for privacy and security activities. The toolkit is a set of templates, white papers, analysis, best practices, and other reference materials that can help you comply with the guiding regulations in managing and securing PHI. It can also help you establish a comprehensive risk management program that would start with the risk assessment. This tool is created and maintained by HIMSS member volunteers and is intentionally vendor-agnostic.

The Information Governance Toolkit

In the United Kingdom, the Information Governance (IG) Toolkit from the Department of Health (DH) integrates the legal requirements and guidance into an information governance application. This tool allows organizations under the purview of the IG requirements to perform self-assessments of their compliance. The goal of the toolkit is to allow healthcare organizations in the United Kingdom to demonstrate that they properly maintain the confidentiality and security of personal information.[14] Using the toolkit, control variance, partial compliance, and remediation activities can be documented, tracked, and communicated. This effectively supports UK healthcare organizations' information governance compliance through continuous improvements. As stated by the UK NHS, using the IG toolkit helps the healthcare organization earn and demonstrate their trustworthiness to their patients.

Chapter Review

In this chapter, we introduced the process of examining information risk in an organized, repeatable way. Some risk can be prevented, detected, and remediated. Where risk must be accepted, actions can be taken to minimize the likelihood of risk occurring or reducing the impact if it does. Sometimes, the elements of risk are so incompatible with the business of healthcare that the risk must be avoided (in other words, the actions cannot be taken). In any event, healthcare organizations are mandated to go through a risk management process. Some frameworks were introduced in this chapter with general applicability scenarios. The most salient point about information risk in healthcare is that it can lead to patient harm. At the same time, implementing information risk controls without regard to the healthcare processes can also result in unintended patient safety issues. Healthcare-savvy information protection programs will understand and factor in these unique concerns. With proper communication of these issues and the findings of the risk management process, information protection can integrate and enable healthcare business strategy, clinical practices, and third-party relationships.

Review Questions

1. Which of these is a variable in considering the risk of a decision?

   A. Controls

   B. Cost

   C. Impact

   D. Frequency

2. At a high level, NIST 800-39 builds a risk management framework around
   _____, _____, _____, and _____ activities of a risk
   management program.

3. Which risk management framework specifically tailors its approach to
   healthcare?

   A. ISO 27001

   B. HITRUST

   C. NIST RMF

   D. Common Criteria

4. (TRUE or FALSE) If you must perform the action that increases risk, you may
   choose to avoid residual risk by implementing one or more administrative,
   physical, and technical controls.

5. An incident report process and the procedures required to comply with it would
   best be described as what form of information asset control?

   A. Preventive

   B. Common

   C. Administrative

   D. Hybrid

6. (TRUE or FALSE) After implementing an intrusion detection system for the
   local area network, collecting data to show the number of attacks detected and
   prevented for future sharing with the information management committee
   is an example of supporting business cases by proper use of corrective action
   plans.

7. Because medical devices have special configuration considerations, the
   information security officer decides to implement a compensating control
   to ensure the company is mitigated against virus infiltration via an enclave, or
   virtual private network architecture. Which of these suggest a valid reason for
   implementing the compensating control?

   A. The architecture solution meets or exceeds the original intent of the prescribed
      control of protecting against virus infiltration.

   B. Medical devices are regulated by an external agency and cannot be
      administered by healthcare organizations.

C. Physicians must approve any changes to medical devices because medical devices often provide diagnostic and treatment support, so patient safety is at issue.

D. Antivirus software is not applicable to systems that do not provide office automation services.

8. At the completion of a risk assessment and development of a corrective action plan, which would be a logical next step in the risk management program?

A. Budgeting for future information security upgrades

B. Filing results with regulatory agencies

C. Creating a risk management archive

D. Communicating results to the organization

9. (TRUE or FALSE) Outsourcing the handling of protected health information to a third-party data center that has specialized procedures for handling sensitive information reduces information risk accountability for a healthcare organization.

10. Much like the first step in any good risk management framework, what is a best first step in managing the risk of third-party relationships?

A. Assessing risk

B. Inventorying third parties

C. Reviewing contracts

D. Communicating findings

Answers

1. **C.** The impact of the exploit of a vulnerability is one of the variables that must be considered in making risk-based decisions. Impact is the expected outcome if the scenario happens. It can be measured in subjective (loss of reputation) and objective (dollars for fines) terms. Controls are the safeguards that may be put in place to reduce risk. Cost is a consideration of alternative controls. Those controls that make sense compared to how much they cost to implement against what value they provide are selected. Frequency may be a variable related to likelihood, which is a variable, but it is not a variable by itself.

2. **Framing, assessing, responding**, and **monitoring** are the prescribed high-level activities found in NIST Special Publication 800-39.

3. **B.** ISO 27001 is an information risk management framework, but it is applicable across any industry that handles sensitive information. The NIST RMF also has applicability across multiple industries, especially U.S. federal government systems. The Common Criteria is an assessment or accreditation program that assigns a level of assurance to common hardware and software security products, not specific to healthcare. HITRUST Common Security

Framework is the only representative in this group that applies specifically to healthcare organizations.

4. **FALSE.** According to the definitions of these valid actions taken to address residual risk in an organization, mitigate is the one where you implement one or more controls to minimize the likelihood and negative impact of a risk. Avoiding a process or action entirely that has risk is one way to address residual risk, but there are no controls added to try to reduce the likelihood or severity of impact.

5. **D.** Because an incident reporting policy should have elements of multiple types of controls, it is considered an example of a hybrid control. The fact that the other answer options could be right in different context illustrates why hybrid is the best answer. Some elements of the incident reporting may be preventive or meant to prevent data loss before it occurs. Because the incident reporting policy is applicable among all organization systems and applications, it could also be considered a common control. Finally, the policy and procedures that communicate the incident reporting requirements to the organization are also an administrative control.

6. **TRUE.** Collecting data to demonstrate objectively that the intended impact is happening for the control that is put in place is a great example of supporting a business case for the cost of implementing and maintaining the intrusion detection system.

7. **A.** The incorrect answers all point to common reasons why some healthcare organizations and medical device manufacturers believe medical devices cannot be secured the same way as office automation computers and networking equipment. Some of the reasons are based in fact. For instance, medical devices are regulated by the U.S. Food and Drug Administration (FDA). But the FDA does allow software configuration for security enhancement as long as the changes are coordinated and approved by the medical device manufacturer. While medical devices are used for diagnostic and treatment purposes often, physicians do not necessarily have a role in approving modifications. However, all clinical personnel should receive communication about such changes and provide concurrence when feasible. Antivirus software is almost always compatible with medical device software because most medical devices use common OS and applications to operate. That said, exception lists and other additional configuration efforts need to be made based on types of file extensions and traffic that medical devices process to ensure legitimate files are not quarantined or blocked inadvertently. Therefore, the correct answer is implementing a compensating control that, while not the prescribed control from a set of standards, is a control with equal rigor that meets or exceeds the original requirement.

8. **D.** A good risk management program is good only if it is present throughout the organization from senior leadership down. Awareness must be built into clinical practices and business processes to ensure corrective actions succeed and

future events are prevented to the extent possible. While getting information security acquisition into future budgets is important, it may not cover all findings because some corrective actions may be no cost or nontechnical to fix. There may not be any requirement to send results to a regulatory agency, so that is not correct. A good risk management program is not static, so simply filing the result away in an archive until the next assessment is not recommended.

9. **FALSE.** A third party that handles healthcare information for the healthcare organization presents an increased direct risk.

10. **B.** A risk assessment is a fundamental action that must be performed against all third parties that handle sensitive healthcare information, but it consists of many actions including the best first step. That best first step is to inventory or list all the third parties with which the healthcare organization has a relationship. Knowing where data resides and who handles it is the first step in good risk management frameworks. That is true for managing risk with third-party entities. Of course, reviewing contracts is important but is an action done after the inventory is complete. And communicating findings is also subsequent to having a comprehensive and up-to-date list.

References

1. Open-source web application security project (OWASP). Risk Rating Methodology. accessed on February 10, at https://www.owasp.org/index.php/OWASP_Risk _Rating_Methodology

2. Adapted from "Managing Information Security Risk: Organization, Mission, and Information System View." NIST Special Publication 800-39, pps 37-45. Accessed on February 25, 2014, at http://nvlpubs.nist.gov/nistpubs/SpecialPublications/ NIST.SP.800-39.pdf

3. "Guide for Applying the Risk Management Framework to Federal Information Systems: A Security Life Cycle Approoach." NIST Special Publication 800-37 rev 1, p. 2. Accessed on February 19, 2014, at http://nvlpubs.nist.gov/nistpubs/ SpecialPublications/NIST.SP.800-37r1.pdf

4. Adapted from "An Introductory Resource Guide for Implementing the Health Insurance Portability and Accountability Act (HIPAA) Security Rule." NIST Special Publication 800-66 rev 1, pps. 12-14. Accessed on February 18, 2014, at http://nvlpubs.nist.gov/nistpubs/SpecialPublications/NIST.SP.800-66r1.pdf

5. Adapted from International Organization for Standardization/International Electrotechnical Commission 27001, "Information Security Management System Requirements," October 2005.

6. About the Common Criteria. Accessed on March 3, 2014, at http://www .commoncriteriaportal.org/ccra

7. ID Experts: Ponemon Study. "Third Annual Benchmark Study on Patient Privacy & Data Security." Dec 2012. Accessed on March 3, 2014, at http://www.ponemon.org/library/third-annual-patient-privacy-data-security-study

8. "Managing Information Security Risk Organization, Mission, and Information System View." NIST Special Publication 800-39, pps. 42-43. Accessed on February 17, 2014, at http://csrc.nist.gov/publications/nistpubs/800-39/SP800-39-final.pdf

9. Adapted from "Recommended Security Controls for Federal Information Systems and Organizations." NIST Special Publication 800-53 rev 3. Accessed on February 14, 2014, at http://csrc.nist.gov/publications/nistpubs/800-53-Rev3/sp800-53-rev3.pdf

10. U.S. Department of Health and Human Services. "HHS Plan of Action and Milestone Guide." 2005. Accessed March 2, 2014, at www.docstoc.com/docs/126410338/CMS-Plan-of-Action-and-Milestones

11. Payment Card Industry (PCI) Data Security Standard. "Requirements and Security Assessment Procedures." Version 2.0. October 2010. page 13.

12. Swire, P. P., S., Bermann, & International Association of Privacy Professionals (2007). Data Sharing and Transfer. In Information privacy: Official reference for the Certified Information Privacy Professional (CIPP). York, ME: International Association of Privacy Professionals.

13. NIST. "HIPAA Security Rule Toolkit User Guide." October 2011. Accessed March 1, 2014, at http://scap.nist.gov/hipaa/NIST_HSR_Toolkit_User_Guide.pdf

14. Information Governance Toolkit. "About the Information Governance Toolkit." Accessed on March 4, 2014, at https://www.igt.hscic.gov.uk

Third-Party Risk Management and Promoting Awareness

In this chapter, you will learn to

- Recognize the importance of managing third-party information risk
- Review and apply leading information risk management frameworks for their use in third-party information risk management
- Describe third parties in the context of healthcare operations
- Consider common administrative tools to control third-party risk
- Examine the role of healthcare information privacy and security professionals in managing third-party risk and developing organizational awareness

In the previous chapter, we introduced some considerations related to risk and the technical interconnections between healthcare organizations and third parties. In short, a valid need to exchange information, a secure type of connection, and an encrypted data flow are fundamental concerns. But there are many more concerns related to managing the risk healthcare organizations face because of the business and clinical imperatives that make third-party relationships a reality. No healthcare organization can efficiently provide all administrative (and some clinical) services using just employed staff. It is too expensive. Outsourcing and contractual arrangements with third-party organizations are efficient and effective relationships to provide certain important services. In this chapter, we will explore these concepts a little more in depth. The studies of data breaches, however, continue to indicate that a large proportion of incidents happen because of the actions and inactions of third parties. A controllable, contributing factor is the lack of risk management that the healthcare organization takes.

One of the components of managing third-party risk adequately is organizational awareness. This chapter looks at some ways in which healthcare information security, particularly the risk management activities, can be promoted throughout the organization. Training and awareness are probably the most cost-effective controls an organization can use to reduce the likelihood and severity of data breaches caused by internal threats, such as employee actions. We will review several established methods for building an awareness program.

Managing the Risk of Third-Party Relationships

This section will cover the context behind the purpose and methodology of managing the risk that is inherent in having third-party organizations handle the sensitive health information on behalf of the healthcare organization. The risk management framework for third parties should not differ greatly from what an organization might use internally. We covered the leading risk management tools healthcare organizations use, including HIPAA controls, the NIST Risk Management Framework, and ISO 27001, to name just a few. Any differences in a framework to assess and manage third-party risk will typically reside in what level of access and control the healthcare organization has with the external organization. The framework choice will also depend on the healthcare organization's ability to enforce any changes.

NOTE In the United States, healthcare organizations have made complaints about the expectations of HIPAA regulators, such as using a cloud service provider to manage electronic health information—levied requirements on major, multinational corporations such as Microsoft, Amazon, and Google. Those types of organizations attract customers from many different industries in almost every country in the world. So, when presented with U.S.-centric, healthcare-specific regulations, the global companies were reluctant to take the steps to comply with third-party HIPAA standards. Their actions indicated reluctance to increase costs to satisfy an industry requirement none of their other customers had. Over time, initial positions evolved, and today there are some major corporations willing to comply with HIPAA as regulatory requirements have been clarified.[1]

Purpose

The responsibility for healthcare organizations as data controllers to manage third-party risk is international. Whether the regulatory reference is HIPAA in the United States or the Data Protection Directive (DPD) in the EU, to name just two, the obligation to protect health information remains with the healthcare organizations that collect the information. Even though they legitimately share the information with third parties, they cannot shift all of the responsibility through contracts. But through risk management, the healthcare organization can provide due diligence in minimizing the risk of data loss caused by the third party. If the risk management is not done or is done badly, third-party vendors can have a negative effect on the healthcare organization's financial health, reputation, and even patient care. Beyond the fines and penalties that result from breaches in the United States and other countries, patients may delay their care, withhold information from their provider, or choose another provider based on data loss caused not by the healthcare organization but one of their third-party vendors.

Managing risk of third parties is a matter of law in countries that have privacy and security regulations. But the imperative also follows the leading privacy and security frameworks. According to the Generally Accepted Privacy Principles (GAPP), "(a health-care) organization may outsource a part of its business process and, with it, some responsibility for privacy; however, the (healthcare) organization cannot outsource its ultimate responsibility for privacy for its business processes. Complexity increases when the entity that performs the outsourced service is in a different country and may be subject to different privacy laws or perhaps no privacy requirements at all."[2] In all circumstances, the organization that outsources a business process will need to ensure it manages its privacy responsibilities appropriately. The healthcare organization (prior to sharing sensitive personal information with a third party), must share the healthcare organization's expectations, policies, or other specific requirements for handling protected health information. In return, the third party must provide written agreement to adhere to these requirements.

NOTE GAPP is recognized internationally and provides criteria and related material for protecting the privacy of personal information and is popular in the United States and Canada to help implement privacy programs. GAPP has been developed from a business perspective, referencing several significant U.S. and international privacy regulations. It should not be confused with GAAP.

As of September 2013, HIPAA through an amendment with the Omnibus Final Rule has formalized and clarified the responsibility of healthcare organizations to conduct security reviews of their third-party subcontractors and vendors that handle protected health information.[3] Additionally, the healthcare organizations are required to audit these business partners for continued compliance. This requirement becomes important when a data breach is caused by a third-party organization losing an unencrypted laptop or having their database hacked by an external adversary. The healthcare organization that did not conduct risk reviews and audits will likely face additional fines and penalties rather than demonstrating due diligence. What is more, the audit would likely uncover a lack of encryption for mobile devices, and mitigation of that finding could take place that would prevent the data loss in the first place.

Methodology

The list of technical controls for connecting with third parties provided in the previous chapter gave a starting point for us to explore managing third-party risk more holistically. We introduced the following basic steps to manage third-party risk in the previous chapter. Here we explain them a bit more as steps in a best-practice process.

1. Inventory third-party vendors that handle PHI.

   - Have an accurate, up-to-date list with valid contact information.
   - Document the data categories (that is, sensitivity levels) and the data flow.
   - Identify the inherent risk of various third parties (the information sensitivity levels related to the perceived likelihood there could be data loss).
   - Know who the healthcare organization's functional representative is for each contract (It may not be someone from information technology).

2. Perform a risk assessment using one of the risk management frameworks or a combination of them.

- Make sure the third party is compliant with relevant data privacy and security regulations (HIPAA, EU DPD, ISO, PCI, and so on).

- Make the effort to review any objective audit review and status of these relevant regulations (SSAE 16, FISMA, and so on).

- Visit the third party's facilities.

3. Conduct due diligence in selecting a third party, including considering industry ratings and past performance.

- Justify choices by evaluating the third party against alternative third-party vendors.

- Be sure to know and understand the financial position of the third party.

- A third party that cannot invest in adequate security is a high risk to the healthcare organization over time.

- A third party that declares bankruptcy or goes out of business after causing a data breach shifts the costs to clean up the breach to the healthcare organization.

4. Select connection controls or a trust model for the interconnection.

- The secure transfer of information relies on a variety of technical controls and identity and authentication management.

- Connections must be overseen so that dormant connections are terminated.

- Encryption is essentially mandatory.

 NOTE In the United States, encryption must be validated according to Federal Information Processing Standards (FIPS) 140-2 to be granted safe harbor status. This status means that a healthcare organization, subject to HIPAA, would not have a requirement to notify regulatory authorities or patients in the event of data loss. Proper encryption satisfies the HIPAA requirement that any data lost is rendered unreadable or indecipherable to unauthorized individuals.

5. Structure the contract and review it as appropriate to the nature of the work performed.

- Terms and conditions must reflect expectations for handling protected health information.

- Assess compliance with the contract terms.

  - Risk assessment, service level agreements, satisfaction ratings

- Evaluate the adequacy of the vendor's training to its employees.
- Conduct anonymous testing of the vendor's service capabilities.
- Assess the terms of liability and indemnification.

  Possible considerations are insurance covering data breach (cybersecurity), responsibility for costs associated with data loss, and clauses to hold harmless the healthcare organization if a data breach is the third party's fault.

TIP When it comes to contractual agreements between a healthcare organization and another healthcare organization or a third-party vendor, there are two prevailing types of documents. The first is relative to HIPAA in the United States, and that is the business associate agreement. You can find a template for these agreements at www.hhs.gov/ocr/privacy/hipaa/understanding/ coveredentities/contractprov.html.

The second template is found in the European Union. It is called a *model contract* or a *model of standard contractual clauses*. Entities that use these standard contractual clauses "offer sufficient safeguards as required by the EU DPD (Article 26 (2))." These clauses allow the organizations to transfer data without any additional approval needed from the data authority (the government). You can find the model contract at http://ec.europa.eu/justice /data-protection/document/international-transfers/transfer/index_en.htm#h2-5.

---

6. Implement oversight by the healthcare organization information protection program.
   - Continuous monitoring by the healthcare organization is essential.
   - As part of the contract, a right to review and audit should be present.
   - Findings should be remediated at no additional cost to the third party.
   - You should test the third-party vendor's business contingency planning.
   - Have periodic meetings with the vendor to review contract performance and operational issues.

NOTE These steps are not a framework for risk assessments per se. Figure 5-1 illustrates these steps in an organized framework. They are, however, borrowed controls from the recognized risk management frameworks we have already covered and referenced. From these overall controls, those that specifically apply to managing third parties are good to know and understand. A secondary source for managing supply chains (another popular term for third-party vendors) is NIST Special Publication 800-161, "Supply Chain Risk Management Practices for Federal Information Systems and Organizations." This publication is specific to U.S. federal agencies and not to healthcare.

Figure 5-1
Basic steps
in managing
third-party risk

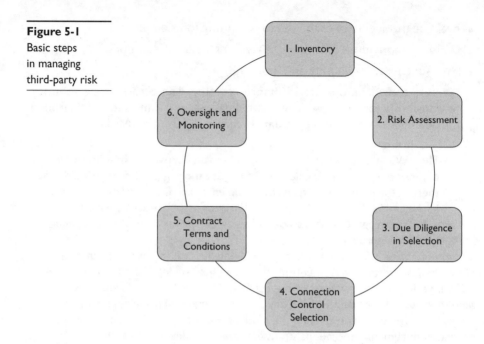

Types of Third-Party Arrangements

A third party may or may not actually perform the work outside of the healthcare organization. Some third parties work right beside the employees of the healthcare organization. In fact, they often do the same job. For example, because many healthcare organizations have implemented EHRs, the work required to connect any existing data systems, engineer the local area network, and prepare physical environments to house the equipment require additional staffing. So, healthcare organizations have to procure the services of contracted staff to help the current workforce accomplish EHR implementation in a timely, cost-effective manner. Some of these services are provided by consultants working on-site, and some are handled remotely by experts who can provision services or transfer data as required. There are several basic forms of third-party services covered next.

Outsourcing

Outsourcing services, functions, and products is popular. Internationally, forecasts say outsourcing of healthcare information technology will expand at about 8 percent annually. That percentage results in expenditures of approximately $50 billion by 2018 compared to $35 billion in 2013.[4] The attractiveness of outsourcing is that it allows healthcare organizations to focus more on their core mission, reduce costs, and increase access to highly skilled staff. While the outsourced model extends beyond information technology, a majority of healthcare information privacy and security concerns with third parties reside in the outsourcing of information technology processes.

The model for outsourcing consists of completely transitioning responsibility for the performance of key objectives to a third party. Again, that does not mean the healthcare organization can transition responsibility for privacy and security concerns. In some cases, the outsourcing is so extensive that the only employee of the healthcare organization who has any contact with the third party is a contract management staff member. That healthcare organization employee may be the person responsible for managing the information risk relative to sharing protected health information. In other cases, the third party is directed by a healthcare organization employee who has the relative qualifications to accomplish the same tasks, but the third party is in place to augment that capability. A great example is a chief information officer who manages the contract and the third-party personnel who provide the entire information technology function for the healthcare organizations. Another example is a patient administration director who oversees all the patient billing functions and accomplishes the process by using a third-party vendor.

The other variance in the total outsourced model is whether the vendor works on-site or off-site. Using the previous patient billing scenario, the likelihood is that the billers work from a location other than the healthcare organization. In fact, it is increasingly probable that they work from home. Another information security–related example is the managed security service provider (MSSP) that is hired to provide outsourced monitoring and management of security devices and systems, such as firewalls and intrusion prevention appliances.[5] Revisiting the outsourced information technology example, help-desk personnel and network administrators are better suited to on-site staff at the healthcare organization. This would facilitate attendance at information governance meetings, which would be appropriate from time to time. There are also tasks that require the information technology staff to be present rather than remotely accessing the local area network or end-user device.

Staff Augmentation

In comparison with totally outsourced services, healthcare organizations can contract for support in a more tailored fashion. The reason staff augmentation is mentioned here is because in some cases contract employees are viewed more as workforce members. They receive all the same training and access to information systems as employed staff. Under HIPAA in the United States, these employees' actions may remain the healthcare organization's liability, not their third-party employer. Under the law, they are considered workforce members.[6] They take day-to-day direction from the healthcare organization rather than from their company. An example of this arrangement would be a consultant hired to help a healthcare organization implement a clinical application, possibly in the emergency department. The contracted employee might accomplish tasks based on the direct supervision of the shift supervisor. Terrific examples of these types of arrangements are contracted nursing personnel and temporary employees. So, an important distinction and implication between an outsourced third-party arrangement and a staff augmentation contract is in how a data breach might be viewed from a regulator's point of view. A data breach caused by the contract staff member who is considered a workforce member under U.S. law may keep sole liability for the data breach within the healthcare organization, not involving the third-party company. To illustrate this, a nursing agency that supplies a nurse temporarily to a hospital may not have liability under HIPAA if that nurse causes a data breach. These distinctions require legal review and interpretation. The intent of introducing them here is as part of managing (and assessing) the risk of third parties and how their support is delivered.

Third Parties in the Healthcare Operations Context

The number/variety of businesses that support the healthcare organization through a contract or financial agreement while not employed by the healthcare organization is sizeable. Several third-parties require more explanation because their relationship with a healthcare organization creates impactful scenarios. Within these scenarios, some interesting concerns arise that those who protect healthcare information must appreciate.

In international data protection terms, a third-party company in EU healthcare provides services or products for a data controller. Under the EU DPD, this is an allowable relationship as long as a safe harbor treaty is in place (for data flow outside of the European Union) or a model contract is in place with already approved clauses from the data authority.[7] In the United States, the relationship is focused on the healthcare sector and formalized using a business associate agreement (a specialized type of contract). This mini-review is important because the relationship between the third party and the healthcare organization may be unusual from the third party's perspective. If they provide similar services to other industries or handle nonpersonal information, the requirements of regulatory guidance such as HIPAA and the EU DPD can be challenging. Figure 5-2 shows how transferring information within U.S. borders is controlled via business associate agreements. Transferring data across U.S. and EU borders requires another type of administrative agreement; safe harbor and model contract standard clauses.

Specific Examples of Third Parties with Healthcare Impact

The number and variety of businesses and entities external to the healthcare organization, yet important to patient care and business success, is almost limitless. Those that handle sensitive health information on behalf of the healthcare organization introduce areas of information risk that must be managed. Some of the specific examples of third-party support and the information risk concerns are as follows.

Cloud Provider   Beginning with one of the emerging third-party relationships in healthcare, the cloud provider example allows you to examine several important considerations. Think about a cloud service provider that supports a healthcare customer as well as those in retail, banking, or education. If the transfer of data includes collecting, storing, or transmitting protected health information, the cloud provider must also meet HIPAA compliance standards in the United States. It must also be able to provide documentation of its independent audit report. This is in addition to any requirements

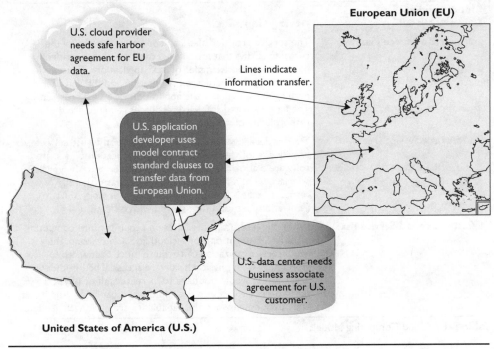

European Union (EU)

U.S. cloud provider needs safe harbor agreement for EU data.

Lines indicate information transfer.

U.S. application developer uses model contract standard clauses to transfer data from European Union.

U.S. data center needs business associate agreement for U.S. customer.

United States of America (U.S.)

Figure 5-2   Third parties in healthcare providing international support

the cloud provider may or may not have with its other customers. Regardless, the move to cloud services for healthcare organizations is happening internationally. There are good reasons for this, such as unprecedented pressures to reduce costs, improve health outcomes, and respond to regulatory changes, to name a few concerns. Cloud solutions promise the ability to help healthcare organizations implement complex health information technology systems at a fraction of the cost. NIST Special Publication 800-144 provides a terrific synopsis of the upsides and downsides of cloud computing from a privacy/security perspective.[8] Things such as improved staff specialization and resource availability are upsides, while Internet-facing systems and multi-net hosting arrangements introduce new vulnerabilities (for some customers). Table 5-1 describes common examples of cloud computing service delivery models to help illustrate the variety of products and services referred to as *cloud computing*. Table 5-2 describes the format that cloud computing can take. In sum, cloud computing offers convenience, rapid innovation, and lower total cost of ownership.

With an understanding of the types of cloud offerings, you can look at some scenarios where healthcare organizations may have challenges using them. This means that information privacy and security issues arise when considering a third party and a type of cloud to use and then evaluating that relationship over time.

Cloud Service Delivery Model	Description
Software as a Service (SaaS)	The service provider offers an application for use by the customer. EHRs that are offered over the Web or patient portals are good examples of SaaS applications. To access the service, the healthcare organization and the end user do nothing more than use the application via a web browser. The hardware and software resources required are the responsibility of the service provider.
Platform as a Service (PaaS)	This model allows a healthcare organization to use service provider resources to run a specific application on a shared software platform in the cloud. The service provider might offer access to a MySQL or Oracle database (shared resource) that is used by the healthcare organization's front-end application (not shared with others).
Infrastructure as a Service (IaaS)	When the healthcare organization requires more computing capability, it might opt for a cloud IaaS. On demand, the healthcare organization can acquire more bandwidth, storage, or even physical hardware access. The healthcare organization would not have to increase staff or physical space on-site to acquire the additional capabilities. And it can scale back down when the capabilities are no longer needed.

Table 5-1 Cloud Computing Models

 TIP Cloud providers and data centers (private clouds) are extremely important third parties in healthcare. With this understanding, you can now begin to apply the same principles to cloud applications such as an EHR, billing operations, or health information exchanges.

Outside Legal Counsel Many healthcare organizations employ lawyers with and without specific healthcare background or experience on the internal staff. But even when they do have employed legal representation, they may choose to retain (on a contract) the services of legal counsel not employed by the healthcare organization, called *outside legal counsel*. These legal professionals and firms perform many different types of services from reviewing contract language, the content of compliance programs (such as the information risk management program), and many other administrative controls the healthcare organization wants to make sure it is properly managing. The outside legal counsel may also help the healthcare organization defend itself in malpractice claims, defend against data breach cases (in the United States), perform forensic investigations, and otherwise represent the healthcare organization in litigation. In the context of managing them as a third party to the healthcare organization, the same types of risk management review must be done on the outside counsel that handles protected health information as any other third party performing similar data use services (A good outside legal counsel will advise their customer to do as much!).

Cloud Architecture (Format)	Characteristics
Private	A private cloud devotes resources to a single customer. It can be a form of intranet with a configuration of servers located behind the customer's firewall. However, a type of private cloud that follows the intent of cloud services is the virtual private cloud, where customer assets are logically provisioned or configured within the service provider's overall cloud offering. Thus, the customer gains all of the dedicated resource aspect with some of the cost reduction. The private cloud in any form is the most expensive type of cloud.
Public	Public clouds offer the most flexibility and scalability. They maximize cost effectiveness and can respond to customer demand rapidly. A public cloud supports multiple customers across any industry, geographic boundary, and type of data involved. For the most part, all resources, processing, and bandwidth are shared among all customers.
Community	A community cloud is a form of combined public and private clouds. In a community cloud, the customers sharing resources are defined and segmented according to predefined criteria. A healthcare-specific example consists of multiple hospitals and provider organizations that collectively make up an integrated delivery network.
Hybrid	A hybrid cloud is actually an integration of some or all of the other cloud types. Instead of having only a community cloud or a private cloud, the healthcare organization may have a public cloud for the patient portal, a private cloud for the EHR, and a community cloud for a health information exchange with its affiliated providers and third parties.

Table 5-2 Cloud Computing Formats

Data Disposition   In the information management life cycle, destroying or disposing of data is the final step. It is also one of the most vulnerable.[9] When data is no longer needed, it often receives less protection because the organization tends to relax control. In many cases, the data destruction or disposal process is conducted by an outsourced company that specializes in this function. Some examples include paper shredding, electronic media erasure, and hardware recycling. Whether the disposal is in paper or electronic format, a healthcare organization needs to ensure the protected healthcare information it marks for disposition is safeguarded all the way through the final steps of making it unreadable and indecipherable. Otherwise, theft and otherwise unauthorized disclosure happen as protected health information is taken from loading docks where medical records await pickup from the data disposition company, for example. As many personal computers are donated to community organizations and schools, a data disposition company may have authority to make the donation, but any sensitive information must be completely removed from the hard drives. A healthcare organization must conduct third-party risk assessment and auditing oversight to make sure its sensitive data is not disclosed under these types of scenarios.

Nonmedical Devices   A special category of third party has evolved as printers, faxes, and scanners have become commonplace in the healthcare environment. If an organization is not careful, these devices can be the source of a data breach. Because these devices copy, e-mail, and transmit data by changing paper documents into electronic images, they often store the images on local storage media. A third-party company contracted to maintain and service these devices may not know the nature of the data the hard drives contain. But, if it is sensitive healthcare information, that data may leave the healthcare organization as the devices move to be serviced or replaced. Similar to the data disposition companies, nonmedical device repair and supply companies must be under contractual obligation to protect the healthcare information that potentially could be present. This means proper destruction, disposal, and reuse provisions are in place. It also means the healthcare organization has risk management responsibilities with respect to the third party that manages nonmedical devices that includes auditing compliance with the use of protected health information.

Of course, these are just a fraction of the types of organizations that provide support to healthcare as third-party vendors. The following list is included for general awareness. All of these could be part of a healthcare organization's third-party risk management responsibility.

- Medical transcription
- Provider answering services
- Patient safety or accreditation organizations
- Billing and claims processing companies
- Health information exchanges (HIEs)
- Third-party health and pharmacy benefit administrators
- Data conversion, de-identification and data analysis service providers
- Utilization review and management companies
- Software vendors and consultants
- Researchers

Third-Party Information Risk Impact on Healthcare Operations

With the data flow for sensitive health information extending beyond the healthcare organization to third parties, new vulnerabilities are present. Add to this the growing mandate from regulators and payers alike to share more data, even among competitors. For a healthcare organization to have a firm information protection program in place, they have to not only know what to do, but why they are doing it. The following sections illustrate why information risk management for third parties is important in the context of scenarios common to healthcare operations.

International Trade Implications Increasingly, companies that support healthcare organizations are international. Going back to the cloud service providers, Amazon, Google, and Microsoft are popular examples. But there are many other third parties that provide data management services through billing, data analytics, and utilization review, for instance, that have entities throughout the globe. Even healthcare organizations themselves have facilities and presence in multiple countries. All of this presents international trade implications related to the transborder exchange of health data. Starting with the EU under the DPD, few countries are approved as having adequate data protection process in place. They are Switzerland, Guernsey, Argentina, Isle of Man, Faroe Islands, Jersey, Andorra, Israel, New Zealand, and Uruguay. Canada has been approved for certain types of personal data.[10] Other countries that want to handle EU DPD protected data must have safe harbor arrangements in place. This book previously introduced and defined this. Within the United States, individual companies must go through safe harbor evaluation under oversight by the U.S. Department of Commerce.

Another way EU healthcare organizations can transfer sensitive data to third parties beyond their own borders is by adopting "model contract" language. This language is pre-approved by the data authority (the EU Commission) and, if not edited, provides adequate safeguards from the commission's perspective.

Regulatory Differences Related to international trade implications, the variations in regulatory standards present concern for healthcare organizations transferring information internationally. The U.S. healthcare organizations, subject to HIPAA, have some concerns where international data management and storage third parties (including cloud providers) do not have the same data segmentation, auditing, and breach notification requirements.[11] International concerns for auditing and monitoring are similar in that data controllers must request the logging of processing operations performed by the provider according to the EU DPD. HIPAA codifies the requirements a bit more in that the healthcare organization must be able to demonstrate authentication, error reporting, and accounting of disclosures. Careful consideration must be made by the healthcare organization using the international third party. If there is a breach of data by the third party, the HIPAA requirement for patient notification in certain circumstances is not relaxed simply because a healthcare organization houses data outside of HIPAA jurisdictional area.

Canadian and EU healthcare organizations particularly have additional privacy concerns even beyond the need for safe harbor or model contract language. These governments and their domestic healthcare organizations in particular have expressed concern with cloud providers that collect, store, and transfer information to and from the United States. The U.S. Patriot Act makes it undesirable—and even illegal—for them to use U.S.-based cloud service providers because the law allows U.S. authorities to look at their data in certain circumstances. That said, remember that under all leading privacy and security regulations, access to health information has provisions for legal authorities to access with additional patient consent. For instance, the United Kingdom's Regulatory of Investigatory Powers Act, much like the U.S. Patriot Act, mandates similar levels of government access.

Disaster Recovery and Continuity of Operations   Because of the criticality of patient care and patient safety issues, healthcare organizations have clinical (and
in many cases regulatory) requirements to have robust disaster recovery and continuity
of operations. System downtime and nonavailability of health information has a terrific impact. Reverting to manual processes and gaining access to health information
that long ago converted to digital format is almost impossible. Medical imaging and
electronic health records (EHRs) are producing unprecedented amounts of data, creating complications in storage, recovery, and security. Think about a radiologist who
needs a relevant prior image for a patient who presents to the emergency room. Those
images are no longer stored on film. Without access to the networked Picture Archiving
and Communications System (PACS), a diagnostic error could be made.

Healthcare organizations that have moved the hosting and storage of their information assets to third parties have to ensure those parties maintain the rigid requirements
for disaster recovery and continuity of operations. Some data centers and cloud providers may claim that healthcare requirements for data availability are more stringent than
prevailing standards such as NIST, ISO, and the EU DPD. In any case, uptime levels
need to be tailored to the healthcare organization's requirements even if that differs
from all other customers of the data center. This must be outlined in contracts and
agreements.

A sound disaster recovery and continuity of operations strategy is essential, and having third-party compliance with the healthcare organization's clinical and regulatory
requirements is important. There are some variables a healthcare organization can use
to help communicate these requirements. They include *recovery point objective* (RPO)
and *recovery time objective* (RTO). RPO is the level of functionality that must be restored
before a healthcare organization can permit operations to continue. Otherwise, the
healthcare organization may consider the system or application offline or experiencing downtime. That condition may be important based on parameters established by a
contract or by regulatory oversight. RTO is the maximum amount of time a healthcare
organization can tolerate downtime. In some disaster recovery plans, a downtime not
to exceed 24 hours may be a best-practice industry standard. In healthcare, 24 hours
of lost data collection or nonavailability of systems is probably unacceptable. Where
RPO and RTO parameters might be more inflexible in healthcare than other industries
and third parties charge more for increased capability and responsiveness, healthcare
organizations consider it a cost of business.

TIP   In considering disaster recovery and continuity of operations
options, a key concept is that more capability or resiliency is available,
but it costs more.

There are several disaster recovery and continuity of operations platforms a healthcare organization can choose to employ. Figure 5-3 shows the cost-benefit trade-off
between the most prevalent options.

- **Hot site** This is the choice for systems and applications with the highest criticality. It is the highest-cost option. A hot site is a redundant capability to the healthcare organization. It can be implemented in an instantaneous switch because it operates in parallel with the production system. At a minimum, it is ready to go in a short period of time.

- **Warm site** This option provides basic infrastructure. It is less expensive than hot site capability, but the healthcare organization can expect a delay in getting the warm site up and running.

- **Cold site** This is the least expensive option. Power and physical security are provided, but equipment must be brought in and configured. Clearly, this option would take some time and probably is not applicable to healthcare organizations unless there is a natural disaster that renders the original healthcare organization site unusable.

Unauthorized Disclosure This may seem obvious, but third parties have significant impact on healthcare organizations because they cause a high percentage of data loss and data breach. Even with robust risk management from the healthcare organization, unauthorized disclose may still happen. With proper contracts and legal agreements in place, financial liability can be properly applied to the third party. But from a reputational perspective, the healthcare organization still is affected negatively. For instance, a patient billing company receives files and has access to databases of healthcare information. If the third party has offices that are burglarized and computer equipment is stolen, the third party may have to pay the fines and penalties. But patient notification will be done by the healthcare organization. Patients will probably not make the distinction between responsible parties.

Figure 5-3
Comparison of disaster recovery and continuity of operations alternatives

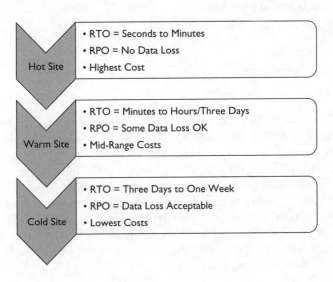

Hot Site
- RTO = Seconds to Minutes
- RPO = No Data Loss
- Highest Cost

Warm Site
- RTO = Minutes to Hours/Three Days
- RPO = Some Data Loss OK
- Mid-Range Costs

Cold Site
- RTO = Three Days to One Week
- RPO = Data Loss Acceptable
- Lowest Costs

NOTE A database of third-party unauthorized disclosures in the United States is publically available at www.privacyrights.org. If nothing else, examining the database presents a clear picture of the frequency and magnitude of the impact that third-party unauthorized disclosure has on healthcare organizations.

Tools to Manage Third-Party Risk

In addition to risk management frameworks that help healthcare organizations oversee third parties that handle protected health information, several other types of documents and agreements are necessary. These help the healthcare organization communicate requirements, evaluate performance, and hold all parties accountable for compliance. Without the use of one or more of these administrative controls, healthcare organizations have little reason to expect a third party will apply appropriate safeguards or be responsive enough, particularly in cases where a healthcare organization's expectations exceed those of the third party's other customers from other industries. The examples that follow are some of the major types. There may be others, and there may be combinations that are valid, but only a few are mentioned here.

Service Level Agreements

Healthcare organizations may choose to use a written agreement between themselves and a third party called a *service level agreement* (SLA). These can be legal contracts with binding conditions enforceable in court, or they can be an informal obligation between the two parties. Either way, SLAs have several provisions.

- Definition of services
- Performance measurement
- Escalation of problems
- Customer duties
- Warranties
- Disaster recovery
- Termination of agreement

The most effective SLAs have scheduled times where the customer and service provider meet to discuss ongoing operations. As we presented earlier, this communication may integrate into the overall risk management process where issues concerning risk assessment and mitigation are also included in the monitoring of the SLA. But the SLA covers more than just the management of risk. Service providers will have obligations to provide availability of information, upgrades to hardware and software, or improvements in general customer service depending on what services are being provided. In short, the SLA can be considered an additional administrative control within the risk management process. The SLA should be enforced, but changes should be permitted as situations warrant. Communication is a vital part of ensuring the SLA is never static and helps the healthcare organization and third party have a successful partnership.

To protect healthcare information for your organization, you may have to manage one or more SLAs. The SLA may be a portion of your overall risk management strategy. The following are some suggestions for properly managing the SLAs under your purview:

- Be proactive and review compliance regularly.
- Establish measurable objectives that
  - Meet business or clinical standards
  - Comply with law or regulatory requirements
  - The service provider agrees to meet
- Monitor these objectives continuously.
- Communicate with the third party.
- Communicate to information governance within the healthcare organization.

Doing these activities can help you succeed in your duties. More importantly, the active oversight will give the SLA the best chance of being efficient and effective. Too many SLAs are signed and shelved only to be reviewed after a data breach or after service levels have reached such low levels the agreement is in jeopardy of being terminated for cause.

Contracts (Standards and Practices)

When a formal, legally binding document is required, a contract may be used. These contracts will have standards, practices, and clauses that exceed the level of formality and enforcement an SLA would have. Contractual provisions are helpful for data security concerns. Every contract has variations, so an overall template is hard to illustrate. Some commonalities exist.

To begin with, the contract should hold the third party to relevant privacy and security standards that the healthcare organization complies with, including internal policies and procedures. Additionally, contracts will consist of terms and conditions related to the following:

- **Compliance** The third party must adhere to relevant regulations. In the United States, this would start with HIPAA. The contract may be the business associate agreement (BAA), or the BAA may be part of the entire contract. The third party will have to comply with relevant state laws. This must be covered specifically in the compliance section. Internationally, this section is where you would find compliance requirements for laws of other countries such as the EU Data Protection Directive if there is transborder data transfer. Beyond compliance with the law, compliance with standards that are not law are included. For example, the Payment Card Industry (PCI) Data Security Standards or applicable National Institute of Standards and Technology (NIST) standards that the third party must adhere to will be included in this section.

- **Confidentiality**   If there is a requirement for a third party to handle sensitive healthcare information, the confidentiality provision must be present. This is the area where the information is defined, permitted uses are explained, prohibited uses are described, and return or disposition provisions are outlined upon the termination of the contract.

- **Data loss prevention and response**   The third party will take on responsibilities for preventing data loss. They will also need to know how to respond to any potential or actual data loss by complying with the healthcare organization's incident response policies as well as any governing regulatory guidelines. The contract should allocate responsibilities and outline procedures accordingly.

- **Indemnification**   Some will argue the sections covering indemnification can be the most impactful in a contract. Indemnification, or the provisions for damages or compensation if things go wrong, becomes crucial in the event of a security breach or abuse of personal information. The contractual language also includes insurance to cover data loss events. If there are notice obligations in the country where the patients reside, they will be provided. Also, the indemnification clause will include a duty to cooperate in investigations and resolution actions. In some cases, the healthcare organization will want to add provisions for controlling these investigations and any notification actions to patients or regulators even if the vendor is responsible for some or all of the related costs.

- **Limits to liability**   In the event the third party causes the data loss or breach, the contract should limit liability (or hold harmless) for the healthcare organization. On the other hand, there can be limits imposed on the liability of the third party because too high of a threshold or unlimited liability may far exceed the value of the contract. Not many third-party vendors would accept that much risk. They might choose not to provide the service to the healthcare organization. It is a delicate balance. But, the healthcare organization needs to be protected from undue litigation resulting from a third party's failure to perform or to comply with applicable laws.

Vendor Management Frameworks

We have introduced and explained several leading risk management frameworks that healthcare organizations can use to evaluate and manage internal risk. By all means, these same tools can be used to evaluate and manage third-party vendors. The same risk assessment and remediation work should be done for each external vendor with respect to their processes, policies, and controls in place to protect your information. We will not repeat the information here concerning the leading risk management tools such as the NIST RMF, the NIST HIPAA Security Rule (HSR) tool, or the ISO 27000 family of standards, but keep in mind that these same tools can be applied to third parties that handle protected health information for your organization.

One leading risk management framework that is presented as a vendor risk-specific framework is the Office of the Comptroller of the Currency (OCC) in the U.S. Department of the Treasury.[12] This is presented here because the framework is used by many leading assessment organizations internationally, for example Shared Assessments.

Shared Assessments was established in 2005 and is present in more than 115 countries worldwide (mostly in the financial industry).[13] It specializes in assessing third-party vendors that handle sensitive information. You can see some similarities in this life-cycle risk management model compared to the ones already discussed. A couple of differences are in contract negotiations (SLAs, for example) and in the termination phases. These phases are as follows:

- **Planning**   Analogous to the risk management phase of inventorying all of your third parties or data systems, planning for outsourcing data handling is the first step.

- **Due diligence and third-party selection**   Looking at alternatives, evaluating past performance (references), and maybe even doing a tailored assessment before contracting with a potential third party all show appropriate management.

- **Contract negotiation**   Going back to using an SLA to define expectations and measure performance or a more formal contract with legally enforceable terms and conditions, the third-party relationship with the healthcare organization must be governed by an administrative control.

- **Ongoing monitoring**   Periodic audits and assessments are necessary to ensure compliance. Remember, the third-party relationship is not a static relationship that is forgotten once the paperwork is signed.

- **Termination**   Once the contract ends (either at the end of the period of performance or because the third party fails to perform), arrangements must be made to continue the service in another way and securely return or dispose of all sensitive health data.

The OCC life cycle (see Figure 5-4) also integrates some overarching concepts that fit into the other risk management frameworks we have covered. Here are some examples:

- **Oversight and accountability**   Of course, someone from the healthcare organization must be responsible for the contract. They should be accountable for results and be integrated into the information governance structure of the healthcare organization.

- **Documentation and reporting**   As part of the information governance structure, the accountable person must be able to communicate relevant details, events, and performance measurements. All of this must be documented and retained.

- **Independent reviews**   In addition to periodic assessments and audits, both on-site and remotely through vendor self-assessment, an objective independent assessment is a best-practice idea as well. Remember, accessing/reviewing objective audits of the third party that they already maintain is a solid risk management component. For example, give credit for FISMA ratings, ISO certifications, SSAE 16, and Sarbanes-Oxley (SOX) audit results.

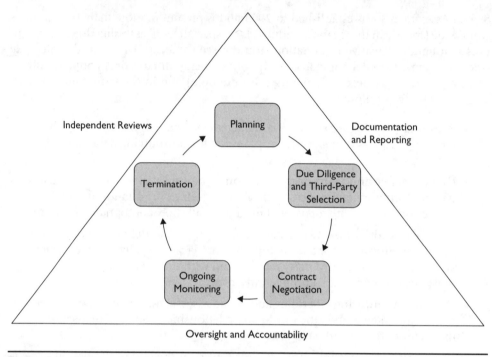

Figure 5-4 OCC version of third-party risk management life cycle

Determining When Third-Party Assessment Is Required

Each organization will have to determine when and how it wants to assess its third parties. Of course, there are some regulatory pressures. Typically, the assessment should be done annually. But in any event, organizational standards for vendor management will set the expectations. Going back to the first step in the assessment of the third party, having an inventory and level of riskiness established will help scope the frequency and nature of the assessments. The organization may choose to allow a self-assessment, support a remote assessment, or insist on an on-site audit.

In addition to regularly scheduled (such as annual) events, sometimes an out-of-cycle assessment might be needed. The following are some of the events that can trigger a third-party assessment:

- Failure to perform to the contract or SLA
- A data breach relative to another organization
- New personnel in key positions
- Information outage and unsatisfactory disaster recovery
- Leadership inquiry or interest item
- Possible recompete for new provider

Support of Third-Party Assessments and Audits

A primary role of a healthcare information privacy and security professional is to help organize and conduct the required assessments and audits of the third parties. The overall consideration for a third-party audit will be whether the activity will be conducted.

- **Self-assessment**   The vendor responds to a survey provided by the healthcare organization.

- **On-site**   This happens on-site by the healthcare organization's employee observing and interviewing.

- **Remote**   With or without a self-assessment, the third-party vendor is reviewed using relevant third-party material such as past performance attestations, marketing material, any legal proceedings against the third party, and so on.

- **Hybrid**   This uses a combination of on-site and off-site approaches.

Based on factors such as how much risk the third party introduces or how familiar the third party is to the organization, one of the assessment approaches will be chosen. This is true for the initial assessment in the planning or selection phase and in the annual or periodic assessment process. If a third-party vendor triggers an out-of-cycle assessment because of a potential data loss incident, a different approach from previous assessments can certainly be chosen. That said, because the SLA or contract is a risk transference vehicle, it can help determine the type of assessment approach.

The next step may be your biggest obstacle in participating in the third-party risk assessment process. Just because the third party is not part of the healthcare organization, there are no special considerations to reducing standards that are internal to the organization. The third party must have the controls in place that are required by contract and by law. For instance, if there are information security and privacy training requirements, it is not acceptable to excuse the vendor from them. Sometimes healthcare organizations are tempted to give credit to the vendor for training provided by the healthcare organization. Unfortunately, under most circumstances, that does not meet the requirements. Remember, a component of the required training is training on that specific organization's policies and procedures, not those of the healthcare organization. This is one example. Another example is not having access to the third party's facilities. If within the contractor SLA the negotiated terms and conditions permit access by the healthcare organization to visit on-site premises and conduct an inspection, that should be part of the audit. Relaxing that standard because of reluctance of the third party to support the inspection adds undue risk to the healthcare organization.

When faced with third-party vendors that do not comply with assessment and audit requirements, your role in the organization will be to document findings and communicate them to more senior leadership. This is an incredibly important role. Properly organizing these types of assessments (correct approach, valid assessment tool, following contracts, and communicating all findings) is a linchpin to reducing the risk of third-party data breaches. Once again, you know that the results of several industry surveys demonstrate that third parties commonly cause data breaches. The underlying causes tend to be the lack of oversight we have just described and desire to avoid.

TIP The best application of this book is by using it as a resource to refine and execute internal processes. This chapter accentuates that focus. While external reporting procedures and awareness of regulatory changes are vital, the day-to-day mission of most healthcare information security and privacy professionals is internally focused. Make sure any compliance efforts integrate with the healthcare clinical and business functions as well as meet cost-benefit analysis concerns. Avoid chasing best-practices and responding to changes in the law or governing directives before examining the impact such concerns have on your organization.

Promoting Information Protection Including Risk Management

According to every leading privacy and security framework or set of regulatory standards, training and awareness are mandatory components of the information security program. As a healthcare information privacy and security professional, you will have responsibility in designing and implementing your organization's program and generating awareness for information protection throughout the organization. Table 5-3 outlines some of the leading frameworks and regulatory standards that require training and awareness. From this perspective, you can look at some common components of proven training and awareness programs.

There are numerous ways to promote awareness of privacy and security within a healthcare organization. Some of the most common ways are through training and internal marketing campaigns.

Training

The entire security awareness program should consist of a number of training opportunities that continually keep information protection on the minds of healthcare organization personnel. Even with the best policies and procedures in place, organizations

Standard	Background
HIPAA	HIPAA requires healthcare organizations and their third-party vendors to implement a security awareness and training program for all members of their workforce (including management).
PCI Data Security Standards	If an organization processes credit cards, it must "implement a formal security awareness program to make all personnel aware of the importance of cardholder data security."
FISMA	FISMA requires organizations that support U.S. federal agencies to provide some type of security awareness training particular to the government organization they support (in other words, that agency's policies and procedures).

Table 5-3 Frameworks and Standards That Require Training and Awareness

may find they are all but useless[14] without proper training on security policies, privacy policies, and incident response policies, especially with respect to managing third-party risk. The following are some of the most common opportunities to provide training (and many of these are required):

- Upon hire (even temporary employees)
- Annually
- After an incident occurs (lessons learned)
- Using current events (through a newsletter or distribution list e-mail)
- Promotions and recognition of personnel
- Ad hoc topics as technology, regulations, or processes change

As part of new employee and annual training programs, most healthcare organizations in the United States will provide HIPAA and information security awareness training. Internationally, the requirements are similar. The EU DPD has an annual requirement for employees to be trained on their duty of confidentiality. The content of the training will certainly differ from country to country and from one U.S. healthcare organization to another. In fact, there is no mandatory curriculum for training. Most of the training is developed internally in the organization. However, these general training topics should be present:

- Name and contact information for responsible individuals (privacy officer, information security officer, and so on)
- History and context behind prevailing regulations (HIPAA, EU DPD, PHIPA, and so on)
- Organization-specific policies related to regulatory requirements
- Definition and examples of sensitive health information (protected health information in the United States) and typical scenarios where such information is present
- Prevention activities related to reducing risk of data loss
- Incident reporting processes in the event of potential and actual data loss

Internal Marketing

Marketing internally to healthcare organization staff and third-party vendors is a form of training. When done correctly, it can help shape the culture of the organization more than training alone. Some of the standard tools marketing professionals use can help create awareness through posters, contests, and logos that will help staff members comply with information protection. Many healthcare organizations will use suggestion programs and hotlines to augment their internal awareness programs to help develop the marketing process. In sum, marketing, as opposed to training, tends to be viewed as a more positive, upbeat communication tool.

Security Awareness Program Essentials

Like with any program, performance must be measured to determine how effective the security awareness program is. When it comes to training classes, the value of testing personnel to ensure they have an acceptable level of understanding is important. So, at least for new hires and annual training on information protection, an exam or assessment test is required. But, there are other ways to assess how effective the security awareness program is. One such way is to conduct mock data breaches.

At first, most healthcare organizations might hesitate to voluntarily experience a data breach. But testing the processes has an added value to learn where improvements can be made. For the awareness program purposes, it can demonstrate and reinforce training and marketing better than just about any other assessment tool. A mock data breach can be conducted by developing a likely scenario using the healthcare organization's risk assessment with typical threats incorporated. If an insider threat is most likely, then develop a scenario around record snooping or loss of a laptop. Make relevant personnel walk through the actions required to report the incident internally, investigate, and remediate the data loss. Third-party vendors could participate if the scenario accommodates their participation.

 NOTE Third parties would not be obligated to participate in mock data breaches per se. However, third parties are obligated to test and evaluate their own backup plans and disaster recovery processes. Healthcare organizations can develop mock data breach scenarios integrated with their third parties' scheduled plans. The result would be no contractual issues and meaningful lessons learned about how a data breach involving a third party might occur.

If there are additional steps to take external to the organization (such as patient notification), they can be simulated. In all cases, the event should be documented. Afterward, a meeting can be held with the information governance stakeholders, possibly the information management council, to review the findings. To conclude, a mock data loss not only helps measure the organization's awareness but satisfies several requirements to test and evaluate relevant information protection procedures, including third parties. If a scenario involves data loss caused by a third party, that third party may discover some areas of improvement as well.

Chapter Review

You now have a more holistic approach to managing the risk of third parties in healthcare. The value of these relationships will continue to grow as technology advances, pressures to control costs continue to mount, and access to specialized personnel is difficult. The healthcare organization will have to outsource many of its services and products and share access to protected health information. However, without exception, the responsibility that healthcare organizations and data collectors have in maintaining the privacy and security of this information cannot be outsourced with the information sharing. So, understanding how to manage third-party risk appropriately is a central competency of the healthcare information privacy and security professional.

Of course, building a culture within a healthcare organization that values managing this risk is no easy task. You also looked at some ways to build awareness in the organization through training and marketing programs. The effectiveness of such programs can be demonstrated through mock data breaches. If all of this is done well, we hope that the only data breaches a healthcare organization will experience will be of the simulated nature.

Review Questions

1. Outsourcing health data management to third parties is:
   A. Not regulated by law in the United States but is in Canada
   B. Illegal in the United States and European Union but not in Canada
   C. Covered in leading privacy and security frameworks
   D. Reduces information risk to the healthcare organization

2. To properly manage third-party information risk, a healthcare organization should:
   A. Inventory all third parties that handle protected healthcare information
   B. Assign an objective clinical staff member to review all service level agreements
   C. Use the same vendor for all services that require the handling of protected health information
   D. Ensure patient consent is obtained that includes sharing information with third parties

3. (TRUE or FALSE) An administrative control used to manage third-party information risk in the United States is an end-user licensing agreement.

4. Contracting with a data center provider to manage off-site storage is an example of:
   A. Staff augmentation
   B. Public cloud
   C. Community cloud
   D. Outsourcing

5. The international trade impact of having a safe harbor agreement in place is:
   A. A U.S. cloud provider could contract with an EU healthcare organization
   B. Data authorities would provide model contract standard clauses
   C. The U.S. government could have access to EU data controller health data
   D. A U.S. healthcare organization could use an EU utilization review firm

6. Health data accessed on a laptop donated to a school is an example of a data breach in which information life cycle phase?

   A. Use

   B. Maintenance

   C. Distribution

   D. Disposition

7. Performance measurement criteria and procedures for escalation of problems would be found in _____.

8. In monitoring third parties, healthcare organizations should:

   A. Ensure outside counsel does inspections

   B. Include them on information governance groups

   C. Conduct annual and periodic audits as needed

   D. Assign a board member to interview them

9. (TRUE or FALSE) The current third-party patient billing company has had a break-in at its office. Nothing was stolen or missing. One possible action for the healthcare organization customer is to audit the current patient billing company.

10. One of the most cost-effective ways to promote organizational awareness of privacy and security concerns with information management by third parties is:

   A. Investing in a software-only data loss prevention application

   B. Conducting audits of third parties with clinical leadership personnel

   C. Publishing service level agreements on an organization's intranet

   D. Providing training upon hire and annually

Answers

1. **C.** The provisions for allowing information sharing with third parties is included in regulatory guidance internationally and in privacy and security principles. Therefore, option A is not correct because both the United States and Canada regulate the third-party use of health information. The use of third parties to support healthcare in the European Union, United States, and Canada is entirely legal, as is proper health information sharing, so option B is incorrect. Finally, the main point of this chapter is that information risk is inherently increased by introducing information sharing with an external, third-party organization, so option D is not the right answer.

2. **A.** The first step the healthcare organization should take is to inventory all third parties that handle health information and what services they provide. Option B is incorrect because involving a clinical staff member is beneficial, but is not an

applicable step in the process. It is highly improbable and likely cost prohibitive to use the same vendor for all required services. Option C is not appropriate. Patient consent is not necessarily needed for transferring health information to a third party that is supporting healthcare operations. Therefore, option D is not the right answer.

3. **FALSE.** The business associate agreement is required by HIPAA; therefore, it is U.S.-centric.

4. **D.** Of the available options, outsourcing is the only one that fits the scenario. Staff augmentation could be correct if the off-site variable were not present. Option A is not the best answer. Options B and C are not correct because both a community cloud offering and a public cloud offering would probably not host protected health information.

5. **A.** Safe harbor allows EU health organizations to transfer sensitive data to U.S. companies that satisfy the requirements. This agreement is for U.S. companies only, not governments, so option C is incorrect. Option B is not right because model contracts are used in place of safe harbor agreements. Option D is irrelevant in that the safe harbor agreement is an EU requirement. The U.S. healthcare organization would be subject to HIPAA, and because the EU utilization review firm would not be, the third-party contract would probably not happen. But that has nothing to do with safe harbor.

6. **D.** Data breaches can happen in any of the information management life-cycle steps, but many happen in the disposition stage because data users relax control when the data is no longer needed and marked for disposal. This scenario describes unauthorized access after the data has gone through the use, maintenance, and distribution phases. Options A, B, and C are not the correct answers.

7. **Service level agreement (SLA).** The service level agreement by definition contains performance measurement criteria against which the third party is evaluated.

8. **C.** Healthcare organizations are required to conduct annual or periodic audits of their third parties that handle protected health information. For this response, options A, B, and D are incorrect in terms of feasibility and cost. There is little chance a board member would interview an individual third-party organization as a risk assessment measure. However, it might be possible to have a board member meet with a collection of third-party vendors as part of an "industry day meeting." Outside counsel is an expensive option, and unless there is a high risk and the healthcare organization wants a more formal interpretation, outside counsel is probably not involved with third-party risk monitoring. While including third parties in some activities of information risk management within the healthcare organization, having them as regular members of any internal boards and committees is not practical.

9. **FALSE.** The scenario illustrates a potential data breach and an out-of-cycle assessment is a good idea.

10. **D.** It is cost effective and too often overlooked, but providing training on managing third-party risk (along with protecting healthcare information in general) is the right answer. Option A might be less costly than hardware technology purchases, but there is no expectation of the application's effectiveness. Option B is a scenario that implies a high cost with using clinical personnel to augment auditing while not providing patient care. And option C is probably not useful in that publishing service level agreements on the Internet provides no context or explanation to the average user of those services. No organizational awareness is increased.

References

1. Kolbasuk-McGee, Marianne. "Google, Amazon Adjust to HIPAA Demands. Cloud Vendors Signing Business Associate Agreements. Healthcare Info Security." October 9, 2013. Accessed on March 10, 2014, at www.healthcareinfosecurity.com/google-amazon-adjust-to-hipaa-demands-a-6133

2. American Institute of Certified Public Accountants (AICPA) and the Canadian Institute of Chartered Accountants (CICA). Generally Accepted Privacy Principles. p. 3. Accessed on March 21, 2014, at www.aicpa.org/InterestAreas /InformationTechnology/Resources/Privacy/GenerallyAcceptedPrivacyPrinciples /DownloadableDocuments/GAPP_BUS_%200909.pdf

3. Omnibus HIPAA Rule. Modifications to the HIPAA Privacy, Security, Enforcement, and Breach Notification Rules Under the Health Information Technology for Economic and Clinical Health Act and the Genetic Information Nondiscrimination Act; Other Modifications to the HIPAA Rules. Executive Summary. Section 1 A (ii). Accessed on March 3, 2014, at www.gpo.gov/fdsys /pkg/FR-2013-01-25/pdf/2013-01073.pdf

4. Markets and Markets. Healthcare IT Outsourcing Market – By Application [Provider (EHR, RCM, LIMS) Payer (CRM, Claims Management, Fraud Detection, Billing) Life Science (ERP, CTMS, CDMS) Operational (SCM, BPM) & Infrastructure (IMS, Cloud Computing)] & Industry – Global Forecast To 2018. August 7, 2103. Accessed on March 13, 2014, at www.rnrmarketresearch .com/healthcare-it-outsourcing-market-by-application-provider-ehr-rcm-lims-payer-crm-claims-management-fraud-detection-billing-life-science-erp-ctms-cdms-operational-scm-bpm-infrastruc-market-report.html

5. Author's note: Gartner is a great resource for healthcare IT issues. Gartner. IT Glossary. Accessed on March 19, 2014, at www.gartner.com/it-glossary/ mssp-managed-security-service-provider

6. U.S. Department of Health and Human Services (HHS) Office of Civil Rights (OCR). Business Associates adapted from HIPAA Privacy Rule (45 CFR 164.502(e), 164.504(e), 164.532(d) and (e)). April 3, 2003. Accessed on March 4, 2014, at www.hhs.gov/ocr/privacy/hipaa/understanding/coveredentities/businessassociates.pdf

7. European Commission. Model Contracts for the transfer of personal data to third countries. Accessed on March 19, 2014, at http://ec.europa.eu/justice/data-protection/document/international-transfers/transfer/index_en.htm

8. NIST Special Publication 800-144. Guidelines on Security and Privacy in Public Cloud Computing. December 2011. Section 3. pps. 8–13. Accessed on March 30, 2014, at www.nist.gov/customcf/get_pdf.cfm?pub_id=909494

9. Swire, Peter P., and Kenesa Ahmad. "Common Principles and Approaches to Information Privacy and Data Protection." Foundations of information privacy and data protection: a survey of global concepts, laws and practices. International Association of Privacy Professionals, 2012. p. 12. Print.

10. European Commission. Commission decisions on the adequacy of the protection of personal data in third countries. Accessed on March 19, 2014, at http://ec.europa.eu/justice/data-protection/document/international-transfers/adequacy/index_en.htm

11. Cloud Standards Customer Council. Impact of Cloud Computing on Healthcare. November 2012. Accessed on March 28, 2014, at www.cloudstandardscustomercouncil.org/cscchealthcare110512.pdf

12. Office of the Comptroller of the Currency (OCC). U.S. Department of Treasury. Third-Party Relationships. Risk Management Guidance. October 2013. Accessed on March 11, 2014, at www.occ.gov/news-issuances/bulletins/2013/bulletin-2013-29.html

13. Shared Assessments. About Shared Assessments. Accessed on March 22, 2014, at https://sharedassessments.org/about

14. Travis, Breaux. "The Roles of Governance and Risk Management in Driving a Culture of Trust." Introduction to IT Privacy. International Association of Privacy Professionals, 2014. p. 247. Print.

Information Security and Privacy Events Management

In this chapter, you will learn to
- Understand the phases of data incident management
- Recognize the difference between incidents, events, and data breaches
- Apply responsibilities of incident response team members
- Comprehend required actions when third parties cause the incident
- Examine external notification requirements for data breaches

Our story begins at the end of the week. It's Friday afternoon and Sally, the health records specialist, is just about finished for the day. Looking forward to a long weekend of rest and relaxation after a busy week, she was almost done adhering with the organization's Clean Desk Policy. Sally chuckles to herself as she remembers the reason she has to make sure her desk and work area are clean of paper, files, and electronic media each day before she leaves is her own doing. After earning her certification in health information privacy and security, Sally helped her organization develop and implement the Clean Desk Policy, along with several other policies, that improved the overall information security program. "Having clutter on a desk or workspace when no one is around is an invitation for after-hour workers or passersby to simply steal paper and electronic health information. Desks must be clutter-free as much as possible," she told the healthcare CIO.

Tonight was a big night. Sally was looking forward to getting out of the office. Then the phone rang. "Hello, this is Sally, health information management. Can I help you?" The voice on the other end of the line sounded worried.

"Yes, I hope so," he stammered. "My name is Jack, and I work in pediatrics."

"OK, Jack, what can I do for you?"

"Well, I was working with a healthcare provider downtown, and I sent her a roster with all of her patients that are seen here."

Sally provided reassurance. "That's OK. Did you encrypt the data?"

"No," Jack replied, "How do I do that?"

"We can cover that later," Sally told him. "We may still be OK. Tell me, did you send it to the doctor and only the one recipient?"

"That is the problem," Jack blurted out. "I meant to send it to Mary Ann Williams at Children's Hospital. But my e-mail autopopulated another Williams—Andrew Williams to be exact." Jack continued, "I hit Send before I noticed the mistake. Andrew Williams is a reporter from the local newspaper. That file had more than 500 patient names, record numbers, appointment dates, and reasons for visit." Jack deflated. "I have no idea how I have his e-mail address, but I do."

Sally sighed. She knew her weekend plans are now canceled. "Jack, we have some work to do," Sally said as she remained calm. "At this point, we have to initiate our organization's incident reporting process."

The story you have just read is fiction. However, it is based in fact and happens often. What Sally does next is extremely important. Sally will initiate (and possibly) lead the healthcare organization's incident reporting process. In this chapter, we will discuss the actions of an incident response team, the notification procedures, and the responsibilities of those who protect information in healthcare organizations.

Anyone who has worked in a position that includes healthcare information security and privacy responsibility has received the late-afternoon or middle-of-the-night phone call announcing a possible data breach. Knowing what to do before the call comes (the incident response process) is vital to the information security program. The best incident response procedures require proper management and adequate resourcing from areas inside and outside of information technology departments. Normally, however, the IT department leads the overall effort. Ahead of time, the personnel responsible for incident reporting must establish and publish guidelines for incident handling. The team should also have the ability to analyze data related to the incidents to improve actions in the future.

Definitions

Starting with some definitions, information security notification involves two main types of concerns. An *event* is any observable occurrence in a system or network. Events can be authorized actions, such as a user sending e-mail or a server receiving a request for a web page. If the event has a negative effect, it is called an *adverse event*. Typically, these are activities related to the functionality of the hardware and software of the system. For instance, the system crashes, there is unauthorized access to sensitive information, or a virus infects the network causing data loss. Events can also be related to physical security concerns such as natural disasters and power failures.

When an action is taken that violates information security policies, acceptable use policies, or standard security practices, that action is an *incident*. Many outsider attacks fall under the definition of an incident (versus an event). A spamming or phishing attempt to fool authorized users into accessing malicious web sites that may install malware onto the network is another example. Incidents (as opposed to events) are typically influenced by human action.

Differentiating between these types of activities is helpful in further determining whether the activity needs to be escalated or reported internally only or whether it requires notification external to the organization (for example, to government regulators or patients). Incidents and events in healthcare information scenarios that require reporting and notifications are called *data breaches*. Not all incidents or events are data breaches, but all breaches start as incidents or events. In the United States, HIPAA guides healthcare organizations in this area by defining breaches as an impermissible use or disclosure of protected health information unless the covered entity or business associate, as applicable, demonstrates that there is a low probability that the protected health information has been compromised based on a risk assessment.[1] If the organization can determine the incident or event does not meet the risk of disclosure threshold, the organization does not have to report the incident or event to patients or regulators.

TIP Again, there are two types of data breaches that exceed the risk of disclosure threshold. The key variable is the number of individual records involved. The important number to remember is 500. A breach of less than 500 records carries less severe reporting requirements outside the healthcare organization. External notification involving immediate federal regulatory notification starts at 500 individual records.

The data breach risk assessment methodology, per HIPAA, is to determine the risk of disclosure of the information. The incident response team, as the first step, will be required to assess the following:

- What was disclosed? Categorize and define the identifiers within the protected health information (PHI) and the likelihood the elements could be combined to identify an individual.

- Who used the data? Identify the person or people who used, received, or accessed the PHI and were unauthorized to do so.

- Was the PHI actually viewed or used? Sometimes, disclosure is not made even though an unauthorized person had access.

- What actions have been taken to limit unauthorized disclosure? Outline what has been done to mitigate the risk of additional PHI disclosure.

Outside of the United States, there is commonly no general requirement to notify affected individuals or the government. Of course, leading privacy frameworks and regulators consider notification of affected individuals and regulators (data authorities) a best practice. They highly encourage reporting data breaches. However, HIPAA equivalent reporting requirements are not internationally in place. This is changing as governments are recognizing notification as a prevention of data loss as well as mitigation actions to reduce the overall impact of the data loss. An example is the United Kingdom Privacy and Electronic Communications (EC Directive) Regulations 2003 (the PECR), which requires providers of public electronic communications services (for example, Internet service providers, telecoms providers, and so on) to notify the data protection authority (government) for personal data breaches. However, notifying customers is still not mandatory.

Timeline of Incident Activities

There are several distinct phases for handling data incidents. These phases begin before an incident has ever happened. In the preparation phase, the organization prepares by establishing and training an incident response team. The team is resourced appropriately and equipped with the tools required. Detecting incidents is the second phase. In this phase, alerts and error reporting occur. The subsequent phase includes all the actions the organization will do in terms of containment, eradication, and recovery. Keep in mind that the organization will continually reassess the systems like they did in the detection and analysis phase because additional exploits may be present. When the organization has recovered and the incident is handled, post-incident activities are conducted. This phase is when lessons learned are reported to help prevent the next data incident. Figure 6-1 shows the timeline of incident activities.

To be a little more descriptive, the phases identified here require further explanation. The following sections contain some examples of activities and outcomes of each phase.

Preparation

This is where policies, processes, procedures, and agreements are established to guide management and response to security incidents. The organizational expectations for priorities and response times are set. The incident response team pre-identifies audits and logs that will be used for future forensics. The team also may assist in preventing incidents during the preparation phase by contributing and documenting information risk assessments. As part of preparation, the incident response team should obtain adequate workspace. They should also acquire hardware (laptops, smartphones, and so on) and software (packet sniffers, digital forensics, and so on) ahead of time for use in their incident response. Again, the key is doing these actions ahead of time because once an incident occurs, there is no time to gather these tools and resources. Finally, during preparation, incident response teams develop and test exercise scenarios to ensure they are ready for the next event. Using previous events and events that have happened to other organizations are extremely helpful.

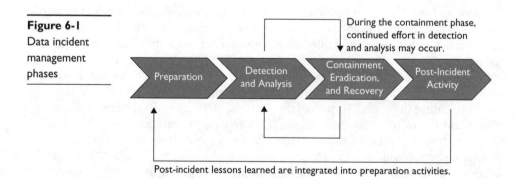

Figure 6-1 Data incident management phases

During the containment phase, continued effort in detection and analysis may occur.

Preparation → Detection and Analysis → Containment, Eradication, and Recovery → Post-Incident Activity

Post-incident lessons learned are integrated into preparation activities.

Detection and Analysis

Healthcare organizations are extremely complex in the number of diverse systems employed, variations in access to these systems, and the function of these systems. This is noted only because, much like all other organizations, incident detection is extremely difficult. There are many false positives that require investigation. Some actual incidents remain undetected because they look like legitimate activity. Nevertheless, accurately detecting and assessing possible incidents is vital, albeit challenging. There are two common ways organizations detect incidents: automated and manual detection. Automated detection includes network and host-based intrusion detection and prevention systems. Manual processes include the employees and end users making an incident report that is a foundational requirement for any good incident reporting process. Automated tools are terrific and effective, but human interrogation of an incident or potential incident is still the most prevalent way incidents are discovered.

It's important to note the detection of an incident includes two classifications: precursor and indicator. A potential incident may be foreshadowed by a sign, which is called a *precursor*. If the incident is happening now or may have already occurred, an *indicator* may be detected. An example of a precursor is evidence of external network scanning of the environment looking for vulnerabilities. An indicator of an incident may be antivirus or network intrusion sensor alerts communicating abnormal activity that requires further investigation. At this point, analysis becomes important. Precursors and indicators do not always result in incidents and events. In fact, many organizations have millions of indicators each day and none that result in an incident or eventual data breach. In fact, one of the key aspects of proper analysis is to know what normal activity and behavior is and identify deviations. Analysis by a qualified individual is imperative to distilling all of the false indicators and precursors down to actual items on which to act.

Within detection and analysis, the incident response timeline will include prioritizing the incident once it is analyzed. Sometimes this is called *triage actions* where the nature of the incident is determined, the initial priority level is assigned, and the documentation of all actions taken is initiated.[2] Ideally, an organization does not have to manage too many incidents that rise to the level of triage or prioritization, but it is important to not handle them as first come, first served. Consideration must include the following:

- Functional impact to the organization (patient care and safety in healthcare)
- Informational impact (PHI data loss)
- Recoverability from the incident (contingency operations)

The detection and analysis phase also includes initial notification. From communicating with senior leadership to coordinating internally with resources related to incident management (such as human resources, IT departments, and possibly public relations), the next step is to start informing key personnel and to provide regular updates. In some cases, the input from the incident response team will be used by organization personnel to interact externally with law enforcement, U.S. CERT, data authorities, other government regulators, the media, and, in some cases, patients. That communication starts to happen sometimes in just the second phase of the complete investigation.

Containment, Eradication, and Recovery

Containment starts with a decision about how to stop an incident from expanding its impact. Once relatively certain an incident is adverse, the initial response should be focused on limiting the damage already done and on preventing further harm. There are several general strategies for initial containment.

- Shutting down a system
- Disconnecting from a network
- Disabling certain functions
- Creating a backup
- Changing passwords
- Altering access control
- Implementing continuity of operations plans

No matter what decision is made, having considered alternatives beforehand is useful. Guidelines and strategies in place in the planning phase can help reduce uncertainty in decision making in the containment activity. Keep in mind that making the wrong decision in containment can increase the negative impact of the incident. For instance, a decision to disconnect a system from the network may launch a type of malware that reacts to not having connectivity to the Internet. If that malware encrypts the entire hard drive of the affected system, it may be worse than simply leaving the system connected while eradication is attempted. What is more, in an emergency situation where an instantaneous containment response is needed, there is no time to weigh options. So, having containment strategies agreed upon for a variety of scenarios is advisable.

While in containment, digital forensic analysis begins. This involves the identification, preservation, extraction, and documentation of computer-based evidence. It is the discipline of assessing and examining an information system for relevant clues even after it has been compromised by an exploit.[3] Whatever evidence is collected during the containment phase and beyond has to be maintained so that it is legally admissible. Using the definitions from NIST SP 800-86, "Guide to Integrating Forensic Techniques into Incident Response,"[4] computer forensics phases involve the following:

- **Collection**   Identifying, labeling, recording, and acquiring data from the possible sources of relevant data, while following procedures that preserve the integrity of the data
- **Examination**   Forensically processing collected data using a combination of automated and manual methods and assessing and extracting data of particular interest, while preserving the integrity of the data

- **Analysis**   Analyzing the results of the examination, using legally justifiable methods and techniques, to derive useful information that addresses the questions that were the impetus for performing the collection and examination

- **Reporting**   Reporting the results of the analysis, which may include describing the actions used, explaining how tools and procedures were selected, determining what other actions need to be performed (for example, forensically examining additional data sources, securing identified vulnerabilities, and improving existing security controls), and providing recommendations for improvement to policies, procedures, tools, and other aspects of the forensic process

Figure 6-2 illustrates the progression and circular nature of the phases. Also included in the illustration is the notion of taking media such as audit logs or tapes and collecting and examining raw data. From the raw data, information comes out of the analysis. Finally, evidence is the result of the forensics phases, if done correctly. These forensics phases certainly may continue or resurface in other phases of the incident response timeline. The important aspect of introducing them in the containment phase of incident response is so that no one begins eradicating, or removing, potential evidence prior to maintaining it appropriately.

Eradication involves removing the cause of the incident and putting measures in place to prevent recurrence. Once the incident has been contained, actions such as deleting malicious code or running antivirus applications to ensure no further infections are taken. If accounts have been compromised, those accounts may be removed from the system or their access credentials changed. Another part of eradication is eliminating or mitigating any vulnerabilities that contributed to the breach or hack. As a simple example, if a user account accesses the system via a virtual private network (VPN) while simultaneously accessing the same account on the local area network and there was no alert, then that vulnerability is closed by adding rules for simultaneous account access. Of course, if multiple systems or accounts were impacted, all evidence of infiltration has to be remediated or the recurrence of the attack is virtually assured. In short, do not move on to system recovery unless and until the eradication is complete.

The final steps of the containment, eradication, and recovery phase is when the systems are put back into operation. In incidents such as losing a physical media with PHI, the recovery activity includes resuming the normal organizational process (for example, tape backup or data destruction). In the recovery activity, additional logging or more tailored controls are put in place because where an incident happens once, it is common for another attack to happen again.

Figure 6-2
Evidence
collection
framework

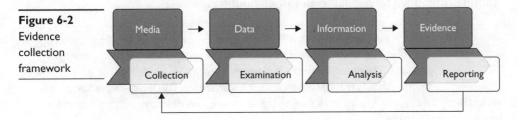

TIP Incident response processes should be integrated with the overall disaster recovery and continuity of operations processes.

Post-incident Activity

The most tempting thing to do after incident response is fully completed is to quickly move on to something else. Think of all the work that has been put on hold while investigations are done, updates are communicated, remediation and recovery actions are taken, and disciplinary actions are discussed. Now that the crisis is past, it is time to get back to "normal." However, after an incident is evaluated and it is determined to be a breach or not, the real final step after recovery is to conduct post-incident activities. This step seems to be omitted more often than not. The incident response team should get together and discuss lessons learned, what happened, what was done well, what could be improved, and what additional resources might be needed to either prevent the next event or help the incident response team work better.

Another perspective on this activity is that all of the information and evidence collected during the incident is useful beyond its use in the case. Things such as the number of hours spent dealing with the incident help decision makers scope resources required and priority of actions taken to prevent the next incident. For instance, the indirect costs of data incidents always include the number of hours staff members are taken from their normal activities to spend on investigation and correction activities. The higher that number and the more it is communicated, the more likely senior decision makers might be to support efforts to prevent recurrence.

Another data point that the team will collect is the nature of the attack, the characteristics of the data, and the root causes of the event (to name a few examples). Any and all relevant factors as to how the incident happened and what occurred can be used to identify weaknesses that were unknown before. Maybe a trend can be identified (such as a cluster of lost or stolen laptops from a certain area or during a specific time). In any case, this type of information is useful for updating risk assessments and evaluating the controls in place.

Finally, the incident response team and process must constantly evaluate itself. In some cases, the team may need to justify itself (resources are always constrained). Using objective data to demonstrate the number of incidents, their duration to close, and (if possible) trend analysis of reducing incidents can influence senior leadership to continue to support an incident response process to the level required. Compliance with having an incident response process and team is equal only to having minimally necessary resources. Successful processes and teams typically need more than what is minimally required by regulators or external influences.

 NOTE Evidence retention is also a function of the post-incident activity. There are usually legal requirements for keeping evidence. Organizations may also have requirements, especially in terms of incidents that do not meet the thresholds for law enforcement involvement. The incident response team would likely be responsible for maintaining the evidence and destroying it appropriately when no longer needed.

Incident Notification and Remediation Efforts

The focus of this chapter is on actions and activities a person working in a healthcare organization who has information privacy and security responsibilities would be expected to take. To that end, most of the concentration in this section is internal notification and remediation. The tasks of actual patient notification and reporting to external regulators are outside the scope of foundational privacy and security responsibilities. However, awareness of what happens once the decision is made to notify patients or involve external regulators is valuable. The linkage between internal and external notification processes demonstrates the importance of the work required by those on the internal incident response team.

Preparation Phase

The first responsibility of an information security and privacy professional is to build a program that stresses reporting errors. No one wants to admit when they have made a mistake. Rarely do people want to get a colleague or co-worker in trouble. Often a potential data breach is first recognized as something that seems out of the ordinary but not alarming. For these reasons, the healthcare workforce may be reluctant to report errors and issues. However, because the first evidence of an incident or event is the people using the systems, their participation is important. Even with sophisticated information technology equipment such as firewalls and intrusion detection systems, human intervention is still a meaningful component of incident notification and remediation. Healthcare organizations can use information technology tools to scan their networks for incidents and events, but people are often the first line of defense. Note that as many as 41 percent of U.S. healthcare organizations have reported data breaches caused by unintentional employee action.[5]

Another aspect to remember when building the incident reporting process is to make it centralized and easy to do and to provide feedback. If the end user has to figure out which office receives PHI incidents versus other types of data incidents, they will be less inclined to report. The easier it is to report, the less likely it is that the end user will rationalize not reporting. And finally, incident reporters require feedback on the initial resolution of their input. A simple acknowledgment of receipt and a contact number to field additional questions (or additional reports) can encourage reporting because the end user sees action upon their concerns.

Participating in incident response requires a sense of urgency. The potential loss of PHI or other sensitive data requires quick and effective actions when security breaches occur. An established team and process in place prior to when they are required can help assure urgency instead of chaos. The team that responds to incidents can do it rapidly and handle incidents systematically (in other words, following a consistent incident handling process). In sum, the role of those responsible for healthcare information security and privacy will be founded upon encouraging error reporting, fostering a sense of urgency, and ensuring the process is conducted systematically.

The following items are a sample of additional responsibilities that are applicable to the preparation phase:

- Reviewing standard operating procedures for incident reporting, system administration, human resource management, and so on, to assure to the greatest extent possible that when an incident occurs, it is handled the same way each time.

- Establishing organizational structure and definition of roles, responsibilities, and levels of authority of the incident reporting team are set in the planning phase. Some relevant levels of authority are

  - The ability to take suspected systems off the network and confiscate equipment as part of the investigation

  - The approval to interview and observe activities in the healthcare organization

Detection and Analysis Phase

In the detection and analysis phase, the incident response team will need to determine the nature of the incident. Incidents can originate from a loss of a laptop, from a web page vulnerability that is exploited, or from an external cyberattack. The examples are almost limitless. Based upon the nature of the incident, the incident response team can fulfill its responsibility to properly determine the actions that are required.

 NOTE Depending on the type of exploit or attack, the incident response team will tailor its actions. If the incident is entirely internal (a lost removable media), certain actions are taken. If the exploit is a malicious piece of software found in an electronic health record (EHR), a different set of actions would be taken. That said, the variety and uncertainty surrounding the nature of the incidents make it imperative to build scenarios and practice the response before the incidents happen.

Here are some examples of relevant responsibilities that are accomplished within the detection and analysis phase:

- Initially evaluating whether there is actually an incident (interrogate false positives)

- Analyzing the precursors and indicators

- Looking for correlating information across the enterprise or complaints from end users

- Searching available incident reporting resources (Internet, internal case files, and so on)

- As more information about the incident surfaces, assessing prioritization or severity ratings

- Determining the internal or external nature of the incident (here will be a variety of possibilities of how much impact the incident is expected to have)

- Escalating results from the incident to keep senior management informed and, if required, getting additional resources or assistance from other departments such as the privacy office, legal review, or human resources

- Engaging system administrators or owners of infiltrated systems, as needed

- Collecting data relative to time and material used to investigate these incidents because they involve so many people from the healthcare organization

  - The "downtime" is often forgotten at the end of a data incident. Even other types of breaches require a great deal of this downtime away from the regular healthcare mission. It comes at a cost.

- Beginning the process of collecting data that may become evidence

Containment, Eradication, and Recovery Phase

There is probably no other responsibility of the incident response team that is more important than evidence collection and preservation, which happens primarily in containment. Of course, information that is collected in the detection phase could serve as evidence too. The responsibilities of the incident response team may now progress into formal digital forensics. As such, the team also serves as the organizational focal point for security incidents as resources are provisioned to triage, respond, and begin to recover.

Evidence gathering and preservation must include proper documentation and handling. The first step is to create a backup of the system that is believed to be infected to be used as evidence. If possible, a second copy could be made to use as a restore copy once vulnerabilities are remediated. The copies need to be stored safely by the incident response team. As mentioned, getting assistance from the healthcare attorney or human resources, for example, can help ensure chain-of-custody elements are preserved or relevant laws are followed. Sometimes, evidence collected in these incidents is used by law enforcement agencies in court cases. Those law enforcement personnel may not have access to the systems as early in the process as the incident response team and will rely on the validity of the evidence collected. A detailed log should be kept for all evidence, including the following:[6]

- Identifying information (for example, the location, serial number, model number, hostname, media access control [MAC] addresses, and IP addresses of a computer)

- Name, title, and phone number of each individual who collected or handled the evidence during the investigation

- Time and date (including time zone) of each occurrence of evidence handling

- Locations where the evidence was stored

Additional activities the healthcare information security and privacy professional can be expected to accomplish include the following:

- Be sure to revisit detection and analysis because it is common to discover additional systems that are impacted by the same incident cause.

- Conduct a thorough investigation.

- Begin eradication once cause and symptoms are considered contained.
- Identify and mitigate all vulnerabilities that were exploited.
- Remove malware, inappropriate materials, and other components.
- Make required changes to information systems (add patches, change code, remove access, and so on).
- Minimize newly discovered vulnerabilities resulting from a security incident.
- Report incident status and resolution information to senior management and the information systems help desk to assist any end users who are reporting concerns.
- Assist senior management in all communications to be made in community updates and notification activities to the media, regulators, and affected individuals.
- Act as liaison with upper management and other teams and organizations, defusing crisis situations, and ensuring that the team continues to have necessary personnel and resources.
- Assist with bringing the systems back to production.
- Confirm normal operations.
  - Unintended consequences can occur. Short-term oversight of active systems is necessary.
- Implement additional or improved monitoring in case of another incident.

Post-incident Activity

Now is when the preparation activity begins for the "next" incident. Of all the resources that are committed to the incident detection and remediation, such as the people, equipment, and skills, each will be compelled to return to normal operations. The healthcare information security and privacy professional will have to assure a proper debriefing is done to gather final data on the metrics collected, assemble lessons learned, and add the latest incident into the scenarios the incident response team will use to train. The following additional, extremely important activities will be required:

- Developing and implementing any new standard operation plans
- Overseeing the corrective action plan if it extends beyond the timeline of the incident
  - For example, a Plan Of Actions and Milestones (POA&M) might include estimated completion dates of certain upgrades or mitigation actions extending out three months, six months, or longer. The tracking and management of these dates cannot be forgotten.
- Issuing a report that details the root cause and total cost of the incident, along with the steps the organization should take to prevent future incidents

- Updating any forms or create new ones based on the efficiency and effectiveness of these communication items during their actual use

- Adding incident causes and outcomes to information security training and awareness programs

TIP A key role for those responsible for information privacy and security in healthcare is to communicate the incident reporting process within the overall security awareness program and user training. Using post-lessons learned helps make the communications relevant to the healthcare organization and the end users.

Incidents Caused by Third Parties

The previous section presupposes incidents that are caused by personnel or contained within systems internal to the healthcare organization. A large percentage of incidents, however, are caused by improper handling of protected health information by a third party (in the United States, a business associate). According to the Ponemon Institute (a privacy and information management research firm) in its fifth annual U.S. Cost of a Data Breach Study, third-party organizations accounted for 41 percent of all breach cases.[7] These remain the most costly form of data breaches because of additional investigation and consulting fees. Similar prevalence of third parties as the cause of the data breach has been found in the European Union. Ponemon also discovered that 33 percent of EU organizations say their data breach involved one or more third parties' "botch," including outsourcers, cloud providers, and business partners.[8] For this reason, incidents that involve actions taken or not taken by third parties are discussed as a separate topic. Keep in mind, the healthcare organizations' incident response team may activate and oversee the overall incident investigation. Based on contractual obligations and legal requirements, the third party will have significant responsibility and should bear the costs of the investigation (and notifications, if required). Figure 6-3 depicts the coordination with third parties that the incident response team may need to oversee.

Preparation Phase

In the preparation phase, responsibilities will include doing the third-party reviews as part of the organizational information risk management program. Making sure you have business associate agreements (U.S.) or model contracts for EU agencies with cross-border data transfer is a preparation activity. Other responsibilities can include the following:

- Implementing and reviewing service level agreements
- Auditing third parties
- Testing third-party data breach scenarios

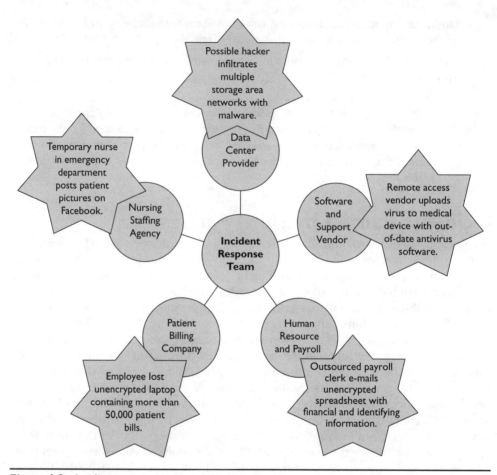

Figure 6-3 Incident response team and third parties

Detection and Analysis Phase

In this phase, the third party suspects a data incident is underway originating in their organization. As they comply with contractual obligations and legal requirements, initial reports come to the healthcare organization in the prescribed timeframe. This report may cause the healthcare organization to activate its incident response team. Additional responsibilities the healthcare information security and privacy professional can expect to perform are as follows:

- Coordinating with the third party during the investigation
- Collaborating any findings of the third party against the healthcare organization's environment
  - In the case of malware, infiltration of the healthcare organization may also be evident as attackers target multiple hosts.

- Escalating the incident within internal reporting processes (senior leadership, vendor management, and so on)
- Assisting the third party in all communications to be made in community updates and notification activities to the media, regulators, and affected individuals
  - The healthcare organization can delegate notification responsibilities but may choose to lead the effort.
- Ensuring third-party actions adhere to contractual obligations and legal requirements
  - Notifications are made in the prescribed manner.
  - Disruptions in services are minimized.

NOTE During incident investigations and data breach notification timeframes, healthcare organizations should implement controls to manage the flow of information through their spokesperson.[9] Normally, one central point of contact is established for any external requests for information. All other employees, including members of the incident response team, are highly discouraged from providing comments to the media or details about the incident to patients. The guidance is to refer these requests to the central point of contact. When there is a toll-free number for patients to call, that number is provided. Having these central contact points readily available (on a web site or broadcast in the media) is not only required but is helpful in controlling rumors, incorrect information, and compromising the investigation.

Containment, Eradication, and Recovery Phase

Much like an incident that originates inside the healthcare organization, the third party will progress to the containment, eradication, and recovery phase. The healthcare organization will closely monitor the progress, whether the incident response team is activated or not. As the third-party determines whether the evidence indicates a data breach, communication with the healthcare organization must continue. The other pertinent responsibilities in monitoring the third-party progress may include the following:

- Assisting with digital forensics to preserve evidence
- Continuing to coordinate any media press releases and notices to regulators and affected individuals once the incident is determined to be a data breach
- If there are interconnections of systems between the third party and the healthcare organization, vulnerability scanning to ensure proper eradication and recovery
- Documenting costs to the healthcare organization as they apply to any downtime, assisting in managing the third-party activities, and checking performance against service level agreements

Post-incident Activity

When the incident is completed, the third party should have a process that is similar to what the healthcare organization has. Lessons learned and additional training on the previous events should be updated into the organization's risk assessments and information security programs. Doing this has been shown to reduce incidents by third-party organizations both in the United States and in the European Union.[10] The following are some other responsibilities to consider in the post-incident phase:

- Including previous incidents in the next risk assessment done by the healthcare organization
- Updating any contractual documents and service level agreements
- Providing any financial data relative to investigation, oversight, and downtime to internal management for possible reimbursement from the third party
- Incorporating third-party incidents into healthcare organization training and awareness as well as incident response team training scenarios

External Reporting Requirements

Responsibilities may be limited to internal activities culminating with notification of senior management. Regardless, an understanding of how the healthcare organization leadership must interact with external agencies during and after an incident is valuable. What follows is an overview of how that interaction should happen and under what conditions.

Law Enforcement

Once an incident is determined to be a crime, senior leadership will want to notify law enforcement. In the United States, this will be authorities like the Federal Bureau of Investigations (FBI) and Secret Service as well as local and state agencies. Internationally, relevant law enforcement agencies will have jurisdiction and should be notified. Law enforcement can assist in the investigation and advise on evidence collection. They also can help determine when additional notification actions might take place, such as delaying notification if it would interfere with an ongoing investigation.

Data Authorities (EU)

As noted, the notification responsibilities in the European Union relate to electronic information and are found in telecommunication industry regulations. However, also noted earlier, this is changing as notification is being integrated into overall privacy doctrine. Currently, when there is a data breach, the data controller (healthcare organization) is encouraged to notify the personal data breach to the competent national authority, much like the provider of commercial telecommunications services is required to do.[11]

Affected Individuals (Patients)

In the United States, healthcare organizations must notify individuals (of any number) once the incident has been evaluated and there has been sufficient risk of disclosure.

 TIP Under HIPAA, the risk of disclosure threshold is important to determine whether the data incident is a breach under the law (impermissible use). According to the U.S. Department of Health and Human Services, "a breach is, generally, an impermissible use or disclosure under the Privacy Rule that compromises the security or privacy of the protected health information." Unless the healthcare organization can show through a risk of disclosure analysis that the protected health information has a low probability of compromise (further disclosure), the disclosure is considered a data breach.

The risk analysis will consist of these considerations:[12]

- The nature and extent of the protected health information involved, including the types of identifiers and the likelihood of re-identification
- The unauthorized person who used the protected health information or to whom the disclosure was made
- Whether the protected health information was actually acquired or viewed
- The extent to which the risk to the protected health information has been mitigated

In the event the risk analysis confirms that the incident is in fact a data breach, healthcare organizations in the United States are mandated to notify affected individuals. Even the form of the notice is prescribed. The individual notice must be within 60 days and in written form by first-class mail or, alternatively, by e-mail if the affected individual has agreed to receive such notices electronically. When the contact information is out of date or incorrect for 10 or more people, the healthcare organization has to take alternative measures. It can post the notice on the organization's web site or engage the media to broadcast the information. The notice in any format must include the following elements:

- A description of the breach
- Types of information that were involved
- What affected individuals can do to reduce chances of additional harm
  - Obtain a credit report, monitor bank accounts, and so on
- A brief description of what the healthcare organization is doing to investigate the breach, mitigate the harm, and prevent further breaches
- Contact information for the covered entity
  - The contact information should include a toll-free number for individuals to call to determine whether they also were affected by the breach.

In the European Union, as the proposed notification rules gain acceptance, the imperative will be to notify the supervisory authorities within 24 hours. The imperative to notify individuals is less stringent. The data controller is permitted to determine whether the data breach is likely to affect the privacy of the individual adversely. If the breach has adverse impact, the data controller may notify the affected individual. The data authorities intend to keep individual notifications to those with adverse impact versus over-notifying individuals and creating notification fatigue.

Media

The media plays a role in broadcasting the nature and extent of the breach. It will also help notify individuals and the community about actions they can take to protect themselves. In the United States, healthcare organizations are required to notify the media (newspapers, television stations, and so on) when the breach impacts 500 residents of a state or jurisdiction. The media press release must happen within 60 days of breach discovery. The content of the media notification will be the same as the elements included in the notification to affected individuals.

Public Relations

While the incident is ongoing, the healthcare organization will continue to interact with the media and the community. Typically, one person serves as the spokesperson for the healthcare organization in front of the media. This helps ensure continuity and reliability of messaging and proper dissemination. Public relations personnel will create press releases to continually update the media and community. These updates may be placed in local newspapers, periodicals, and social media outlets. The public relations personnel may oversee the content that is placed on any web site created and dedicated to communicate data breach issues with affected individuals and other interested parties. In some cases, the lessons learned from the data breach can be shared with other healthcare organizations. Public relations personnel may contribute to this process to help develop the message for others to present or deliver it firsthand at professional organizations' meetings, seminars, and other educational events.

Secretary Health and Human Services

This is very specific to the United States. The notification to regulators includes the Secretary of Health and Human Services (HHS). This notification is done in the event of breaches of 500 or more individuals. Healthcare organizations report the event on the HHS web site and submit an electronic breach form. The 60-day timeline also applies to notifying the HHS. Breaches that involve fewer than 500 individuals are reported in aggregate to HHS on an annual basis no later than 60 days after the end of the same calendar year of the breach.

Health Information Exchanges

In some circumstances, a data breach by a healthcare organization may result in the need to notify other external stakeholders. For instance, in the event a healthcare organization participates in a health information exchange (HIE), the healthcare organization may need to notify the exchange or other member institutions. For now, health information in the HIEs is not considered at risk because the patient records are supposed to be de-identified. However, because of the new organizational relationship resulting from HIEs, healthcare organizations may incur new notification responsibilities.

International Breach Notification

In the United States, unauthorized disclosure of protected health information by organizations subject to HIPAA has straightforward requirements for external notification. In other countries, the external reporting requirements vary. Some of the variations are noted here:

- **Canada**   According to PIPEDA, the external notification of the affected individuals and the Privacy Commissioner is a beneficial practice but voluntary. In select provinces, such as Alberta and Ontario, rules are in place to make external notification mandatory.[13]

- **European Union**   European Commission Regulation (EU) Number 611/2013 of June 2013 mentions appreciation for interest "to notify the competent national authority within 24 hours of all personal data breaches" under the telecommunications law. As far as affected individual notice, the EU deems it necessary only when the personal data breach is likely to adversely affect the personal data or privacy of individuals.[14]

- **China**   There is no general data protection law in China to notify data breaches to the affected individuals or to the regulator. However, there is a national standard of data protection, namely, the Information Security Technology Guideline for Personal Information Protection within Information Systems for Public and Commercial Services (GB/Z 28828-2012, or the "Guideline"), which became effective on February 1, 2013. This is only a technical guidance and has no compulsory legal effect.

- **Israel**   The main data protection national law is the Protection of Privacy Law, 1981. Notification of the affected individuals is recommended but as a preemptive measure to help reduce legal and regulatory damages and fines. There is no obligation.

Chapter Review

The scenario that begins this chapter is familiar to anyone who works in protecting information in healthcare. Identifying incidents is an important component of the overall information security program. Having a proper response through a multidisciplinary team to deal with incidents is crucial once the incident is identified. Some incidents are not data breaches. Other incidents, once they are investigated, are determined to be data breaches, and additional actions are required to manage these activities. An individual who is employed to protect information in a healthcare organization can have numerous responsibilities in these scenarios. Knowing what to do and practicing it beforehand can mean less downtime of systems, minimal lost patient data, and fewer costs to the healthcare organization. This chapter focuses on internal responsibilities, yet an awareness of how internal investigations and reports are used externally is valuable. The healthcare organization, in cases of data breach, has external responsibilities to notify stakeholders such as the community, media, regulators, and patients. Properly conducting the internal incident response processes facilitates future external reporting and notifications.

Review Questions

1. An action that is taken that violates information security policies, acceptable use policies, or standard security practices is a data _____.

   A. event

   B. breach

   C. incident

   D. attack

2. United Kingdom Privacy and Electronic Communications (EC Directive) Regulations 2003 (the PECR) requires who to be notified for personal data breaches?

   A. Affected individuals

   B. Data authorities

   C. Data controllers

   D. European Commission

3. (TRUE or FALSE) In the preparation data incident management phase, policies, processes, procedures, and agreements are established to guide management and response to security incidents.

4. In the containment activities of the incident management process, _____ is accomplished.

5. In digital forensics, which of these best describes a valid activity in the overall process?

   A. Gathering facts to prove the incident is not a breach

   B. Determining the cause for future disciplinary action

   C. Preserving the integrity of the data for later use

   D. Collecting data to ensure manufacturers will honor warranty service

6. An effective healthcare organization incident reporting process should:

   A. Be easy to use

   B. Allow input over the Internet

    C. Be decentralized

    D. Provide cash incentives

7. During an incident, if an individual is reviewing syslogs from other systems across the hospital, you could assume they are performing which responsibility?

    A. Engaging system administrators

    B. Escalating results from the incident

    C. Collecting data relative to time and material

    D. Looking for correlating information

8. (TRUE or FALSE) After a malware attack was contained and remediated, a note to employees was sent by the hospital CIO. The note had instructions about what to do if the employee received a suspicious e-mail that could be a phishing attack. This activity is best described minimizing litigation.

9. Which of these statements is most accurate concerning a risk assessment of third parties that handle protected health information for the healthcare organization?

    A. As a detection phase activity, the risk assessment can find vulnerabilities.

    B. As a post-incident activity, the risk assessment determines whether the incident is a data breach.

    C. As a preparation phase activity, the risk assessment prevents data breaches.

    D. As a containment, eradication, and recovery activity, the risk assessment documents all actions are complete.

10. The key difference between U.S. and international data breach notification laws is:

    A. Affected individual notification

    B. Regulatory fines

    C. Encryption standards

    D. Damage to reputation

Answers

1. C. This is the definition of a data incident. If the incident, after investigation, proves to have impermissible disclosure, then it could be a data breach. However, not all incidents are data breaches. An event is any observable occurrence in a system or network, which can include legitimate events. An attack implies external action and does not adequately satisfy the definition in the question.

2. B. The regulation specifically requires notification to the supervisory data authorities. The regulation does not require notification to affected individuals. The European Commission may receive the notification, but there

are supervisory data authorities that should receive the notifications. Data controllers are the entities that actually make the notifications to the data authorities.

3. **TRUE.** In the preparation phase, the responsible individuals on the incident response team should collect and compile the relevant documentation that will guide the incident response process.

4. **Collecting evidence.** Evidence is collected and preserved during the containment activity within the containment, eradication, and recovery phase of incident management.

5. **C.** In digital forensics, there are several activities that take place. While there may be an indirect benefit to supporting disciplinary actions or preserving warranties, these are not valid reasons to conduct digital forensics. In fact, digital forensics should be accomplished without a goal of proving a data breach or disproving one. The evidence should be collected to determine cause and impact. Preserving the integrity of the data for future use (such as legal proceedings) is the only valid answer of these choices.

6. **A.** While cash incentives might encourage incident reporting, it is probably not necessary. Being able to input suspected data incidents over the Internet is not as useful as simply having an easy-to-use process that includes all the different ways to report incidents. In fact, some personnel may be frustrated by having to use a web site to report incidents. The incident reporting process should also be centralized, not decentralized. In sum, the process must be easy or it will not be used.

7. **D.** During an incident, the incident response team will check for additional incidents and any indications that an incident is occurring. The other options are also responsibilities accomplished during an incident, but not by reviewing activity on the syslog.

8. **FALSE.** In post-incident activity phase, adding lessons learned to new training and awareness communications is important. The action described in this question would not have much effect on any pending litigation or fines.

9. **C.** All risk assessments of third parties who handle health information should be conducted in the preparation phase. All of the other phases happen after the incident occurs. The risk assessment can help prevent data breaches in that vulnerabilities may be found and fixed before they are exploited.

10. **A.** The major difference in U.S. and international data breach notification law is the fact that the United States mandates that affected individuals are notified, and internationally the requirement is by and large voluntary (but encouraged). As far as regulatory fines and encryption standards go, these are similar considerations for the United States and international healthcare providers. Damage to reputation happens to any organization that has a data breach, although some data suggests the damage is not as bad as it was in previous years.

PART I

References

1. U.S. Department of Health and Human Services. "Modifications to the HIPAA Privacy, Security, Enforcement, and Breach Notification Rules Under the Health Information Technology for Economic and Clinical Health Act and the Genetic Information Nondiscrimination Act; Other Modifications to the HIPAA Rules." 45 CFR Parts 160 and 164. p. 74. 2013. Accessed on April 2, 2014, at www.gpo .gov/fdsys/pkg/FR-2013-01-25/pdf/2013-01073.pdf

2. European Union Agency for Network and Information Security. "Triage." Accessed on April 3, 2014, at https://www.enisa.europa.eu/activities/cert/support/incident-management/browsable/incident-handling-process/incident-handling-phases/triage-1

3. Swire, Peter, and Sol Bermann. Information Privacy Official Reference for the Certified Information Privacy Professional (CIPP) International Association of Privacy Professionals. Paperback Publisher, 2007. p. 193.

4. NIST Special Publication 800-86. Guide to Integrating Forensic Techniques into Incident Response. August 2006. p. ES-1. Accessed on April 1, 2014, at http://csrc.nist.gov/publications/nistpubs/800-86/SP800-86.pdf

5. Swire, Peter P., Kenesa Ahmad, and Terry McQuay. Foundations of Information Privacy and Data Protection: A Survey of Global Concepts, Laws and Practices. International Association of Privacy Professionals, 2012. p. 106.

6. NIST Special Publication 800-61 rev 2. Computer Security Incident Handling Guide. August 2012. p. 45. Accessed on April 1, 2014, at http://csrc.nist.gov/publications/nistpubs/800-61rev2/SP800-61rev2.pdf

7. Ponemon Institute. "2011 Cost of Data Breach Study: United States." March 2012. p.8. Accessed April 19, 2014, at www.ponemon.org/local/upload/file/2011_US_CODB_FINAL_5.pdf

8. Ponemon Institute. "2011 Cost of Data Breach Study: United Kingdom." March 2012. p.9. Accessed on April 19, 2014, at www.symantec.com/content/en/us/about/media/pdfs/b-ponemon-2011-cost-of-data-breach-uk.en-us.pdf

9. European Network and Information Security Agency (ENISA), "Good Practice Guide for Incident Management." 2010. p.76. Accessed on April 20, 2014, at https://www.enisa.europa.eu/activities/cert/support/incident-management/files/good-practice-guide-for-incident-management?searchterm=incident+management

10. Ponemon Institute. "2011 Cost of Data Breach Study: United States." March 2012. p.1. Accessed on April 19, 2014, at www.ponemon.org/local/upload/file/2011_US_CODB_FINAL_5.pdf and Ponemon Institute. "2011 Cost of Data Breach Study: United Kingdom." March 2012. p.1. Accessed on April 19, 2014, at www.symantec.com/content/en/us/about/media/pdfs/b-ponemon-2011-cost-of-data-breach-uk.en-us.pdf

11. Directive 2009/136/EC10 of the European Parliament of the Council of 25 November 2009. Accessed on April 6, 2014, at http://eur-lex.europa.eu/ LexUriServ/LexUriServ.do?uri=OJ:L:2009:337:0011:01:EN:HTML

12. Department of Health and Human Services. "Breach Notification Rule: Definition of a Breach." Accessed on April 14, 2014, at www.hhs.gov/ocr/ privacy/hipaa/administrative/breachnotificationrule

13. DeJesus, Ron. The Privacy Advisor (IAPP). "Exploring Federal Privacy Breach Notification in Canada." April 1, 2013. Accessed on April 10, 2014, at https:// www.privacyassociation.org/publications/2013_04_01_exploring_federal_privacy_ breach_notification_in

14. Vivet-Tana, Laura. The Privacy Advisor (IAPP). "EU Data Breach Notification Rule: The Key Elements." August 27, 2013. Accessed on April 2, 2014, at https:// www.privacyassociation.org/publications/eu_data_breach_notification_rule_ the_key_elements

PART II

Healthcare Information Privacy and Security Management

CHAPTER 7

Information Privacy: Patient Rights and Healthcare Responsibilities

In this chapter, you will learn to

- Distinguish among the relevant general privacy terms applicable to healthcare
- Recognize how privacy protects patient rights and supports the confidentiality of the healthcare information
- Appreciate the role of and requirement for the healthcare privacy officer
- Understand the prevailing data privacy concepts that make up leading privacy frameworks
- Comprehend measures required under privacy principles related to data breach, including requirements for notifying affected individuals

This book is very clear in its intentions. Within healthcare, the roles and responsibilities of those who are charged with protecting information converge around distinct roles that may or may not have involved working with digital or electronic information previously. Some roles originate from traditional privacy or legal roles in health information management, where there is a shift from information being stored on paper to being stored in digital format; others come from information technology support backgrounds, such as local area networking, application management, and end-user support, where new concerns over protected health information is relevant. Still others may come from the clinical engineering or biomedical technician professions, where the interconnectivity of medical devices to each other and to internal and external networks is rapidly evolving. To help you visualize this convergence, Figure 7-1 depicts the intersection. For these previously distinct and somewhat separated communities, a primer is needed, both in privacy compliance for those with stronger backgrounds in security and in security for those with stronger backgrounds in privacy compliance. Chapter 7 provides such a primer for those who now have a responsibility for complying with information privacy in healthcare, and Chapter 8 does the same for those with traditional privacy or legal compliance roles in healthcare who now have increasing roles in protecting digital information through information security management.

Figure 7-1
Convergence
of healthcare
competencies
with information
privacy and
security
responsibilities

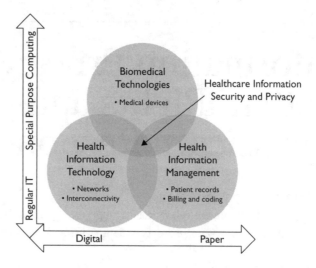

 NOTE The distinction between privacy and security has begun to narrow. Some advocate that privacy is a concept embedded in the practice of providing information security or cybersecurity. However, for purposes of this text, we will maintain a distinction. This chapter presents information privacy as a function of what is being protected and why. Chapter 8 will address security by defining how an organization can protect the information.

U.S. Approach to Privacy

The United States does not apply a data privacy policy across all industries and data collectors. Due to a variety of factors, and to maintain a free-market economy, the United States approaches data privacy from a sector, or functional perspective. The central principle in this approach is that government does not set a singular policy that transcends the industries. Instead, each industry is governed by a combination of self-imposed guidelines and government-originated regulations specific to that industry. What results is incremental legislation that is focused on specific concerns (for example, the Video Privacy Protection Act of 1988, the Cable Television Protection and Competition Act of 1992, the Fair Credit Reporting Act, and the 2010 Massachusetts Data Privacy Regulations).

The reasoning behind this approach stems from the U.S. Constitution and traditional American laissez-faire economics. Additionally, privacy in the United States tends to be defined as what society is willing to accept, and that can change significantly over time. Under the construct of the U.S. Constitution, it has always been seen as outside the purview of the federal government to regulate privacy. Privacy laws are most effective at the state level. Within industries like healthcare and with legislation such as HIPAA, laws are best implemented with a focus on the purpose and use of the information.

European Approach to Privacy

The European Union approached the concept of privacy from a very different perspective than the United States. Because of historical experiences such as World War II, fascist government regimes, and post–World War II Communist regimes, Europeans have a natural suspicion and fear of intrusive, unnecessary, unfettered access to personal information. This is not only reflected in the over-arching data protection approach in the European Union's Data Protection Directive (DPD) but also in how the European Union sees data transfer to non-EU nations. Additionally, there is a variation between the European Union and other nations in what identifiers are considered personal information. For instance, the European Union includes race, ethnicity, and union status as protected, sensitive information. The impact of identifying someone based on these was once the catalyst for secret denunciations from neighbors and friends in the 1930s. This led to apprehensions of select individuals and groups (for example, Jewish citizens) that sent friends and neighbors to work camps and concentration camps. The European Union takes significant steps to protect personal information from abuses by implementing and enforcing comprehensive data protection laws.

Information Privacy Concepts and Terms

Maintaining the privacy of individuals is a concern that spans the globe, is important in all industries, and has long been a focus. Collecting the required information to perform a needed or desired service and share the information appropriately while maintaining an individual's privacy is a challenge. We see the importance of an individual's privacy as more than a political or business imperative. In some communities it is a moral or religious concern. The Koran, the Bible, and Jewish law, historically, all have provisions for protecting an individual's privacy. In 1948, the United Nations published the *Universal Declaration of Human Rights*. In Article 12, they agreed, in part, that, no one "shall be subjected to arbitrary interference with his privacy, …."[1]

The importance of protecting the privacy of the individual in healthcare is no less universal and no less fundamental. The need for the physician to maintain physician-patient privilege by keeping the examination, diagnosis, and treatment of the patient confidential and not divulging information about them to the caregivers is found as far back as the Hippocratic Oath (believed to have originated in the fifth century, B.C.) and has survived antiquity to become a moral compass for providers of healthcare even today: "What I may see or hear in the course of the treatment or even outside of the treatment in regard to the life of men, which on no account one must spread abroad, I will keep to myself, holding such things shameful to be spoken about."[2]

We can draw the conclusion from these data points in and outside of healthcare that having an understanding of the concepts and terms that underlie information privacy is essential. In many countries today, protection of individual privacy is seen as a fundamental human right.

The following concepts and definitions are found in the leading privacy frameworks and regulations. Minor differences may exist across these, particularly where terms are combined to make one principle rather than two distinct principles in the framework.

Once you have read and understood the general concepts and terms, you will certainly want to familiarize yourself with the various frameworks and regulations that originate and promulgate them. This is not a comprehensive list, but a starting point:

- Health Insurance Portability and Accountability Act (HIPAA) Privacy Rule
- Asia-Pacific Economic Cooperation (APEC)
- European Union's Data Protection Directive (DPD)
- Fair Credit Reporting Act (FCRA)
- Organisation for Economic Co-operation and Development (OECD)
- Generally Accepted Privacy Principles (GAPP): Designed by the Canadian Institute of Chartered Accountants (CICA) and the American Institute of Certified Public Accountants (AICPA)
- Personal Information Protection and Electronic Documents Act (PIPEDA)

Consent

The sharing of an individual's personal information is initially governed by the individual, as consent must be obtained from the individual to do so. Consent is an action typically taken prior to the release of information, whereby the individual pre-approves such a release. For consent to be legal, a few conditions must be satisfied: Individuals must provide consent voluntarily and must also be informed about their rights, one of which is that it is okay to change their minds after they provide consent. Of course, individuals must also be able to understand these conditions and be capable of communicating their decisions. In healthcare, consent generally is not required for purposes of treatment, payment, and operations. In the United States, the HIPAA Privacy Rule[3] makes that clear. However, for other uses and disclosures for research and public health reporting, additional patient consent may be required. This differs from international healthcare information sharing in that the data privacy rules, such as those established in the European Union by the DPD, tend not to make a healthcare exclusion. Consent is required for collecting, storing, and using data that identifies the individual for patient care or otherwise. Where consent by the individual is impossible, patient care is not impeded, however, because under such circumstances next of kin or a competent official may provide the level of consent required. As soon as individuals are able to provide consent for themselves, they do. Along with informed consent, a data collector under the DPD has to disclose any specific intent in order to best inform the individual of how the information is to be used and by whom.

 NOTE *Consent* and *informed consent* are related terms. *Consent* is a term that applies across industries and privacy frameworks. Although *informed consent* also has broad implications, within healthcare it relates to giving permission to perform a procedure or test on the individual.

Choice

Choice is defined under various privacy standards as giving an individual the option of whether to freely provide the information or withhold it. The distinction between *choice* and *consent* is that choice is about providing options, whereas consent is about providing permission. The choice offered to an individual must be between legitimate options, and the options must be presented in a clear manner without deception. Choice is offered through opt-in and opt-out provisions. One version of opt-in or opt-out provisions for legitimate data collection and sharing is where the healthcare organization provides a statement about the choice. An organization can structure their opt-in and opt-out processes in multiple ways to obtain patient choice. If the individual does nothing, it is an implicit opt-in or opt-out choice by default; if the individual makes an active choice (by selecting or unselecting an option), it is an explicit choice. When collecting sensitive information, it is best to require the individual to make an explicit opt-in or opt-out choice. Examples of implicit and explicit opt-in and opt-out statements are shown in Figure 7-2.

With the growing adoption of electronic health records (EHRs), the opt-in or opt-out choice can have a profound impact. When providing consent to receive care, patients should be offered an informed choice if that information is collected into the EHR and then automatically shared as part of a health information exchange (HIE). This additional sharing is outside of what the patient may expect. Therefore, added consent is required. To receive such informed consent, either by opting in or opting out, providers might have to provide notice to thousands of patients, which is logistically difficult and costly.[4]

 TIP It is easy to confuse the appropriate use of the terms *opt in* and *opt out*. For instance, a patient portal web site might provide a choice for patients to opt in to the healthcare organization's data collection and storage system by selecting a check box that reads, "I agree to the terms and conditions found in the hospital privacy statement." In this case, the check box should not be prechecked, as a preselected, affirmative statement would be more appropriately defined as an explicit opt-out choice.

Figure 7-2
Examples of implicit and explicit opt-in and opt-out statements

Preselected (must be unselected to indicate choice):

> ☑ I understand the privacy practices terms and conditions. (Opt-in, implicit)
> ☑ Do not share my information with third parties. (Opt-in, implicit)

Not preselected (must be selected to indicate choice):

> ☐ I understand the privacy practices terms and conditions. (Opt-in, explicit)
> ☐ Do not share my information with third parties. (Opt-in, explicit)

The explicit statements are best when collecting or using sensitive data.

Notice

The ability to provide choice and consent is related very closely to the organization's responsibility to provide notice to the affected individual. In the United States, health-care organizations are required to provide notice to patients upon enrollment, at the time of the first appointment, when receiving healthcare services (for example, before undergoing procedures), and any time a patient asks to see such documentation. Notice, as a privacy principle, is satisfied when the patient signs an acknowledgment of understanding of the Notice of Privacy Practices (NPP) published by that healthcare organization. The NPP contains the following:

- An explanation of how the covered entity's protected health information may be used and disclosed. (If the healthcare organization is required to use it in any other way, it will get the patient's permission or authorization first.)
- The healthcare organization's acknowledgement of its duties to protect health information privacy.
- The patient's privacy rights, which include the right to view the information on hand, the right to file a complaint with the U.S. Federal Government (specifically, the Department of Health and Human Services) if a violation is suspected, and the right to request an amendment to the record if it is incorrect.
- Contact information relative to the privacy practices and complaint process.

The NPP is generally in paper form and presented to the patient at the required occasions, but the NPP must also be prominently displayed on a web site providing information about the healthcare organization's services or benefits.

In contrast to a *healthcare* privacy framework, the *data* privacy framework of the European Union's DPD seeks notice every time data subjects have their data collected. Depending on the individual's preference for the content and frequency of these notices, the DPD allows for a data collector to provide a choice to data subjects to "opt in" or "opt out" of notices based on various criteria. This can help allow the individual to receive notice at a level of detail or frequency that is manageable and meaningful.

Collection Limitation

A principle common across data protection best practices and regulations is the *collection limitation principle,* which adheres to a basic tenet regarding data protection: Only collect what is necessary and nothing more. Numerous data breaches are caused or exacerbated by persistent data that was never really needed but was collected, stored, maintained, and ultimately lost along with the necessary data sets. Think about the forms we ask patients to fill out while waiting, or the web forms we ask our customers to fill out prior to gaining access to an online service. If all of that information is required—or relevant, as the collection limitation principle generally states—then it probably follows the collection limitation principle. However, if some of that information is not needed or the data collector used it for a purpose other than that intended by the individual providing it, the practice is inappropriate. The inappropriate use of such information is addressed by the collection limitation principle, which states that data should be collected by fair and lawful means and that, when necessary, notice should be given to the individual or their consent obtained.[5]

Frameworks such as the European Union's DPD mandate collection limitation via a purpose specification provided to the individual, and the data collector is constrained to using the data only for those stated purposes. In the United States, HIPAA introduces the concept of a *limited data set* under the Privacy Rule; this is one in which the unneeded protected health information elements are either stripped out or are never collected. Elements such as one's name, social security number, and date of birth, for example, combined with some form of health information, are selectively collected and retained. Other elements that are also present in the record, but not needed by the data recipient, for instance, home address, are selectively extracted and transferred. The similarity between this and other privacy control sets is the focus on collecting only what is needed and only for a stated purpose.

Disclosure Limitation

In addition to the healthcare organization collecting only relevant health-related information, it must limit the disclosure of that information. The constraints of that limitation are twofold. First, the information can be disclosed only based on prevailing law. For instance, the HIPAA Privacy Rule permits a covered healthcare provider to use or disclose protected health information for treatment, payment, or operations. Second, disclosure can be made only if the organization has obtained consent from the individual. Any use or disclosure outside of these parameters is either illegal (HIPAA) or a violation of the consent authorization provided by the individual. That said, just because it is legal to disclose information does not necessarily mean the use of such information cannot be further limited. As noted, HIPAA allows providers to share information for purposes of treatment. Instances exist where health information related to one individual may assist a second provider in the treatment of another person. If the initial patient specified that this use or disclosure was impermissible, that disclosure should not be made. This applies, for example, in cases of genetic testing or predisposition of patients to certain diseases. While such information may or may not be relevant to family members for their own treatment, the individual may restrict disclosure. In short, HIPAA may authorize such disclosure, but it does not mandate it. Disclosure can be further limited by patient-provider agreement.

Minimum Use and Proportionality

When using protected health information (PHI), the healthcare organization must first determine that the disclosure does not violate the disclosure limitation principle, and then it must disclose only the minimum necessary information. For instance, if an audit log is required by law enforcement because a hospital employee is suspected of snooping in a medical record, producing an entire access log for all personnel on a certain day, showing all accessed or modified patient information, would be inappropriate because it would involve not only disclosure of the name of the hospital employee and the PHI he or she accessed but possibly also a tremendous amount of PHI irrelevant to the investigation. The idea of "proportionality" is related very closely to minimum use and is actually a term found in the DPD. Under European law, data collectors must ensure that personal data may be processed only insofar as it is adequate, relevant, and not excessive in relation to the purposes for which it is collected and/or further processed.[6] While the additional data might be useful at a later date or for another purpose unrelated to the patient's current visit, that data should not be collected.

Retention of Data

A very important step in the life cycle of information, especially sensitive information, is the destruction of data that is no longer needed. For a variety of reasons, institutions that collect and store data often make the mistake of retaining the data well past the time that it is remains useful. One reason for this is that data has evolved from paper-based to digital information, and space considerations for storage have become minimal concerns. Even the cost of storing increasing amounts of data has decreased over time. Conversely, in the past, when actual physical space was required to house paper records, organizations had a significant motivation to set standards for how long information could be retained. Once it was no longer useful or required to be maintained due to a regulatory requirement, policies would require data destruction, shredding, burning, or off-site archival of paper records. Then additional space was made available for newer records or for other purposes. Another reason that excessively lengthy data retention is often overlooked is that once information is no longer useful, data collectors forget about it. If there are years and years of data on a hard drive or storage area network, the older data may be completely forgotten in terms of who the data identifies, why it is being maintained, if it is still accurate, and so on. Yet the data remains in the possession of the data collector. Additional reasons exist as to why data retention is often overlooked, but the point is, it cannot be. A significant risk for data breach is caused by the fact that data retention policies and procedures do not keep pace with the transfer of information to digital storage systems and with digital technology.

Retention of data should begin with identifying what types of data are being stored and how long the data must be retained. In some cases, there are regulations that govern this. HIPAA, the DPD, and other global guidelines have various requirements. In healthcare, how long the information is considered clinically relevant also matters. Some pediatric radiology images are required to be kept at least 18 years. Other radiology images are required to be maintained for 99 years in the case of asbestos-related lung disease. These are outside of privacy guidelines but extremely important for anyone with data retention policy and procedure responsibilities.

Legitimate Purpose

If we are to state the purpose of the data collection, collect it in a lawful or fair manner, and only use the data for the stated purpose, we must also be sure the purpose is a legitimate one. *Legitimate purpose* is a principle that takes collection limitation a step further. A healthcare organization in the United States must collect the patient information only as that information assists in the provision of treatment, payment, or operations. If the organization is sharing that information, it must still limit disclosure to reasons that are defined as legitimate under the law. One such provision is in public health information sharing.[7] To carry out public health and safety responsibilities, healthcare organizations are permitted to provide data access to public health authorities and those who have a public health mission. This provision extends to those third parties who handle PHI for the healthcare organization. If the third party is required to disclose PHI to public health entities, that disclosure expectation should be stated in the business associate agreement. Legitimate purpose is comparable to the European Union's DPD in that the DPD allows personal data to be processed only for specified explicit and legitimate purposes. If the purpose of collecting or processing the data changes over time, the DPD mentions a related privacy concept called *fair processing*, which basically instructs the data collector to get an additional or updated consent from the individual if the processing of the data changes from the legitimate purpose originally presented to the individual.

Individual Participation

One of the central tenants of all privacy principles is the acknowledgment that privacy works best when the affected individuals are active and involved in the use of their data. The Organisation for Economic Co-operation and Development (OECD) privacy principles clearly outline the privacy rights individuals have in this regard, many of which are reflected in subtopics such as notice, consent, choice, and access and correction—the topic that follows. In short, HIPAA, for example, was enacted in 1996 in large part because the principle of individual participation in the use and disclosure of a patient's health information was too often seen as the property of the healthcare organization. HIPAA helped to rectify this by clearly outlining the rights of the individuals to have access to, and to participate in, the use of their healthcare information.

Access and Correction

Whether you are referencing the Personal Information Protection and Electronic Documents Act (PIPEDA) in Canadian law, the DPD in the European Union, or the HIPAA Privacy Rule in the United States, you will find provisions around the right of individuals to request access to their personal information that the organization collected. Furthermore, individuals should be given the ability to correct, or rectify, any such information that they believe to be in error. In a healthcare setting, changing some information may not be permissible under other governing medical-legal considerations. However, the annotation of the individual record can be done to highlight the alleged discrepancy. In other cases, if the record can be fixed, there are provisions to do so. In the European Union, data subjects also have the right to have the data controller notify all third parties that received the data in error, in order to correct the record. When we see the havoc that medical identity theft can have on an individual's life and financial state, having the right to access health information and correct the record is a very important right. Imagine a person whose insurance rates increase because someone is receiving care under his or her identity. That individual may initially be the only one to suspect something is wrong. Only by individuals having the right to access their information in a timely manner and without excessive cost can fraud and personal distress be limited.

NOTE Accounting of disclosures is a concept related to the right of access under HIPAA. Along with a right to access the record, the individual has the right to know to whom their PHI was disclosed.

Complaints and Enforcement

Within the privacy frameworks and laws, requirements exist that allow individuals to file complaints if they suspect their information is breached. The regulatory agencies must also investigate these claims and enforce the rules and laws as they pertain. In the United States, the Department of Health and Human Services (HHS) hosts a web site that has collected over 84,000[8] complaints since 2003, the year the HIPAA Privacy Rule went into effect. In the European Union, as in the United States, these privacy laws have provisions for individuals to bring civil law suits against providers. The regulatory agencies can bring criminal charges as well. Figure 7-3 shows the increase over time of these complaints from individuals in the U.S. to the HHS, especially after amendments to HIPAA were enacted via the HITECH Act/American Recovery and Reinvestment Act (ARRA)in 2009 and the Omnibus HIPAA Final Rule in 2013.

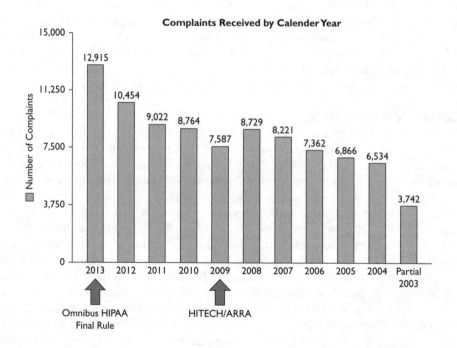

Figure 7-3 Graph showing complaints received by calendar year

Quality of Data

While we collect and disclose data appropriately and give patients the ability to review and request rectification of errors, we also must be proactive. To this end, another principle that is important in information privacy is the *quality* of the data, which comprises three main considerations:

- Accuracy
- Integrity
- Completeness

Accuracy of the data is vital in that patient safety and patient care will be at risk if the accuracy of data is not verified and protected. Imagine if data elements such as height, weight, and date of birth were not accurate and medication dosage decisions were based on these parameters. Related to accuracy is data *integrity*. There must be methods in place to check to see if data that was collected and recorded accurately at some point was changed or altered. One of the fears about medical devices becoming infected with malicious software has to do with the possibility that data integrity may be at risk. A virus that alters time stamps of files and corrupts them can wreak havoc on patient monitoring systems. Finally, *completeness* of data is referenced in the DPD, which requires that member states ensure that data is accurate but also kept up-to-date. Over time, additional data may be required to complete the data record or correct any inaccuracy. These additions or rectifications must be included in the record with the same focus on privacy as the original data set.

Accountability

The entities that collect privacy-protected data are held accountable to adhere to the provisions that govern them. Under HIPAA, healthcare organizations in the United States are held accountable to protect the confidentiality of PHI. Fair information practices that originated in the United States also guide data collectors to be accountable. In the DPD, data subjects are expected to have a method available to them to hold data collectors accountable. Accountability is the reason why fines and penalties often result when data collectors do not adequately protect the information they collect.

Openness and Transparency

Because personally identifying information can be sensitive, especially to the person who is providing it, best practices in privacy and data collection tend to insist on both openness and transparency. At the core is trust. Patients can be reluctant to seek care or may withhold relevant information from their providers when they do not trust that the information is protected during use. They may not trust the process simply because they are not informed of how the healthcare organization manages the sensitive information on their behalf. Therefore, to better assure individuals how their information is collected, used, and disclosed, openness and transparency by the data collector is imperative. In healthcare, it can be a patient care issue if the patient is not made aware of the relevant practices, as well as how they may make reasonable choices about how their information is used.

According to the HIPAA Privacy Rule, compliance with the Notice of Privacy Practices (NPP) helps a healthcare organization provide openness and transparency. The content of the NPP discloses the following in plain language to individuals[9]:

- The various ways in which the healthcare organization will use and disclose the individual's protected health information.

- What rights the individual has and what he or she can do to if the individual wishes to exercise his or her rights. A process for filing a complaint with the healthcare organization, for example, must be described in the event the individual believes his or her information has been used in an unauthorized manner.

- A statement asserting the healthcare organization has legal obligations to protect the individual's information.

- A contact within the healthcare organization from whom the individual can get more information about the healthcare organization's privacy policies.

An effective date must be included. For openness and transparency to be relevant, such notice of policies and procedures should be provided in a timely manner prior to collecting or disclosing the information. Moreover, because healthcare information is increasingly kept or created in digital format and increasingly shared among organizations (payers and other providers), a framework that specifically addresses openness and transparency between external agencies is complementary to building the trust that an NPP supports internally between patient and provider. In the United States, a HIPAA-related framework that helps implement the openness and transparency principles (among other privacy and security principles) is the Nationwide Privacy and Security Framework for Electronic Exchange of Individually Identifiable Health Information.[10] This framework recognizes how the privacy principles must be extended and expected between unaffiliated healthcare organizations for the benefit of patient trust and patient care.

Openness

We should make the distinction between openness and transparency. The concept of *openness* maintains that organizations that collect personal information should disclose that the information exists, that it is kept secure, how it is processed, or with whom it is shared. The OECD privacy principles require a general policy of openness about "developments, practices, and policies"[11] relative to individually identifiable data that an organization collects and uses. This principle includes the ability of individuals to know who has their data, where it is located, and how it is primarily used. In comparison, the United States Privacy Act of 1974 requires federal government agencies to publish a system of records notice (SORN) in the Federal Register. A *system of records*[12] is one or more records in a collection that is started or maintained by a federal government agency using personally identifiable information to store and retrieve the information. Publishing the existence of such databases helps the U.S. Government to achieve openness.

Transparency

When a patient discloses a significant amount of sensitive information that may include social security number, date of birth, or a history of mental illness he or she has endured, one can imagine the general reluctance and fear that accompanies it. This is, in part, due to the fact that the patient is not sure who will see the information or how it will be shared. Once the information is provided, the patient loses control. *Transparency,* as a privacy concept, requires organizations to address the mystery of how the information will be used. Although it is not healthcare specific, the DPD includes the right of individuals to know specifically how their data is maintained, processed, and shared. Under U.S. law (HIPAA), the provision for providing patients the right to receive an accounting of PHI disclosures would satisfy the principle of transparency.

Designation of Privacy Officer

Many of the regulatory requirements found in different countries (including HIPAA in the United States) require that organizations appoint (in writing) a privacy officer. This position usually requires a very specific background, including appropriate education, experience, and training. This individual's job is to ensure compliance with laws and regulations regarding privacy requirements, and to include developing policies and processes supporting compliance. Of course, that is not all they must do. Privacy officers must ensure that NPPs are used, that they are prominently displayed, and that patients acknowledge them. The privacy officer is a main point of contact on issues related to using PHI for marketing, research, and fundraising. He or she also centrally administers policies and procedures related to requests for correction or amendment of health records by patients, or requests for additional protection of PHI that is shared confidentially. Patients and staff who have questions or concerns about privacy matters can rely on advice and guidance from the privacy officer.

Probably the most important responsibility of the privacy officer is handling complaints from patients about data handling. In addition, when data breaches occur, the privacy officer becomes the central resource in the healthcare organization's response internally, to regulators, sometimes to patients, and often to the board.

The organization's privacy officer faces a monumental task. That person has the responsibility to develop an organizational culture working toward data protection. The privacy officer requires help in order to achieve this, starting with the appropriate privacy and security policies developed, approved, and promulgated throughout the organization. This officer also requires a workforce that is trained and aware of the importance of data protection and privacy. Note, however, that it's not just the privacy officer's responsibility to protect data; everyone in the organization has the responsibility to protect privacy.

Assisting the privacy officer should be a support staff that handles the day-to-day administrative tasks and issues associated with regulatory compliance and investigations, and manages the overall privacy program in the organization. Depending on the size of the organization, the staff may be very small or very large. As managers, privacy officers must delegate some of the day-to-day tasks and responsibilities to their staff. However, the staff must understand that the privacy officer holds the ultimate responsibility and accountability for the program.

Promises and Obligations

To make privacy principles work, an organization must understand that its actions in providing information privacy amount to making promises, which result in obligations. Remember, if privacy principles describe what we are to protect, the acknowledgment of those principles is often contained in a written document such as an NPP or a contract, either one of which is legally enforceable. Although not specifically found in the privacy principles and concepts covered in this chapter, information privacy in practice requires an understanding of a few additional concepts.

Data Protection Governing Authority

In the United States, the governing body for the protection of healthcare data is primarily the Department of Health and Human Services (HHS). Enforcement actions reside in the Office of Civil Rights (OCR)—an entity under HHS direction. In contrast, the European Union requires that each member state set up an independent body to monitor the data protection level in that member state. These governing entities are called *data protection authorities* or *supervisory authorities*.[13] They govern data controllers who collect the individually identifiable information in their states and advise the government about compliance with the DPD. When there are violations, the data protection authority has jurisdiction and reports infractions to the European Union. Individuals have the right and the ability to directly complain to the data protection authority. When a data controller is going to collect data, it must register this process in a public register, with the data protection authority aware of this collection. Relevant rationale and specific data to be collected must be included in the registration. This includes the purpose for collection and a description of the data to be collected. Two additional important disclosures the data collector must make are whether or not transfers of data to foreign countries are proposed and how the data will be protected while being processed.

The data protection authority must also oversee any transfer of sensitive data from a data collector to another entity, making sure that appropriate safeguards are in place. Data collectors must seek and receive specific authorization in order to minimize risks of unauthorized disclosure. In the event the data collector desires to transfer sensitive data across borders from the European Union to another nation (for example, the United States), the data protection authority seeks and requires compliance with the Safe Harbor treaty, as defined in Chapter 3, or obtains other equivalent assurance that data will be processed with the same or better standards as those required under European Union law.

Breach Notification

Data breach notification is part of the overall process of enforcing privacy guidelines and laws. The term *breach*, in this context, is used to describe an unauthorized disclosure, whether intentional or not. Most often, data breach requires notification to authorities or to the affected individual. Each individual country, state, and other region (as in the European Union) has its own specific requirements for breach notifications. You should deftly understand the requirements for breach notification in your geographical area. Frankly, not properly reporting a data breach internally, and then externally, as applicable, will put your organization in a position that is indefensible and that can incur additional, unnecessary fines and penalties.

United States

To comply with HIPAA as it has been amended most recently by the Omnibus HIPAA Final Rule (2013), healthcare providers have very specific notification requirements. First, the threshold for when to notify is very clear. The law establishes a "risk of disclosure"[14] standard that a healthcare organization must measure against. For instance, when a healthcare organization suspects that health information may have been disclosed in an unauthorized manner, it must determine how great a risk exists that the information was actually viewed or used by an unauthorized recipient. An unencrypted e-mail sent to a valid recipient may not necessarily constitute a reportable breach if the e-mail was not intercepted or sent to other unauthorized recipients. In that case, there is no risk of unauthorized disclosure, and no additional reporting is required. However, if the information may have been disclosed (for example, as a result of a lost, unencrypted laptop), the healthcare organization would be required to promptly notify affected individuals of a breach. If a breach involves more than 500 individuals, the organization *must* notify HHS and the media. Where the breach affects fewer than 500 individuals, the healthcare organization is required only to report these in aggregate on a yearly basis.

European Union

While many European nations have likely had their share of breaches, data breach notification traditionally has tended to depend on the rules of each independent nation. That is beginning to change, however. The latest amendments to the DPD introduce a compulsory obligation to inform EU regulators when data breaches occur across the European Union. The report must be immediate. With a few exceptions, the report must be filed within 24 hours of a security breach of personal data. The new directive standardizes the data breach notification process across EU member states.

Canada

Canadian breach notification rules vary across national privacy guidance rules (PIPEDA) and provincial-level privacy rules. Where provinces have guidance that is considered substantially similar to PIPEDA, Canada's federal law, the provincial guidance is sufficient according to federal regulators. That said, PIPEDA currently has limited requirements for notifying individuals. However, some provincial laws do have mandates. Those that require data breach notification are Ontario's Personal Health Information Protection Act, Newfoundland and Labrador's Personal Health Information Act, New Brunswick's Personal Health Information Privacy and Access Act, and Alberta's Personal Information Protection Act.

 TIP There is a data breach notification balance. You can be negligent in failing to notify individuals and regulators in adequate timeframes when required. There are fines and penalties in most countries for such negligence. You can also contribute to data breach notification fatigue if you over-notify. This can open your organization to undue scrutiny and needless bad publicity. Remember that data breaches have an impact on the financial bottom line of organizations, on patient care, and on organizational reputation. Knowing the rules and actions to take, therefore, will likely position you in a key role in your organization's data breach notification procedure.

Chapter Review

Privacy in a healthcare setting is a traditional concern that dates back to the very beginnings of medicine, where information confidentiality and identity protections are a professional mandate. In today's digital healthcare organization, new communities of interest, such as information technology and biomedical equipment maintenance departments, are joining health information management and compliance functional areas with emerging privacy considerations in their work with health information.

The overall definition of information privacy is found in many different sources. Some define information privacy as *what* we are protecting. Others might describe information privacy as a desired state of information protection. In any case, healthcare organizations must enact numerous privacy controls to safeguard sensitive personal health information they collect, transfer, store, and ultimately discard. Remember that a large number of data breaches happen just as retention requirements end and information protection safeguards are inadvertently relaxed. This chapter introduced privacy concepts and terms with which you need to be familiar. These concepts are rooted in legal guidance, such as HIPAA in the United States. They are foundational to leading privacy frameworks as well. Under most regulatory requirements, regardless of national, state, and regional boundaries, there normally is a requirement that organizations designate a privacy officer, who is responsible for legal compliance, assuring the privacy of data, assisting "customers" with issues or complaints, and monitoring the quality and coordination of sensitive healthcare within and outside of the organization.

In the event that privacy data is disclosed in an unintended or unauthorized way, regulatory requirements include mandatory actions to advise those affected by the loss or breach. Knowing the correct procedures and enacting them for data breaches is a core competency of the information privacy and security professional in any healthcare organization.

Review Questions

1. The concept that allows an individual who has a legitimate interest to be provided information about the processing of data is

   A. Transparency

   B. Access

   C. Openness

   D. Accountability

2. To be permitted to share patient information with a marketing firm, which of the following would a healthcare organization want to obtain prior to information disclosure?

   A. Consent

   B. Choice

   C. Accuracy

   D. Notice

3. Which of the following nations developed the Personal Information Protection and Electronic Documents Act (PIPEDA)?

   A. Japan

   B. Switzerland

   C. Canada

   D. Great Britain

4. Which of these apply to the privacy officer position?

   A. Must be a lawyer

   B. Must report to the senior information technology officer

   C. Must be designated in writing

   D. Must oversee third-party partner negotiations

5. (TRUE or FALSE) Within the construct of the European Union's Data Protection Directive, consent must be both voluntary, informed, and given by a competent individual.

6. Under U.S. healthcare law (HIPAA), a data breach occurs when what threshold is exceeded?

   A. Risk of harm

   B. Risk of unauthorized access

   C. Risk of disclosure

   D. Risk of patient care

7. (TRUE or FALSE) To provide the most assurance that an organization has received patient consent, the organization should use a preselected check box so that the patient does not inadvertently miss the consent statement.

Answers

1. C. Transparency refers to permitting an individual to be aware of specifically how their data is maintained. Access means data subjects should be allowed to access their data and request corrections to any inaccurate data. Accountability means data subjects should have a method available to them to hold data collectors accountable for following privacy principles. Therefore, openness, which allows for any member of the public who has legitimate interest to be provided information about the processing of data, is the correct answer.

2. A. To share information for reasons other than patient treatment, payment for services, or hospital operations, a healthcare organization must receive consent from the patient. Choice is a related concept, but it is not relevant to getting approval for information sharing. Accuracy of the data would be important, but without consent the information still could not be shared. Notice would also be insufficient because the hospital does not have the right to share the information after the information is collected and the patient has consented to only specific uses.

3. C. The Personal Information Protection and Electronic Documents Act (PIPEDA) is a Canadian law that is not specific to healthcare and that protects the privacy of Canadian citizens.

4. C. Except for the requirement that most frameworks and laws have for a privacy officer to be designated in writing, the options presented are not necessarily required.

5. TRUE. The DPD requires that consent be both voluntary and informed, but it must also be granted only by competent individuals.

6. C. With the passage of the Omnibus HIPAA Final Rule in 2013, risk of disclosure has become the assessment threshold under HIPAA. Risk of harm to the patient was the previous standard.

7. FALSE. The best measure of assuring consent is to make it an active choice to opt in or opt out. In other words, patients should be forced to choose the option by selecting a check box. If the option is preselected, it is possible they will not have understood their options.

References

1. UN General Assembly. "The Universal Declaration of Human Rights." December 10, 1948. United Nations. Accessed August 1, 2014, at http://www.un.org/en/documents/udhr/

2. Tyson, Peter. "The Hippocratic Oath Today." Nova Beta. March 27, 2001. Accessed July 17, 2014, at http://www.pbs.org/wgbh/nova/body/hippocratic-oath-today.html

3. U.S. Department of Health and Human Services. "HIPAA Privacy Rule (45 CFR, Part 160)." Accessed April 28, 2014, at www.hhs.gov/ocr/privacy/hipaa/administrative/privacyrule/index.html

4. Manos, Diana. "Policy Group Wrestles with Opt-in versus Opt-out." Healthcare IT News. July 22, 2010. Accessed May 7, 2014, at http://www.healthcareitnews.com/news/policy-group-wrestles-opt-versus-opt-out

5. Organisation for Economic Co-operation and Development (OECD). "OECD Guidelines Governing the Protection of Privacy and Transborder Flows of Personal Data: Collection Limitation Principle." Part 2: Basic Principles of National Application. 2013. p. 14. Accessed August 20, 2014, at http://www.oecd.org/sti/ieconomy/2013-oecd-privacy-guidelines.pdf

6. Directive 95/46/EC of the European Parliament and of the Council of 24 October 1995 on the Protection of Individuals with Regard to the Processing of Personal Data and on the Free Movement of Such Data. Section 28. Accessed August 3, 2014, at http://eur-lex.europa.eu/legal-content/en/ALL/?uri=CELEX:31995L0046

7. U.S. Department of Health and Human Services. "Disclosures for Public Health Activities." 45 CFR 164.512(b). 2003. Accessed May 7, 2014, at http://www.hhs.gov/ocr/privacy/hipaa/understanding/coveredentities/publichealth.html

8. U.S. Department of Health & Human Services. "Health Information Privacy: Enforcement Results by Year." Accessed July 31, 2014, at http://www.hhs.gov/ocr/privacy/hipaa/enforcement/data/historicalnumbers.html

9. U.S. Department of Health and Human Services, "Notice of Privacy Practices for Protected Health Information." 45 CFR 164.520. 2003. Accessed July 30, 2014, at http://www.hhs.gov/ocr/privacy/hipaa/understanding/coveredentities/notice.html

10. "Nationwide Privacy and Security Framework for Electronic Exchange." HealthIT.gov. Accessed May 7, 2014, at http://healthit.gov/policy-researchers-implementers/nationwide-privacy-and-security-framework-electronic-exchange

11. Gurría, Angel. "Openness and Transparency – Pillars for Democracy, Trust and Progress." Organisation for Economic Co-operation and Development (OECD). Accessed May 7, 2014, at www.oecd.org/fr/etatsunis/opennessandtransparency-pillarsfordemocracytrustandprogress.htm

12. United States Office of Personnel Management. "System of Records Notice (SORN) Guide." April 22, 2010. Section 2.1, p. 1. Accessed July 22, 2014, at https://www.opm.gov/information-management/privacy-policy/privacy-references/sornguide.pdf

13. Swire, Peter P., and Sol Bermann. *Information Privacy: Official Reference for the Certified Information Privacy Professional (CIPP)*. (York, ME: International Association of Privacy Professionals, 2007), p. 13.

14. U.S. Department of Health and Human Services. "Breach Notification Rule: Administrative Requirements and Burden of Proof." 45 CFR 164.400-414. 2013. Accessed August 3, 2014, at http://www.hhs.gov/ocr/privacy/hipaa/administrative/breachnotificationrule/index.html

PART II

Protecting Digital Health Information: Cybersecurity Fundamentals

In this chapter, you will learn to

- Appreciate the evolution from information security to cybersecurity
- Recognize application of information confidentiality, integrity, and availability
- Understand fundamental cybersecurity terms
- Explain data encryption and identity access management
- Become familiar with information assurance practices such as business continuity and systems recovery

Some people who read this book will already have years of experience in information technology or security. Some may even have certifications such as CISSP (Certified Information Systems Security Professional) or CISA (Certified Information Systems Auditor). This chapter will be a refresher for those readers, but do not bypass it. One of the changes taking place, even as this book is written, is the evolution (or revolution) from information security to cybersecurity. As mentioned previously, this text brings together readers from other traditional areas of information protection that principally applied to privacy concerns or medical device technology that is now more networked. Therefore, the focus of Chapter 8 is on providing a solid foundational understanding of cybersecurity concepts, especially with non-cybersecurity professionals in mind. So, if you come to this chapter with a healthcare professional background that now includes responsibility for cybersecurity, you will benefit.

Healthcare organizations are similar to every other industry that must collect and use sensitive information to produce a good or perform a service. As such, healthcare organizations generally must adhere to information protection practices. What increases the importance of risk management in healthcare is the merging of a traditionally robust effort to protect patient privacy and the digitization of health information. With digitization brings cybersecurity requirements and new professional skill requirements for healthcare workers. There is a terrific amount of information to try to understand, and it may be too much to expect anyone to be an expert in both privacy and cybersecurity. However, healthcare employees are finding it almost impossible to be successful with privacy responsibilities without a fundamental understanding of cybersecurity and vice versa.

Evolving Information Security to Cybersecurity

The difference between information security and cybersecurity is a subject of debate. For many, there is really no difference except that cybersecurity as a term recognizes the evolution from paper-based record collection to digital information collection, storage, use, and transfer in just about every organization across the globe. *Cybersecurity* is increasingly the more appropriate term for how such information is protected, and this is especially true in the United States. This text would not be current if it did not at least address the terminology. The next two sections of this chapter present relevant sources for information security and cybersecurity, providing the focus and definitions for each. Depending on the location of your organization, in the United States or internationally, the terms may be used synonymously or a distinction may still exist between the two.

Information Security

ISO/IEC 27001, Information Security Management, is an information security standard published by the International Organization for Standardization (ISO) and the International Electrotechnical Commission (IEC). It is a leading source for information security controls and principles, and it presents a holistic approach to securing the information resources of an organization. Some differences in this approach may be found among human resources, system acquisition, and asset management controls. These differences are not addressed by the cybersecurity framework discussed in the next section to the extent that ISO/IEC 27001 does in its most recent update in 2013.

At the risk of oversimplifying the definition, it may be that the distinction between information security and cybersecurity is that information security holds a more expansive view of protecting information from unauthorized access and use, regardless of whether the information is paper based or digital. Cybersecurity, in this case, comprises a smaller component of the practice of maintaining information security. However, the distinction between the two terms increasingly rests in whether you are working in the United States or internationally.

Cybersecurity

If we acknowledge that the term "cybersecurity" is increasingly synonymous with the term "information security," especially in the United States, we can best define cybersecurity around the reality of information digitization. Protecting digital information requires many of the same safeguards as protecting paper-based information. For example, many physical and administrative controls are applicable to both. A data center housing digital information requires cipher locks, surveillance, and environmental controls much the same as a paper records room requires. Access to and transfer of sensitive information must be governed by policies and procedures for the same confidentiality, integrity, and availability concerns that existed with paper-based correspondence or faxes. An excellent resource we can use to examine a cybersecurity framework that applies to healthcare is the Framework for Improving Critical Infrastructure Cybersecurity, published by National Institute of Standards and Technology (NIST) in 2014. It is a response to U.S. Presidential Executive Order 13636, Improving Critical Infrastructure Cybersecurity, issued in February of 2013. The NIST framework is a voluntary framework of control standards and practices that address cybersecurity of critical infrastructure, which includes U.S. healthcare IT networks.[1]

The context provided by this framework leads to a definition of cybersecurity that involves the use of information technology solutions to attack, defend, and counter any information technology threats. Cybersecurity focuses more on technical controls such as network architecture than does information security. Cybersecurity practices use layered defenses using firewalls, intrusion detection, and data loss prevention appliances. Of course, physical and administrative controls are included in cybersecurity risk management, but the fact is that cybersecurity focuses primarily on IT risks.

NOTE As this text intends to reach a broad, international healthcare professional audience, it will use the term "information security," with the understanding that future editions may evolve to replace the term with "cybersecurity."

The Guiding Principles of Security: Confidentiality, Integrity, Availability, and Accountability

The triad of information security—confidentiality, integrity, and availability (CIA)—is applicable to healthcare. In Chapter 9, we will discuss the balancing act in healthcare among the three, but for now we need to have a solid understanding of each. These make up the famed triad of information security: the CIA triad. Another term that is related to CIA and should be a part of this discussion is accountability. Accountability as an information security concern is highly relevant in healthcare.

To put these guiding principles into perspective, each and every safeguard, control, and practice that is put in place to protect information has the purpose of protecting confidentiality, integrity, or availability (or a combination of these). When we conduct our risk management program, our efforts are aimed at preventing any vulnerability from being exploited. When a threat exploits a vulnerability, the resulting risk has an adverse impact on the confidentiality, integrity, and availability of the information.

Confidentiality

Confidentiality is the protection of sensitive data from unauthorized disclosure. Two of the controls used to provide confidentiality are encryption and access control. In healthcare, confidentiality is not only important to protect individuals from medical and financial identity theft, research shows that a breach of confidentiality can impact patient care. In the UK, breaches are common enough that some patients are worried information will fall into the wrong hands.[2] Patients who fear their healthcare provider might disclose or lose their information outside of the allowable disclosures fear embarrassment and may withhold information from their provider[3]. Worse, these patients may delay seeking care. There are additional confidentiality considerations in certain circumstances. For example, patient care information related to the Human Immunodeficiency Virus (HIV), behavioral health, and children often require even more restrictive confidentiality requirements. Whether in the United States under HIPAA or in the European Union under the DPD, confidentiality requirements often extend beyond the patient care relationship. The data collector is responsible for maintaining the confidentiality of the information forever, even if the patient discloses the information.[4] Of course, the patient can give consent for specific disclosures, but generally the healthcare organization cannot disclose the information ever. Further, the organization must protect the information from disclosure until it can legally and properly destroy it.

Integrity

Imagine a scenario in which malicious code (a software virus) is introduced via a malware software application into a medical device. If that medical device is responsible for dosing medications to a patient and that virus has the impact of moving all decimal points to the right one space, the results can be significant to the patient. A dose of 0.5 ml may have a disastrous effect if only 0.05 ml is indicated. The integrity of data is important for this and many other reasons. Integrity of information is maintained by assuring that changes made are authorized and correct or not made at all. In fact, integrity of data relates to protecting the accuracy, quality, and completeness of the information.

One concern with integrity of data involves the data flow and life cycle of the information. When you examine the process of data collection and use in a healthcare setting, the data often changes format and various data elements are combined, parsed out, or even aggregated. Nevertheless, the integrity of the data must remain. A patient name or date of birth, for instance, must remain the same even if it is collected as Jane Doe, December 14, at admissions and then transformed into Doe, Jane, 12/14, once it gets transcribed into the billing system. Although this is an exceedingly simplified example, maintaining data integrity across data flow is one reason for the existence of international standards such as ICD-10, for coding patient encounters, and HL7, for transmitting health information across organizations and systems. Using standard data sets and transaction codes help to assure data integrity.

Availability

Information is only valuable if it is accessible and timely. The data can be accurate and kept private, but if it is not available when it is needed, the third part of the CIA triad has failed. *Availability* of data is generally described as proper access at the time the information is needed. In healthcare, we can certainly understand the failure of protecting patient identity and ensuring that the record is accurate, but having network downtime and no contingency operations plan means the information is not available at the point of care. This scenario can lead to patient care and patient safety risks because the provider does not have the ability to use the information he or she needs. Exacerbating the problem, paper-based records and manual processes are not easily retrieved or enacted as information becomes increasingly digital. Not having availability of information can result in improper diagnosis, inefficient or redundant tests, and in some cases adverse drug-drug interactions.

Before moving on to the next concept, it is important to note that availability also relates to having only the necessary information available. Often, having too much information available or having unorganized raw data is a security issue. The privacy and security frameworks such as the DPD and HIPAA, for instance, address the issue of having relevant information versus having more than is needed. A provider that requires a relevant prior MRI image when treating an orthopedic injury must certainly have the last MRI on the affected body part to compare against the latest image. However, that provider would be overwhelmed by having to search through all the images for unrelated care of that patient. If nothing else, the search would be time consuming and wasteful. By limiting availability, we can prevent unauthorized disclosures or data breaches simply by not sharing unused or extra data in the transaction. For illustration, consider an example from the past. There was a time in the United States when personal bank checks commonly were printed with the individual's social security number on them. This was useful for identification purposes, but ultimately the practice ceased because vendors could determine identity in more discrete ways. The practice of including the social security number on checks introduced too much risk of data loss and identity theft, and it is a good example of the information security impact of over-availability.

Accountability

Accountability as an information security concern is not one of the goals of the CIA triad; however, it is related and worth including in the general discussion. To be compliant with information security laws and guidance, an element of accountability typically must be present. An organization must demonstrate accountability for the information it collects and uses. The individual who uses the information likewise is responsible for his or her actions. These actions must be logged and audited to various degrees to prove that measures of accountability are in place to safeguard information from data breach. *Accountability* is the assignment of responsibility and the capability of proving proper data use. It is also a mechanism for tracing or tracking actions and responsible parties with respect to information security. Access logging by a computer system helps trace and track users of a system. Auditing information disclosure reports allows us to view and remediate any disclosures that may have been unauthorized, or at least prove to government regulators that disclosures are tracked as required. *Nonrepudiation*, the ability to ensure that someone cannot deny something, also is an element of accountability. By providing safeguards such as digital signatures and encryption algorithms, an organization can ensure that the sender of an electronic message cannot deny sending it and that the receiver cannot deny receiving it. In this way, nonrepudiation assists organizations by providing ways to prove accountability.

TIP Depending on your role in the organization, the relative importance of each component of the CIA triad and of accountability may change. For instance, as a system administrator, providing accountability and availability may be more within your job description than is confidentiality. This is typical, so although the prevailing illustration for the CIA triad is an equilateral triangle, the reality is that the shape depends on some situational factors, including organizational role.

Shaping Information Security

Without question, the first step in understanding information security is getting an introduction to the relevant terms. To make the terms meaningful, it helps to provide some context for how to shape, or incorporate, information safeguards in an organization. Our starting point is to define some overarching concepts that will help frame the terms and definitions that follow. We start with some leading information security approaches and practices: security controls, security categorization, and defense-in-depth.

Security Controls

To protect information, the organization must, of course, employ security controls. Security controls, it is important to note, refer to standards or technologies that are generally accepted as effective. Cost is also a concern in that a security control is not effective if it costs more to implement and maintain than the information asset it protects. Controls outlined in NIST guidance or ISO publications meet the requirement for properly implementing security controls. The nature of the controls, as introduced in Chapter 4, can be physical (a lock), administrative (a policy), or technical (encryption). The benefit of implementing a control can be realized at various stages in the function-based organization of controls:

- **Preventive**   Avoid the incident.
- **Detective**   Identify the event as it happens.
- **Corrective**   Rectify the situation.
- **Deterrent**   Discourage attacks and violations.
- **Recovery**   Restore operations.
- **Compensation**   Provide alternative or complementary controls.

Security Categorization

To determine what controls should or should not be implemented, the organization must shape its approach around the types of information it collects and uses. According to NIST's Federal Information Processing Standards Publication (FIPS PUB) 199, "Standards for Security Categorization of Federal Information and Information Systems,"[5] security categorization is a process of evaluating the information against confidentiality, integrity, and availability. A simple low, medium, or high valuation of the importance of each component can be used to determine a subjective score. For example, if we believe availability is the most important component of CIA for protected health information (PHI), we might have an equation like this:

Security categorization = confidentiality (low) + integrity (low) + availability (high)

This valuation may lead an organization to provide controls that assure availability, such as investing in a generator and providing continuous power to information systems. In this case, investment in confidentiality and integrity controls may be secondary and more conservative.

Figure 8-1 illustrates this simple process that can be followed to provide information security categorization. To determine the security categorization in healthcare, we use this equation for PHI and for personally identifiable information (PII) once we identify where this data is and how it moves through the organization. At that point, the information is categorized and the level of protection required can be determined.

Now that you have a basic understanding of how information security levels are categorized, it's important to acknowledge the complexity of the categorization process. As noted in NIST SP 800-60, a certain system may actually use various types of data with multiple levels of impact to the organization if the data is breached. Take the electronic health record (EHR), for instance. That system will have PHI, insurance data, and contact information. Some occupational health services will even include employment records. The categorization formula remains the same: using the categories of confidentiality, integrity, and availability, the organization must assess each type of information in the same way, albeit independently for high, medium, and low values, depending on their criticality in each of these three areas. When it comes to an organization's EHR system, this is a team effort. Representatives from clinical service departments, finance,

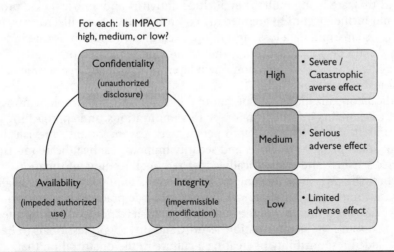

Figure 8-1 Categorizing information for safeguarding

IT, and clinical engineering (medical devices) should be included to ensure the best outcome. The controls that are put in place may be tailored to the type of information that is at risk. For example, a separate access control or log-in credential may be required to access the finance module of the application. This process is tedious and often overlooked; however, the Data Protection Supervisor review under the European Union's DPD and the audits conducted by HIPAA enforcement regulators in the United States seek evidence of such controls. The other way to look at this process is from an overall risk management standpoint. Because the first step in any good risk management process is to inventory assets, categorizing information security is a means of taking inventory for sensitive data and facilitates other risk management activities.

Defense-in-Depth

The SysAdmin, Audit, Networking, and Security (SANS) Institute describes defense-in-depth as the "concept of protecting a computer network with a series of defensive mechanisms such that if one mechanism fails another will already be in place to thwart an attack."[6] Basically the concept is to use as many security controls as is feasible to provide layers of protection. While many will argue that defense-in-depth does not protect very well against the fully authorized or elevated, privileged end user with appropriate credentials who is doing something wrong. According to Ponemon[7], mistakes by people and system glitches are costly and still highly prevalent in healthcare. However, malicious actors are beginning to spoof or steal valid end-user credentials though social engineering, phishing e-mails, and other criminal theft activities. In the end, the external threat becomes an internal threat. The argument against defense-in-depth is that the architecture and safeguards may not provide any detection or deterrence. While this may be true, an understanding of defense-in-depth is fundamental. The salient points about the ways in which defense-in-depth falls short can be discussed elsewhere.

Specific defense-in-depth controls should be designed into new systems and applications as they are being built. They include antivirus and anti-malware protections, and should include technical architecture controls such as firewalls, routers, intrusion detection systems, and data loss prevention. Even more important is that independent controls should be able to work together to provide integrated protection. Figure 8-2 illustrates the defense-in-depth component layers and provides an example of the types of controls that might be used.

Healthcare organizations cannot ignore the requirements of implementing security controls, categorizing information for security implications, and approaching information security from a defense-in-depth perspective. It is important to revisit the reality of international privacy principles and security frameworks: healthcare information is considered sensitive and is specifically addressed in all leading information protection approaches. The processes, technologies, and actions required to protect health information are components of today's healthcare strategic practices and tomorrow's core competencies. Every member of the organization has a responsibility for protecting the information—and we, as information security and privacy professionals in healthcare, have the added responsibility of creating a culture in the organization that, at a mini-

Figure 8-2
Defense-in-depth
approach

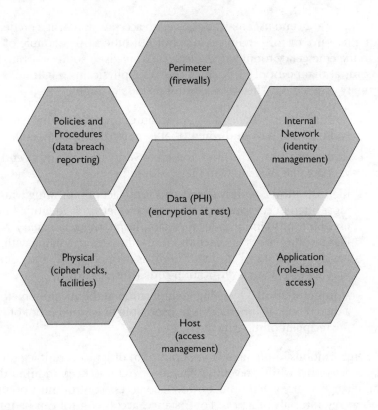

mum, drives security controls, categorization of information, and defense-in-depth. Otherwise, the organization will fail to meet regulatory compliance with laws such as HIPAA and PIPEDA, and the organization will likely suffer one or more data breaches, causing an erosion of patient trust.

General Security Definitions

The concepts that shape information security can be abstract and complex. To help you understand the approaches and practices of information security, being familiar with pertinent definitions is clearly a fundamental step. These definitions are included here because they are central to information security practices and compliance, and because more progressive security processes are designed from them.

Access Control

Access control protects sensitive information and is made up of all of the actions and controls put in place to regulate viewing, storing, copying, modifying, transferring, and deleting information. Controlling access also includes limitations of time and situation.

For instance, an end user may be allowed to access a system at a predetermined time but not afterward, or for certain reasons but not others. An example of situational access is in the emergency room where physicians are given some access to behavioral health records at that point of care, which the same physicians might not have access to in a primary care setting. The access control process includes:

- **Authorization**   Policies and procedures for determining which permissions an end user will have and when (that is, a user's level of access).

- **Authentication**   The process used to verify the identity of end users and validate that they are who they claim to be.

- **Identification**   Simply stated, this is the act of indicating who a person is. Most often in computing technologies, a person is identified by the use of a username or identity code (for example, *firstname, lastname*). Note that the identification does not include combining this username with a password, which is considered authentication, as defined above, and combines a simple identity code with a verification code (the password).

- **Nonrepudiation**   By using identification authentication methods and tools in a digital transaction, there is indisputable or assured proof of who the sender or the recipient of the data is.

Organizations implement access control in order to permit legitimate use by authorized personnel while preventing unauthorized use. Keep in mind that legitimate use can change at any given time, however, so access control must occur at various levels and at key intervals of access. For instance, access control can be implemented at the operating system level to safeguard files and storage media, and at the database level to guard against unauthorized access and potential corruption of data. In addition, well-designed applications and web services typically enforce several independent access controls to layer the protection, even if a single sign-on (SSO) technology is used. To be clear, access control is an effort to prevent unauthorized use, but the practice also allows sharing of sensitive information at an acceptable level of risk to the organization. Without access controls in place, most organizations would consider it too risky to share PHI or PII; and that would prevent or degrade patient care in a digitized healthcare environment.

For access control to be effective, an authentication process must support the controls. To properly identify personnel and grant them appropriate access levels, it's useful to understand two types of authentication: Multifactor authentication is present when at least two conditions are satisfied independently by the same individual who wants to access a network, system, or application. In many contexts, multifactor authentication and two-factor authentication are synonymous based on how many conditions must be satisfied. When an organization implements proper multifactor authentication, the process is recognized as strong authentication.

To gain access, an end user must provide something a person knows (password/PIN), something they have (a physical token/badge), something they are (biometrics), or some combination of those three factors. To be clear, this means the person can verify at least two of the following things[8]:

- What I know (authentication by knowledge)
- What I have (authentication by ownership)
- Who I am (authentication by characteristic)

Access Control Models

Several access control models are used to enforce authentication and authorization guidelines, and the controls used are automated. (Imagine how difficult it would be to manually check the credentials of each end user every time they desired access to data or to a system!) The common models for access control are mandatory, discretionary, and role-based. There are some hybrid models that combine features of each, but these three are fundamental ones.

NOTE Although these models are enforced by computer policies and configurations, some information security guidelines have provisions for overriding these policies and configurations, or for emergency access. The best example is the provision in HIPAA to provide "break glass" access in emergency situations. In other words, the system has a method for providing access to someone who may not have authorization or access under normal circumstances.

Mandatory Access Control   The first type of access control model is *mandatory access control*, in which a central authority such as the organization's CIO makes the access control policy, which is implemented by the IT department. The actual access control is enforced at the hardware or operating system level as a technical control. Most often, mandatory access control is used in organizations that handle classified information—for example, a military organization. It is valid to include mandatory access control in this context because it is relative to a healthcare organization where rigid, centralized controls are used in some applications and networked resources. In this model, individual system or data owners do not have the ability to change the level of access allowed. A mandatory access control model depends on proper security categorization of information because the access policy in this case most likely will be determined by the sensitivity of the information. In some organizations, there may be confidential information, in which case the central authority can determine who is allowed access to this type of information. Improperly categorized information can lock out individuals who may need access, or it may allow access to those who have no need to know the information. Neither case is desired. On the positive side, having a central authority enforce the access control makes standard, equitable policies possible.

Discretionary Access Control   A *discretionary access control* model is used if access control is more decentralized or delegated to the owner of the individual system or to the owner of the data itself. Privileges are granted by the system owner or data owner to whomever he or she considers authorized to access the information. Discretionary access control is more flexible than mandatory access control, but it introduces greater risk. For instance, once someone has access to view a file, the system owner has no control over whether that person decides to copy it and allow others to view the file.

Role-Based Access Control   Probably the most prevalent type of nondiscretionary access control model is *role-based access control,* in which system owners determine the level of access based on a user's or group's job function or organizational role. For instance, there may be one type of access control for physicians in pediatrics and another for nurses in the same department. One component of a role-based access model is *an access control list (ACL),* a list that indicates which personnel have access rights to certain objects or delineates which personnel have specific types of access rights, such as read, write, or delete access. An ACL is the most common way of implementing role-based access controls.

NOTE   Another use of the term ACL relates to firewall or router rules, and the concept is very similar. A firewall ACL is a list of ports and Internet Protocol (IP) addresses that are allowed to access the organization IT resources under predetermined circumstances (using certain protocols). This type of ACL could be thought of as role-based access control for IT systems instead of personnel.

Data Encryption

Data encryption is a technical control or solution to protect information confidentiality. Strictly speaking, encryption does not focus on protecting or providing data integrity or availability; however, cryptographic algorithms, called *hashing algorithms,* do provide for data integrity. Sensitive data, such as PHI and PII, must be encrypted under the prevailing information security standards, such as HIPAA and ISO 27001, to name just two. There are two states in which data can (and should) be encrypted: when it is "at rest" and when it is "in transit." The first state, *at rest,* refers to data that is stored on any media and is not currently being processed or transmitted. If data at rest has been encrypted, media that is lost or stolen and recovered by someone unauthorized to view the data will be unusable or unreadable to the person who finds it. In this case, the only people who can access the data are those who possess the cryptographic key to decrypt the information. There are two common ways of applying this type of encryption using encryption applications. One is to encrypt the entire volume of information on the disk with the same encryption key, and the other is to encrypt at the file level. Encrypting the entire volume of the disk has benefits in that human error is minimized because users may forget or neglect to encrypt data if any part of the process is manual or discretionary, as file-level encryption can be.

The second state of data is that which is *in transit:* Some sensitive data must be transferred via an e-mail message; other data must be transferred over a secure connection. During these transfer processes, the data must be protected by encryption. The cryptographic key process is similar whether the data is at rest or in transit. The principle concept is that the data is protected from unauthorized access and disclosure by being rendered unusable to anyone other than the intended recipient. In order to achieve this, an encryption key is attached to a digital certificate related to public and private keys for each sender and recipient. The private key is secret. The public key, however, is not and can be used by anyone to encrypt the message. Only the private key of the intended recipient can decipher the message. These keys are different, but they are related by a mathematical algorithm that makes this process possible. A certificate is the mechanism used to uniquely identify an encryption key and associate it with the claimed owner[9]—assuring confidentiality and preventing unauthorized disclosure. It is important to note that the leading standard for encryption keys is found in FIPS 140-2. If an encryption key has been tested and certified under FIPS 140-2, it can be used to provide safe harbor protection under HIPAA in the United States. Keep in mind the distinction between HIPAA safe harbor and the DPD safe harbor provisions, as described in Chapter 3.

Figure 8-3 depicts a simple e-mail transfer using encryption for data in transit. It illustrates components of public key infrastructure (PKI), which consists of all technology, personnel, and policies that work together to create, manage, and share digital certificates.[10]

Training and Awareness

One of the most cost-effective security controls that any organization can put into place is an active employee training and awareness program. Training and awareness can help prevent the breaches caused by employee mistakes and reduce complacency around handling PHI and PII. *Training* is the act of instructing employees or teaching skills or topics to them that are focused on specific improvements in job performance. The target audience approaches the learning process at a purpose-oriented level. The subject matter typically covers what needs to be done and then includes steps or procedures on how to do the right things. As training topics are specific, so is the target audience. An example of a training scenario is an annual training class on information security procedures for the organization. Often, these types of classes are delivered based on the level of access the end user has, whether a system administrator or standard end user, for example. Training is most effective when delivered regularly. Many required training

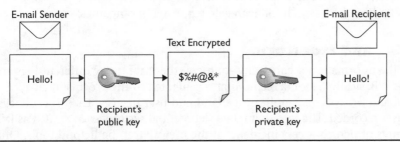

Figure 8-3   Transfer of encrypted data in transit

courses are mandated for annual recurrence. That type of training is tracked, and compliance is reported to relevant leadership. Sometimes the training is required by law. In the case of HIPAA, a healthcare organization is required to provide training to all workforce members on relevant security policies and procedures.[11] However, training is also extremely effective when offered on an ad hoc or as-needed basis. A class on how to encrypt an e-mail with PHI may be helpful as a weekly in-service topic for a specific audience. The more often ad hoc trainings are offered on a variety of timely topics, the more effective they are at influencing proper information security behavior and avoiding employee-caused data breaches.

Awareness is part of an overall strategy to increase employee understanding and, again, motivate correct behavior. Training is closely related to awareness; in fact, security awareness is the preferred outcome of training activities. Most awareness programs include marketing and communication of relevant information through information security campaigns using posters displayed in prominent areas, newsletters, banners that pop up during log-in, or announcements made in staff meetings, to name just a few delivery methods. While many would argue this delivery of information is really just a form of ad hoc training, the more targeted nature of the message and audience of these awareness examples provides a distinction. In sum, these security controls, training, and awareness practices must be used in tandem to conduct a comprehensive workforce information security program.

Sanction Policy

Even the best training and awareness programs do not prevent every employee incident. To address situations when an employee violates the organization's privacy and security practices and policies, a sanction policy is required. A *sanction policy* is best described as a set of prescribed actions that management can take with regard to such violations. While some incidents are so serious that immediate termination is appropriate, the majority of incidents are accidental by nature. Therefore, the policy should outline progressive levels of discipline and allow management discretion whenever possible. To facilitate this, the organization must categorize the types of infractions and match them against the various types of penalties to be considered. In the end, a good sanction policy will be fair and consistent, not only with regard to who commits a violation but also with the rest of the organization's policies for human resource types of disciplinary actions. As a part of the organization's training and awareness program, data from the sanction policy enforcement process is invaluable in determining trending issues and reasons for breaches, as well for aggregate reporting of outcomes.

Logging and Monitoring

Within the information security environment, there are many different logs and types of logging. Basically, a *log* is a record that is generated by the processing of events on the network and on systems, applications, and end-user devices. Each specific event that happens is recorded. The logs that relate to potential security events, such as failed log-in attempts or denied access incidents at the firewall, can be helpful tools. One of the principle duties of an information security and privacy professional is to actively review logs and take action on any events that trigger alerts. As this is a daunting task due to the sheer volume and complexity of such logs, the ability to monitor the computing environment is necessary. *Monitoring* is typically an automated method by which rules of behavior or parameters are set to distinguish normal network behavior from potential incidents or events. For instance, a good monitoring process would alert when there is simultaneous logon by the same end user on the network inside the computing domain and on the virtual private network. That indicates a spoofed or stolen set of credentials more often than not. Although monitoring is an automated function using security technology, hard work is necessary to set up the monitoring tools and to educate the training personnel to know and understand the complex rules of behavior, what normal behavior is, and what should alert action.

A growing trend within logging and monitoring, because of improved automated tools and process in security automation, is information security continuous monitoring (ISCM). NIST SP 800-137, Information Security Continuous Monitoring for Federal Information Systems and Organizations, defines ISCM as maintaining ongoing awareness of information security, vulnerabilities, and threats to support organizational risk management decisions. More important is that the directive outlines domains of potential automation and best practice philosophy around the domains depicted in Figure 8-4. While this text only introduces these domains, the key point is that logging and monitoring in these domains is increasingly automated and continuous.

Figure 8-4
NIST 800-137
security
automated
domains

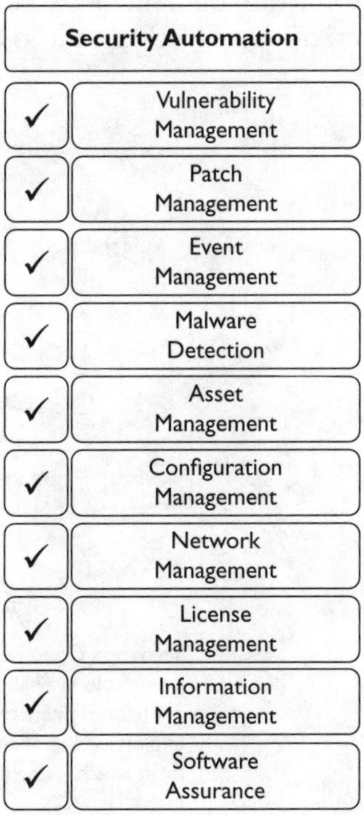

Security Automation
✓ Vulnerability Management
✓ Patch Management
✓ Event Management
✓ Malware Detection
✓ Asset Management
✓ Configuration Management
✓ Network Management
✓ License Management
✓ Information Management
✓ Software Assurance

Vulnerability Management

Wherever an organization has a gap in information security controls, a weakness or a potential opportunity for exploit exists. Such an area or condition in which a security control is not present, or the control is inadequate, is an area of *vulnerability,* a weakness that presents a risk that might be exploited; however, there is not always a high probability the risk will be exploited. Additionally, the asset that could be exploited may not present a level of impact that necessitates expensive controls be put in place. Vulnerabilities are simply indicators that alert risk managers to consider actions and to balance risk, factoring in the likelihood of occurrence versus cost implications. For these reasons, whether to implement a safeguard or choose one safeguard over another is a consideration that information security and privacy professionals must make carefully. Another name for safeguard is security control, which we introduced earlier in this chapter. There is a definite relationship between vulnerability, threats, safeguards, and assets, and this relationship is illustrated in Figure 8-5.

Within the practice of vulnerability management is the process of patching systems and applications with updated code or software changes to mitigate vulnerabilities. This process is called *patch management* and is vital to maintaining a properly safeguarded network and computing environment. Operating systems and various applications all are designed and implemented with a secure configuration when they are introduced to the marketplace. However, vulnerability management, in this case specifically patch management, is a dynamic, ongoing process. Periodically, a vulnerability is found in established code. Sometimes the vulnerability is found because a threat, such as a hacking attempt or the introduction of malicious code, exploited it. Other times, the vulnerability is discovered by software developers who bring the vulnerability to light before

Figure 8-5
Relationships among assets, vulnerabilities, threats, and safeguards

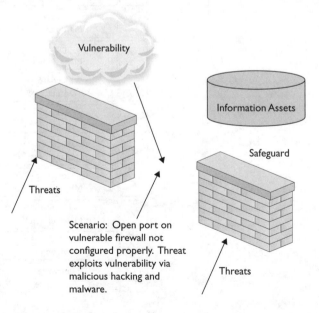

Vulnerability

Information Assets

Safeguard

Threats

Scenario: Open port on vulnerable firewall not configured properly. Threat exploits vulnerability via malicious hacking and malware.

Threats

anyone exploits it (the preferred scenario, of course). In such cases, the patch required to fix the vulnerability is coded, developed, tested, and distributed to the marketplace before any exploit. The patch management process concludes with system administrators and network operators applying the patch or patches to their systems. The process of patch management is an area of security automation. Patches (once tested and validated) can be automatically distributed across a local area network and automatically updated on all networked resources. This is efficient and effective.

 TIP For FDA-regulated medical devices, the process should not be automatic. Each patch must be evaluated and approved for use on all medical devices by that device's manufacturer. In short, medical devices may be able to receive a patch, but the manufacturer must first test and approve the patch. Otherwise, the addition of a patch, which is in reality a piece of third-party software, can result in a patient safety issue if the medical device malfunctions after the patch is applied.

Segregation of Duties

Good information security practices dictate that no single person should have the ability to violate critical process or security functions. The system administrator may have the ability to review audit logs and system maintenance files; however, the ability to actually edit these may not exist, or someone else may have that privilege assigned. This compartmentalizing of privileges is known as segregation of duties (SOD). SOD is a separation of the roles and responsibilities within management of computing environments, systems, and networks. The intent is to ensure that there are checks and balances in providing information security. Otherwise, the integrity of the process is jeopardized in that one individual can inadvertently or intentionally become a vulnerability to the overall information security program. Having these checks and balances ultimately increases the organization's ability to detect threats much earlier and more reliably.

Least Privilege

Least privilege refers to having only the permissions, rights, and privileges necessary to perform your assigned duties, and no more. Many of the concepts within information security (and privacy) relate to avoiding too much access or too much disclosure, where such access or disclosure is not needed. Not to complicate the discussion, but it is always best to allow the least amount of access to information. Only as much information as is needed should be disclosed, transferred, used, and stored, and as soon as the information is no longer required, it should be destroyed. (Data destruction is discussed later in this chapter.) Generally, least privilege or minimal use concepts must support every information protection program. It is infeasible and cost prohibitive to protect information from individuals who have no need for it, have no reason to use it, or no longer need it. Regarding least privilege, it is appropriate to limit access, both initial and elevated, to only those individuals who have the need to access the information in order to do their jobs. One of the distinctive elements of providing information protection in a healthcare environment is that least privilege concerns can be highly dynamic. For example, a physician may have access to records one day due to a specific case or responsibility, and the next day that access may be restricted. This commonly happens as physicians see patients in emergency situations, such as when a behavioral health patient presents in the emergency room. Another example is that sometimes, for peer review under medical records management processes, physicians may be granted temporary access to pediatric records where their normal clinical duties would not include children under the age of 18.

Business Continuity

There is probably no industry more compelled to always function than healthcare. Not only are there regulatory pressures, but many governments at national, provincial (Canada), and state (United States) levels have required reporting procedures even when the healthcare organization is not functioning. For our purposes, we concentrate on the information asset functioning, so network or application down time is at issue. In the United States, healthcare networks are included in the NIST Framework for Improving Critical Infrastructure Cybersecurity, which includes rigid guidelines to help assure continuity of operations. Business continuity, or continuity of operations, includes all the actions taken to enable a healthcare organization to perform clinical and business services with minimal to no interruption or degradation. Continuity can be impacted by natural causes such as natural disasters or man-made problems like cybersecurity attacks, electrical outages, or construction accidents (for example, severing a fiber line to the data center).

As with all security controls, business continuity also includes time-based elements. For instance, having a continuity of operations plan (COOP) for disasters is a preventive aspect of security control. Monitoring network activity is a detection function of this control. However, once a disaster happens, the optimal method for business continuity is a redundant system or an alternative source. For example, if there is an electrical outage, a healthcare organization may temporarily switch to power provided by generators running diesel fuel. In that way, disruption of care and business processes are least likely to be interrupted. When network resources are not available, whether due to power outages or because the actual resources just do not work, manual processes should be implemented. As an example, a lab system that processes samples using bar code technology may also have a manual process that uses hand-written intake forms. Personnel should be trained and able to implement the manual forms in the event that the bar code scanning system is unavailable.

 NOTE As organizations become more digital, the manual processes that preceded current electronic processes are often long forgotten. Information security and privacy professionals will be challenged to foster training and periodic testing of COOPs.

System Recovery

The security control that supports business continuity is system recovery, or disaster recovery. After a power outage or malware attack, the systems may be down or may be compromised. Once the systems have been remediated (that is, once the threat is no longer present), a process for bringing the systems back into business and clinical operation is needed. This is true for every system or application. For example, if a database server is corrupted by an attack, it is obvious that the server must be tested and evaluated prior to putting it back into the computing environment. However, special care and procedures must be in place to prioritize and stagger all systems back online. In the event of a total network outage, there is always the potential that if you restart all systems immediately and at the same time, unintended failures can happen at other network locations. This can be due to electrical surges or load balancing issues, for example. The best COOP, specifically for system recovery, includes a plan for a scheduled, prioritized restart. First, select clinical systems and business systems would be restarted. Then additional systems could be started while the impact of the restarts is monitored. That said, if a system recovery plan involves a switchover from a redundant computing site (a *hot site*) or an alternate site started as the result of the disaster (a *cold site*), you will need to factor in the procedures for transferring reliance from either of those sites back to the normal organizational computing environment, at which point data transfer and integration must be done securely. Depending on the duration of the outage or system failure, a significant amount of new, sensitive healthcare information may have been collected. That data will need to be integrated into the entirety of the patient record and related business records.

Data Retention and Destruction

While digital information has drastically reduced the overall cost of stewardship of data, organizations still must have policies and procedures in place to appropriately retain information they need and then destroy information when it is no longer needed. Just a few decades ago, 5,000 medical records comprised of paper-based images, charts, notes, and printouts might encompass a 1,000 square foot records room stacked from floor to ceiling with medical records on shelves. Clearly, that amount of geographic space can be expensive and could be put to use for more valuable purposes. To constrain costs and properly protect and use all assets, both physical and informational, the focus was on minimizing how many records were retained, and proper destruction policies were designed. However, today, the same number of records fit easily on an inexpensive USB "thumb" drive. In some cases, the fact that space or real estate is no longer required encourages retention of all information for yet-undetermined uses. It's important to look at reasons for maintaining robust and enforced constraints on data retention and destruction.

Retention of Data

First and foremost, the retention of data is regulated by local or national law. This establishes a minimum amount of time a record must be maintained. A maximum limit should also be established, with a caveat that allows longer limits if the information is determined to be valuable to business processes or clinical treatment. Regarding minimum limits, an example would be the seven-year minimum requirement for certain health records that exists under HIPAA in the United States[12]. There are international standards in place as well. The Canadian Privacy Act is less prescriptive in that no specific number of years is mandated; however, if the information is collected by the government, the act charges data collectors with retaining the information for a minimum time period, set by additional regulation. This time period must be sufficient for the data subject to have access to the information. Because healthcare is funded by the government in Canada, this provision can impact records retention by forcing longer retention periods.[13] In the European Union, the DPD also has a provision that describes maximum limits for how long the information should be retained, so that it is kept no longer than necessary. At the same time, the DPD allows member states to establish longer retention periods if they have historical, statistical, or scientific uses for the information that are valid and otherwise permitted by the DPD.

 NOTE Make sure medical and legal liability issues are addressed in retention policies. Whether an organization is solely a provider in the United States or has international reach, there may be financial implications if, due to lack of retention compliance, records are not available when they are supposed to be. Conversely, records that are maintained longer than any requirement exists remain discoverable in judicial proceedings. This can add unnecessary cost, delay, and liability to the discovery process.

Secure Disposal of Electronic Media

In the information management life cycle, data at the disposal or destruction stage is highly vulnerable. Breaches and loss happen far too often just at the time when the organization has decided the information is no longer valuable to it. Even at this stage, the information remains sensitive, whether it is payment related or contains health data for an individual. Proper disposal and destruction methods, collectively called "sanitization methods," can prevent unauthorized disclosure. Those methods include physical destruction of storage media, secure overwriting, and degaussing. A sanitization method can be a technical action, involving the use software, or it can be a physical action such as drilling holes in the hardware. The best methods use both approaches as needed based on the level of sensitivity of the information and the desire to possibly reuse the media. The goal of sanitization as an information security control is to render the data so that it is impossible or impractical for someone ever to retrieve it.

 NOTE Disposal and destruction methods apply to paper-based sensitive records as well as electronic records. The available methods aren't covered in depth in this text, but shredding and incinerating documents are commonly accepted procedures. The key is protecting the information as the paper-based records are transported from storage to destruction.

Physical Media Destruction   Somewhat analogous to physical destruction of paper-based records, media that contains sensitive data can be destroyed completely as opposed to securely removing the data while leaving the physical media asset (back-up tape, hard drive, and so on) intact. The processes for physically destroying the media are not very technical or elegant, but they are highly effective. For instance, drilling holes into a hard drive through the spinning disk is effective. This method may not actually destroy the data, but the data will become unreadable or unrecoverable. Large shredders can also be used to actually shred the physical assets into small pieces. Some other methods that can be used are disintegration, incineration, pulverization, melting, sanding, and treatment with chemicals.

Secure Overwriting   Secure overwriting renders data unusable by destroying just the data. Other methods render the drive completely unusable, even those that do not destroy the physical asset. If an organization wants to reuse storage assets, such as expensive storage area network components, it will choose to use securely overwrite the data. This process consists of writing meaningless data over and over onto each of the sectors on an asset's hard drive. The meaningless pattern typically consists of combinations of 1s and 0s. The number of times this process must happen to be effective varies across a number of standards. Probably the most often referenced standard is the U.S. Department of Defense Sanitizing (DOD 5220.22-M) guidance, which calls for three overwriting passes to completely overwrite the data the organization wants to destroy.

Degaussing   *Degaussing* is a process used to erase all data on magnetic field types of media, such as backup tapes or hard drives. The device used to degausse the media generates a magnetic field that completely randomizes the 1s and 0s on the media with no preference to orientation, thereby rendering previous data unrecoverable. The magnet used in degaussing acts much like a magnet used on a compass. The magnet changes the compass's notion of where north is so that the data on the media is no longer in a retrievable pattern. This process is useful in sanitizing large amounts of data quickly. It is also very effective to use when the media is damaged and is inoperable. However, for optical media such as CDs and DVDs, degaussing has no effect because it results in an effect known as *bias*, in which many argue it is impossible to completely remove the magnetic field and thereby fully randomize all the 1s and 0s. A remnant can remain, making it theoretically possible for some of the data to be recovered. For this reason, much like secure overwriting, information security best practices require multiple degaussing for each piece of media. Using the U.S. Department of Defense as an example standard, once again, at least seven degaussing passes are considered enough. Degaussing has an added advantage in that the media can be reused. Proper degaussing is sufficient to securely dispose of or destroy sensitive information.

Configuration or Change Management

To help ensure integrity within the parameters of the CIA triad, organizations establish a configuration, or change management process. Usually under the information governance purview of a formal configuration control board or equivalent, the organization can have consistency in how changes are made to the network, systems, and applications. Change management guidelines are well known as important information security controls. For example, within the Information Technology Infrastructure Library (ITIL) framework, the controls are part of "service transition." ITIL recognizes the value of having an efficient, organized methodology for taking new products or updates of existing products from design to operations without adding risk.[14] These phases in ITIL are called service design and service operation. An example of the change management process in action is where the laboratory department decides to purchase a new information system for processing lab results. This system would require network access and interfacing with current legacy systems such as the EHR. Imagine if the acquisition and implementation of such a system did not include a formal, management-level review of the operating system, interfacing requirements, physical installation environment, and other very significant factors. In this case, if the system worked at all, it would certainly work in a less than operable manner. There would be significantly more information risk added to the overall architecture. Another, more basic, scenario for configuration management would be changes required to the perimeter security defenses, such as border firewalls. If a networked system needs to communicate with external entities across the Internet, the data traffic devices would exit the organization's network through the firewall via distinct ports using specific protocols. Outside of the ACL, with its approved ports and protocols, all other traffic would be blocked. For example, special-purpose computing systems, such as medical devices, often might require a port to be opened that is not on the current ACL. To request or ultimately make those changes, a change request should be made formally, such as verbally over the phone.

Incident Response

We conclude this chapter by revisiting the concept of incident response, which we introduced in Chapter 6. In this context, we are presenting proper incident response as a security control that is effective as a corrective measure. Incident response can limit the duration and impact of an exploited vulnerability from a threat. NIST SP 800-61 rev2, Computer Security Incident Handling Guide, defines incident response as a mitigation strategy that approaches security incidents with practical guidelines. The guide presents direction for establishing a solid incident response program that accomplishes detection, analysis, prioritization, and handling of security events, such as data breach. In these days in which data breaches seem almost inevitable no matter how well you implement security processes and controls, the one security control that may make the most difference is incident response. As Experian, a leading global credit reporting and identity theft organization claims, "how you react in the first 72 hours can be critical to the outcome"[15] of a data breach. This is based on significant regulatory pressures around notification, both with HIPAA and HITECH in the United States, and internationally, for example with the European Union's DPD.

Chapter Review

The evolution from information security to cybersecurity in some ways reflects the evolution of healthcare from a paper-based system to a digital one. The protection of health information now involves several communities in the healthcare workforce that had traditional responsibilities in handling health information. Their duties now include or involve electronic information security (cybersecurity) roles and responsibilities. That convergence makes this chapter central to the overall understanding of healthcare information security and privacy. There are many types of security controls, such as access models, encryption, business continuity, data disposal, and incident response, to name a few. Each control has a focus on preventing, detecting, or correcting data incidents, or any combination of those. Mastering implementation and management of information security controls is fundamental, yet the skills required can be complex and challenging.

Review Questions

1. You have chosen to delete data from a storage device. You want to ensure that the data is fully destroyed, but you also want to reuse the storage media. Which of the following methods should you use?

    A. Degaussing

    B. Sanitization

    C. Shredding

    D. Either A or B

2. In a healthcare office environment, which of the following applications must be considered as possibly having sensitive data included within its storage media?

    A. E-mail

    B. Scheduling

    C. Billing

    D. All of the above

3. Which of the following are elements of business continuity?

    A. Continuing mission capabilities after a power loss

    B. Continuing contact with a patient who moves from the care area

    C. Keeping in contact with a former business associate

    D. Preparing for an external assessment while continuing to see patients

4. Which of the following describes the ability to do something with a computer resource, such as permission to review, edit, or delete?

    A. Least privilege

    B. Logging

    C. Monitoring

    D. Access control

5. Which of the following is defined as a condition or weakness in (or absences of) security procedures or technical, physical, or other controls?

   A. Threat

   B. Risk

   C. Vulnerability

   D. Exploitation

6. The principles of security, often referred to as CIA, are

   A. Confidentiality, integrity, accountability

   B. Contingency, integrity, accountability

   C. Confidentiality, integrity, availability

   D. Confidentiality, interoperability, availability

7. To protect health information in an e-mail sent to a colleague, which would be a proper security control?

   A. Logical controls

   B. Strong authentication

   C. Encryption

   D. Least privilege

Answers

1. **D.** Because shredding makes the media unusable, it is not an option. Degaussing will remove all data but still make the storage media reusable. Sanitization removes PII but does not affect the use of the media.

2. **D.** Even though an organization may have policies in place that prohibit the use of e-mail for communications with the patient about specific sensitive healthcare diagnoses, and so on, the fact is that users and patients could be including e-mail in their communications. As a result, you should assume that e-mail data should be stored with the same security controls as other sensitive data systems. Clearly, patient scheduling and billing data contain personally identifiable data as well as protected health information.

3. **A.** Business continuity addresses the organization's ability to deliver its mission (healthcare, for example) when it might be affected by electrical outages, weather-related events, community-based events such as riots, accidents, or even a serious outbreak of influenza that affects staffing levels. While maintaining contact with former patients or business associates and preparing for external assessments are part of doing business, they are not part of business continuity.

4. **D.** Access control defines the technical ability to perform a function within a computer resource. While least privilege does cover the level of access, it defines an overall scope and is not specific to a user or role. Logging and monitoring are processes that are preformed to detect proper access and use of computer resources.

5. **C.** A vulnerability is a condition of weakness that can be exploited by a threat. While a threat, a risk, and exploitation can be caused by a weakness in procedures or controls, only vulnerability matches the definition.

6. **C.** The principles of security are confidentiality, integrity, and availability. While accountability has been discussed often as a principle, especially in the healthcare setting, it is not considered a primary principle. Contingency and interoperability are also discussed, but again they are not primary principles.

7. **C.** Encryption using PKI and digital certificates to enhance encryption and decryption keys is what is necessary to properly protect information "in transit." Logical controls do not apply to e-mail. Strong authentication may be related to password protection but does not apply to e-mails in transit. While least privilege is needed to make sure the recipient has a need to know, it is not the most relevant information security control based on the scenario.

References

1. National Institute of Standards and Technology. "Framework for Improving Critical Infrastructure Cybersecurity." Version 1.0. February 12, 2014. Accessed August 25, 2014, at http://www.nist.gov/cyberframework/upload/cybersecurity-framework-021214-final.pdf

2. Borland, Sophie. "2,000 NHS patients' records are lost every day with more than two million serious data breaches logged since the start of 2011." *Mail Online*, Feb. 14, 2014. Accessed August 1, 2014, at http://www.dailymail.co.uk/news/article-2559876/2-000-NHS-patients-records-lost-day-two-million-data-breaches-logged-start-2011.html#ixzz3CgQ3zTL9

3. Ponemon Institute. "Third Annual Survey on Medical Identity Theft." June 2012. p. 31. Accessed August 1, 2014, at http://www.ponemon.org/local/upload/file/Third_Annual_Survey_on_Medical_Identity_Theft_FINAL.pdf

4. European Union. "Directive 95/46/EC of the European Parliament and of the Council on the Protection of Individuals with Regard to the Processing of Personal Data and on the Free Movement of Such Data." Oct. 24, 1995. Article 28, Section 7. Accessed August 13, 2014, at http://eur-lex.europa.eu/legal-content/EN/TXT/PDF/?uri=CELEX:31995L0046&from=en

5. National Institute of Standards and Technology. FIPS PUB 199. "Standards for Security Categorization of Federal Information and Information Systems." February 2004. p. 2. Accessed August 20, 2014, at http://csrc.nist.gov/publications/fips/fips199/FIPS-PUB-199-final.pdf

6. McGuiness, Todd. SANS Institute InfoSec Reading Room. "Defense in Depth." 2001. p. 1. Accessed August 28, 2014, at http://www.sans.org/reading-room/whitepapers/basics/defense-in-depth-525

7. Ponemon Institute. "2013 Cost of Data Breach Study: Global Analysis." May 2013. p. 7. Accessed August 28, 2014, at https://www4.symantec.com/mktginfo/whitepaper/053013_GL_NA_WP_Ponemon-2013-Cost-of-a-Data-Breach-Report_daiNA_cta72382.pdf

8. Harris, Shon. "Access Control." *CISSP: Exam Guide.* 6th ed. (New York: McGraw-Hill, 2012), p. 163.

9. Harris, Shon. "Cryptography." *CISSP: Exam Guide.* 6th ed. (New York: McGraw-Hill, 2012), p. 836.

10. Breaux, Travis. "Encryption and Other Technologies." *Introduction to IT Privacy: A Handbook for Technologists.* (Portsmouth, NH: International Association of Privacy Professionals, 2014), p. 126.

11. U.S. Department of Health and Human Services. Federal Register 78, no. 17. 45 C.F.R. part 164.308(a)(5)(i). p. 713. October 1, 2003 edition. Accessed September 1, 2014, at http://www.gpo.gov/fdsys/pkg/CFR-2003-title45-vol1/pdf/CFR-2003-title45-vol1-sec164-308.pdf

12. U.S. Department of Health and Human Services. Federal Register 78, no. 17 part II. 45 CFR parts 160 and 164. January 25, 2013. Accessed January 7, 2014, at http://www.gpo.gov/fdsys/pkg/FR-2013-01-25/pdf/2013-01073.pdf

13. *Privacy Act.* R.S.C., 1985, c. P-21. Accessed January 3, 2014, at http://laws-lois.justice.gc.ca/eng/acts/p-21/page-2.html

14. UCISA. "ITIL – Introducing Service Transition." p. 4. Accessed August 29, 2014, at https://www.ucisa.ac.uk/~/media/Files/members/activities/ITIL/servicetransition/ITIL_introducing%20service%20transition%20pdf.ashx

15. Cividanes, Emilio, Paul Luehr, and Bob Krenek. "Best Practices for a Healthcare Data Breach: What You Don't Know Will Cost You." Experian. May 2011. Accessed August 10, 2014, at https://privacyassociation.org/media/pdf/knowledge_center/Best_Practices_Healthcare_Data_Breach.pdf

Impact of Information Privacy and Security on Health IT

In this chapter, you will learn to
- Recognize the influence of data ownership rights in healthcare
- Comprehend the intertwined relationship between privacy and security in healthcare organizations
- Understand information protection challenges of electronic health records
- Identify information security concerns about medical devices relative to patient safety
- Appreciate the risk of medical and financial identity theft, and understand patient care issues related to data breach

In this chapter, you will learn how privacy and information security are separate disciplines that work very much together. In markets and industries, such as the military or industrial corporations, as in healthcare, privacy and security goals are often implemented for different purposes. Outside of healthcare, privacy controls are often implemented more for compliance with protecting employee or customer information the organization collects for business purposes than about protection of individual rights. Security controls are sometimes focused more on protecting the assets of the organization, rather than the individual's personal information. In the healthcare field, however, this is not true; security is tasked with the goal of protecting healthcare information both as a business product of the healthcare provider or facility *and* as a privacy right of individuals. The practice of each discipline brings together various workforce personnel in the healthcare organization. Within the complex computing environment that is healthcare information technology, many special types of equipment, systems, and applications are considered business critical and clinically essential. In fact, in the United States, the entire healthcare network is deemed critical infrastructure, so privacy and information security concerns have a direct and often dramatic impact on the healthcare organization.

Ownership of Healthcare Information

When it comes to healthcare, traditional expertise grew independently around privacy (for example, protecting identity) and information security (for example, protecting resources). Over time, both disciplines evolved and developed into specific competencies found in the workforce. Today that reality has changed. Privacy and security have integrated into an almost singular competency that every person handling protected health information (PHI) or personally identifiable information (PII) requires. The reasons for the integration have been discussed already—the digitization of health information, networking of medical systems and devices, and regulatory pressures to safeguard health information, to review a few. This is a global reality. We begin this chapter with a quick look at privacy and security of health information according to international law and customs, and focus on the key concern of ownership of the information once it is collected by a healthcare organization. This concern is addressed differently in different countries, based on the country's own views on data ownership and laws. Recognizing how authorities view this concern helps explain how relevant guidelines, laws, and customs can help make sense of the overall privacy and security approaches the country expects healthcare organizations (or data collectors) to take.

United States (HIPAA)

True ownership of health information is hard to determine. If we try to make a comparison between how the United States regulates property rights against a notion of data ownership, the comparison is flawed. To clarify, the issue is what level of control a patient in the United States actually has over use of their information. Property rights offer owners control as to how their property is used or not used. The rights enforced by U.S. law provide guidance about how the information is used; but patients don't have ownership rights in that some nonconsensual uses are authorized, such as for public health reasons or for use under purview of an Institutional Review Board (IRB). An IRB, an internal organization in an academic healthcare environment where research is conducted, would be in place in the event that clinical trials are performed with the use of human subjects. The IRB governs some baseline consent and authorization guidelines that would not necessarily include additional input from the patient. Patients do have the right to know what information is collected about them, the right to access that information, to request amendment when the information is believed to be incorrect, and to know who else has seen the information. Once the data is collected, however, the healthcare organization owns the information in the recorded format, whether written or electronic, such as a file folder or a digital e-file. The legal responsibility to safeguard the information under HIPAA stems from a perspective of proper caretaking of the data, but the law favors healthcare organization ownership.

European Union (DPD)

In the European Union, the Data Protection Directive (DPD) makes it very clear that the individuals who provide their personal information are the data owners. Data collectors have a responsibility to continually protect sensitive information, but the rights individuals have over their information do not change as the information changes hands. There are strict provisions for gathering personal data, which only allow collection of data for legitimate purposes. Once collected, the healthcare organization must respect the rights of the individuals as the data owners. Chief among the rights of data owners under EU law is the right to complain and obtain redress if an individual believes his or her information is not being used in a way the data collector indicated.

United Kingdom

Because healthcare is funded and provided almost exclusively by the National Health Service (the United Kingdom's government healthcare system), health data and medical records in the United Kingdom are seen as government property. Controls must be in place to safeguard the information, of course. There are provisions for patients to view and address perceived discrepancies in their records, but the philosophy of ownership leans toward the government. The overall responsibility for the records lies in the authority of the Secretary of State for Health.

Germany

Germany is presented here outside of the governance of the DPD because Germany has recently passed its own new law, Act Improving the Rights of Patients, in 2013. The law serves to clarify and strengthen the obligation of the provider not only to safeguard the information, but to completely document all health information. For example, the provider must document information such as patient history, diagnoses, treatment, and prognoses. The law mandates the provider to properly maintain the records (whether paper or electronic) for ten years and preserves ownership with the individual. For example, the law mandates that any and all information be made available for the patient upon his or her request.

The Relationship Between Privacy and Security

There is a danger in predicting a day when privacy and security are combined into one general category of information protection. Some people think that is the progression of things as we find more and more texts and seminars on healthcare privacy and security with the terms used synonymously. However, there remains a distinction between the two. Primarily, information security will really never focus on privacy principles such as notice, consent, and accounting of disclosures, for example. Privacy, it can be argued, will focus on more than just digital assets; it will also fulfill obligations to the patient. For example, the organization's promise in the notice of privacy practice may indicate obligations it has that are not related to ensuring confidentiality, integrity, and availability of the data. Maybe its obligations are focused on ensuring the relevancy of the information it collects. This consideration may not have any impact on information security concerns for the same information. Granted, the terms are closely related, and increasingly so. However, it is unlikely we will ever get to a point where they are indistinguishable and synonymous. That said, there are a couple of concepts that demonstrate the interconnected nature of privacy and security, particularly in health-care, where an unbreakable bond exists between the two.

Dependency

The relationship between security and privacy has developed into one of dependency. To achieve security in the healthcare industry, there are certainly elements of privacy that must be addressed. At the same time, privacy is often provided through one or more information security controls. Within the regulatory process for protecting pri-vacy of personal information (for example, under HIPAA), encryption is seen as an adequate information security control for ensuring the confidentiality of the informa-tion transferred via an e-mail. Integrated within this security control is the ability to make sure that the person to whom you want to send the e-mail is authorized to view it. This illustrates how privacy is dependent on the use of information security controls.

Privacy is also dependent on good information security practices to preserve the right of individuals to choose who has access to their information. In fact, maintaining the right to refuse to share the information at all is an element of privacy that informa-tion security is designed and implemented to protect. In the use of electronic health records (EHRs), identification, authentication, and access management technologies serve to allow credentialed access to defined amounts of data. Without proper creden-tials, access is denied. Based on the patient's choice and consent, access is even more defined. For example, when patients choose to disallow any requests for their patient status, information found in the EHR cannot be shared with friends, family, or indi-viduals calling the reception desk. Of course, there are usually additional instructions provided to allow specific family members or powers of attorney to receive patient status updates. In short, information security tools are used to protect unauthorized disclosure from a privacy perspective.

Integration

Privacy and security depend on each other, and that dependence results in an integration of the two. In other words, providing information security may involve privacy issues. Conversely, providing privacy can introduce unintended information security concerns that may have nothing to do with whatever privacy protection is being implemented. For example, a number of security safeguards (surveillance cameras and facility access logs, for example) require monitoring people or collecting personal information. These safeguards introduce privacy concerns because, not only do they keep data and people more secure, they collect personal data in the process. So, while initially you may be concerned with unauthorized access to a patient portal, you may end up having an additional concern with privacy controls. As information privacy and security pro-fessionals, we must balance such information security measures against the privacy impacts of collecting personal information. Almost daily, we see integration of privacy and security processes. The goal is to ensure that we understand the implications of privacy and security actions on each other, as well as on the problem we intended to address.

Another example, and a timely one, of how privacy concerns are integrated with information security involves the bring-your-own-device (BYOD) initiatives. While healthcare organizations are increasingly allowing individuals to bring their own smartphones, laptops, tablets, and so on, under these initiatives, they are also instituting information security policies and procedures to protect the PHI and PII on their networks—the same networks these devices are accessing. One such procedure is *data wiping*: In the event an employee quits or is terminated and that person used his or her own device to access the organization's network resources, the BYOD policy likely gives the organization the right to remotely and completely erase everything on the device. This would include the work-related information along with any potential PHI or PII. It could also include pictures, personal information, and personal property.[1] Because of this, the healthcare organization's effort to protect privacy through information security may actually infringe on the privacy of the employee. When implementing the BYOD policy, the integration of privacy and security issues should be considered.

This is not to say that integration necessarily produces a negative consequence or integration effect. Most integration of privacy and security is positive. Information security controls in a digital environment successfully provide privacy as they automate routine processes like access management. They also reduce errors in enforcement that would exist in paper-based environments where policy adherence or human action is the only line of defense. For instance, a network firewall or access control list programmed into a router certainly is less fallible than a records room clerk in charge of clearing individuals for facility entry. Moreover, privacy is the intended consequence of many information security practices. Where organizations enforce role-based access configuration of their EHR system, the privacy of the individual's information is protected by allowing access only to those providers who have a requirement to use the data. In a paper-based records system, this level of data segmentation and constrained availability is nearly impossible. Eavesdropping and easy access to data in plain view is too likely.

Information Protection and Healthcare Technologies and Initiatives

The special-purpose computing resources used to implement privacy and security within healthcare have specific implications that impact numerous initiatives underway in various areas to improve healthcare. At the same time, these special-purpose computing resources and healthcare initiatives introduce new privacy and security concerns that healthcare organizations must wrestle with.

Medical Devices

Central to the concern we have about implementing information security and privacy in the healthcare environment are medical devices. A medical device can be anything from a thermometer to a digital X-ray machine; some are stand-alone machines and tools. Increasingly, medical devices are networked (to each other or to larger networks), and they are continuously communicating. The future predicts even more types of medical devices that we wear, with some devices implanted or ingested; many already exist and are providing patient care today.

Medical devices entered the medical marketplace under the purview of a U.S. government agency now known as the U.S. Food and Drug Administration (FDA), and Figure 9-1 depicts some important events in the history of medical device privacy and security.

 TIP The U.S. Food and Drug Administration (FDA) hosts the MedWatch web site (https://www.accessdata.fda.gov/scripts/medwatch), where anyone— including healthcare organizations and patients—can submit a complaint about the potential misuse or faulty operation of a medical device. In the past few years in which cybersecurity concerns have begun populating the MedWatch database, the FDA has recognized the impact of malware on medical devices.

Medical devices introduce issues around privacy and security that are primarily tied to patient safety. In the pursuit of implementing good privacy and security practices, unintended consequences can occur with medical devices. Medical devices have been defined by the FDA as being (in part) "an instrument, apparatus, implement, machine,

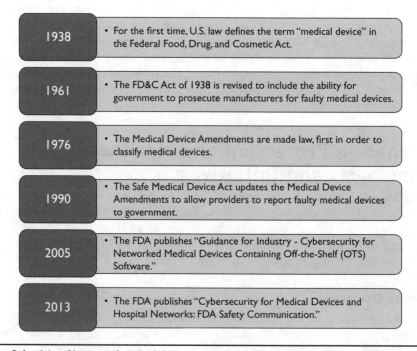

1938	• For the first time, U.S. law defines the term "medical device" in the Federal Food, Drug, and Cosmetic Act.
1961	• The FD&C Act of 1938 is revised to include the ability for government to prosecute manufacturers for faulty medical devices.
1976	• The Medical Device Amendments are made law, first in order to classify medical devices.
1990	• The Safe Medical Device Act updates the Medical Device Amendments to allow providers to report faulty medical devices to government.
2005	• The FDA publishes "Guidance for Industry - Cybersecurity for Networked Medical Devices Containing Off-the-Shelf (OTS) Software."
2013	• The FDA publishes "Cybersecurity for Medical Devices and Hospital Networks: FDA Safety Communication."

Figure 9-1 A brief history of medical device law and associated privacy and security guidance provided by the U.S. Food and Drug Administration (FDA)

contrivance, implant, in vitro reagent, or other similar or related article, including a component part, or accessory which is intended for use in the diagnosis of disease or other conditions, or in the cure, mitigation, treatment, or prevention of disease, in man."[2] As such, medical devices are essential to direct patient care and are highly regulated by the FDA.

 TIP The impact the FDA has internationally is growing. Cybersecurity issues and the relevant governance that FDA publishes are applicable to an international audience of privacy and security professionals. Following are two terrific references for those who have responsibility for managing the cybersecurity of medical devices:
"Guidance for Industry - Cybersecurity for Networked Medical Devices Containing Off-the-Shelf (OTS) Software" (U.S. Food and Drug Administration, January 14, 2005. http://www.fda.gov/MedicalDevices/DeviceRegulationandGuidance/GuidanceDocuments/ucm077812.htm)
"Content of Premarket Submissions for Management of Cybersecurity in Medical Devices - Draft Guidance for Industry and Food and Drug Administration Staff" (U.S. Food and Drug Administration, June 14, 2013. http://www.fda.gov/MedicalDevices/DeviceRegulationandGuidance/GuidanceDocuments/ucm356186.htm)

If one of these devices fails to perform or performs in an unsafe manner, it can mean patient injury or death. The reverse is also true. Where good privacy and information security practices exclude medical devices, vulnerabilities can evolve; and this can introduce patient safety risk. The proper way to address the privacy and security of medical devices is to implement, whenever possible, good privacy and security practices that understand and account for special considerations relative to medical devices. These devices may have IP addresses, operating systems, and relational databases, but they are not identical to office automation end points or servers performing office automation tasks or business functions. If a prescribed information security control may cause unintended issues, seek alternative controls and tailored safeguards. For instance, sometimes a medical device uses an operating system that is no longer supported by the software manufacturer, yet the device manufacturer can't upgrade the software unless it upgrades the device to the next model. This is often expensive, and the current model may work sufficiently for its intended clinical purpose. Upgrading to a newer model simply because the operating system cannot be updated with future vulnerability patches likely is not justified from a cost-benefit perspective. A better control to put in place is to segment the device into a separate enclave that is firewalled (quarantined) from the rest of the network but still able to access the network. In these types of cases, the required skill for a healthcare information security and privacy professional is having the savvy to know when to implement the prescribed control (for example, upgrading to new operating system) and when to seek a compensating or alternative control (for example, quarantining the device).

NOTE The growing field of clinical engineering that covers "wearable," implantable, and ingestible types of networked medical devices is called *biomedical telemetry*. The leading professional organization governing this technology is the Institute of Electrical and Electronics Engineers (IEEE), at https://www.ieee.org. More information on this topic can be found there.

Here is another scenario to help illustrate the concept. Imagine you have the job of configuring and performing the periodic software vulnerability updates to your local area network (LAN). Typically, once the prescribed updates are tested against your standard computing configuration for end points (desktops, laptops, and so on), you are authorized to accomplish this through automated routines across the network. The efficiency and effectiveness of this push-button approach are clear industry best practices. However, imagine some of those end points on your networks are in a cardiac catheterization lab. Sure, they look like desktop computers running standard operating systems, and they have a network IP address assigned to them. However, these special-purpose computers also run medical applications that serve up diagnostic-quality (high-resolution) video and imaging that enable physicians to perform complex cardiac procedures. If, in the middle of such procedures, your automatic push of the software vulnerability patch causes the system to reboot involuntarily (as patches often do), that unanticipated downtime may cause a patient safety issue.

Even if the incident does not actually harm the patient, the healthcare organization may have to face consequences. The Joint Commission, a nongovernment organization in the United States that inspects, accredits, and certifies hospitals, would require reporting of this "imaginary" event as a *sentinel event*, an unexpected occurrence involving death or serious physical or psychological injury, or the risk thereof.[3] Our imagined scenario would fall under the condition "or the risk thereof." Having a medical device reboot in the middle of a patient procedure can certainly be considered a near-miss event, because it is also easy to imagine how the process or procedure could go wrong and cause a serious adverse outcome for the patient next time. In sum, the best information security practices as applied to the healthcare industry must include a risk-reward consideration with the number one rule of healthcare at the core: first, do no harm.

NOTE Although the Joint Commission is U.S.-centric, it has peer organizations in most advanced nations. In fact, the Joint Commission itself has had an International component since 1994, with almost 700 organizations—certified in South Korea, Italy, Spain, Turkey, and Brazil, to name a select few.[4]

The main concerns about integrating networked medical devices into the overall information security program without much regard for their unique characteristics are the following:

- *Medical devices are used in direct patient care scenarios.* Medical devices that malfunction can put patients at risk and impede the diagnosis or treatment by clinicians.

- *Medical devices depend on special applications with unique protocols and standards.* Although most devices run on known operating systems and use common database technologies, they also depend on or use special-purpose applications and use distinctive protocols. The use of Health Level Seven International (HL7) data transfer protocols and Digital Imaging and Communications in Medicine (DICOM) as an imaging standard are just two examples.

- *Medical device manufacturers play a major role.* Unlike other computing device manufacturers, medical device manufacturers retain a great deal of responsibility for their devices even after they are sold to a healthcare organization. The reason for this has to do with safety rather than cybersecurity, and this responsibility can actually introduce security risks. Because medical devices are FDA-regulated and patient safety is a concern, medical device manufacturers must test and approve all third-party software before a healthcare organization can update a medical device. This process can, at best, delay the software vulnerability patch management process; at worst, it can cause medical devices to remain unpatched and vulnerable to exploit on the hospital LAN.

- *Medical devices often exist on legacy operating systems and "sunsetted" applications (those no longer supported by their developers).* The cost of upgrading a medical device to a newer model simply because the operating system or database application is no longer supported, for example, is sometimes cost prohibitive.

The point of discussing medical devices and their privacy and security implications is not to say that medical devices cannot or should not be fully integrated into the overall information security program. In fact, the opposite is true. If medical devices are not part of the enterprise information security program, it is certain that the LAN will be extremely susceptible to attack. The FBI recently conducted an investigation on healthcare organizations in the United States and found some profoundly disturbing levels of vulnerability related to poorly managed medical devices.[5] Medical devices offer information security and privacy professionals an opportunity to truly protect information by developing appropriate compensating or tailored controls. Here are some of the approaches you should consider:

- *Include the medical devices in the information security program.* Medical devices are often managed by biomedical technicians. Sometimes the department is completely outsourced to a third-party management team. However, proper communication and coordination must be made to include the devices in the overall asset inventory and vulnerability management process. According to the FBI report, simply knowing which devices have up-to-date software configurations and which do not is a big first step toward solving the problems.

- *Segment the LAN.* Quarantining medical devices or segregating them in a defense-in-depth architecture in a firewalled enclave, for example, is helpful. Because software vulnerability patch management can be on a different compliance schedule than the medical devices can support, segmentation not only provides a series of subnets and an additional line of defense from

PART II

external infiltration, it also protects the rest of the organization's network from these vulnerable devices while the testing and approval steps are taken and the manual patching process is completed.

- *Ensure that medical devices are included in the organization's data incident response policy.* When a medical device malfunctions or performance degrades, it may not be obvious that the cause is related to malware or security. As repair actions are taken, a data incident must be considered as a potential source of the problem. Additionally, the data incident policy must viably allow for biomedical technicians to report potential and actual issues. This also means that the healthcare organization will notify the medical device manufacturer and the FDA as part of normal data incident processes. Make sure to use the FDA reporting channels.

 TIP *Botnets* are the most common type of malware found on infected medical devices. Botnets lodge inside the computer and communicate back to command-and-control (C2) servers. They can act immediately or wait for a specified period of time to begin sending spam or conducting other types of attacks on a medical device. Often the goal of the botnet is to attack other networked resources on the healthcare organization's network, using the medical device as the launching pad.

Cloud Computing

In an effort to increase efficiency, reduce costs, and garner expert IT support, healthcare organizations are rapidly moving toward the "cloud." A working definition of *cloud computing* is one in which resources, software, processing power, and storage are shared and accessible on the Internet. In short, IT services are delivered much like utilities such as electricity are delivered. As with many other industries, healthcare organizations are moving to these virtual computing environments and away from the traditional information technology environment, which suffered from single-purpose server and storage resources. In traditional IT environments, costs can be prohibitive. Also, they can often result in low device utilization, gross inefficiency, and inflexibility in responding to changing organizational initiatives. By contrast, the return on investment with these cloud-based, IT-as-a-service arrangements are promising. Because future IT costs seem to be boundless, savings from initiatives like cloud computing are very attractive.

Some of the benefits, besides storage, that cloud computing promises to provide to healthcare organizations include:

- EHR technologies
- Improved data exchange or sharing
- Availability of large amounts of data for analytics ("big data")
- Patient enrollment

- Home health, telehealth, and picture archiving and communication system (PACS) technology

Going to the cloud introduces concerns relative to privacy and security, however. Some of these concerns involve privacy laws, and others are unique to healthcare. There are many concerns that all organizations face with regard to cloud computing, not just healthcare organizations. Included in this chapter are some of the most prevalent concerns that have a healthcare impact. Among these issues are multiple tenants, trans-border concerns, and third-party risk. Figure 9-2 helps to provide a visual representation of overall guidance found in NIST Special Publication 800-144, "Guidelines on Security and Privacy in Public Cloud Computing," which cautions those who rush to the cloud services model that building in the proper privacy and security safeguards can prevent the adversaries from gaining access[6], because they, too, see the cloud as a terrific business opportunity—for a very different and untoward purpose.

Multiple-Tenant Environments

By definition, the cloud computing environment has many different customers inter-mingling within the same architecture. These customers can come from banking, retail, academic organizations, as well as healthcare. Each industry may have varying manda-tory information security requirements. For example, the healthcare industry in the United States responds to HIPAA, while a retail organization is aligned with the Fair and Accurate Credit Transaction Act (FACTA) and the Red Flags Rule. Certainly, there is overlap or common ground between these regulations focused on protecting informa-tion. Sometimes there are safeguards that may limit the amount of sharing of resources, thereby reducing the return on investment of the cloud. For instance, under HIPAA,

Figure 9-2
Build in privacy
and security
when you
make strategic
decisions to
implement
cloud computing
solutions.

Carefully plan the security and privacy aspects of cloud computing solutions before engaging them.

PART II

disclosure of healthcare information is prohibited outside of treatment, payment, and operations. HIPAA prohibits health data from being accessible by other tenants because that would be unauthorized disclosure. However, data stored in shared space in the cloud may not adhere to this requirement. Therefore, cloud providers must physically segregate health data from shared virtual machines (VMs) and physical servers with multiple clients.

Cloud providers that want to support healthcare organizations must be able to provide networks that are logically partitioned enclaves with segmented database and storage layers. Healthcare organizations require enforcement of data access policy by cloud providers that is equivalent to the policy they would enforce if the healthcare organization housed the data. For some cloud providers, these requirements may be more stringent than what their other customers require, adding costs and uncertainty as to whether the cloud provider's workforce is competent to handle healthcare data. This also relates to a common concern about identity and access management, where the policies and procedures in place at the organization may be difficult or impossible to implement and enforce in the cloud. Another issue is whether the healthcare organization can restore or delete the organization's data on demand. If the data is not properly segmented, restoration or data disposal is improbable. Due to the privacy and security concern about intermingling of multiple tenants databases on shared resources in the cloud, healthcare organizations have been slower to move to cloud adoption, generally.

Trans-Border Issues

As discussed in Chapter 3, cloud providers present challenges to privacy and security in healthcare organizations due to concerns with data being transported across international boundaries. A quick examination of the major regulatory influences in this area:

- **United States**   HIPAA does not require data to remain in the United States. However, data does not escape the law by leaving the country, and healthcare organizations cannot export their obligation to comply with HIPAA. Many healthcare providers find it most manageable to mandate in the business agreement that their cloud providers offer U.S.-based cloud storage. They recognize the challenges of trans-border data in the event of a data breach or other jurisdiction problems. An inability to comply with HIPAA after a data breach exacerbates the notification process and likely will result in additional fines and penalties that could easily be avoided with a cautious approach to cloud adoption.

- **Canada**   Across all Canadian provinces, as in the United States, there is no prohibition against sharing personal data across the border; that is, PIPEDA does not specifically forbid the transfer. However, the common practice in Canada is not to share personal data outside of Canada. Canadian officials have jurisdictional concerns with trans-border data flows, much like their American counterparts. In particular, the U.S. Patriot Act, enacted after September 11, 2011, as a response to acts of terrorism, presents issues. Data pertaining to Canadian citizens that crosses the border and resides in a U.S. company for storage or other use falls under U.S. regulatory jurisdiction. In this case, the U.S.

Patriot Act may allow U.S. Government access to the personal information of Canadian individuals without their knowledge, a violation of Canada's PIPEDA. Therefore, contracts negotiated with Canadian healthcare organizations will likely mandate that data remain within Canadian jurisdiction.

- **European Union**   With respect to the DPD, trans-border data flow is expressly regulated. The DPD says "the transfer of personal data to a third country which does not ensure an adequate level of protection must be prohibited."[7] In earlier chapters, we discussed the Safe Harbor provisions, which must be in place and approved by the EU data authority before any foreign country and its data safeguards are deemed appropriate for data sharing. Alternatives in the European Union to the Safe Harbor treaty that allow data transfer are the Model Contract Clauses and the Binding Corporate Rules (BCRs). The Model Contract Clauses are standard data protection clauses approved by the regulatory authority and can be used in cloud computing contracts. BCRs apply to multinational companies that have sufficient internal data protection rules, implemented globally for the international transfers of personal data within the company. In some ways, the BCRs act as sufficient safeguard provisions in non-EU countries where inadequate or no government policies exist.

Regardless of which country the data originates from, an additional concern exists for all healthcare organizations, which is that they must all consider the location and governance of the data. One of the benefits of cloud computing is having multiple copies of data in multiple locations. This helps to mitigate any downtime or reduce time to recovery for organizations. However, these multiple copies across multiple geographic locations can be extremely problematic if the data is sensitive healthcare data. Not only is there real potential for uncontrolled copying or access, but when the requirement no longer exists for the cloud provider to maintain the information, it is practically impossible to certify full return of the data to the healthcare organization. If the data cannot be fully returned, the cloud provider would have to maintain appropriate safeguards (including incident reporting) for as long as it has the data, and that timeline can far exceed the contract the cloud provider has with the healthcare organization. As another option, if the cloud provider cannot return the data, it can certify that all copies are destroyed once the statutory limit for maintaining the data is exceeded and the contract is no longer in effect. However, if the cloud provider cannot return the data because multiple copies of the data exist, it is likely that it can never certify that all copies are destroyed.

Third-Party Risk in the Cloud

While it's true that cloud providers introduce levels of risk to healthcare organizations in terms of information privacy and security, as described in Chapter 5, the risk can be worth it because cloud computing does offer measurable benefits. Most healthcare organizations do not have or desire to have in house the capabilities that cloud providers can quickly provide (large storage facilities, processing power, resource provisioning, and network redundancy). In as much as healthcare organizations have to understand the cloud computing process to assess risks, many cloud providers do not fully understand the unique privacy and security pressures for healthcare. This mutual lack of understanding can be a source of information risk. The healthcare organization needs to make sure the cloud provider can meet the applicable regulatory standards. If it cannot, it must continue to evaluate cloud providers until it finds one that can comply and deliver all the other benefits, too.

 TIP In the United States, cloud providers must sign business associate agreements. In the past, cloud providers often did not enter into these agreements. Their position was that, as cloud providers, they did not access the data and therefore were not subject to HIPAA. The recent passage of the Omnibus HIPAA Final Rule in 2013 clarified the definition of business associate with specific regard to naming cloud providers and data centers as business associates, whether the cloud provider signs a business associate agreement or not.

In sum, healthcare organizations must carefully consider the issues and evaluate potential cloud solutions before leaping into binding agreements. Healthcare organizations that do not heed this advice will encounter problems when regulators remind them that compliance cannot be outsourced to a third party—in this case, to the cloud. What your cloud provider does or does not do will be your responsibility in terms of privacy and security of sensitive information.

Mobile Device Management

Bring your own device (BYOD) is a popular strategy that end users are embracing and organizations are trying to adopt. The positive aspects of BYOD, including reducing inventory costs and maintenance for the IT department, are evident. End users like the flexibility of using a device that they can personalize and customize (for improved productivity). These BYOD environments typically include laptops, tablets, and smart-phones that run operating systems and mobile applications the organization cannot provide resources to support. Because of the information privacy and security implications with BYOD, a mobile device management (MDM) process must be in place. The MDM policy will include access management, user rights and responsibilities, as well as what actions the organization can take with respect to these privately owned devices. Since healthcare organizations use PHI and PII that needs to be protected, they will have to address mobile device management. For instance, a growing number of healthcare providers are finding they have better productivity accessing the organization's EHR, as well as ordering tests and medication, using computerized provider order entry (CPOE) via their own personal mobile devices.

BYOD presents unique challenges in healthcare in that the PHI or PII that is located on these devices are outside the information protection reach of the organization. There is little control an organization can have over third-party software that may be loaded on a device. Further, the devices are easily lost or stolen. If the devices are not encrypted, the data loss may require patient notifications as well as government intervention. The loss of such devices is likely; as a recent article on healthcare and mobile devices put it, "$429,000 … [was] the typical large company loss due to mobile computing mishaps in 2011."[8]

One control that healthcare organizations can implement is network access control (NAC), which can identify an end user's device when the end user tries to access the healthcare organization's network. Prior to allowing the device any level of access, the device can be scanned for compliance with the latest antivirus version and to make sure other software is up-to-date with vulnerability patches. Network access control technologies can support all brands of mobile devices. This is important in healthcare, as there is a wide variety of mobile devices that try to access the network. (A growing number of these mobile devices are also medical devices.)

 NOTE There is a significant overlap among mobile device management, BYOD, and medical devices. For instance, handheld ultrasound machines are commercially available that are smartphones, medical applications, and scanning peripheral devices with Wi-Fi capability in one. An example of such a device can be found at http://www.mobisante.com/products/product-overview.

Another architecture solution that is facilitating mobile device management is the implementation of the virtual desktop interface (VDI). This configuration, relying on VM equipment and software, basically allows an authenticated user access to network resources without delivering those resources to the end device. In the past, "dumb terminals" were used to access mainframes in a mainframe computing environment, which bears some similarity to how mobile devices now access VDIs.

Health Information Exchange

We are in an age in which the digitization of patient information has made sharing the information much easier. However, constraints for using sensitive health information must still be followed. A patient who seeks treatment at Hospital A doesn't necessarily give consent for Hospital A to share that information with Hospital B unless the use is for treatment, payment, or operations. However, advantages exist for sharing health information beyond treatment, payment, and operations; and they are the basis of health information exchange (HIE). Healthcare organizations see value in HIE in that it can improve access to clinical data by providing safer, timelier, and more equitable care, with better outcomes. Sometimes the exchange is part of treatment, payment, and operations; other times, the exchange can be for research, public health, or another valid clinical reason. However, HIEs bring in privacy and security concerns, namely the creation of multiple copies of data, much like those mentioned relative to cloud service providers. Decentralized database locations with overall system awareness can help keep control localized and safeguarded.

Before we go further, rest assured that HIEs are not just a U.S.-centric movement. Although United States' healthcare organizations are implementing HIEs, globally HIEs are increasing by 10 percent per year and should reach an estimated $980 million spent on HIEs by 2019.[9] The global demand for HIEs is based on similar motivating factors as in the United States: cloud computing, mobile devices (BYOD), and emerging economies across the world. With rising economic levels, EHR implementation is spreading; thus, so is information sharing through HIEs.

If HIEs are implemented correctly, with protection of properly collected PHI or PII, their international evolution will give healthcare organizations unbelievable access to public health reporting, outcome measures, biomedical surveillance capability, and research. However, patients and regulatory authorities will be the judges when it comes to determining whether or not the HIEs can share information safely and securely. To build the necessary trust, HIEs will want to guide themselves by standards such as the U.S. Office of the National Coordinator for Health Information Technology (ONC)'s "Nationwide Privacy and Security Framework for Electronic Exchange of Individually Identifiable Health Information." This set of standards, which has international applicability as well, helps HIEs demonstrate good stewardship of PHI on behalf of the patient in terms of secure collection, use, and disclosure of PHI. Along with the ONC framework, the U.S. Department of Health and Human Services' Office for Civil Rights (OCR) published a series of fact sheets to assist HIEs in building privacy policies and to explain how HIPAA applies.

Implementation of Electronic Health Records

An EHR alters the mix of security needed to keep patient health information confidential, provide data integrity, and assure availability. Technology also brings new responsibilities for safeguarding your patients' health information that was once paper based but now is in an electronic form. The healthcare industry did not see widespread adoption of EHRs until stimulus funds were provided via U.S. Government reimbursement for their adoption as a result of the American Recovery and Reinvestment Act (ARRA) of 2009. Of course, prior to that date, some healthcare data was being collected in digital format, such as with PACS and teleradiology systems, but electronic order entry and digitization of the majority of the patient record was still the exception, not the rule. Post-ARRA, in the United States the EHR is very common today. There are two privacy and security concerns that EHR implementation introduces, and they involve access management and data management.

Access Management: Create, Write, Update, Delete (CRUD)

In Chapter 8, when we covered identity, access, and authorization within the context of information security controls, we highlighted the importance of establishing controls around who has access to what resources and when. Specific to EHRs, it's necessary to make sure the digitized information has the appropriate administrative, physical, and technical controls in place to protect the information. For EHRs, end-user rights concerning view, write, and delete permissions must be protected. In a healthcare environment with physicians, nurses, and clinicians filling multiple roles, often based on temporary responsibilities, we can expect a highly dynamic access management environment around the EHR. An example of such a scenario would be when a cardiologist wants access to a pediatric record. If that patient is not one she is currently treating, that access should be denied; but if that same cardiologist were serving on a peer review panel or held the CMO position in the hospital, access to that record may be authorized for purposes of fulfilling those responsibilities. Just because the EHR is a medically unique application or system, it is not infeasible to implement certain access control methods.

To begin with, access can be controlled by physical safeguards. Never overlook or underestimate the use of locked doors, surveillance cameras, or even security guards to augment other controls. Making resources physically unavailable to those who are not authorized to access the systems is important and effective. A likely scenario in healthcare is when an unauthorized person obtains authorized credentials and attempts to access health information. This illegal access is called *snooping*. With the proper credentials, unauthorized users can access information and network resources unless they are physically prevented from accessing them.

After putting physical barriers in place, having an active and continuous monitoring process will help control access. The process may start with coworkers who are vigilant in monitoring who is accessing systems in their view or work area. Questioning people who are not known or do not behave normally for the work conditions (for example, someone who seems nervous and rushed) is the first line of defense. Next, EHR administrators should maintain an up-to-date access list with designated roles or levels of access specified. The individuals who are on the list should be supplied with unique IDs and mandated to create a strong password or personal identification number (PIN) unless another form of multifactor authentication is available.

An often-overlooked control that can help prevent unauthorized access is an automatic shutdown routine. When an authorized user is done working or simply walks away from his or her access point (for example, desktop, laptop, smartphone, or medical device), the device should log off or shut down after a short, but reasonable, amount of time. This forced termination of access can reduce the likelihood that someone who is not authorized could piggyback or continue the session under the authorized user's credentials. In fact, even if the second person is authorized, conducting business on the network under another person's credentials is not acceptable because it violates the information security principles of authentication, authorization, and nonrepudiation.

A final consideration for healthcare organizations relative to access management is to periodically audit access and user activity logs. Having an active monitoring process that is reviewed and analyzed can help prevent and detect security incidents. Additionally, when it comes to providing data subjects or patients an accurate history of who has accessed their data or what actions may have been taken, the access management process can support that disclosure, which is required by privacy and security frameworks. In the United States, this disclosure supports a healthcare organization's obligation to provide, upon request, a full accounting of the use of a patient's PHI upon request.

Data Management

Secure data lifecycle management must be a priority when converting from paper to digital records. Many organizations tend to relax controls on the amounts of data collected or maintained as they convert to digital information. One of the prevalent reasons for this is because companies do not need to procure rooms or buildings to house the information to the extent they had to with paper records. The ease of data collection and storage that an EHR provides is also a glaring vulnerability. To put it simply, the ability for a healthcare organization to lose more than 500 individual medical records at one time has increased immeasurably. Whereas 500 medical records might have taken up an entire small records room, floor to ceiling, when all records were paper based, today that same amount easily fits on a USB thumb drive. Remember, 500 individual medical records is the threshold at which a data breach requires increased levels of government notification under HIPAA. This number illustrates how easy it is to have significant data breaches with electronic health information. While the paper-based records would have to be transported in numerous (and noticeable) trips in and out of the records room, the 500 digital records can be downloaded and transported out of the hospital door in mere minutes and completely undetected by onlookers. Therefore, with the implementation of EHRs, information security and privacy professionals must continue to educate and communicate the importance and proper management of sensitive data—in this case, PHI and PII.

Data Breach Impact

When it comes to protecting healthcare information, nothing influences the perception of success or failure like a data breach. It may be unfair to use data breaches as an outcome measure of program effectiveness since some believe it is not a matter of "if," but "when," you will have a data breach.[10] Organizational reputation is affected by a data breach. Data breaches may also cause patients to lose trust in the organization, which would have patient care implications. In addition, a breach may cause an organization to lose revenue if patients choose to switch to a competitor as a result. All these impacts may occur with a data breach, in addition to the most publicized impact of data breaches in healthcare, which are fines and penalties from regulators. These impacts are not unique to the United States; internationally, aggressive scrutiny on protection of healthcare information and increasing government fines for data breaches of sensitive information are making the headlines. Organizations that have data breaches lose more than just patient data, and Figure 9-3 helps illustrate this by presenting some of the data from surveys from organizations such as Ponemon, which has conducted an independent assessment of organizations relative to data breaches and their impact. There is no shortage of these data points, and they are often shocking.

Figure 9-3
A small sample of results from data breach surveys and investigations

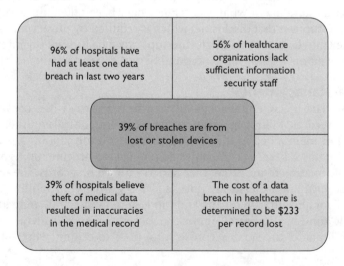

96% of hospitals have had at least one data breach in last two years

56% of healthcare organizations lack sufficient information security staff

39% of breaches are from lost or stolen devices

39% of hospitals believe theft of medical data resulted in inaccuracies in the medical record

The cost of a data breach in healthcare is determined to be $233 per record lost

Organization Reputation

Nobody wants to be the subject of headlines that read, "Hospital Loses 200,000 Medical Records," or "Healthcare Organization Fined $5 Million for Data Breach." Such headlines have a negative impact on the organization's reputation. Many organizations invest heavily to cultivate and promote the assets of public perception, brand image, and reputation. These can have a high intrinsic value for an organization. Something like a data breach can have immediate and lasting effects on reputation, whereas a good reputation may have taken years to earn.

Depending on its size and what industry it serves, the reputation of an organization has been valued as high as over a billion U.S. dollars.[11] Although not specific to healthcare organizations, the same study revealed that data breach decreased that value by as much as 31 percent, which results in a dollar reduction of as much as $330 million. In an industry such as healthcare, where trust is so important, reputation value is on the higher side of these ranges.

To help soften the blow of a data breach and mitigate the negative effects it has on reputation, several actions can be taken by the organization. One is for the organization to do what is necessary to investigate and understand why the data breach happened. Applying forensics to determine the root cause will help restore trust that at least the organization will not experience another data breach for the same reason next time. Also, how closely and openly the organization works with law enforcement, complies with regulatory inquiry, and communicates to the media propels the organization in the right direction from a public perception perspective. Finally, organizations fare much better after a breach if they provide support mechanisms such as call centers for customer inquiry, identity protection, credit monitoring, and tips on other actions affected individuals can take.

Financial Impact

The easiest way to measure the impact of a data breach in healthcare is by looking at the financial impact. In fact, our previous topic on reputation is actually measured in dollars and financial loss. All told, the amount of money lost to the organization as a result of losing information can be staggering. Between lost productivity, fines and penalties, investigation costs, and lost revenue after a breach, the financial impact is direct.

Once the data incident response process goes into action, the costs begin to mount. Even if the investigation ultimately reveals there was no breach, the cost of having employees divert from their normal duties and conduct forensics has a measurable impact. The lost opportunity to pursue normal duties or other initiatives while investigating potential and actual data breaches is where the financial impact also starts to become evident.

As soon as an actual breach is determined, costs begin to be incurred in notifying patients. In almost any breach scenario, notifying patients of the circumstances of the breach and what actions they can take is appropriate, if not mandated. If the breach involves more than 500 individual records (in the United States) or regulations otherwise require notification, notifying regulators and the media will have a cost. Advertising, setting up a toll-free call center, and direct-mail campaigns take significant financing.

If the proper course of action is to set up credit monitoring or if some other form of identity management protection for affected individuals is needed, more financial cost will be added.

Once the event is mitigated and notification actions have been taken, the possibility of fines and penalties from regulators exists. These dollar amounts tend to get the biggest headlines. However, for as much as the fines are (the average U.S. fine under HIPAA/HITECH is $2.5 million), the fact is that the fines and penalties are only roughly half of the total financial cost of a data breach, which is $5.4 million.[12]

Another component of financial cost is the resulting loss of future revenue. For publically traded companies, the stock price can decrease after a breach occurs. For non-profit healthcare organizations, the risk of having a bond rating lowered is a possibility. The impact of a lower bond rating makes it more expensive to invest in capital improvements and can make an otherwise solvent healthcare organization a better target for acquisition or merger. These are somewhat extreme outcomes, but they are very real possibilities if information protection is not a focus of the healthcare organization and data breach is a periodic occurrence rather than a rare one.

The final future state impact of a data breach that can have a financial impact on healthcare organizations is increased turnover. Every organization has turnover in patients year to year; that is normal, but the hope is that the net turnover results in a positive or increase in overall patients that use the healthcare organization. Studies show that healthcare organizations that have suffered a data breach actually experience turnover at a rate of four percent more than they expected.[13]

Medical and Financial Identity Theft

The information found in a medical record can be worth as much as four times the amount of a stolen credit card file or stolen bank account information. This is due, in large part, to two factors:

- Medical records tend to include financial data as well as health information.
- Elements in the medical record can be sold separately for maximum gain.

In either scenario, the probable use of stolen health information is to fraudulently gain access to medical services and prescription medication. In the case of prescription medication, it can be sold once it is obtained illegally. An emergency department, where patient care is delivered rapidly, is a likely source of the illegal medication or service procurement. A patient presents with an injury (even if self-inflicted) and offers a fake ID made from data they stole or uses social engineering tactics to gain access. In an effort to care for the patient first, diagnosis and treatment is made. It is common for at least a small amount of medication to be provided even when insurance or identity is in question. In the case of a prescription that must be filled later with another instance or proof of identity, for example at a retail pharmacy, chances are that the fraudulent identity will fool the dispensary. The actual person who the identity belongs to may not know any of this has happened until his or her insurance company provides an accounting of the benefits paid. This may result in increased premiums. Although the effect on insurance is germane mainly to the United States, the effect of medical identity theft on an international audience with a single payer-system where insurance fraud is nonexistent is nonetheless impactful. Where resources are limited, such fraud can make treatment or resources unavailable to those that truly need it.

Healthcare organizations, especially in the United States, handle sensitive financial information such as bank card information, credit card numbers, home addresses, and birthdates. Even in cases where the criminal does not care about the healthcare data, the access to viable financial data makes healthcare organizations a target. To date, there have been few cases where patients have been able to win lawsuits based on the loss of their PHI or PII as a result of a healthcare organization's data breach. This is mostly because it is difficult to prove harm that is directly attributable to the data loss by the healthcare organization. That can change quickly, and in the event that healthcare organizations are seen as willfully negligent in the data breach, class action lawsuits may be won by patients as time goes on. In growing numbers, however, the general public unfortunately is complacent about the loss of their financial data. Far too often, individuals who have their information stolen or compromised view cancelling their accounts and cards and setting up credit monitoring as the remedy to an inevitable reality of having the convenience of digital banking and retail. The costs incurred to banks and credit card companies for account recreation and card issuance are passed back to organizations (healthcare organizations, for example) that lose the data in the first place. This is a good reason for companies to increase efforts to protect the information.

Patient Embarrassment

The idea that patient embarrassment is a factor in data breach impact helps to illustrate the convergence of biomedical engineers, clinical system administrators, health information managers, and health information technology professionals in the practice of healthcare information security and privacy. To those who have come into information protection from a clinical background, patient care and patient safety have always been at the core of risk management (including information risk management), but the digitizing of patient information with its ease of access to huge amounts of data in a short period of time has shed new focus on the patient safety and patient care impact of data breach. Data suggests that patients may delay care or not seek it at all due to fear of healthcare organizations improperly safeguarding their sensitive information, or to fear of their sharing it.[14] This is in addition to any patients that decide to seek care at a competitor or alternate healthcare organization simply because of lack of trust.

The fear of embarrassment when sensitive healthcare information is breached is different than any emotional reaction to financial information being lost or stolen. In fact, according to Ponemon, an oft-cited source on this subject, when healthcare providers are asked what they believe to be the greatest fear patients have with respect to the potential unauthorized disclosure of their health data, they respond that public exposure or embarrassment rank above both medical identity theft and financial identity theft.[15] Figure 9-4 puts these responses into perspective.

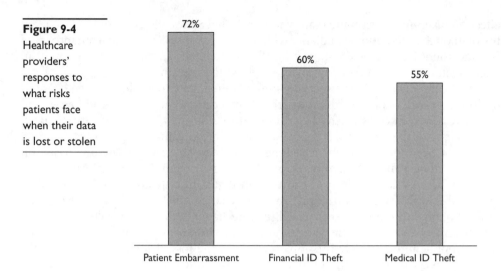

Figure 9-4
Healthcare providers' responses to what risks patients face when their data is lost or stolen

72%

60%

55%

Patient Embarrassment   Financial ID Theft   Medical ID Theft

Patients may have good, personal reasons for wanting information protected from employers, friends, family, and people in the community. Disclosing medical history and status should be their choice because once that information is disclosed in an unauthorized manner, it cannot be retrieved, reversed, or forgotten. Unlike financial information, one cannot "cancel" a medical record or change the number and make the old information useless. No monitoring service exists that can determine if any of the sensitive information is further disclosed, if employment or personal reputational decisions are made, or if actions are taken using the information. So there is no way to prove a level of harm; if there were, maybe affected individuals could better execute class action lawsuits on the basis of embarrassment alone. The RAND Corporation, which did a study of service members returning from Iraq and Afghanistan, provides a couple of examples of when public exposure and stigma figured into patient care and patient safety. Of those service members with possible post-traumatic stress disorder (PTSD) or traumatic brain injury (620,000 veterans), it is estimated that only about half of them actually seek care; and the study showed that the most common reason they delay or do not seek care is because of concerns that the information will be disclosed. In some cases of military service, disclosure to a patient's commanding officer is necessary, but not all study participants were on active duty. Their privacy concerns also involved fear of disclosure to family, friends, employers, and even fellow veterans.

When it comes to sensitive health data, the impact of delaying or not seeking care is worrisome enough where the harm is to the affected individual alone. However, it is more common that the delay or failure to seek care is more of a public health issue at the immediate family level and to the community at large. Conditions such as PTSD and other behavioral health issues can result in the patient harming themselves and others around them. Domestic violence and mass shootings top the list of tragic outcomes of a failure to get or comply with treatment. Even if the patients do seek care, they often withhold relevant parts of their medical history from their providers, mask their identity, or frequently change providers, all of which can actually sabotage the care plan.[16]

Of course, not all of the incidents of domestic violence or mass shootings have as the root cause patients delaying or not seeking care because of privacy concerns; but this is the case for some, and the stigma placed on many behavioral health conditions does influence the outcomes. For some diseases, such as sexually transmitted diseases (STDs) and some other communicable diseases, community or public health outbreaks can result if patient delay due to fear of exposure is not addressed. Again, not all delays of care in these areas can be directly attributed to patient privacy or data breach fears; but we cannot simply ignore them as major factors because in many cases they are the reasons or are contributing factors, and we end up with patient safety or patient care risks.

Special Categories of Sensitive Health Data

Health data in general is internationally protected by regulation or law. Almost every privacy and security framework makes specific mention of healthcare data. Within the general category of healthcare information (for example, PHI), there are some noteworthy subtypes that bear mentioning because they have additional or even separate handling provisions for those that require access or use. As a representative sample, the following subsections present DPD public health information protection requirements and some U.S.-specific requirements.

European Union

The DPD gives member states—the data collection agencies—the authority to deviate from regular handling procedures for privacy-protected information in matters of public health and safety. Specifically, where there are concerns for the welfare of the public at large, data collectors have some discretion. The Data Protection Act (DPA) allows for special handling considerations for health data that should be disclosed in the interest of public safety. The directive also clearly outlines an acceptance of member states that decide to deviate from normal processes for the purposes of scientific research, gathering of government statistics, and settling claims for benefits and services in the health insurance system. However, data collectors must otherwise continue to provide safeguards for protecting sensitive data from other, unauthorized disclosure.

United States

Although it is too common to assume that HIPAA contains the complete set of regulatory concerns and controls relative to healthcare, some other regulatory laws and sets of controls exist that have special purposes relative to specific patient populations. These laws include the Comprehensive Alcohol Abuse and Alcoholism Prevention, Treatment, and Rehabilitation Act of 1970 and the language amended by the Drug Abuse Office and Treatment Act of 1972.

Substance Abuse In this context, healthcare organizations that treat patients for drug and alcohol abuse must not only comply with HIPAA, and as amended, they must also comply with the Comprehensive Alcohol Abuse and Alcoholism Prevention, Treatment, and Rehabilitation Act of 1970, as well as the language amended by the Drug Abuse Office and Treatment Act of 1972. The considerations addressed by these regulations center around providing additional confidentiality. For example, even providers that treat a patient in one care setting, such as primary care, have to obtain an additional privilege to access the drug and alcohol treatment record from another care setting, such as drug and alcohol treatment, if that record is relevant to the primary care treatment. Typically, substance abuse treatment and records are regulated under behavioral health laws, and additional access clearance is required.

Protection of the Education Records of Minors The Family Educational Rights and Privacy Act (FERPA) governs the use and disclosure of the PII of minor students and, where applicable, PHI. For the most part, FERPA disallows an educational entity from disclosing any information to a third party without parental consent. While FERPA would not at first seem to have any overlap with HIPAA, it does because schools in the United States commonly employ a nurse or healthcare provider. The data collected by these individuals is covered under FERPA, even if the school has no obligation under HIPAA. The HIPAA privacy and security rules exclude from additional or redundant governance any PHI collected by school healthcare providers. FERPA is generally considered sufficient to protect the health information of minor students as part of securing the defined education record. In short, properly safeguarded information under FERPA would be compliant with HIPAA if the school is under U.S. Department of Health and Human Services (HHS) regulatory control.

Chapter Review

Upon completion of this chapter, you should have a better understanding of how privacy and security disciplines and practices have evolved into a dependency on each other, resulting in an integration of the two. Not only are the practices converging, but so are the professional competencies of the workforce members that have traditionally provided information services. As clinical engineers, biomedical technicians, health information managers, clinical system administrators, and information technology personnel have moved from paper-based information and stand-alone systems to digital, interconnected architectures, the role of and relationship between privacy and security have moved to the forefront of healthcare organization and management. This chapter covered some very important topics related to this role and relationship. To begin with, how your regulatory authority views the ownership of patient information has some bearing on what requirements you will have for safeguarding it and for ensuring that any patient rights to that information exist. From there, we looked at a couple of key factors in the evolving relationship between privacy and security that apply particularly to healthcare. As previously stated, privacy is often described as having to do with what we protect, and security as having to do with how we accomplish the task of protection.

The majority of this chapter focused on specific healthcare information technology issues as they relate to privacy and security. If you work in a healthcare setting, you certainly have familiarity with medical devices, mobile devices, EHRs, HIEs, and cloud computing. These represent clinical and business imperatives because they present specific and unique challenges to privacy and security program. If patient safety and patient care requirements are not factored into information privacy and security best practices—from the planning stages of the initiatives, through the operations phase, to decommissioning or discontinuation of the services and technologies—data breach and risk of patient harm can result.

With respect to data breach, the chapter covered the medical and financial identity theft concerns involving lost and stolen data. The value of the health information is about four times the value of the financial data obtained. This is because the data can be used to commit financial identity fraud as well as to obtain medical services, including prescriptions for use or for sale. These are not the biggest fears patients have concerning data breach, however. Public exposure and embarrassment resulting from their data being disclosed in an unauthorized manner are listed as their most prevalent fears when asked.

Data breach takes a financial and reputational toll on healthcare organizations. It is important to note that even the investigation and eventual determination that no data breach has occurred has associated direct costs and opportunity costs. Man hours spent doing forensics instead of other important tasks have a financial impact. The attention data breaches get, however, comes from the fines and penalties that are announced publicly. As those who have ever experienced a data breach and had to account for the costs know, those fines and penalties add up to about half of the total cost, which also includes notification actions, mitigation costs, and expenses for implementing patient-focused actions (for example, toll-free call centers and credit monitoring). In the end, if a data breach does occur, the evidence indicates that organizations that handle the breach quickly and openly, and work to keep the patients from getting further harmed, fare better after the breach.

Review Questions

1. The use of encryption to ensure the confidentiality of information is an example of privacy and security _____.

    A. integrity

    B. interoperability

    C. dependency

    D. nonrepudiation

PART II

2. When implemented, which of the following technical safeguards can create privacy issues if it involves collecting private information about users of the system?

   A. Malware protection

   B. System performance monitoring

   C. Audit of access logs

   D. Release of information requests

3. (TRUE or FALSE) In an effort to manage medical devices and protect them from the patient safety risks of malware exploitation, a valid information security practice is to ensure that all medical devices have the standard enterprise antivirus application implemented.

4. To apply a software vulnerability patch to a medical device, which of the following would have to be contacted for evaluation and approval?

   A. Biomedical technician

   B. Food and Drug Administration

   C. Chief Information Officer

   D. Medical device manufacturer

5. (TRUE or FALSE) Segmenting medical devices as part of a strategy to address risk is ineffective because it defeats the benefits of information availability by disconnecting the devices on a logical level.

6. Which is a privacy and security concern healthcare organizations face with cloud computing that results in people without authorization accessing data?

   A. Multitenet environments

   B. Shared costs

   C. Increased storage

   D. Federated access

7. Which is an information security control that, when implemented, can enable a healthcare organization to support a BYOD policy for physicians?

   A. Indemnification

   B. Encryption

   C. Wiping

   D. Passwords

8. (TRUE or FALSE) Periodically auditing access logs of the EHR is an effective way to help protect unauthorized CRUD access.

9. A woman receives a bill for cardiac surgery and rehabilitation in excess of $350,000. She has never received these services. When she contacts the healthcare organization to inquire about the bill, she is provided a photocopy of her driver's license, which was provided to patient administration when she was admitted to the hospital. The picture is not of her, but the address and other information are hers. What has happened?

   A. Financial identity theft

   B. Medical identity theft

   C. Medical impersonation fraud

   D. Social engineering

10. Of the following, which describes the impact of a data breach?

   A. Increased patient care costs

   B. Lost opportunity for mergers

   C. Disclosure of patient information

   D. Withholding of medical history

Answers

1. **C.** The use of encryption, an information security control, provides adequate protection of the individual's privacy. In this way, privacy is *dependent* on the information security control. Integrity and nonrepudiation are not ensured by encryption. Interoperability would be relevant among information systems, but not between privacy and security controls.

2. **C.** Only audit logging stores data specific to users that could create issues concerning privacy while properly implementing a valid information security control. Malware protection and system performance monitoring only monitor system-level issues, and release of information requests would not collect personal information without consent.

3. **FALSE.** This is false only because the medical device manufacturer must evaluate and approve any third-party software that might be added to their medical device. For this reason, it is common for some medical devices not to have the same enterprise antivirus application installed as the standard enterprise solution. Some have other applications that the vendor can support; others have no application and must have alternative or compensating controls applied.

4. **D.** The only correct answer is the medical device manufacturer, which is the only entity that must evaluate and approve any third-party software before it can be applied to a medical device. There will be some coordination with biomedical technicians for updates that impact medical devices, but they are not necessarily responsible for evaluation and approval of software vulnerability patches. The Food and Drug administration requires compliance

with vulnerability patch management, but they are not in a position to evaluate and approve specific patches for specific devices. The Chief Information Officer likely has no day-to-day role in the process.

5. **FALSE.** Segmenting medical devices into a protected enclave or a private LAN, for instance, is a proven best practice for protecting both the medical devices from exploit and the rest of the healthcare organization network from vulnerable medical devices. The segmentation has no impact on data availability.

6. **A.** Multitenet environments with cloud customers from different companies and industries, who may have access to someone else's data, inadvertently often cause concern for healthcare organizations, which have rigid access requirements. Shared costs and increased storage have no bearing on access. Federated access is a concept that does relate to decentralized access management, but it is not specific to cloud computing.

7. **B.** Encryption is the correct answer because an encrypted mobile device that is lost or stolen is not a reportable data breach: the information is considered unreadable or indecipherable to anyone other than the authorized user. Indemnification is a legal term for contracts with no relevancy to BYOD, unless the healthcare organization wants end users to have no ability to sue if their device malfunctions. Wiping is a control that is useful as a response to a lost or stolen device, but a healthcare organization should not permit BYOD with the use of PHI and PII without encryption. Password-enabled devices are important, but they do little to protect a healthcare organization from the real possibility of a data breach if a device containing PHI or PII is lost or stolen.

8. **TRUE.** Monitoring access is a best-practice method for detecting and correcting unauthorized access in a timely manner.

9. **B.** While social engineering may have augmented the type of fraud that took place, this is a clear example of medical identity theft. Financial identity theft would have been the correct answer had the scenario included the use of proper, real identification. Medical impersonation fraud, such as the use of a stolen credit card, is not applicable.

10. **D.** The only correct answer is withholding of medical history. Data breaches, or the fear that the healthcare organization will lose patient data, can cause patients to withhold some of their medical history, potentially having a negative effect on their care. Data breaches may result in increased patient care costs in that the entire healthcare system suffers from the cost of data breaches, but they have no real, immediate impact on costs. While it possible for a healthcare organization that suffers a data breach to be considered less valuable, some data suggest that in certain cases those healthcare organizations become more attractive as merger and acquisition targets. Unauthorized disclosure of patient information is actually the definition, rather than the impact of, data breaches.

References

1. National Institute of Standards and Technology. "Guidelines for Managing the Security of Mobile Devices in the Enterprise." By Murugiah Souppaya and Karen Scarfone. Special Publication 800-124, Revision 1. June 2013. p. 8. Accessed September 20, 2014, at http://nvlpubs.nist.gov/nistpubs/SpecialPublications/NIST.SP.800-124r1.pdf

2. U.S. Food and Drug Administration. "Is the Product a Medical Device?" Accessed September 16, 2014, at http://www.fda.gov/MedicalDevices/DeviceRegulationandGuidance/Overview/ClassifyYourDevice/ucm051512.htm

3. The Joint Commission. "Sentinel Event Policy and Procedures." June 10, 2013. Accessed September 13, 2014, at http://www.jointcommission.org/Sentinel_Event_Policy_and_Procedures

4. Joint Commission International. "JCI-Accredited Organizations." Accessed September 19, 2014, at http://www.jointcommissioninternational.org/about-jci/jci-accredited-organizations

5. Finkle, Jim. "Exclusive: FBI Warns Healthcare Sector Vulnerable to Cyber Attacks." Reuters. April 23, 2014. Accessed September 23, 2014, at http://www.reuters.com/article/2014/04/23/us-cybersecurity-healthcare-fbi-exclusiv-idUSBREA3M1Q920140423

6. National Institute of Standards and Technology. "Guidelines on Security and Privacy in Public Cloud Computing." By Wayne Jansen and Timothy Grance. Special Publication 800-144. Section 4.3, "Key Security and Privacy Issues." p. 21. December 2011. Accessed October 15, 2014, at http://csrc.nist.gov/publications/nistpubs/800-144/SP800-144.pdf

7. Directive 95/46/EC of the European Parliament and of the Council of 24 October 1995 on the Protection of Individuals with Regard to the Processing of Personal Data and on the Free Movement of Such Data. Section 57. Accessed September 18, 2014, at http://eur-lex.europa.eu/legal-content/en/ALL/?uri=CELEX:31995L0046

8. Hoglund, David. "The BYOD Healthcare Challenge - 2012." *Healthcare Wireless and Device Connectivity.* May 22, 2012. Accessed September 25, 2014, at http://davidhoglund.typepad.com/integra_systems_inc_david/2012/05/the-byod-healthcare-challenge-2012.html

9. "Health Information Exchange Global Market - Forecast to 2020." *Research and Markets.* To be published in March 2015. Content description accessed September 25, 2014, at http://www.researchandmarkets.com/research/3pckwq/health

PART II

10. Greenberg, Adam. "Plan ahead: Prepare for the Inevitable Data Breach." *SC Magazine.* September 2, 2014. Accessed September 21, 2014, at http://www.scmagazine.com/plan-ahead-prepare-for-the-inevitable-data-breach/article/366348

11. Ponemon Institute. "Reputation Impact of a Data Breach, U.S. Study of Executives & Managers." *Experian.* November, 2011. Accessed September 1, 2014, at http://www.experian.com/assets/data-breach/white-papers/reputation-study.pdf

12. Ponemon Institute. "2013 Cost of Data Breach Study: Global Analysis." *Symantec.* May, 2013. Accessed September 10, 2014, at https://www4.symantec.com/mktginfo/whitepaper/053013_GL_NA_WP_Ponemon-2013-Cost-of-a-Data-Breach-Report_daiNA_cta72382.pdf

13. Ponemon Institute. "2011 Cost of Data Breach Study: United States." *Symantec.* March 2012. Accessed September 3, 2014, at http://www.symantec.com/content/en/us/about/media/pdfs/b-ponemon-2011-cost-of-data-breach-us.en-us.pdf

14. Agaku, Israel T., Akinyele O. Adisa, Olalekan A. Ayo-Yusuf, and Gregory N. Connolly. "Concern About Security and Privacy, and Perceived Control over Collection and Use of Health Information Are Related to Withholding of Health Information from Healthcare Providers. *Journal of the American Medical Informatics Association.* August 23, 2013. Accessed September 16, 2014, at http://jamia.bmj.com/content/early/2013/08/23/amiajnl-2013-002079.full

15. Ponemon Institute. "Fourth Annual Benchmark Study on Patient Privacy and Data Security, Ponemon Institute Research Report." *ID Experts.* March 12, 2014. Accessed September 25, 2014, at http://www2.idexpertscorp.com/ponemon-report-on-patient-privacy-data-security-incidents/

16. Felt-Lisk, Suzanne, and Jennifer Humensky. "Privacy Issues in Mental Health and Substance Abuse Treatment: Information Sharing Between Providers and Managed Care Organizations: Final Report." Mathematica Policy Research, Inc. January 17, 2003. Accessed September 2, 2014, at http://aspe.hhs.gov/datacncl/reports/MHPrivacy/MHPrivacy.pdf

Workforce Competency in Healthcare

In this chapter, you will learn to

- Understand the status of the U.S. and international information privacy and security workforce
- Recognize implications of cybersecurity workforce status on healthcare
- Understand the convergence of traditional healthcare skill sets into cybersecurity responsibilities
- Identify knowledge domains required for healthcare cybersecurity competency
- Describe government and educator initiatives to improve cybersecurity workforce competency

With the increase in the number and severity of data breaches happening globally, many call for measures to provide for and ensure that healthcare has trained and competent workforce members protecting sensitive information. Of course, the need for measures of competency is not necessarily unique to healthcare; however, many of the information privacy and security competencies are specific to healthcare. The advances in healthcare information technology and the increasingly complex systems and interconnections, coupled with the value of the data—all used and shared within the healthcare environment—have initiated an imperative in healthcare. Not only must we put programs and technology in place to protect the information assets from unauthorized disclosure, but we must also make sure we have employees equipped and trained to succeed sufficiently in their responsibilities.

Cybersecurity Workforce

Many of us remember the days leading up to the year 2000, or "Y2K," as the world came to know it. At that time, we began to realize just how dependent we were on integrated and interconnected computers. Banks, retailers, and even healthcare organizations had to examine any machine containing a microprocessor to find those that might react and fail due to a date change from a year ending in 99 or 00. The fear was that computers and software that had only a two-digit year field size would "think" the date had changed back to the year 1900. Critical calculations, such as in the banking industry, for example, would miscalculate things like interest accrued or owed. In healthcare, the worry was that devices such as telemetry units or ultrasound machines would simply stop working. Billions of dollars were spent worldwide to patch systems or replace them with newer versions of software that used four-digit year field sizes. If you are too young to remember this Y2K effort, now you know why we always use four digits in an application's year field. Maybe you never gave it a second thought, until now.

In the end, either because of the focus and attention paid to this problem or because the computers were never at much risk in reality, there were no catastrophic events that occurred when the clock struck 12:00 a.m. on January 1, 2000. In the process, we developed disaster recovery plans, refined backup strategies, and mandated continuity of operations disciplines. Most of these concepts remain integral parts of every information security and privacy professional's responsibilities; however, the level of interconnection among systems and the degree of our reliance on them has changed almost immeasurably since the Y2K era. Continuity of operations plans (COOPs) do not involve manual processes—those are long forgotten. It usually means a redundant, or backup, system. Disaster recovery in the year 2000 might have been sufficient within 24 hours. Today, as industries (including healthcare) are identified as critical infrastructure, disaster recovery is measured in seconds, minutes, or hours, at most.

This critical infrastructure is also a viable target for attacks. Threats are real, and attacks come from many sources, including hackers, nation states, terrorists, and organized crime. To provide cybersecurity defenses, we must have the right people equipped and trained in the right positions in the organization. This was true in order to get us through the Y2K crisis, and it is still true in order to help us leverage the power of interconnection and digital information while not losing sensitive personal information to the adversary in the process.

Even if we determine that we have the quantity of individuals needed for cybersecurity jobs worldwide, those people need to be qualified. This is a profession requiring a high-level skills (not all of them technical) to maintain systems, secure networks, make safe applications, and monitor compliance, to name just a few. The shortage is found both on a global scale and in the United States.

Global

Where there is a shortage of skilled cybersecurity workers, some countries are approaching the issue and having some success. For instance, the United Kingdom published a "Cyber Security Strategy" document in 2011 that established a blueprint for how its government wanted to protect and defend against these cyberattacks from terrorists, organized crime, and so on. Of course, we cannot forget that cyber vulnerabilities are often internal, and strategies for avoiding these internal vulnerabilities are included in the strategies described in the document. The objective most relevant to cybersecurity workforce competency is the fourth one, titled "Building the UK's cross-cutting knowledge, skills and capability to underpin all cyber security objectives." To carry out this objective, subobjectives are discussed that include establishing a framework for certifying the competency levels of information security professionals. The strategy also has as a goal the requirement to certify training programs for cybersecurity.[1]

What is important to note is that the United Kingdom government made an assessment and determined that it did not have enough cybersecurity workers. This scarcity was impeding their ability to reach their cybersecurity strategy goals. They found that students were leaving educational programs that could prepare them for cybersecurity jobs. Those individuals that did enter the market opted for higher-paying positions as contractors or opted to work in private firms. This is primarily because the government could not compete with the salaries the private sector can offer.

Along with building specialized programs and establishing competency measures for the workforce, the United Kingdom is trying to reach potential cybersecurity workers much earlier in their education. In fact, government agencies are providing special learning materials in the curriculum for the nation's 11- to 14-year-olds in order to increase cybersecurity skills. Another successful approach employed by the British government is to sponsor cybersecurity apprenticeships to provide on-the-job training and mentorship for potential workers.

The country of Ireland offers a second global example of how nations deal with their own cybersecurity workforce shortages and related competency concerns. Ireland seems to be doing very well in the cybersecurity arena, as organizations such as McAfee and Symantec have opened locations there and been able to attract and train qualified workers. In all, the nation employs around 6,000 people in those two organizations, and other security firms have since established a business presence in Ireland. The investment by these private security companies has increased the pool of qualified cybersecurity workers, either by relocating talent from other places or recruiting Irish citizens and training them.

As a major financial center in Asia, and Southeast Asia's only truly developed nation, Singapore is also finding cybersecurity to be a challenge. As its government links corporations with public facilities and infrastructure to obtain real-time data, the risks and vulnerabilities are huge. Recent attacks on government web sites and data breaches of sensitive company data have the potential to tarnish Singapore's reputation as a safe and secure business climate. For this reason, Singapore has committed to a public-private partnership to train and develop a workforce for cybersecurity through the Singapore Economic Development Board (EDB). The country is starting from almost zero, as only 0.8 percent of Singapore's entire information technology workforce is competent in cybersecurity responsibilities, such as malware detection and prevention.

United States

The shortage of cybersecurity professionals is just as prevalent in the United States as it is globally. Some estimates indicate that only about 10 percent of the required qualified (competent) cybersecurity workforce is in place. Leading cybersecurity experts and organizations such as the Department of Defense are very forthcoming about the fact that demand far exceeds supply. If the United States truly has only 10 percent of the personnel it needs, imagine how underserved the nation's critical infrastructure is. In descriptive terms, more than 300,000 manufacturing plants, 50,000 water utilities, thousands of electric utilities, 200 natural gas utilities controlling 2.4 million miles of distribution pipes, 28,000 food processing plants, 100 urban rail systems, and 140,000 miles of freight rail tracks make up the nations' critical infrastructure in the United States,[2] and those numbers likely represent just a portion of the infrastructure. Other components, such as healthcare networks, are not included in those numbers. The requirement for competent cybersecurity professionals across all industries with critical infrastructure ties is enormous. As previously stated, the risk of industrial control systems sustaining cyberattacks is getting higher, and the results can be life-threatening. When it comes to healthcare, any exploit of the healthcare infrastructure, interconnected medical devices, and sensitive data traversing the network can be a matter of life and death.

To respond to these threats and to best maintain the critical infrastructure, organizations including the U.S. Federal Government have established position descriptions that list required duties and skills. Each positon is filled with personnel who best match the particular job requirements, of course. It has become clear, however, that more needs to be done to better prepare, train, educate, recruit, and retain competent cybersecurity personnel. The focus is becoming more proactive than reactive.

A groundbreaking effort is underway at the National Institute of Standards and Technology (NIST), the Department of Homeland Security (DHS), and the Office of Personnel Management (OPM). These organizations have established the National Initiative for Cybersecurity Education (NICE), a group that classifies cybersecurity job functions so that personnel can be trained to meet those requirements. The categorization and standardization of the requirements will also help those organizations that need cybersecurity professionals better predict and fill cybersecurity skill-set shortages. Although NICE is primarily focused on the U.S. Federal Government workforce, it does have applicability in the private sector. Not only is NICE working with the entire U.S. public education system, including universities and colleges, in some ways it is shaping private sector business approaches to the same competency issues. NICE is examined in greater depth later in this chapter.

Healthcare Cybersecurity Workforce

The status of the healthcare cybersecurity workforce is at a shortage, and it fares worse than other industries. Many healthcare industry surveys indicate that healthcare is lagging in terms of adopting security controls and practices. It stands to reason that healthcare also lags behind in employing competent cybersecurity workforce members. There are well-documented reasons for this. First, the business of healthcare is healthcare, not cybersecurity. For this reason, C-level executives (CEOs, CFOs, and so on) traditionally focused on initiatives that drove revenue or improved clinical outcomes, and legitimately so. Healthcare information technology began to see increased investment over the last 20–25 years, as electronic health record (EHR) implementation and picture archiving and communication system (PACS) technology demonstrated return on investment (ROI). (In the case of EHRs, the ROI came from reimbursement by the American Recovery and Reinvestment Act.) Information security was always a cost at best, and at worst seen as an impediment to initiatives focused on increased revenue or improved clinical outcomes. Not any longer: the consequences of poor cybersecurity investment, or lack thereof, has executive board–level attention. The need to demonstrate

ROI still exits, but that is becoming easier, considering the costs of a breach. Knowing that the average data breach in the United States costs a healthcare organization approximately $5.4 million for investigation, remediation, and notification is a significant data point.[3] Also included in that number are the fines and penalties from government regulators, which, when published, harms an organization's reputation and negatively influences future revenue as patients choose other care options.

Within that context, 56 percent of information technology leaders estimate that they have too few information security workers.[4] Four percent of those respondents were in healthcare. Other studies show that a small percentage of the total IT budget is allocated to information security spending, although the trend is moving upward. This lack of investment can be related to or result in a lack of competent personnel in key positions for cybersecurity in healthcare. Because insider threats or the actions of employees, as well as third-party business partners, are still the causes of most data breaches in healthcare, lack of competency can be attributed to these information loss and theft problems.

Similar to what NICE is doing, healthcare cybersecurity workforce competency is being addressed by the National Health Information Sharing and Analysis Center (NH-ISAC). NH-ISAC is developing a framework using NICE's guidelines, but one that is specific to preparing future healthcare cybersecurity workers. The goals of the NH-ISAC are to

- Increase security resilience (Prevention, Protection, Mitigation, Response & Recovery) in the private and public sectors

- Expand security awareness and workforce education (Growing a National Cybersecurity Workforce)

- Enhance security leading practices (NIST Cybersecurity Framework, Standards and Certification Bodies, Security Technology Innovators)[5]

The need for cybersecurity professionals across all industries internationally includes the recognition that such talent is needed in healthcare. As data breaches increase in frequency and severity, as well as the public embarrassment to data collectors and government officials, a sense of urgency grows. This is in addition to the fines and penalties the government has begun to levy on healthcare agencies. In 2013, the government of the United Kingdom assessed £200,000 against the National Health Service for improperly disposing of obsolete computers with over 3,000 records. The computers ended up on eBay for sale.[6]

Another example from the myriad of information privacy and security misadventures comes from Canada. In 2013, an unencrypted laptop was stolen that had personal health information identifying 620,000 patients from Alberta. Human errors, lack of policies and procedures, and immature information security governance are cited by government officials as evidence for the need not only to better educate all workers on health information protection but to recruit and retain competent information security and privacy professionals in healthcare organizations.

Convergence of Skill Sets

Unlike most other industries that handle sensitive information and that made the jump from paper to digital, healthcare has developed most of its cybersecurity workforce internally. Many professionals who have assumed cybersecurity responsibilities were trained, and gained experience, in areas often unrelated to information technology. Other industries, such as banking and retail, most likely gained cybersecurity resources—even ones that were developed from within the organization—from help desk personnel, network operations, or software developers. In healthcare, today's cybersecurity workforce may come from an information technology background, even if it is from outside the healthcare industry. However, it may just as likely come from a background of biomedical engineering or health information management. In addition, it is not uncommon for non-IT or non-cybersecurity personnel, such as risk managers, legal staff, and compliance office personnel, to have a key role in the organization's incident response process and hold key positions within the information governance structure relative to information security issues.

Biomedical Engineers

Biomedical engineering is the profession that designs, installs, sustains, secures, and helps to safely operate medical devices, systems, and networks. These professionals are trained and experienced in systems design work and engineering problem solving. They are also specifically adept at applying these concepts to healthcare devices for the safe treatment of patients. As medical devices have become more digital, more connected, and more complex, biomedical engineering staff have evolved competencies similar to those of information technology and cybersecurity professionals. For these reasons, it is best when an inclusive relationship exists among these three communities in a healthcare organization.

Biomedical engineers have always been concerned with the safe operation of medical devices. When these were stand-alone devices, not connected to anything other than a patient, safety had more to do with mechanical failure than anything else. As medical devices integrated microprocessors, used IP addresses on the network, and evolved into special-purpose computers, they took on cybersecurity implications. Because those cybersecurity implications can often result in patient safety issues when the devices produce inaccurate results or fail to operate at all, biomedical engineers needed to gain cybersecurity competencies. For example, biomedical engineers now are responsible for access and authentication processes involved with medical devices. They can also be responsible for perimeter security devices protecting medical device enclaves on a segmented hospital network. Most importantly, biomedical engineers are the key component in a safe and secure medical device software vulnerability management program. Biomedical engineers have a responsibility to coordinate with medical device manufacturers to ensure that patches are tested and approved. Once approved, the patches can be applied to the medical devices, either by the manufacturer or by the in-house biomedical engineering team. The proper inclusion of biomedical engineers in decision-making processes concerning various information security issues as they impact medical devices can avoid frustration, patient safety issues, and frustrated clinicians.[7]

NOTE The title of biomedical engineer is sufficient to cover all the types of job functions this community performs. However, there are different core competencies within this field. There are clinical engineers who design devices and systems, and there are biomedical technicians who typically maintain the medical devices and networks. That said, while a biomedical technician is more likely to have the cybersecurity role, it's not entirely accurate to assume that clinical engineers will be excluded from this discussion.

Information Technology

Information security skills and responsibilities often develop with the information technology department as a byproduct of normal information technology tasks (implementing authentication, reviewing access logs, provisioning users with privileges, and so on). However, information security requires different skill sets, so IT workers can't be expected simply to absorb cybersecurity tasks. For instance, senior leaders in information technology indicate that cybersecurity workers are needed and sometimes have more broad-based skills.

In healthcare, information technology personnel often make the transition to information security personnel as new regulatory requirements have added pressures on healthcare organizations. While the healthcare organization long ago implemented certain security controls such as firewalls, secure routers, or antivirus software, the advent of laws like HIPAA in the United States made having formal positions to fulfill information privacy and security roles a requirement. Some of the first information technology professionals in healthcare to make the evolution to cybersecurity did so as a response to HIPAA and related categories of legislation, as much as for any other reason.

Outside Industry Because healthcare as an industry has been slower than most to incorporate cybersecurity, it is common to see healthcare organizations reach out to other industries for talent. The benefit to this approach is quicker implementation of cybersecurity discipline. It is also useful to seek results from industries that are benchmarked for cybersecurity, such as banking. However, the drawback to this, as those who have worked in healthcare cybersecurity know, is that even proven cybersecurity practices in other industries cannot always be implemented in healthcare without careful consideration of the healthcare environment.

That said, it is unrealistic to expect healthcare organizations to train, develop, and retain cybersecurity professionals without some level of prior experience. The fact remains, healthcare organizations are not cybersecurity centers of excellence. While they need to comply with cybersecurity to the extent of protecting patient information, their primary efforts toward building and investing in a competent workforce will be within patient care areas. Whether through outsourcing or simply hiring already trained cybersecurity professionals, industries outside of healthcare are an important source of cybersecurity healthcare workers that contribute to advancing the healthcare information technology department.

Health Information Management

Another example of the convergence of different healthcare professions for cybersecurity purposes is in the area of health information management (HIM). HIM professionals have long been central to compliance with managing patient records, coding processes, and billing procedures. These professionals require formal education and can be certified as registered health information technicians (RHITs) and registered health information administrators (RHIAs). Competency measures are nothing new to these professionals, who have always been central to the healthcare organization's privacy and security programs because of their expertise in medical records and health information in all formats. The advent of EHRs, electronic coding and billing systems, and web-based patient portals, for example, have pushed HIM professionals into increasing roles relative to cybersecurity. One of the interesting side effects of the changes is how HIM personnel must now be proficient in a decentralized environment, whereas traditionally they were stewards of centralized medical record areas or in-house departments.

Compliance (Risk Management, Legal Department, Privacy Office)

It may not be obvious how professionals in the areas of compliance and risk have taken on more responsibilities in cybersecurity. These personnel, in healthcare, are the risk managers, legal professionals, and privacy officers. All have roles and responsibilities that extend back many decades as healthcare organizations developed. Their roles and responsibilities would be critical even without any additional concerns with cybersecurity; but as the information handled by the healthcare organization has become more prolific, digital, and pervasive, these professionals have turned their attention to helping with cybersecurity concerns involving location of data, governing access to data, and managing third-party risk. Of course, changing regulations and patient privacy issues are their area of expertise (especially with compliance and legal personnel). As part of the data breach incident investigations and reporting processes, compliance and legal personnel understand reporting obligations. Finally, these individuals also lead most contract negotiations and help the organization obtain cybersecurity insurance.

TIP Cybersecurity insurance is a type of protection healthcare organizations may choose to purchase to mitigate some of the financial impact of a data breach. Some advisors claim that cybersecurity insurance has a positive impact. For example, coverage premiums and liability limits can be favorable for organizations that have strong data breach prevention and cybersecurity programs. In short, cybersecurity insurance is beneficial but is not a substitute for having cybersecurity policies and procedures in place.

The historical significance of risk management personnel is just as impressive as that of compliance and legal personnel. In addition, the roles and responsibilities of risk management personnel are related to the work done in compliance and legal departments. In fact, many risk managers are considered part of the overall compliance team. In some instances, the risk management group reports directly to the Chief Nursing

Officer because of his or her focus on patient care and patient safety issues. A risk manager designs and implements a plan for those clinical and administrative activities that healthcare organizations perform to identify, evaluate, and reduce the risk of injury to patients, staff, and visitors, as well as the risk of loss to the organization itself.[8]

The responsibilities a risk manager has in healthcare include putting processes and procedures in place to avoid risk in the first place. For example, before a patient has surgery to remove a limb, a process exists to have more than one person verify the appropriate surgical area. The area is marked and several people participate in the process, including surgical staff and the patient, and all agree to the correctness of the marked site prior to the patient receiving anesthesia. The surgeon also verifies which limb is to be removed prior to entering surgery. All of this sounds extreme, but as a result of lessons learned from medical errors, risk managers have helped develop these checks and balances to prevent mistakes or miscommunication. If an adverse event or disaster happens, a risk manager would have the responsibility to minimize the loss or damage such events cause. For instance, after a hurricane, a risk manager would be part of the responsible team to put the disaster recovery plan in place or implement emergency mass casualty procedures. In times of disaster and crisis, risk management is particularly useful in maintaining order and helping the organization adhere to standard operating procedures.

Because healthcare organizations are considered critical infrastructure, the worlds of risk management and IT collide when there is any IT-related event that affects patient care. One such example might be network downtime, since it can be considered an adverse event and must be documented for potential reporting to various agencies, such as state public health departments in the United States.

TIP In healthcare, risk management is a function that may not include primary responsibility for *information* risk management. That responsibility may reside with IT, but this is an example of how various communities in the healthcare organization are closely related in terms of implementing cybersecurity and privacy.

Clinical Professions with New Cybersecurity Concerns

Since everyone in healthcare is responsible for protecting sensitive healthcare information, clinical professionals of all kinds who use protected health information (PHI) and personally identifiable information (PII) have found new obligations in doing their jobs. The concept of having the responsibility to maintain patient privacy is not new, but the technologies and communication abilities that clinicians employ to better provide patient care often have information security and privacy considerations. Clinicians must understand and be mindful of these considerations. Although this responsibility for cybersecurity is not the same as the responsibilities described relative to biomedical engineers, information technology staff, compliance officers, and risk managers, the role of clinical personnel is changing and is worth noting.

Healthcare Providers

The requirement for physicians, nurse practitioners, and physicians' assistants to incorporate cybersecurity into their practice of medicine is twofold. First, healthcare business owners have a legal responsibility not only to ensure that they follow relevant guidance, but to ensure that their offices are in compliance. This means that their EHR and IT infrastructure must have the necessary controls in place to protect digital information. Second, physicians who own their own practices, as well as partners in group practices, have the responsibility to ensure that their staff meets requirements for initial, annual, and recurring training on privacy and security practices. Additionally, the correct policies and procedures, such as an information security plan, for example, must be in place to comply with regulations such as the HIPAA privacy and security rules.

In the rush to implement the latest technologies, including smartphones and EHRs, providers must contend with risks of data loss and theft that were not part of their practice prior to the digitizing of patient data. A telephone or verbal order for a medication or an exam does not exist in an interconnected world of computerized order entry. That communication needs to be secure from point to point. Simply losing an unencrypted mobile device with gigabytes worth of PHI or PII data on it is more likely than losing the same number of records in paper format.

To illustrate another facet of the way cybersecurity issues have influenced practice patterns, social media (Facebook, Twitter, and Instagram, for example) has created challenges for healthcare providers. In an effort to better connect with patients, many providers are open to communicating with patients through personal e-mail, text messages, and social media. However, because these methods often are not encrypted, extreme caution must be taken to obtain patient consent, as required, and to limit the amount of any PHI or PII transmitted. In fact, the best policy is not to use these communication methods for transmitting PHI or PII, even *with* patient consent.

Nurses and Clinical Data Analytics

A growing initiative in healthcare, as well as in other industries, is the concept of "big data." While *big data* is hard to define, within healthcare it refers to the aggregation of vast stores of years' worth of research and development data from drug companies, mixed with EHR information, and integrated into enormous government databases. Big data offers never previously conceived possibilities for data access, storage, and analytics. The promise of big data, including improved outcomes and increased quality of healthcare practices, encourage data sharing among many different organizations. The nursing profession and clinical researchers are working hard to assemble these large quantities of data, and are attempting to analyze it all in new and meaningful ways. Nurses, in particular, are using this data and new algorithms to create care plans for conditions such as sepsis and congestive heart failure, as well as determine the best interventions for older adults who are fall risks. Using data analysis, providers are improving the quality of life for patients and decreasing costs for healthcare organizations by reducing readmissions (typically not reimbursed) and improving practices.

Big data, data sharing, and reporting, however, bring new risks of data de-identification and unauthorized disclosure of PHI or PII. Much of the promise of big data really does not depend on the individual identities of the data subjects, so care must be taken to properly remove or obfuscate identifiers. When that does not happen, the risk of unauthorized disclosure is great. The nursing community and clinical researchers, to name a few, are at the forefront of this work involving identifiers.

Additionally, nurses have a leadership role in ensuring that patients are notified of privacy practices. This notification includes explaining the potential for information sharing as a result of initiatives similar to big data, such as health information exchanges (HIEs). While HIEs are allowed under the treatment, payment, and operations provision of HIPAA, healthcare organizations that participate in HIEs nevertheless are required to indicate this participation on patient consent forms. Nurses, in their distinct role as patient educators, are often essential in helping patients understand their rights and the obligations of the healthcare organization.

Government Initiatives

The governments of most every nation have acknowledged the shortage of qualified cybersecurity workers. They understand the need for competency measures to find and retain qualified cybersecurity workers. All industries have a need for these workers, and healthcare is no exception. To provide examples of this, we don't have to look any further than the United States and the United Kingdom. Their governments are creating organizations to assemble thought leaders to help develop the next generation of cybersecurity professionals. In both of these countries, this effort extends into healthcare specifically.

NICE

The National Initiative for Cybersecurity Education (NICE) is an organization that was established to create and advance the National Cybersecurity Workforce Framework, which can be used by educators at all levels, but particularly in secondary schools (high schools), to help shape curricula for science, technology, engineering, and math (STEM) programs. Within these disciplines, cybersecurity education should be provided in a consistent, standardized way. The outcomes of such curricula will be a future workforce with a common level of competency from which to recruit, develop, and retain employees. Over time, and with experience, these individuals can grow into the types of highly qualified cybersecurity professionals we do not have enough of today. The impetus for NICE and the workforce framework is U.S. Executive Order 13636, signed by President Barack Obama, which calls for "the development of a framework to reduce cyber risks to critical infrastructure."[9] This framework is called the "Cybersecurity Framework."

Regardless of the organization for which a person works, a framework for workforce competency should be possible. The NICE model is structured around distinct categories and specialty areas,[10] which are further broken down into typical tasks, and knowledge, skills, and abilities (KSA) expected of those working in the specialty areas. Breaking the areas down into KSAs serves mainly to provide order and arrangement. Cybersecurity workers are often expected to be versatile; they have duties that cut across specialty areas and can have multiple KSAs. This is especially true in smaller organizations.

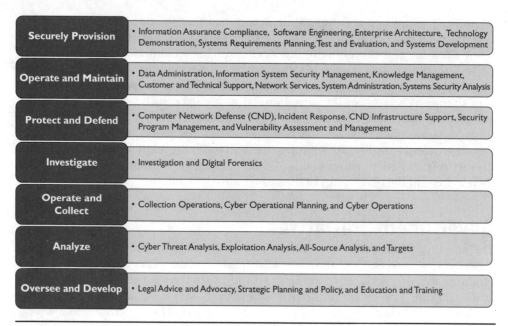

Figure 10-1   NICE Framework with associated specialty areas

In larger organizations, specialization may be possible, but the mission of the organization may dictate cross-training and performance of multiple, shared key tasks. Figure 10-1 illustrates the NICE Framework's categories and specialty areas.

NHS Cyber Initiative

Hiring officials and government data authorities recognize the shortage in required competencies relative to cybersecurity. This is true even within the National Health System (NHS), where poor security practices and lack of skilled workers are considered root causes for highly publicized data breaches. For this reason, the NHS has initiated a program to recruit and train future workforce members. The lack of skilled cybersecurity staff leaves healthcare organizations prone to external hackers' attacks. However, internal processes and threats continue to be problems. The numbers are somewhat staggering. Between 2008 and 2011, a watchdog group in the United Kingdom gathered data using a freedom of information request from the NHS. They found that an average of five data incidents occurred per week in the UK healthcare system during that time frame.[11]

It appears the shortage will be a reality for some time to come unless there is intervention. For instance, currently less than one percent of recent graduates in the United Kingdom go into cybersecurity careers, according to the International Information Systems Security Certification Consortium, (ISC).[2] This percentage translates to 7,635 graduates who took cybersecurity jobs after completing their first IT-related degree. Even at that rate, business officials claim that the individuals they do hire are not adequately prepared for cybersecurity roles in their organizations. This claim is backed up by an examination of UK computer science curricula, which averages less than five percent coverage of cybersecurity topics.[12] In a 120-credit degree, that would be six credits or possibly just two classes.

Experience and exposure to cybersecurity operations have no substitute—notwithstanding the average of two classes offered in the curricula. Cybersecurity graduates lack familiarity with relevant knowledge of risk management and information governance. The effort and attention is in programming, web development, and software application creation—all data collection, use, transfer, and storages actions. Not enough emphasis is made on protecting the data assets once they are in the possession of the data collectors.

NH-ISAC

In response to the U.S. Presidential Memorandum establishing a call to action for protecting the nation's critical information infrastructure, Information Sharing and Analysis Centers (ISACs) were established. These are public and private sector organizations working together on industry-specific issues. Individual ISACs comprise the overall organization; and one of those ISACs, the National Health ISAC (NH-ISAC), is focused on U.S. healthcare organizations. This group looks at healthcare and public health critical infrastructure and develops recommendations for security protection, cybersecurity approaches, continuity of operations, and disaster recovery. The National Council of ISACs (NCI) establishes a communication and sharing framework to assist individual ISACs in collaborating and in advancing their respective initiatives. Of course, ISACs interact with each other and leverage best practices as much as possible. Following are some of the specific products NH-ISAC provides healthcare organizations:

- Trusted, timely, and actionable cyber intelligence
- Situational awareness (threat and vulnerability monitoring)
- Countermeasure solutions, incident response, best practice, and education[13]

Competency Measures

The function competency measures have played in information technology and cybersecurity are established, accepted, and some may argue indispensable. New measures enter the marketplace every year, and some older measures become obsolete due to technology changes or market saturation. Regulations such as HIPAA and implementation guidance such as that provided by NIST Special Publication 800-66 address the need to have a qualified workforce doing the work (in this case, handling electronic PHI).[14] Formal education has the most persistence and longevity of available competency measures. A college degree holds its value over a much longer period of time than a credential or specific information technology training that will change and perhaps become obsolete. Yet formal education is less dynamic and less flexible when it comes to technology and market changes. Consider the earlier example of how little cybersecurity practicum is offered in UK formal education. It takes considerable time to establish coursework with the appropriate academic rigor necessary.

PART II

Measures such as credentials and certifications are extremely popular in the IT and cybersecurity industries because of their speed to market and responsiveness to industry needs. However, the quality of credentials and certifications is often suspect because they can be relatively easy to create and sell. In these cases, the credential or certification provides no legitimate measure of competency.

The need for competency measures for the healthcare-specific cybersecurity and privacy workforce is a mounting imperative. With the increasing complexity of healthcare information infrastructure and the impact data breaches have, hiring officials, healthcare leaders, and government regulators all have a growing interest in the topic. Figure 10-2 depicts various competency measures and serves as a reminder that they are not intended to be checklists. The goal is not to have a set number of certified or degree-holding personnel, or a certain number of people who belong to a professional organization or have continuing education, but the workforce competency process should be responsive to the following:

- **Organization**   The size and scope of the healthcare organization, along with services provided, level of technology maturity, and third-party business relationships

- **Education**   Offerings and quality of curriculum delivery that either anticipates or at least reacts to business requirements

- **Industry**   Regulatory concerns, market pressures, clinical practices, and local and national competition

- **Privacy and security**   Changes in controls and standards, technologies that better support information protection, and policy and procedural effectiveness

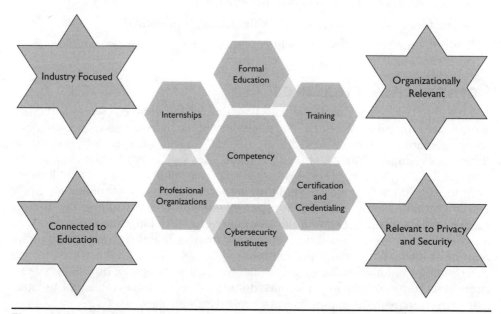

Figure 10-2   Workforce competency components and external considerations

Formal Education

To assist those individuals who wish to enter the cybersecurity workforce, the United Kingdom built a program complementary to it national curriculum, not only to enhance its computer science programs with cybersecurity resources but also to create resources to help teachers improve lesson plans. This investment in the formal education system is called the National Cyber Security Programme, and it makes clear to educators and learners alike that cybersecurity is of national interest. Because healthcare is funded by the UK government, some of this investment certainly benefits the government via healthcare organizations. To influence students at the right time in their learning about potential careers they might have in cybersecurity, innovative strategies such as online competitions and scenario-based tools are used. In the end, students begin to develop the practical tools and experiences they will need once they enter the workforce. One such practical lesson involves the use of encryption, and ultimately the students are asked to create an indecipherable encryption sequence to be posted online to see if their fellow students can crack the code. If they can, they earn points for their school in an effort to win the overall scholastic competition.

When it comes to formal education in cybersecurity and even healthcare cybersecurity, the United States leads the way in on-campus, online, and hybrid degree plans. Formal degrees in all delivery methods can be found at the associate's (two-year), baccalaureate (four-year), master's, and doctorate degree level alike. Degree plans can feature a major in cybersecurity, and some degree plans feature a major in business, healthcare management, or computer science, with cybersecurity offered as a concentration within the degree. A concentration typically equates to a set number of classes or credit hours obtained in the focus area (cybersecurity), which ordinarily is outside of the degree itself. A university business student obtaining a master's in business administration may need to acquire five or more classes from the school of information sciences to get a concentration, or minor, to go along with his or her major degree.

The real significance of the role of formal education in measuring the competency of cybersecurity workforce members (and, by extension, healthcare cybersecurity) has to do with the ways in which the degree offerings have changed. Specifically, an evolution has taken place in terminology and practice from information security to cybersecurity that reflects a change in perspective: curricula are now built around the changing nature of digital information protection. Cybersecurity focuses on attacks or threats that use information technology tools and techniques (hacking, malware, and so on) to access information technology assets. Many colleges and universities still offer both information security and cybersecurity degree plans; however, the distinction between the two is shrinking.

Although not a formal degree itself, formal education curricula in information assurance (IA)/cyber defense (CD) in U.S. colleges and universities at the doctorate, baccalaureate, and associate's degree levels are earning distinction as National Centers of Academic Excellence (CAEs). The accreditation is done by the U.S. National Security Agency (NSA) and the Department of Homeland Security (DHS). Colleges and universities seek this designation to differentiate their programs. The NSA/DHS "seal of approval" signifies a level of academic rigor and quality of course content relative to IA/CD. The program, from the NSA and DHS points of view, is meant to try to establish and expand the use of standards in the content and delivery of IA/CD curricula across the nation. Potential students and employers can be assured that studying and graduating from one of the identified schools provides the desired level of competency. To date, there are over 180 degree-granting institutions in the United States and Puerto Rico that have earned the NSA/DHS certification as a CAE in IA/CD. If these programs are implemented correctly, the nation will have better-prepared workers with a higher-level education ready to address cybersecurity issues in their respective organizations, including government agencies such as NSA and DHS.

Associate's Degrees

It makes sense to specifically mention the special role community colleges play in the formal education measure of competency by offering two-year associate's degrees in cybersecurity. Community colleges and accredited training programs were encouraged by the U.S. federal government to apply for portions of the American Recovery and Reinvestment Act (ARRA) of 2009 to receive stimulus funds to set up programs in health information technology and cybersecurity. ARRA also made available increased student aid to complement the new or expanded programs. The rapidly developed degree programs were terrific avenues for the United States to begin to meet the well-documented shortage of qualified cybersecurity workers.

A significant benefit of investing in the associate's degree programs nationwide is that the institutions granting these degrees train the next generation of cybersecurity workers very efficiently. An added benefit is that the institutions are experienced in training current workforce members in additional skills as well as brand-new skills, so experienced workers can potentially gain cybersecurity skills or retrain into new cybersecurity positions. Typically, community colleges offer more trade or industry-practical education—in other words, less theory and academic broadening coursework, and more practical training with an employment focus.

Cybersecurity Institutes

Numerous cybersecurity institutes have been established over the last couple of years, and they provide continuing education and thought leadership. The education can be used as competency measures depending on the credibility of the institute. Some institutes are an extension of degree-granting colleges and universities, which better positions them as competency assessors or measurers. Normally, a goal of these institutes is to bring together subject matter experts from one or more industries and conduct seminars, round table discussions, and conferences for cybersecurity professionals to attend. Some cybersecurity institutes publish books by their subject matter experts and white papers on specific topics of interest. Some cybersecurity institutes are affiliated with colleges and universities, while others are established independently or are based on specific industries.

Training

Specific training on various cybersecurity subjects, as well as those that lead to a certificate of completed training, are helpful in measuring competency. Such courses may be offered as non-degree education by formal education institutions as well as cybersecurity institutes. Certificates offered by these types of training programs should not be confused with formal cybersecurity certification. A key difference between the two is that a training certificate may or may not require passing a test or completing any additional continuing education in order to maintain the certificate. Think of a certificate of completed training as a special type of diploma awarded to the student. This type of training also differs from formal education leading to a degree in the amount of coursework required and in its focus. Typically, in formal education, more coursework would be focused on the major, the concentration, or the topic of cybersecurity. Cybersecurity training may have one course that results in course completion, whereas formal education might have between five and ten. In addition, a multifaceted degree plan offered by a formal education institution mandates "breadth" coursework, which includes subjects such as English, Literature, Math, and so on. These types of courses would not be required in a training program, which focuses on specific topics.

Trainings are offered in various time intervals—initial, annual, recurring, and ad hoc (as needed). When offered in the workplace and when employees comply with training requirements, the organization can expect a minimum level of competency based on the topics delivered. In some cases, exams given at the end of trainings are kept in the employee record to bolster the measure's reliability.

Credentials and Certifications

The introduction of this topic on competency measures mentioned the benefits of credentialing and certification. The recent establishment of several healthcare-specific privacy and information security certifications illustrate how credentials and certifications respond to market pressures and requirements. Historically, no other measures of competency have been able to move as rapidly as these healthcare-specific certifications to address the need to identify individuals with appropriate skill levels; and these credentials have had international acceptance, depending on the credential-granting entity. Usually, a credential is developed and offered by a professional organization that has membership, a requirement for direct experience, an examination, and a continuing education requirement. Another credentialing entity may be a product vendor such as Microsoft or Cisco, both of which have offered industry-recognized certifications.

Measuring security and privacy competencies in healthcare is growing in acceptance. Cybersecurity professional associations are beginning to recognize the unique nature of the healthcare environment, and healthcare professional organizations are seeing their constituencies take on roles including cybersecurity responsibilities that necessitate competency measures. With the number and severity of PHI data breaches that have occurred over the past three to five years, the need to measure competency for cybersecurity awareness and capability in the healthcare setting has never been greater.

With respect to how multiple communities within a healthcare organization have begun to converge around privacy and security requirements, several relevant certifications and credentials are worth noting. A leading credential is called American Health Information Management Association, Certified in Healthcare Privacy and Security (CHPS). This credential certifies personnel who have competence in designing, implementing, and administering comprehensive privacy and security protection programs in all types of healthcare organizations. The CHPS credential is special because it originates from a leading healthcare information management organization that recognizes the digitization of the medical record. The International Information Systems Security Certification Consortium, Inc., or (ISC)², has recently established a credential for healthcare cybersecurity practitioners called the Healthcare Information Security and Privacy Practitioner (HCISPP). The leading cybersecurity credential from (ISC)², however, is the Certified Information Systems Security Professional (CISSP). An example of a certification for the biomedical engineering community that incorporates cybersecurity is offered by the Association for the Advancement of Medical Instrumentation (AAMI) and is called the Certified Biomedical Equipment Technician (CBET).

For the privacy profession, which includes legal and privacy officers, the International Association of Privacy Professionals (IAPP) offers the Certified Information Privacy Technologist (CIPT), which includes the Certification Foundation course, a foundation in privacy principles that is part of the Certified Information Privacy Professional (CIPP) credential. One must take the Certification Foundation exam first, and then the CIPT exam. The IAPP does not offer a healthcare-specific credential, but it certainly evaluates competency against regulatory guidelines such as HIPAA. Lastly, a relevant certification that applies to healthcare risk managers is the Certified Professional in Healthcare Risk Management (CPHRM) from the American Society for Healthcare Risk Management (ASHRM), an organization that is associated with the American Hospital Association. Using these leading examples from each constituent group that has come together to provide cybersecurity in the healthcare context, we can examine their domain areas of interest.

NOTE The professional groups and certifications listed here are not endorsed by the author or the publisher of this text. Of course there are other examples of professional groups and certifications, and you are encouraged to explore them. Even the groups listed in this section, chosen to represent the availability of competency measures in healthcare and cybersecurity, offer multiple other credentials that may be more applicable to your daily job responsibilities.

Knowledge Domains and Expertise Areas

Cybersecurity professionals who work in healthcare are expected to have broad knowledge in several key domains. The individual certification credentials overlap in some areas, and biomedical engineers, information technology staff, health information managers, and compliance officers all may obtain these credentials. It is true that any two knowledge domains may have some common subelements or dependencies. It is also true that an individual may have greater experience or competency in one or more domains than in others. At the same time, there may be domains where the individual has limited or even no experience. Depending on the profession, each knowledge area carries a different emphasis or degree of importance. Figure 10-3 depicts examples of expected areas of competency and areas of overlap. These common knowledge domain areas are further

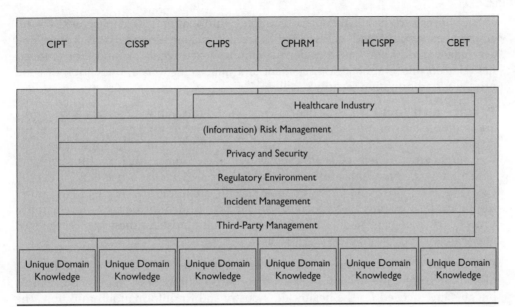

CIPT	CISSP	CHPS	CPHRM	HCISPP	CBET

		Healthcare Industry			
	(Information) Risk Management				
	Privacy and Security				
	Regulatory Environment				
	Incident Management				
	Third-Party Management				
Unique Domain Knowledge	Unique Domain Knowledge	Unique Domain Knowledge	Unique Domain Knowledge	Unique Domain Knowledge	Unique Domain Knowledge

Figure 10-3 Domains of knowledge shared across professions

described next, and they result from several previously disparate healthcare professional communities coming together to properly protect healthcare information.

Healthcare Industry and Organizations   Each of the credentials that apply to healthcare professions evaluates the competencies of candidates on how well they understand healthcare operations and their industry. This applies to the CBET, CHPS, HCISPP, and CPHRM credentials, which cover patient safety, healthcare IT systems, organizational structures, and clinical and business functions such as coding and billing. With regard to measuring privacy and security competency in healthcare organizations, it's important for practitioners to understand that healthcare organizations are different than other organizations in other industries with privacy and security concerns due to healthcare organizations' distinctive organizational missions, structures, and cultures.

Risk Management   For this domain, information risk management knowledge is measured. Someone with CPHRM certification has domain expertise in risk management that not only involves security concerns, but other risk management issues as well, such as surgical procedures, emergency operations, workforce concerns, and so forth. Information risk professionals must also exhibit competency in structuring organizational approaches for preventing, mitigating, detecting, correcting, and recovering from information risk. While this book doesn't advocate any one risk management approach, all risk management credentialing programs evaluate their candidates in terms of their knowledge of established standards and industry best practices (from organizations such as NIST, ISO, for example). Information risk management knowledge and expertise extends across all of the credentials mentioned in this chapter, and this makes sense when you consider the emphasis that regulators and experts in the field put on information risk assessment and management as a foundation of good privacy and information security practices.

Privacy and Security The dependency on and integration of privacy and security are common areas of expertise that are expected within the industry. Knowledge of the distinctive elements of privacy and security is also important. With an emphasis on the unique environment of healthcare, as well as the impact that patient safety and patient care have on healthcare privacy and security, credentials such as CBET, CPHRM, CISSP, HCISPP, CIPT, and CHPS evaluate specific qualifications. The CBET measures the biomedical engineer's competency in managing medical devices—for example, software patch management and managing information risk for these highly regulated and patient-critical computers and systems.

Regulatory Environment Whether the emphasis is on HIPAA or another regulatory pressure, candidates for any of these certifications must know the overarching guidance needed for the healthcare industry and for information protection. The external pressures on an organization can potentially influence the risk management framework, and changes in or implementation of laws impact many facets of privacy and security practices. For example, changes in data breach laws may result in increased fines, a redefining of terms, or additional notification actions. For this reason, having an awareness of the regulatory environment prepares the healthcare organization for compliance and helps avoid unnecessary scrutiny and costs. This then results in the ability to create and implement organizational policies and procedures that are in line with external regulations and guidance.

Incident Management Related to regulatory awareness, one of the most significant ways the disparate healthcare communities have come together is in terms of incident discovery, investigation, and reporting. Prior to the digitization and interconnection of healthcare records and systems, all of these communities had traditional lines of communication for reporting incidents. For instance, CBETs may have had a responsibility to report medical device incidents to the U.S. Food and Drug Administration. With data incidents, this responsibility does not preclude a responsibility under the HIPAA and under organizational policy to report the incident as part of the established organization incident management process. In fact, it is imperative that CBETs are represented on the multidisciplinary organizational incident management team.

Someone with a CPHRM or CHPS is likely familiar with U.S. state or federal government public health requirements to notify certain agencies in the event of sentinel (adverse) patient care events. Now that healthcare organization networks are considered critical infrastructure, reports to the regulators might include cybersecurity events, such as network outages due to malware, for example. This reality illustrates why the CPHRM and CHPS professional certifications should be represented in the organizational incident management process as well.

Individuals with CISSP, HCISPP, and CIPT certification and expertise have long been expected to master the development and implementation of digital forensics, as well as timely reporting of incidents to appropriate officials (internally and externally, if required).

Third-Party Management Whether it is the CBET who interacts with medical device manufacturers or the CISSPs, HCISPPs, and CIPTs who must deal with their business associates in the United States, credentialed personnel should have a demonstrated understanding of the risk third parties introduce to a healthcare organization. Since there is no legal way to outsource the responsibility of protecting sensitive personal information a healthcare organization collects, the organization has a legal obligation to assess and measure the third-party business partners with whom it shares this sensitive information when it depends on the third party to perform a service or provide a product.

Credentials and certifications are an industry-recognized way to measure competency of healthcare information security and privacy professionals. Many established organizations have embraced the need to sponsor the process of credentialing and help validate the competency of individuals who work in the healthcare industry, both in the United States and internationally.

 NOTE Credential holders seek and attain the measures to differentiate themselves to hiring authorities, which often value the credentials as the most dynamic measures of minimum competency. Certification generally is not government mandated, with one exception. The U.S. Department of Defense (DoD) Directive 8570.01M, titled "Information Assurance Workforce Improvement Program" and updated in January 24, 2012, outlines mandatory minimum workforce competency requirements for personnel with information assurance responsibilities.

Professional Organizations

As previously mentioned, the professional organizations and credentials discussed in this chapter provide only a sample of those available. When assessing the value of a credential or certification, it is important to consider the authority behind it. Most industry-recognized credentials have several things in common. Starting with having a professional organization behind it, the credential or certification should include a membership or affiliation with an organization of professionals. Second, the credential or certification should go through an objective, third-party audit such as ANSI or ISO. In that way, you know that the process involved in establishing and maintaining the credential or certification has the appropriate integrity and rigor. Another consideration is whether or not the granting of the credential or certification is contingent on requirements such as a demonstrated minimum experience level, formal education, and recommendations. The most meaningful credentials have maintenance requirements, usually annual. Finally, although some valid credentials have no continuing education requirement, a good credential or certification from a professional organization is one that requires recipients to achieve a certain number of continuing education credits each year. In this way, the measure of competency has some assurance of remaining current in the areas of technology, processes, regulatory compliance, and other changes in the healthcare privacy and cybersecurity industry. The opportunity for continuing education should come from the professional organization, and credit should be offered for other related education and participation in the industry.

TIP Many leading credentials and certifications require candidates to agree to abide by an organizational statement of ethical behavior. This is particularly true when the credential is offered by a professional organization that the candidate can join as an affiliated member. The ethics statement and policies are usually required knowledge for exam takers and members. See www.ahima.org, www.isc2.org, www.privacyassociation.org, and www.himss.org, as examples.

Internships

Internships for cybersecurity employees provide an on-the-job training and awareness platform to help address the shortage of qualified individuals. They are an innovative way to let newly graduated students get a small amount of experience, while allowing employers to evaluate the students as possible job candidates, thereby reducing the risk of hiring someone who does not fit into the organization or cannot acquire the required competencies over time. There is no substitute for real-life experience, and internships provide a good way for future job candidates to get it with relatively low risk to the company. Internships are also a way for employees, especially new graduates, to see if they like the work or the workplace. Many colleges and universities offer internships, and some government agencies in the United States and abroad sponsor such arrangements to help build their workforce.

Chapter Review

This chapter introduced the challenge of recruiting, hiring, and retaining qualified cybersecurity workers. A shortage of qualified professionals exists, both in the United States and globally across most industries where information protection is important, and healthcare is no exception. There is an increasing need for healthcare organizations to have privacy and cybersecurity professionals on staff, yet in the urgent pursuit to fill these needs, emphasis must be placed on qualifications. Relying on unqualified privacy and cybersecurity individuals is almost as disastrous as having no one on staff. For this reason, industries, including healthcare, have championed multiple methods for measuring the competency of their cybersecurity and privacy workforce. In general terms, accepted competency measures include formal education at the collegiate level, credentialing and certification, and internships. Due to the dynamic, highly technical nature of information technology, cybersecurity, and healthcare in general, certifications and credentialing tend to be a very useful way of measuring competency in this specialized workforce. Several leading professional organizations have recently created relevant measures of competency in the form of credentials that are gaining industry recognition and acceptance. This is reflected in position descriptions and hiring decisions.

Review Questions

1. Because healthcare networks are considered _____, the need for a competent cybersecurity workforce is essential.

   A. medical devices

   B. critical infrastructure

   C. patient care

   D. special purpose

2. Which of the following statements regarding the supply of qualified cybersecurity workers is true?

   A. The United States has been able to supply enough cybersecurity workers because it has a large supply of academic institutions.

   B. Singapore has a reputation for being a safe and secure business climate because it has an ample supply of cybersecurity workers.

   C. Because qualified cybersecurity workers find private-sector employment more lucrative, the UK government has difficulty attracting and retaining cybersecurity professionals.

   D. Private-sector employers cannot recruit and train cybersecurity employees, as is evidenced in Ireland.

3. Which of the following describes NICE?

   A. A cybersecurity workforce education framework

   B. An educational risk assessment

   C. A standard for national compliance

   D. A prescribed curriculum for cybersecurity education

4. How have biomedical engineers gained cybersecurity responsibilities?

   A. They are not responsible for cybersecurity due to FDA regulations.

   B. CIOs delegated the responsibilities to bioengineers because there is so much work to do.

   C. Medical device manufacturers need remote site support.

   D. Medical devices often contain individually identifiable health information.

5. (TRUE or FALSE) Information technology personnel who have worked in cybersecurity in the banking industry are extremely well qualified to work in healthcare organizations.

6. If an organization wanted to take steps to assure the cybersecurity competency of its workforce, generally speaking, which is the fastest method for accomplishing this?

    A. Certification

    B. Associate's degree

    C. Baccalaureate degree

    D. Continuing education

7. In which of these areas would a certified healthcare risk manager have the most domain expertise?

    A. Perimeter network security

    B. Third-party liability risk

    C. Use of encryption

    D. Information risk assessment

8. (TRUE or FALSE). Because of the unique nature of healthcare organizations and the industry-specific requirements they have for data breach reporting, incident reporting is the sole responsibility of compliance officers, specifically the privacy officer.

9. Which of the following is a good example of a criterion for evaluating professional organizations and any certifications or credentials they offer?

    A. Reasonable dues that indicate low administrative costs

    B. Multiple credentials across many different topics

    C. Required continuing education to maintain the certifications or credentials

    D. An essay component to the exam rather than all multiple choice questions

10. Which of the following is a benefit of internship?

    A. The organization gets a low-cost chance to try out workers.

    B. Workers get chance to see if they will enjoy the work.

    C. It reduces human resource policies in case of employee termination.

    D. It offers special protection under the law for data breach by an intern.

Answers

1. **B.** U.S. Executive Order 13636 now defines critical infrastructure networks that need cybersecurity protection, and healthcare networks are included. Medical devices also need cybersecurity protection, but healthcare networks are not regulated by the U.S. Food and Drug Administration (FDA) and are not generally considered healthcare networks, although they can be end points and enclaves *on* the healthcare network. Patient care and special purpose are

characteristics of the healthcare network or devices that use it, but they are not applicable in this scenario.

2. **C.** The economic reality is that private-sector cybersecurity for qualified individuals generally is more lucrative in the United Kingdom (and other countries, too). The other statements are false according to the chapter readings.

3. **A.** NICE is intended as a framework around which educational organizations can build curriculum to achieve standard knowledge, skills, and abilities (KSAs). NICE is not designed to assess risk or to be a mandatory compliance standard. NICE does not prescribe an exact curriculum, just a set of KSAs to use as goals.

4. **D.** With the digitization of information and the interconnection of medical devices, medical devices often contain individually identifiable health information, and biomedical engineers therefore have a large and increasing role in privacy and information security. The FDA does not prohibit biomedical engineers from having responsibility; in fact, it advised that biomedical engineers be included in the organization's information security plan. While CIOs may delegate some responsibilities and medical device manufacturers may need help with remote site support, these two choices are not applicable.

5. **FALSE.** Not automatically. While IT personnel coming from any industry with cybersecurity backgrounds, especially banking, can be great additions to the IT team at every level of a healthcare organization, implementing outside-industry best practices can have serious unintended consequences in healthcare. Additional awareness of and savvy about privacy and security implications for the healthcare environment are key.

6. **A.** Certification of the workforce would be the quickest, most accepted method of measuring and assuring a level of competence in cybersecurity. Baccalaureate degrees take approximately four years to achieve, and associate's degrees take two. Continuing education is extremely important, but it is not a competency measure by itself. It is a means to an end. A transcript showing required continuing education or specific education topics that result in a certificate of training may be more valid as measures of competency.

7. **D.** While it depends to some degree on an individual's background, certified healthcare risk managers have more domain expertise in protecting health information as part of the organizational management of all types of risk, and this involves assessing risk, including information risk. They probably do not have as much expertise in networking, structuring risk mitigation with third parties, and using encryption.

8. **FALSE.** Due to the unique nature of healthcare and regulatory requirements, multiple people have major roles in the incident reporting process. It is true that a privacy officer must be identified within the organization and probably is the point of contact for the process, but the process itself is a multidisciplinary, shared responsibility.

9. **C.** A good credential or certification requires holders to maintain their status by completing accredited continuing education offered by the professional organization, another similar organization, or via self-study. The cost of dues, while a good measure of value, has nothing to do with the value of the credential. In some cases, multiple credentials actually indicate lack of focus by the organization and lack of credibility as a credential mill. Finally, the addition of an essay has little to do with the quality of the credential.

10. **B.** By definition, internships allow employees, especially new graduates, a chance to see if they like the work. The other answers may have an element of truth to them, but none of them are appropriate benefits of internship.

References

1. UK Cabinet Office. "The UK Cyber Security Strategy: Protecting and Promoting the UK in a Digital World." November, 2011. p. 42. Accessed October 1, 2014, at https://www.gov.uk/government/uploads/system/uploads/attachment_data /file/60961/uk-cyber-security-strategy-final.pdf

2. Verton, Dan. "New Concerns about Cybersecurity Workforce Shortage in Critical Infrastructure Sectors." *FedScoop*. June 26, 2014. Accessed September 28, 2014, at http://fedscoop.com/cybersecurity-workforce-shortage-impacting-critical-infrastructure

3. Ponemon Institute. "2013 Cost of Data Breach Study: Global Analysis." May, 2013. p. 5. Accessed September 22, 2014, at https://www4.symantec.com /mktginfo/whitepaper/053013_GL_NA_WP_Ponemon-2013-Cost-of-a-Data-Breach-Report_daiNA_cta72382.pdf

4. Suby, Michael. "The 2013 (ISC)^2 Global Information Security Workforce Study." Frost & Sullivan. p. 12. Accessed September 24, 2014, at https://www.isc2cares .org/uploadedFiles/wwwisc2caresorg/Content/2013-ISC2-Global-Information-Security-Workforce-Study.pdf

5. The National Health Information Sharing & Analysis Center (NH-ISAC). "Initiatives." Accessed September 27, 2014, at http://www.nhisac.org/initiatives/

6. BBC News Technology. "NHS Surrey Fined £200,000 after Losing Patients' Records." July 12, 2013. Accessed September 20, 2014, at http://www.bbc.com /news/technology-23286231

7. ECRI Institute. *Medical Technology for the IT Professional: An Essential Guide for Working in Today's Healthcare Setting.* (Plymouth Meeting, PA: ECRI Institute, 2009), p. 8.

8. ECRI Institute. "Sample Risk Management Plan for a Community Health Center Patient Safety and Risk Management Program." 2010. p. 1. Accessed September 28, 2014, at http://bphc.hrsa.gov/ftca/riskmanagement/riskmgmtplan.pdf

9. Executive Order 13636, "Improving Critical Infrastructure Cybersecurity." *Federal Register* 78, no. 33. (February 19, 2013). Accessed October 24, 2014, at http://www.whitehouse.gov/the-press-office/2013/02/12/executive-order-improving-critical-infrastructure-cybersecurity

10. National Initiative for Cybersecurity Education (NICE). "DRAFT National Cybersecurity Workforce Framework." Accessed October 24, 2014, at http://niccs.us-cert.gov/sites/default/files/documents/files/DraftNationalCybersecurityWorkforceFrameworkV2.xlsx

11. Big Brother Watch. "NHS Breaches of Data Protection Law: How Patient Confidentiality Was Compromised Five Times Every Week." October, 2011. p. 2. Accessed October 24, 2014, at http://www.bigbrotherwatch.org.uk/files/NHS_Breaches_Data_Protection.pdf

12. Sparkes, Matthew. "Poorly Trained IT Workers Are 'Gateway for Hackers'." *The Telegraph*. August 6, 2014. Accessed September 28, 2014, at http://www.telegraph.co.uk/technology/internet-security/11011249/Poorly-trained-IT-workers-are-gateway-for-hackers.html

13. The National Health Information Sharing & Analysis Center (NH-ISAC). "Membership Services." Accessed September 20, 2014, at http://www.nhisac.org/membershipservices

14. National Institute of Standards and Technology. "An Introductory Resource Guide for Implementing the Health Insurance Portability and Accountability Act (HIPAA) Security Rule." By Matthew Scholl, Kevin Stine, Joan Hash, Pauline Bowen, Arnold Johnson, Carla Dancy Smith, and Daniel I. Steinberg. Special Publication 800-66, Revision 1. Section 4.3, p. 21. October, 2008. Accessed September 24, 2014, at http://csrc.nist.gov/publications/nistpubs/800-66-Rev1/SP-800-66-Revision1.pdf

Administering Risk Management and Cybersecurity

Rob Davis

In this chapter, you will learn to

- Understand the anatomy of an external cybersecurity attack using an organized approach
- Appreciate the cyber operations application of risk management frameworks
- Comprehend what a detection capability can provide for risk mitigation
- Understand incident response and recovery for the entire organization
- Apply tailored risk assessment consideration and balance to compensating controls in healthcare

Healthcare has seen a tremendous explosion of technology become integrated into the everyday care of patients. Traditional computing of desktops, laptops, and servers centrally managed by the information technology (IT) department is rapidly evaporating. Smartphones, medical devices, and so on, are blurring the lines of computing and communications capabilities, spreading information from countless sources all over the network. The result is that professionals outside of traditional IT are involved in security at all levels. Most healthcare organizations are delivering care 24 hours a day, which means that the network is humming all the time. Personal health information (PHI) is also being stored, accessed, and transmitted continuously. So we have the ingredients of a critical mission, many different perspectives, a large network footprint, and personal information coming from everywhere to make a recipe for the perfect storm for cybersecurity.

In this chapter, we tackle this difficult challenge in a practical manner given the resources and tools available. The anatomy of a cyberattack will be laid out to better understand the problem. For many healthcare privacy and security professionals, this may be their first up-close look at cybersecurity attacks in action. Finally, a practitioner's view of applying risk management frameworks for protecting a network will be provided.

The Attack

In cybersecurity we tend to focus on ourselves because the attackers seem almost like mythical creatures that come to pillage and plunder while we are not looking. The immediate reaction is to fortify our defenses and stop this injustice. However, this is only one side of the equation, and we must give an equal amount of consideration to the adversary. The anatomy of a cyberattack is illustrated in Figure 11-1 and referenced throughout the rest of the chapter.

The Anatomy of a Cyberattack

The procedure outlined in Figure 11-1 is the result of incorporating several best-practice framework descriptions of cyber events, such as Lockheed Martin's "Cyber Kill Chain," a term that is actually borrowed from commonly used jargon in the United States Air Force when it references a mission such as an air strike that will be launched from far away.[1] In cybersecurity, the term has long been applied to the surface area of attack by external threats. The way the Air Force describes the kill chain process is similar to how cyberattacks happen, as most of the adversaries against healthcare networks originate in other networks that are far away. The term "kill chain" as a descriptor sounds cool and really gets attention, and the latter is probably the reason it is sometimes used. Another example to which the anatomy of a cyberattack is related is Carnegie Mellon University's cyber situation awareness (cyberSA). CyberSA means having recognition of the computing environment and events over time, and what their impact is. Situation recognition consists of the following elements: the perception of the type of cyberattack, the source (who, what) of the attack, and the target of the attack; situation comprehension, which is the understanding of why and how the current situation occurred, and its impact; and situation projection, which involves determining the expectations of a future attack, its location, and its impact.[2] Also included in the framework presented here are personal experiences by the author and others. In sum, the attack sequence outlined in this chapter is intended to include several industry best practices.

Figure 11-1

Overview of the anatomy of a cyberattack

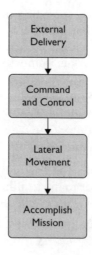

NOTE This is a general, high-level depiction of how cyberattacks take place. Please refer to other kill chain or cyberattack models, as desired, for a full introduction to the processes.

A general misconception exists about the duration and steps needed to successfully execute an attack, because details of attacks get glossed over in our current 140-character media and 24-hour news cycle. To keep stories simple, too much focus is placed on the end of the attack. Usually, many steps precede the headline-grabbing action.

External Delivery

If absolute protection from all the malicious actions on the World Wide Web is the goal, then simply disconnect from the Internet, but we all know that is impossible in today's ever-connected world. We all rely on e-mail, third-party providers, bank transfers, and so on, to get business done every day, and it is almost inevitable that some level of malware will get into a network from this connectivity to the outside world.

The attack process can start in several different ways. For example, users could get blasted with a phishing e-mail with a very enticing link embedded, or they could get some malware from a popular web site, also known as a "drive-by." We all have some level of servers that are accessible from the Internet (patient portals, webmail, and so on). These systems are getting scanned every day for weaknesses and vulnerabilities. These are just a few of the almost limitless ways that an attacker can try to initiate an attack.

NOTE A drive-by is analogous to your computer catching a cold from a web site. Any web site (even popular, trusted ones) can have its program altered to host up malware in the background automatically while you visit the site.

Once a weak link in the armor is found, the initial malware is deployed to finish this stage of the attack. This is the opening shot in the battle, and multitudes of adversaries are firing it every day. All the tools, techniques, and people required to perform this beginning attack are very inexpensive. Compromised assets at this stage are generally low-value targets, such as an employee's laptop, web page front end, or ordinary user credentials. The value to the attacker is in what can be done with these assets once infected.

Command and Control

A presence is now established with this initial delivery of malware. The attacker then gets to work. The malware tries to contact its owner that it has accomplished its mission and waits for further instructions. The attacker then attempts to elevate privileges, gain user credentials, map the system, or carry out other various actions, depending on how much the system is compromised and what the goals of the attacker are. The term used for this is "command and control," and it gives the attacker ultimate control over the machine to execute later steps in the attack. What is particularly frustrating is that, in this scenario, malware could reside undetected for long periods of time because it stays dormant or can be executed immediately. In recent reports, healthcare organizations had a high number of these types of attacks on medical devices and end-user devices alike.[3]

Lateral Movement

Once the attacker has established a solid connection to and a solid presence on the system, the next actions the attacker takes focus on making the most of this advantage. The network is documented by scanning any accessible systems. Results will be used to compromise additional machines through vulnerabilities and weaknesses. More legitimate user credentials are picked up and stored. This is where the intruder tries to start to use the built-in trust of the internal network against it. This trust could go all the way to the core if the intruder gets administrator credentials in the access control system. Now the attacker can grant administrator access to any system on the network, bypassing almost all the security controls in place.

Accomplish the Mission

The attacker has the deck stacked in his or her favor at this point in the process and has obtained a solid presence, user credentials, and a thorough knowledge of the network. Headlines can now be made. The mission could be anything from denial of service to retrieving data for monetary gain. Stopping an attack at this point in the process is very difficult because the attack can actually look like normal user activity to defense-in-depth architecture controls, such as intrusion detection systems. Also, the attacker will have a presence on multiple machines all over the network, phoning home to multiple IP addresses outside of the network for commands. These steps give the attacker obscurity as the proverbial needle in the haystack.

Summary of the Attacks

Attacks can come in many shapes and sizes from anywhere in the world. This is almost like guerilla warfare, and it leads to a lot of confusion. The anatomy of a cyberattack as presented is a very high-level overview to merely illustrate a couple of things: First, that these actions most of the time are not as swift as the media reports would like people to believe. They can be drawn out over months, even years, without detection. However, as the attacker gets further down the procedure, the attack becomes harder and harder to defend against using traditional cybersecurity tactics such as defense-in-depth type of layered architecture. Second, within this process is a glimmer of hope for cybersecurity professionals. Detection, deterrence, remediation, and recovery, albeit painful and difficult, are achievable goals with the right security program.

Defense Against the Attacks: Art and Science

Security is a little bit of both art and science, but people tend to focus on the science because it is easy to measure. It feels good when an auditor comes in and goes through a checklist of controls and all of them have been checked. This chapter focuses a little more on the art and less on the science. As discussed in Chapter 4, great frameworks from organizations such as NIST or ISO are regularly used in assessments to make risk decisions. These scientific endeavors should be encouraged and done on a regular basis. However, an active defense process that moves away from solely relying on controls while implementing some much-needed artistry in the way of tailored controls, compensating controls, and continuous approaches in a security program are next-generation solutions that are needed in healthcare. In many cases, integrating a better understanding of attack procedures, accompanied by solid and continuous control checks brings the security program alive.

A Framework for the Process

There is a saying in the Zen philosophy that goes, "Before enlightenment, chop wood, carry water. After enlightenment, chop wood, carry water." This saying applies here in that often it does not matter which risk management framework you choose; it only matters that the process is the focus and is followed with discipline. An equal mixture of planning, doing, and improvement must be present for any program to be effective. There is no need to get too concerned with which framework is chosen because it will be modified to fit the organization as its processes are executed.

As stated in previous chapters, there are many organizations (ISO and NIST, for example) spanning many countries in the world that have published frameworks that can be used. NIST's Cybersecurity Framework (CSF) will be used as the reference model here simply because of its international applicability. Thoughts expressed here will center on the process and can be applicable to any of the frameworks.

Cybersecurity Framework (CSF)

The Cybersecurity Framework was a direct result of U.S. presidential Executive Order 13636, titled "Improving Critical Infrastructure Cybersecurity." The goal of this framework is to provide a guide for risk management outcomes that can be used by organizations of any size to manage risk. The creation of this framework was a collaboration between the U.S. government and the private sector.[4]

Figure 11-2 represents the core of the framework, which is divided into five functions. Each function is then divided further into categories and subcategories. The framework also has a guide for the following four implementation tiers:

- Tier 1: Partial
- Tier 2: Risk-informed
- Tier 3: Repeatable
- Tier 4: Adaptive

The CSF is meant as a guide. The interesting thing about these implementation tiers is that they are not meant as a maturity diagram. The expectation is that they are to be left up to the organization based on its unique business and risk tolerance. All individual business units within the organization should operate at the maximum risk tolerance allowed. In healthcare, patient care should be the number one priority and

Figure 11-2
NIST
cybersecurity
framework

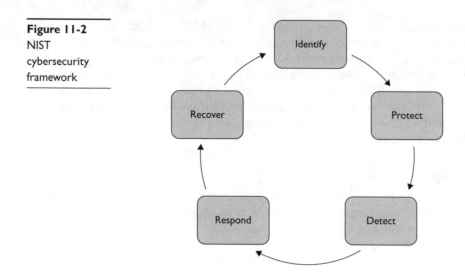

security should be delivered as a best effort given individual resource restraints. Security programs shouldn't consume more resources (manpower, money, and so on) than absolutely necessary because that would impact the primary mission.

 NOTE   The complete CSF can be found at http://nist.gov/cyberframework.

Detect

Conventional wisdom would have this section start with the identify phase. We will start in the middle, however, because as of this writing this is a giant hole, or vulnerability, in healthcare. Plus, if there is one aspect of a security program that it is better to be good at than another this is it. The "Anatomy of a Cyberattack" section previously described some common steps that an attacker takes. All those steps not only take time but also leave a trail, which enables a robust detection ability to make up for some deficiencies in other areas of the process.

This may immediately raise a few questions. Where is the starting point? What is affordable? This segues into a discussion about the building blocks for deploying a detection capability, as shown in Figure 11-3.

Logging   Logging is the most basic element of detection that every organization should be doing. Most of the devices on your network have built-in functionality to perform logging, and this functionality is probably already being used to perform health and status monitoring on most of these devices. Syslog is the most common format for the logs, but vendors sometimes choose to log in another format. Regardless, this should be fairly straightforward to set up. A central repository, called a *log aggregation*

Figure 11-3
Elements of
detection
in order of
complexity

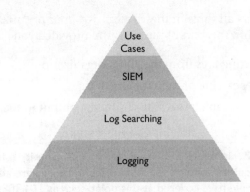

Use
Cases

SIEM

Log Searching

Logging

point, is needed to collect these logs. A storage area network (SAN) is most likely already in existence, and a slice of that storage can be used. Try to pull every log that can be collected without an extreme workload. These logs could also utilize cloud computing if that is used in the environment today. The goal is to get the logs into a central location as easily as possible to provide a base of information used later in the program.

Log Searching Now that logs are centrally stored somewhere, the next step in the detection process can be executed. Collecting all the logs may seem a little overwhelming, as the typical healthcare network puts out millions of log events a day. This is where the searching capability comes into play. There are numerous tools on the marketplace that can provide this functionality. Some notable vendors are Splunk, McAfee, Alert Logic, and HP, all of which come with preconfigured alerting functionality, graphical interfaces, and various training resources.

 NOTE Do not forget about open source tools such as OSSEC or Syslog-ng. These are great tools with good community support that will work for a smaller organization with a limited budget.

Once the tools are installed, the people with network monitoring responsibilities can begin by getting familiar with the ebb and flow of the network. Repeatable patterns in the data will begin to emerge, leading to the next step, which is eliminating the routine traffic from view. This removes a great deal of noise from the log searching. Next is to look for unusual occurrences such as failures, errors, administrative access, and changes. This hunting process may seem daunting at first, but with time it can be done effectively. An example might be an IP from the DMZ using administrative accounts on the access control system in another network segment. This odd behavior is the kind of thing that should be sought out and addressed.

Within the CSF, the detect phase has three parts: anomalies and events, security continuous monitoring, and detection processes. The functionality described in the preceding paragraph covers all three of these categories. Your organization would be at tier three of the CSF, within this part of the program, provided you

- Are collecting logs from the entire organization
- Have a repeatable process for searching
- Have a repeatable process for using the output in the incident response process

---

TIP   In the United States, the HIPAA security rule doesn't currently have any required controls for monitoring, but there are addressable ones that you would have covered at this point, such as 164.308(a)(5)(ii)(B), Protection from Malicious Software.

Security Information and Event Management (SIEM)   Taking detection to a more sophisticated level involves additional tools, processes, and people and will consume a great deal more resources. The biggest tool needed is a security information and event management (SIEM) system. SIEM systems start by ingesting all of the logs just like the log management systems previously described, but then they add intelligence analytics on top that would have been done manually without it. They are able to correlate all the logs that are related during network activity. Alerting is done off of this using common, behavior-based use cases built in to the system. Custom use cases can also be created and added to the system in order to alert based on specific things in the environment. Use cases will be covered in the next section. Along with alerting of potential incidents, policy violations, compliance, and so on, is reporting capability through a dashboard.

Tools like this can absolutely catapult the detection capabilities of an organization, but there is more to the puzzle. People and processes need to be in place to maximize the benefit of tools like this. Most often when these tools have been deployed people aren't using them because they didn't have the necessary supporting structure. In these cases, a good log management solution would have provided the same functional benefit at a much lower resource consumption. People needed to run these devices would need skills in areas such as SIEM management, database management, and threat intelligence. Separate people, usually referred to as analysts, would be needed to spend ample time hunting through the alerts to find the incidents that need to be worked through the incident management process. All of these systems and job duties require solid, repeatable processes and procedures to be generated.

This level of commitment is not for the faint of heart. Best practices for any organization thinking of this must have a solid plan around risk tolerance, resource availability, and total cost of ownership for this endeavor. If the organization is very large and has highly valuable assets, then this is something that might be a good investment. With the right plan and funding, this can be extremely valuable in hunting and remediating the items discussed earlier in the anatomy of a cyberattack. If the organization is small, there are ways to get this functionality. For example, there are many vendors that will perform this service using their tools, providing the benefit at a fraction of the cost of doing it in house. Owning the centralized logging gives you all the information and provides options for getting SIEM functionality. If the outsourced engagement for monitoring via a SIEM is not working out, then switching vendors will have minimal impact. The logs collected are the basis for any monitoring that takes place and these are what should always be controlled by the organization.

Use Cases   The next level of detection involves the generation of unique use cases for the environment. The option of implementing these should be available no matter which technology is picked to get the SIEM functionality. Almost all of the products have a standard way of doing this, and most vendors providing the service do as well. Use cases are becoming pretty standard in the market because there is a limit to applying standard vendor content across different networks. Every network has a flow to it. Medical devices communicate in a certain way depending on the proprietary manufacturer code and clinical purpose. That provides the baseline, and a use case can be generated to look for things outside of that baseline. Any number of factors could be used, such as packet size, port, protocol, and destination IP, for example.

TIP   Outside of the baseline information, there are groups that supply threat intelligence for the healthcare community, such as NH-ISAC at nhisac.org. NH-ISAC is a great information source to be used as the basis for adaptive use cases.

Work like this does take some effort, but is made extremely more attainable with the use of a SIEM, which can be set up and then monitored for a period of time to determine the effectiveness. From there, the use case can be deleted or tweaked to yield better results. Trial and error in this realm is the very definition of being adaptive.

Respond

Let's move on to incident response with the anatomy of a cyberattack in mind. Chapter 6 talked exclusively about the incident management process for all types of incidents. This section will focus on incident response related to cyber intrusions. The collection of data mentioned earlier provides a path to track down all of those nuggets of evidence left by the adversary during the attack process.

The CSF calls for five outcome categories in the respond phase: response planning, communications, analysis, mitigation, and improvements. A direct correlation of ability should exist between the detect and respond phases of the process. Every entity in the organization that is being monitored should be covered in this part of the program. Coverage may vary depending on the mission impact of that particular entity, but it must still be thought about. For example, the billing system being unable to operate because of a denial of service attack has a different response level than an infusion pump. Thinking of response in this way will lead to a less generic overarching process.

Planning   Most healthcare industry regulations across the world provide some guidance for responding to incidents. HIPAA, for example, calls for response, mitigation, and documentation of incidents in 164.308(a)(6), as required.[5] In establishing an incident response process, you need to keep in mind the size and capability of the organization. Plans provide for vital structure, but sometimes they can be too complex to work. For this reason, a plan should be drafted, tested, and reworked. Working through the process over time and constantly improving it is more important than the actual plan. Don't get too bogged down in getting the first plan perfect. Here are some general items that should be considered in the plan:

- What is the goal of the plan?
- What resources/departments will be actively involved in an incident?
- What capabilities/limitations will affect the response?
- What makes the incident reportable externally?
- Who owns the plan?
- How does the response fit in to other areas of the framework?

Tremendous value is to be had once the plan is thought through and written out. It naturally engages others because they have a role to play in security. It has what's called a "forcing function" psychologically. A *forcing function* is something that forces a change in behavior. A simple example would be the microwave not working when the door is open. In this case, once the process is visual and the work is assigned, it forces the process out of abstract thought and into concrete steps.

Communications   Communications is vital during an incident and has an internal and an external component. Internally there must be a common place to share and document the incident. If a ticketing system is in place for change management, that system could be used to provide this function; or a more rudimentary (stored Word/ Excel files) or more advanced system (incident-handling software) could be used. The goal should be to have all the steps taken in the process documented and accessible to all parties involved in the response.

 NOTE   Remember that occasionally an incident may involve sensitive data, and that needs to be accounted for in the tool used for internal documentation and communication.

The external component is the part that handles anything that constitutes a breach, which is any unauthorized access to protected health information. Any incident response plan should account for this early on in the incident response activities. In the healthcare setting, one of the first things to do is establish if a breach has occurred. This determines whether or not a separate plan needs to be initiated to externally communicate the situation. The outline for these required actions is dictated by national and local regulatory bodies.

Analysis   Analysis during incident response in healthcare is essential because of the critical nature of the work that could be affected by a cyber incident. Response and containment are primary jobs of the incident response team. Is this an incident early in the anatomy of a cyberattack, with limited impact, or is it late in the procedure, where the most harm can be done? For example, a single laptop that has malware exhibiting command and control tendencies could be a minor incident with no breach to report.

Mitigations With the analysis above done, you move to mitigation. Having an organization-owned central log management system pays dividends here because it makes it possible to search through the organization for other signs of the attacker's presence in the environment. Since your team has this tool at its disposal, the team can control the process. The goal is to keep the attacker from moving further along the attack procedures by finding other infections, mitigating effects, and eradicating the foothold.

Improvements Working through the process of an incident, even a minor one, yields positive results unattainable any other way. Practice runs of the plan are useful but can't provide the same impact as live fire. Any major incident should bring about an immediate, lessons-learned session with all the findings documented. Most of the items identified for investigation during the detection phase will not be major incidents. Some organizations don't refer to these investigations as incidents. For simplification purposes, all investigations from the detection process will be referred to as incidents. Monthly reviews of all incidents (even false positives) are sufficient to get usable lessons learned. Most of the material for this review should be easily accessible in the system chosen for incident documentation. The lessons learned should include the following:

- High-level review of the incident
- What went right
- What could be improved
- What outputs from the process could have helped other areas of the framework
- What inputs from the other areas of the framework could have helped the process

Recover

It is well know that John D. Rockefeller made a fortune in the oil business. Most would probably assume that he pumped all the oil out of the ground and then took it to market. Actually, in the beginning he decided that he would rather be in the refinery part of the business. One of the biggest concerns for anyone in the refining business is fire. Rockefeller once said in relation to this fear, "So we kept ourselves like the firemen, with their horses and hose carts always ready for immediate action."[6] This story is relevant because his thoughts date back to the late 1800s. People in business have been thinking about disaster recovery arguably since the beginning of business. Recovery in a healthcare organization is a business imperative as well as a patient safety issue. Much like Rockefeller prepositioning fire suppression near his drilling areas to speed recovery, healthcare organizations need to have, ready to go, recovery mechanisms and processes such as backups, generators, and hot or cold sites for disaster recovery.

Planning   Healthcare is no different than most industries in the sense that major failures, fire, power outages, and the like have been thought about and recovery plans put in place. The recovery process is straightforward in these instances: get the system or service back into a state equivalent to operations prior to the incident. Of course, worst-case scenario planning involves having uninterrupted, quality patient care when the system cannot be recovered quickly.

What about the all the smaller processes that work together to deliver quality healthcare to the patient? Doctors and nurses have come to rely on things like diagnostic tablets, heart rate monitors, and MRI scanners, to name just a few devices in an ever-growing field. Is there a plan for recovery when it comes to those devices, which have software on them and therefore are at risk of being infected by malware? If, for example, the vendor that does the updates is using a generic username and password, attackers can leverage this weakness and use the devices to get a new place to further the progression down the attack sequence.

Understanding what processes are critical to each major department in the business is the first recommendation. Is there a critical process that needs IT functionality to work in oncology? How long can the finance department's accounting system be out before there are major issues with getting bills out? These are just some of the high-level questions that generate valuable thought processes to further planning. Use this dialog to baseline the entire organization's processes to prioritize actions in various places. The goal should be to have recovery plans in place at an organizational level for each department and to ensure that the plans have all stakeholders included to enable effective recovery in the event of an incident or outage.

TIP   Make sure that departments communicate to security prior to enabling new systems. Baselines in the priorities of systems within a given business unit tend to change as new technologies are deployed.

Testing the Plan   To reach an adaptive planning stage, use regular exercises to test the plans. As mentioned earlier, healthcare understands how to carry out its mission in the face of almost any internal or external emergency, and good planning and routine practice are the main reasons for this. Being accustomed to procedures and drills puts healthcare in a great position to prepare for and respond to a cyberattack.

Major business processes will have been defined and recovery planning accomplished during the baseline period. Now a small number of those processes should start to be regularly tested through drills. Key to this is living within a constraint of testing only the absolute critical pieces of the business so that it is not taxing on the individuals involved. Most people understand the importance of occasional fire drill testing, but if it occurred every week people would get agitated. The law of diminishing returns suggests that drill effectiveness would then deteriorate rapidly. Use caution and restraint when choosing which plans to focus on during testing.

Improvement   The work of planning, recovering, and testing is a forcing function that forces organizations to think critically about all the systems and processes that are needed to deliver healthcare. Even minimal investment in this area brings great rewards because the mindset and viewpoint are proactive, which in security is typically less expensive than reactive. Improvements in this phase and other phases automatically come out of this process with almost no regard to how much is invested. Let's say one hour-long conversation with the pediatrics department reveals a system that is critical for it, in which case the risk assessment of that system gets a little more scrutiny. That extra care may reveal that vulnerabilities exist with no direct mitigation, leading to increased monitoring of those systems for both cyber risks and performance. All the pieces and parts of the process are important because of interconnectivity.

Identify

Now we talk about the identify phase of the framework and why it wasn't discussed first. Many people start and end here because of motions that these checklists can generate. Asset management, business environment, governance, risk assessment, and risk management strategy make up the main components of this phase. A mental trap is set physiologically when the beginning of the improvement process involves the identification of items such as risk or asset management. Complexity in today's healthcare computing environment creates an overwhelming amount of "work" that could be done. Think about how many machines on the network are minicomputers adding to the already large number of traditional IT components (servers, desktops, printers, and so on). You do not want to fail to act because you get bogged down in assessments.

In the book *Getting Things Done*, David Allen talks about the "mind like water"[7] concept in karate: "Imagine throwing a pebble into a still pond. How does the water respond? The answer is totally appropriate to the force and mass of the input; then it returns to calm. It doesn't overreact or underreact." This is great visual imagery for why this chapter started with the anatomy of an attack and detection.

Action in the detection, response, and mitigation phases provides effective thought processes during identify and protection. Endless amounts of time and effort can be spent on potential risks, vulnerabilities, asset identification, and so on. It is like a boxer preparing for a fight but never getting in one. Instead, a boxer fights and then starts the preparation process over again with the real feedback from the outcome.

Asset Management   The two aspects of asset management to understand are what exists and its importance. Knowing what you have can be a daunting task in today's computing environment, as departments probably purchase and deploy products without involving the IT department. Don't get too excessive with trying to find everything. Remember that there will be other points in the process where critical items will be found in the detection, responding, and recovering phases. Focus on getting a good picture of the entire organization, starting with the traditional IT assets such as networking equipment, desktops, laptops, and servers. Then layer in what is found out during the communication with the departments on the critical business systems.

The Pareto principle, or 80/20 rule, applies in this phase. The rule states that 80 percent of the effects come from 20 percent of the causes. If we think about this in terms of today's interconnected communication among devices, then it is evident that nothing operates autonomously. Everything needs to traverse the network using the established channels, and access databases and servers that house data for the organization. These elements are part of the IT scope of work and are very simple to identify.

With the solid understanding of the key components of the infrastructure identified and the critical business processes understood, prioritization can now occur. Focus on the inputs received from the recovery phase. All the key processes should be identified and the key data flows mapped. For example, if radiology states that it has some imaging equipment that is absolutely key, then all the parts that make this work should be thought about. Where and how do the images get stored? Does the equipment get accessed from outside the network for maintenance? What amount of PHI is attached to the data stored, transmitted, and accessed? Focus on identifying the most critical organizational assets to avoid wasted time.

Business Environment   The identification is taken up a level here and viewed from an organizational point of view. How do all the departments roll up to the overall mission of the organization? Who and what are the relevant stakeholders and critical resources to carry out the overall mission? As an example, a hospital might have facilities items (power) as very high priority and administrative items (benefits systems) as very low priority. Such identification drives the overall cybersecurity roles, responsibilities, and risk management identification. Efforts should be focused on identifying the individual business components' high priorities relevant to the entire organization and its mission. Priority derived from risk tolerance is used to develop constraints. Cybersecurity resources are finite, and priority determines which constraints have the best chance to interrupt the procedures outlined in the anatomy of a cyberattack.

Governance   Policies, processes, and procedures do not affect an organization's security on their own, although they are the foundation of organizational security. These elements are only effective if they are followed, and therefore they must always keep the user in mind. For example, having strenuous access control on a system that a user needs to access multiple times a day might not make much sense. The user will just find a way around the policy for the sake of convenience. Convenience will always win over security when it comes to technology. This is why most people, in their personal life, use the same username and password for every account that they have. Everyone understands that it would be more secure to use different ones, but it is difficult to remember multiple usernames and passwords.

Consider the user's viewpoint related to governance a little further. Governance is the formal channel for communication between the organization and users. Too many times developing an abundance of governance is very enticing because it feels good to show auditors and assessors that thought has been used to develop documents, but then the communication gets too one sided and the receiver either tunes out or does something else. Communication has to be sent, received, understood, agreed to, and turned into action.

Look at all governance documents and think about this as communication between people. Have the major elements of the business been accounted for? Does everyone understand the documents? Is there training associated with the guidance to further the communication process? Is there a feedback process to improve the communication?

These are just some of the questions that come to mind, and others will come up using this lens to evaluate current governance. Sticking to these constraints forces good communication within the organization and keeps the governance at a level of emphasis that will be most effective.

Cyber Threat Vectors

Trust is the word that comes to mind when thinking about risk because one depends on the other. Our current digitally connected world only works because of the millions of connections happening between computing devices. In 1992, Dave Clark said about the Internet, "We reject kings, presidents, and voting. We believe in: rough consensus and running code."[8] This was during the predawn of today's Internet and echoes the original thoughts of the Internet's founders. The thought was that the Internet would be a self-governed utopia where people could exist and communicate freely. Today's Internet is much different than what it was in 1992, but the underlying theme is still present. All the communications are done using widely accepted standards, and there is virtually no barrier to entry. Therefore, a certain amount of trust and risk exists when tapping in to the power of the Internet.

Many naturally think of the cyber threat vector risk from a "them" and "us" perspective, as shown in Figure 11-4. The Internet serves as the "them" and the internal network becomes the "us." This is a natural tendency because our systems and people are the known entity and are therefore considered trustworthy. Cyberspace, on the other hand is large, unknown, and cannot be trusted. Think about when people travel to a large city such as New York, Paris, or Sydney for the first time. They most likely are very hesitant to go exploring by themselves because it is overwhelming, unknown, and risky. It is very easy for risk assessments to fall into this trap because humans perform them and apply the same risk methodology. The problem with today's computing environment is that so much in an organization is connected directly to the Internet. Think about all the e-mail messages, bank transfers, web browsing, patient portals, and cloud services, all of which are connected. Borders can only provide so much protection with all these communications happening.

All the interconnectivity is why it is best practice to do a full organizational wide-risk assessment. Some industry-governing regulations focus on only the systems and support architecture for sensitive data such as credit card info or PHI. Understanding these key elements certainly is vital, but this narrow focus limits the ability to see the rest of the vulnerabilities that might exist in the network. Once an attacker finds vulnerability, that vulnerability is exploited. We can't stop everything, but the goal is to make it as difficult as possible.

Figure 11-4
The "them" and
"us" Internet
perspective

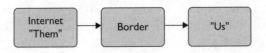

External

The anatomy of a cyberattack illustrated all the possible levels of penetration that could occur during an attack. The first step is the attacker establishing a foothold through a directly connected system. This could be through vectors such as e-mail, operating system vulnerabilities, weak passwords, and so on. A risk assessment should start with assessing these directly connected assets and their data flows. Some of the questions that should be asked are as follows:

- Which servers are externally facing?
- How good is the access control to those systems?
- What access do those systems have to other parts of the network?
- What architectural protections or control points are available between these systems and the inside network?
- Is there a standard image for these systems?
- What are the configuration management and patch management processes, and how fast do critical patches get applied?
- What are the protections in place for e-mail (filtering and data loss prevention)?

These are just some of the types of questions that should be asked during the external piece of the assessment. Taking a step back and looking at the organizational communication to the outside world is the goal. Don't get too invested in trying to find every communication path that might exist. Instead, start with the major ones and work the process. Central monitoring through logs or SIEM provides a safety net if something is missed.

TIP Don't forget about the wireless networks, which are an access point into the network. The access points need to be routinely checked for vulnerabilities.

Internal

Focus internally on the keys to the kingdom to separate the critical assets from everything else. Where is the central repository of data housed within the network? What are the key processes that must function to carry out the mission? These are the kinds of common-sense questions that should be answered during an assessment of the internal network.

After priorities are established, look at the protections around these critical elements. What are the access control mechanisms? How secure are the systems themselves? Do these systems have control points in the architecture from which effective monitoring data can be derived? Find all the potential cracks in the foundations of these systems, data flows, and services.

The practice stated above assumes that solid policies are in place and that there is adherence to the storage of sensitive data in the correct places. There absolutely should be an effort in the assessment to cover this risk. Solid communication between the organization and the users of data storage must be present to cover all the associated policies, processes, and procedures. An additional step should be taken to talk with users and ensure that the communication is well received. It is imperative that any poorly designed pieces are uncovered. If there are insufficient pieces, people will work around them, and this will lead to data being stored all over the network, making securing it next to impossible.

Penetration Testing

A penetration test, or *pen test,* is a purposeful attempt by an authorized person (a contract worker or employee) to access protected resources without using credentials and permissions. The point of this effort is to see if there are vulnerabilities to be exploited and begin to consider what needs to be fixed, so that a real adversary, as opposed to the pen tester, cannot exploit these risks next time. These tests are becoming more prevalent as a step in the risk assessment process across all industries. Many entities hire a third party to perform these tasks because of the specialized skill set needed. Most firms providing this service use the same methodology as an attacker, scanning the network to look for information about the systems, such as IP addresses, operating systems, and so on. Then they exploit any vulnerability found during reconnaissance. There are also what are called *social engineering tests* that use methods such as phishing e-mails, calling users for credentials, following users through gates to gain access ("tailgating"), and so on.

Tests like these are extremely valuable tools to use in the risk assessment process. As discussed earlier, today's Internet is highly interconnected, and every network has reconnaissance performed against it relentlessly every day. Reconnaissance is very cheap for attackers because it can be automated and therefore takes very little manpower. The reality is that hackers conduct their own pen tests on organizations every day. That is the nature of their reconnaissance, looking for vulnerabilities to exploit. Organizations that are proactive and conduct their own pen tests get to see the results and prevent potential exploit.

The final thought about pen tests is that they provide some reality to the risk assessment. People sometimes have a tendency to brush off findings in a report. Remember that we as humans inherently trust what we know. This natural instinct makes us second-guess findings. However, findings in a pen test report illustrating that the team successfully accessed several key servers are much harder to ignore.

 NOTE   Every healthcare regulatory body globally requires that a risk assessment be done periodically on the systems that handle PHI. The thoughts outlined above call for an organization-wide assessment, but local industry regulations specific to assessments should be accounted for as well.

Who Should Perform a Risk Assessment?

Let's conclude this topic with an interesting question that is posed often. Who should perform the risk assessment? Should it be an external third-party organization, or should it be done internally? Some industry regulations across the globe may mandate that an external third-party organization perform periodic risk assessments, and some leave it up to the individual organization. In the United States, as of this writing, it is left up to the organization to make the determination. Best practices would be that at least once per year an external third party would perform the assessment covering the entire organization. However, more frequent risk assessments should take place using internal resources. Answering the original question, both internal and external resources should be used to perform risk assessments whenever possible.

 TIP Risk assessments should be done any time a significant change is made to the computing environment—for example, if a third-party provider has modified the system, a new heavily used medical device has been implemented, or cloud services have been added. This most likely won't be a full organizational assessment, but more of a mini-assessment of the affected parts.

Controlling for Cyberattack

Information and visibility are discovered through all the processes that have been described thus far. We all know that resources are finite. The tricky part is how to react to information correctly. A well thought-out risk management strategy is the key. A solid strategy includes priorities, risk tolerances, constraints, and assumptions. For example, patient care is the number one priority in a healthcare setting. Most likely, a healthcare organization will accept some amount of risk when setting up access controls for doctors, for example, and a multifactor authentication system is a very secure and low-risk option that could be used. However, we all know that current multifactor authentication technology is often too cumbersome and that it inhibits patient care in most situations. A healthcare organization may establish compensating controls such as better physical security around the end point device, rather than enforce multifactor authentication. Some amount of risk always has to be accepted in every organization, and it is up to each organization to set that limit.

Protect

How to look for, react to, recover from, and prepare for an attack have been covered, but how to put up a defense has not. We now turn to putting obstacles in the way in order to make it difficult for the attacker. It is impossible to stop every intrusion because vulnerabilities, phishing, mistakes, and so on, happen faster than an organization can keep up with them. Protection is important, however, because it limits the scope of what has to be attended to during the other parts of the process. The CSF groups protection elements into the following general areas:

- Access control
- Awareness and training
- Data security
- Information protection processes and procedures
- Maintenance
- Protective technology

Access Control

Access control can be a very tricky endeavor because most organizations utilize Microsoft Active Directory (AD) technology to provide access to all the Microsoft products. For non-Microsoft products, Lightweight Directory Access Protocol (LDAP) is enabled from within the AD product. This allows administrators to give users different levels of access through features such as groups. An example of this would be the administrators group for AD. This is a popular method for providing access for users to all the various systems and applications. This method has flaws, however. Too often the tendency is for access to be given but never taken away. When this is coupled with too much access granted, the dormant accounts create vulnerability. What happens if a nurse moves from pediatrics to radiology? Most organizations don't have the information technology support resources to keep up with highly granular access control. The nurse ends up with access to records specific to both patient populations.

This problem can be solved through technology with the adoption of access-specific control tools. Sometimes these tools are built in to the specific applications but not used; other times, the tools are much more expensive than the AD solution and require specific processes and procedures for effective utilization. In large organizations, however, additional access-specific control solutions make sense because they provide significant resource savings in administrative tasks such as account provisioning.

Small organizations have some options, utilizing AD, for making the access control more secure. All the work done in other parts of the process yields valuable information on the most critical systems and data. Focus access controls on the most critical information, such as PHI or credit card data. Limiting the scope will make manual auditing of the access rights manageable.

 NOTE Many of the electronic health record (EHR) applications come with access auditing functionality built in to the system, and you can make use of this to further maximize efficiency in the process.

The AD system itself should be routinely audited for administrator access privileges. Attackers will try to gain access to this system in order to greatly accelerate the attack process. With access to this system, they can grant any access level they want on any system, and that gives them a great deal of power to circumvent most security protections in place. They will look like a normal user to the security measures.

Awareness and Training

Earlier we discussed an organization's use of policies as the communication medium for providing guidance. Every policy should have corresponding training associated with it. Training should be crafted with the audience of students in mind to affect user behavior in a positive way. For example, you could internally send a crafted phishing e-mail with an imbedded link to some of your user community and then have the link take them to a web page that explains that they just clicked on a phishing e-mail. The page should also have information on the dangers of phishing e-mails, providing simple examples that can be understood by anyone in the organization. Another example would be to post signs in areas where employees congregate, such as break rooms. From a distance, such a sign generally looks like something out of a high school classroom, but it contains a simple message that teaches adherence to a critical policy. There are countless ways to use messages to provide training to educate people about policies; just remember the receiver of the communication when crafting training and awareness.

Data Security

Data can be defined in three states while it is under control of an organization: at rest, in active use, and in motion. Data *at rest* would be data that is stored somewhere such as a laptop, desktop, or server. Data *in active use* would be data that is being actively accessed and used by an application. Data *in motion* would be data on the network that is being moved from one place to another. A nurse accessing a patient's record from the local computer would be an example of this. He or she calls up the record from the central system that stores the record, and the data is then transmitted across the network to be presented to the nurse. Confidentiality, integrity, and availability (CIA) must be adhered to in each of these states.

Physical locks, encryption, and access control are just some of the ways data can be secured when it is at rest. The key is to account for all the areas where sensitive data is stored and then evaluate the most effective way to secure the data. Minimizing the number of locations where sensitive data is stored will make this task less daunting.

Data in motion is a little trickier because it could consist of communication within the network or from one network to another. Encryption is the most common way to protect data in transit that is being sent out of the organization. Using a third-party cloud services provider is one example of how data might be sent outbound. In this case, a virtual private network (VPN) is the most common link to ensure encrypted communications. Communication within the network is most commonly secured through access control and continuous monitoring. Technical solutions such as the very popular data loss prevention (DLP) technology also exist to aid in the security of data in transit. DLP can be deployed at the network or end-point level. Its basic functionality is to prevent sensitive data from being removed or accessed by unauthorized persons. For example, it could search e-mails to see if PHI is contained in the messages. Similar to data at rest, all the communication channels for processes in this state must be understood and evaluated to apply proper security.

The underlying systems that house and transmit sensitive data through applications must also be accounted for. These systems have to be available for the information to be accessed. Every one of these systems should have some basic questions asked about it. What do we do if the system fails? How often is the data backed up? Is there a spare system? What happens if the network link fails? From questions like these, adequate resources can be deployed to ensure the availability of these critical systems.

 NOTE Medical systems are computers, and they will at some point need a refresh. That means there will need to be a secure process for disposing of systems that housed critical data.

Information Protection Processes and Procedures

All the systems in the organization should have a standard way that information processes and procedures are carried out. A standard configuration guide should be employed for the most common systems, such as desktops and servers running Microsoft Windows. The guide doesn't need to be overly granular, but it should include major security tenets such as access control, user account privileges, and encryption.

All systems, even those with a standard configuration, should have a lifecycle model applied to them. Lifecycle models plan out how stages such as testing, deployment, production, and disposal will happen in a secure manner to ensure that actions such as changes, data destruction, and backup are handled in the proper way. For example, every system change might go through the organization's formal process, which would include checks and balances such as approvals, change-time windows, and communication channels. These protection processes and procedures force risk mitigation into actions that could potentially impact the CIA triad.

Maintenance

Maintenance of systems is often overlooked when it comes to security. For example, healthcare organizations often contact a third party, such as a medical device manufacturer that provides a service technician to remotely service medical devices on the hospital network. These devices have become huge security vulnerabilities for many organizations, even though they may function perfectly well clinically. What happens if the vendor uses a common password for access to these devices or the password is hard-coded into the system? These are very common issues because multiple technicians could be servicing multiple accounts, making password management difficult for the vendor.[9] Then, all an attacker needs to do is scan the environment for these devices and go look up the common passwords used. Malware can then be installed on the devices to establish the foothold mentioned in the anatomy of a cyberattack. Maintenance of all devices with access to the network should be understood and controlled.

Protective Technology

The protective technology industry is vast today and it is ever expanding as the use of technology is evolving. Years ago there was no Smartphone or cloud services and most networks only used perimeter devices like firewalls and intrusion detection systems (IDS). Now data has the ability to be accessed from anywhere by a multitude of device types. Due to new evolution of technology and the way people use it specialized protection is being developed. At the time of this writing, several different types of software can be installed on a Smartphone to protect it and the data. Security thought processes should be adaptive to how current technology is used and not try to control every device that could be on the network.

Everything that happens on the network can be logged and tracked, but in today's expansive networks it is impossible to do this for everything. Prioritization is more important today than ever before. Every attacker moves through the attack procedure and leaves evidence behind. Protective technology should first make sure no large blind spots in the network exist. For example, does the internal network have the ability to apply security to zone-to-zone communications? All the protection in the world will fail if someone gets inside the network and then moves laterally and locates or creates legitimate network credentials. At that point, the attacker becomes a normal user and blends into the other millions of transactions that take place every day.

Finally, specialized technology should be deployed to individual systems when the return on investment makes sense. Having encryption and antivirus software on all laptops, desktops, and mobile phones makes sense because the cost is low compared to the risk. However, deploying a complex suite of protection software on these same devices might not mitigate enough risk to justify the resource expenditure. Just like everything else in technology, there are always more security products available than budget. Successfully protecting the organization should rely on maximizing the effectiveness of every resource allocated.

 TIP Don't overlook the power of the open source community in this area. Snort, for example, is a great IDS product.

Chapter Review

In this chapter, the anatomy of a cyberattack was introduced to provide some insight into how an attack works, and this insight is critical because it lays the groundwork for trying to apply a security framework that will put up a solid defense. Attackers have the advantage by always throwing the first punch, and today's advancements in computer technology make this easy and cheap. Mitigating this risk calls for an organization-wide process that is alive and that adapts to the world. Lines of demarcation between networks are only going to get blurrier as we bend technology to suite our needs. We won't be able to deploy Superman-like powers to stop adversaries, but with hard work, training, and diligence we can be Batman.

About the Contributing Author

Rob Davis leads strategic cybersecurity services at Leidos, Inc. As such, he has spent the last decade advising organizations in industries with critical infrastructure and has helped them guard against millions of cyber events each day. His expertise is recognized by the U.S. Department of Defense, energy and utilities sectors, and several commercial retail companies. With the advent of HIPAA, HITECH, and the Omnibus HIPAA Final Rule, Rob has dedicated his talents and attention to the U.S. private-sector healthcare market. He brings a practitioner's focus, with real-life experience, to advancing education on cybersecurity.

Review Questions

1. (TRUE or FALSE) The anatomy of a cyberattack illustrates how to stop any attacker from penetrating the environment with malicious software.

2. What technology will need to be in place to perform active log monitoring for potential threats to the environment?

    A. SIEM

    B. IDS

    C. Firewalls

    D. Central logging

3. The method of planning and documenting actions is used as a _____ to enable people to think in terms of concrete steps that need to be taken.

    A. Mind meld

    B. Diagram

    C. Forcing function

    D. Passive function

4. What is the first step to perform in the analysis phase of incident response?

    A. Determine the attacker's IP address

    B. Check the logs for traces of how the attacker gained access

    C. Determine if a breach of sensitive data has occurred

    D. Reverse engineer the malware

5. (TRUE or FALSE) Recovery planning of systems after an incident is primarily an IT department responsibility with little involvement from other departments.

6. (TRUE or FALSE) Risk assessments should be performed as frequently as local industry regulations call for it, or annually if not covered under applicable regulations.

7. Data that is stored on a server, laptop, or mobile device is considered _____.

   A. In motion

   B. At peace

   C. At rest

   D. In limbo

8. What is the most common way to encrypt the connection between an organization's network and cloud services?

   A. IDS

   B. DLP

   C. VPN

   D. AD

9. (TRUE or FALSE) Risk assessments should always include a penetration test.

10. What should correspond to every policy instituted in an organization?

    A. A poster

    B. A penalty

    C. Monitoring

    D. Training

Answers

1. **FALSE.** The anatomy of a cyberattack is an interesting illustration of the most likely steps an attacker will need to carry out the mission. An attacker cannot always be stopped, but the illustration shows that there is more to an attack than what is usually reported. The attacker must get a foothold in the environment and then figure out how to exploit the weaknesses. This takes time and effort. Even if the attacker penetrates the environment, the impact can be minimized, in most cases, with a proper security program.

2. **D.** The minimum amount of technology needed to perform monitoring is central logging. This will provide the capability to collect and search logs from all the devices on the network in one place. Security products such as firewalls and IDS provide great value but are not key to the monitoring technology itself.

3. **C.** A forcing function changes behavior. Working on plans as an organization forces people to take abstract ideas and apply concrete steps. This will expose assumptions that might yield critical flaws in the process. The other choices are irrelevant to driving behavior.

4. **C.** The initial focus should be on determining if a breach of sensitive data has occurred. This will determine what steps need to be taken first in the recovery process. While all of the actions may be valid, the other answers can be implemented later in the process.

5. **FALSE.** Any planning that takes place should be done at an organizational level. Computing environments are far too expansive for the IT department to operate in a vacuum.

6. **FALSE.** Risk assessments should occur numerous times during the year. For example, if there is a major change to the computing environment, then a risk assessment should be done on the change.

7. **C.** When data is stored, it is considered at rest. Encryption and access control are the primary ways data is protected in this state. The other answers are not legitimate security terminology.

8. **C.** A VPN is the primary way to establish an encryption connection between an organization's network and cloud services providers. Encryption provides a secure link and can be accomplished with any number of devices such as a firewall, VPN, or gateway device. IDS, DLP, and AD are not connectivity technologies.

9. **FALSE.** Penetration tests should always be considered when doing a risk assessment but not necessarily performed. They should be done only when it makes sense.

10. **D.** Training should accompany every policy that is created for an organization. Policies are directions to provide level guidance to an organization, and this direction should be strengthened with training. Posters may be part of the training. Monitoring would be helpful for compliance with training. Of course, penalties may be in place when training is ignored.

References

1. Hutchins, Eric M., Michael J. Cloppert, and Rohan M. Amin, Ph.D. "Intelligence-Driven Computer Network Defense Informed by Analysis of Adversary Campaigns and Intrusion Kill Chains" Lockheed Martin Corporation, 2011. p. 2. Accessed October 1, 2014, at http://www.lockheedmartin.com/content/dam/lockheed/data/corporate/documents/LM-White-Paper-Intel-Driven-Defense.pdf

2. Dutt, Varun, Young-Suk Ahn, and Cleotilde Gonzalez. "Cyber Situation Awareness: Modeling Detection of Cyber Attacks with Instance-Based Learning Theory." Carnegie Mellon University Research Showcase @ CMU. June, 2013. p. 5. Accessed October 3, 2014, at http://repository.cmu.edu/cgi/viewcontent.cgi?article=1124&context=sds

3. Talbot, David. "Computer Viruses Are 'Rampant' on Medical Devices in Hospitals." *MIT Technology Review.* October 17, 2012. Accessed October 1, 2014, at http://www.technologyreview.com/news/429616/computer-viruses-are-rampant-on-medical-devices-in-hospitals

4. Executive Order 13636. "Improving Critical Infrastructure Cybersecurity." *Federal Register* 78, no. 33. February 19, 2013. Accessed September 30, 2014, at http://www.gpo.gov/fdsys/pkg/FR-2013-02-19/pdf/2013-03915.pdf

5. Centers for Medicare & Medicaid Services. "Security Standards: Administrative Safeguards." HIPAA Security Series. Volume 2, Paper 2. May, 2005, rev. March, 2007. p. 17. Accessed September 30, 2014, at http://www.hhs.gov/ocr/privacy/hipaa/administrative/securityrule/adminsafeguards.pdf

6. Chernow, Ron. *Titan: The Life of John D. Rockefeller, Sr.* (New York: Vintage Books, 2007), p. 101.

7. Allen, David. *Ready for Anything: 52 Productivity Principles for Getting Things Done.* (New York: Penguin Group, 2004), p. 37.

8. Deek, Fadi P., and James A. M. McHugh. *Open Source: Technology and Policy.* (Cambridge: Cambridge University Press, 2007), p. 29.

9. U.S. Food and Drug Administration. "Cybersecurity for Medical Devices and Hospital Networks: FDA Safety Communication." June 13, 2013. Accessed October 2, 2014, at http://www.fda.gov/medicaldevices/safety/alertsandnotices/ucm356423.htm

INDEX